D1693476

Kraemer Sieverts & Partner   Bauten und Projekte

CIP-Kurztitelaufnahme der Deutschen Bibliothek
Architekten Professor Kraemer, Sieverts & Partner ‹Braunschweig / Köln›:
Kraemer, Sieverts & Partner, Bauten und Projekte
Friedrich Wilhelm Kraemer; Ernst Sieverts. –
Stuttgart: Krämer, 1983
  ISBN 3-7828-1468-1
  NE: Kraemer, Friedrich Wilhelm [Mitarb.]; HST

© **Karl Krämer Verlag Stuttgart 1983**
Alle Rechte vorbehalten

Druck: Heinrich Fink GmbH + Co., Stuttgart 80
Printed in Germany
ISBN 3-7828-1468-1

KSP Kraemer Sieverts & Partner
Bauten und Projekte

Karl Krämer Verlag Stuttgart

Inhalt / Contents

5 Vorwort

Bauten der Denkmalpflege / Historic buildings and conservation

10 Gewandhaus Braunschweig
12 Herzog August Bibliothek Wolfenbüttel
13 Lessinghaus Wolfenbüttel
14 Zeughaus Wolfenbüttel
16 Büro- und Wohnhaus Am Römerturm 3 Köln
18 Deutsche Bank Düsseldorf (Königsallee 49/51)
20 Hörfunkzentrale Westdeutscher Rundfunk Köln

Wohnungsbauten, Heime, Hotels / Housing, homes, hotels

24 Haus Wolff-Limper Braunschweig
24 Haus Hoeck Braunschweig
24 Gaststätte »Unter den Eichen« Bad Harzburg
24 Haus Hess Braunschweig
25 Haus Flebbe Braunschweig
25 Haus Luther Braunschweig
25 Kaserne Nienburg-Langendamm
26 Haus Sandforth Braunschweig
27 Haus Munte Braunschweig
27 Haus Roedenbeck Stöckheim
28 Haus Kraemer 1 Braunschweig
28 Haus Kraemer 2 Braunschweig
29 Studentenwohnheime Berlin
30 Atriumhotel Braunschweig
33 Wohnbebauung am Alsterufer Hamburg
33 Hotel Holiday-Inn Wolfsburg
34 Eifelhöhenklinik Marmagen
34 Studentenwohnheim Berlin-Schlachtensee
35 Studentenwohnheim Würzburg-Keesburg
35 Studentenwohnheim Bamberg
36 Studentisches Wohnen
36 Studentenwohnheim Würzburg Zweierweg
38 Wohn- und Geschäftshaus Am Römerturm 2 Köln
39 Musikerhaus in Monte Leon bei Maspalomas Gran Canaria
39 Altenheim St. Vinzenz Köln

Schul- und Hochschulbauten / School and university buildings

42 Oberschule Wolfsburg
42 Aufbau- und Abendgymnasium Dortmund
43 Mittelschule Peine
43 Handelsschule Heidelberg
44 Auditorium Maximum TH Braunschweig (Hochschulforum)
45 Rektorat und Fakultät 1 TH Braunschweig (Hochschulforum)
46 Bibliothek TH Braunschweig (Hochschulforum)
48 Elektrotechnische Institute TH Braunschweig
48 Volksschule Dortmund-Rahm
49 Hörsaalgebäude Universität Münster
49 Fakultät III TH Braunschweig
49 Universität Bremen
49 Universität Bielefeld
50 Mensa und Studentenhaus Universität Kiel
51 Sportforum Universität Kiel
52 Ingenieurschule Gelsenkirchen
54 Bildungsstätte Nümbrecht
56 Schulzentrum Gifhorn
58 Bildungszentrum Südwest Karlsruhe
60 Internal Security Forces College Riyadh Saudi-Arabien
62 WDR College Gebäude Köln-Bocklemünd
62 Schulzentrum Hankensbüttel
62 Bundesakademien Brühl
62 Paul Ehrlich Institut Langen
63 Civil Defence Institute Riyadh Saudi-Arabien
68 Pharmazeutische Institute TU Braunschweig
70 Forschungsgebäude Leibnizhaus Wolfenbüttel
72 Hochschule für Bildende Künste Braunschweig
74 Technische Universität Hamburg-Harburg
74 Imam Mohammed Bin Saud Islamic University Riyadh Saudi-Arabien
75 Girls' College Riyadh Saudi-Arabien

Innerstädtische Zentren / Urban centres

78 Iduna Zentrum Braunschweig
79 Fußgängerbrücke Berliner Platz Braunschweig
80 Altstadtsanierung Karlsruhe
80 Wohnbebauung Fontenay Hamburg
81 Innerstädtisches Zentrum Neustadt/Weinstraße
82 Research and Study Centres Saudi-Arabien
86 Wohn- und Geschäftszentrum Kreishaus-Galerie St. Apern Straße Köln
88 Wadi Saqra Circle Project Amman Jordanien
90 Berliner Platz Mülheim/Ruhr
91 Kleiner Schloßplatz Stuttgart
92 Gürzenich I und Gürzenich II Köln

Industriebauten / Industrial buildings

96 Fabrikanlage Unger und Sohn Braunschweig
96 Rolleiflex Werkstattgebäude VII Braunschweig
96 Sozialgebäude Büssing Braunschweig
96 NSM Spielautomatenfabrik Bingen
97 Volkswagengroßhandlung Max Voets Braunschweig
98 Rolleiflex Werkstattgebäude VIII Braunschweig
98 Rolleiflex Werkstattgebäude IX Braunschweig
99 Maschinenfabrik Wohlenberg Hannover
99 Prüflabor Rheinisch-Westfälische Kalkwerke Dornap
99 Gemeinschaftshaus Aluminium-Walzwerke Singen
100 Kantine Veba Chemie Gelsenkirchen-Buer
101 Heidelberger Druckmaschinenfabrik Heidelberg
101 Fernmeldeturm Düsseldorf
102 Braunschweiger Zeitung Braunschweig

Büro- und Geschäftshäuser / Office and commercial buildings

108 Flebbe Braunschweig
108 Vereinigte Leben Bremen
108 Hamburg Mannheimer Versicherung Hannover Friedrichswall
108 Staatskanzlei Hannover
109 Pfeiffer und Schmidt Braunschweig
109 Wasser- und Schiffahrtsdirektion und Kataster- und Vermessungsamt Bremen
110 Hauptverwaltung Unterharzer Berg- und Hüttenwerke Goslar
112 Wullbrandt und Seele Braunschweig
113 Iduna Versicherung Braunschweig
113 Iduna Versicherung Osnabrück
113 Iduna Versicherung Münster
113 Iduna Versicherung Essen
114 Perschmann Braunschweig
114 Iduna Versicherung Schweinfurt
114 Erweiterungsbau Preussag Hannover
115 Rechenzentrum eines Chemiekonzerns
116 Rathaus Essen
118 Hauptverwaltung BP Hamburg
120 Bayer Verkaufsabteilungen Leverkusen
121 Preussag Berlin
121 Stadthaus Bonn
121 Iduna Versicherung Gelsenkirchen
122 Hauptverwaltung DKV Köln
126 Iduna Versicherung Hamburg
126 Rathaus Castrop-Rauxel
126 Hauptverwaltung Shell Hamburg
127 Vorstandsgebäude Bayer Leverkusen
128 Hauptverwaltung Philips Wien
128 Hauptverwaltung Veba Chemie Gelsenkirchen-Buer
129 Hauptverwaltung Colonia Versicherung Köln
129 Unternehmensbereich D Siemens München-Perlach
130 Hauptverwaltung VEW Dortmund
136 Hauptverwaltung Vorwerk Wuppertal
136 Hauptverwaltung Klöckner Duisburg
137 Deutsche Botschaft Helsinki
137 Hauptverwaltung ÖVA-Versicherung Mannheim
138 Hauptverwaltung Bayern Versicherung München
139 Rathauserweiterung Wolfsburg
140 Hauptverwaltung Getreideimportgesellschaft Duisburg

140 Hauptverwaltung Tchibo Hamburg
141 Hauptverwaltung Norddeutsche und Hamburg Bremer Versicherung Hamburg
141 Hauptverwaltung Röhrenwerke Mannesmann Lintorf
142 Technisches Rathaus Köln 1. Stufe
143 Technisches Rathaus Köln 2. Stufe
144 Deutsche Botschaft Moskau
144 Regionalverwaltung Salzgitter Stahl Düsseldorf
145 Hauptverwaltung Vereinigte Versicherungsgruppe München-Perlach
146 Kreishaus Warendorf
146 Rathaus Hattingen
146 Hauptverwaltung DEVK Köln
148 Hauptverwaltung Thyssengas Duisburg-Hamborn
151 Verwaltungszentrum eines Chemiekonzerns
151 Erweiterung Hauptverwaltung Hamburg-Mannheimer Versicherung Hamburg
152 Ministry of Public Works and Housing Riyadh Saudi-Arabien
156 Hauptverwaltung GEW Köln
164 Arbeitsamt Hannover
165 Hillmannkomplex Bremen
166 Hauptverwaltung Veba Oel AG Gelsenkirchen
170 Hauptverwaltung VW Wolfsburg
171 Kreishaus Hofheim
171 Bundespostministerium Bonn
171 Municipality Abu Dhabi
172 Arbeitsamt Bochum
174 Rathaus Oldenburg
175 Arbeitsamt Hagen
178 Hauptverwaltung DEVK Köln Ausführung
179 Arbeitsamt Bielefeld
179 Landratsamt Goslar
179 Boehringer Mannheim
180 BASF Espagnola Barcelona
181 Rathauserweiterung Wilhelmshaven
181 Landratsamt Starnberg
182 Verwaltungsgebäude 3 Krupp AG Essen
184 Arbeitsamt Essen
185 Erweiterungsbau VIAG Bonn
185 Bürogebäude St. Augustin
185 Residential Commercial Complexes of Abu Dhabi
186 Hauptverwaltung Schloemann-Siemag Düsseldorf
187 Hauptverwaltung Lurgi Frankfurt

Banken / Banks

190 Braunschweigische Staatsbank Lebenstedt
190 Stadtsparkasse Düsseldorf
191 Landeszentralbank Nordrhein-Westfalen Düsseldorf
192 Stadtsparkasse Einbeck
193 Simonbank Düsseldorf
196 Deutsche Bank Düsseldorf
202 Dresdner Bank Düsseldorf
205 Bremer Bank Bremen
205 Landeszentralbank Wiesbaden

Kulturbauten / Buildings for the arts and cultural activities

208 Norddeutscher Rundfunk Funkhaus Hannover
209 Norddeutscher Rundfunk Großer Sendesaal Hannover
209 Studiobühne Universität Kiel
210 Sprengel Museum Hannover
210 Wallraf Richartz Museum und Museum Sammlung Ludwig Köln
210 Neue Pinakothek München
210 Wilhelm Hack Museum Ludwigshafen
211 Jahrhunderthalle Hoechst

Anhang / Appendix

214 Werksverzeichnis / List of projects
221 Publikationen / List of publications
224 Mitarbeiter / Assistents
225 Fotografen / Photographs by
225 Perspektivzeichner / Perspectives by

Anmerkungen zur Arbeit der Architekten Kraemer Sieverts und Partner

Was hier vorliegt, gibt einen Überblick über fünf Jahrzehnte eines Architektenlebens, das Architektenbüro wurde 1935 von Kraemer begründet und seit 1960 in Partnerschaft mit langjährigen Mitarbeitern geführt. Das Buch ist ein Rechenschaftsbericht über das, was das Büro in diesen Jahrzehnten an Entwürfen und Bauten geleistet hat.

Die Übersicht gibt zugleich einen Einblick in die Architekturabschnitte der Zeit nach dem Krieg, anfangs Wiederaufbau und Baulückenschließung, dann erste Aufträge der Öffentlichen Hand (wie Funkhaus, Schul- und Hochschulbauten) in den sechziger Jahren Aufgaben der expandierenden Wirtschaft mit ihrer wirtschaftswunderhaften Dynamik (Verwaltungsgebäude der Versicherungen, Banken, Industrie) und schließlich die Wandlung zu mehr Behutsamkeit, Einfühlung und Einpassung in die Umgebung, zu mehr Identifikation mit Aufgabe und Ort.

Die Bürogeschichte begann damit, daß sich Kraemer nach Studium und Assistententätigkeit an der TH Braunschweig, achtundzwanzig Jahre alt, selbständig machte. Zunächst entstanden Einfamilienhäuser, einfache Baukörper mit knapp aufgesetztem Steildach, sorgfältig detailliert und mit klaren Raumbezügen, in denen sich Einflüsse von Bonatz und Schmitthenner erkennen lassen. Diese Linie setzt sich mit Einfamilienhäusern nach 1945 fort, und wenn sich diese Bauten von den früheren unterscheiden, dann in der Grundrißposition und im Ausgreifen von Bauteilen in die Natur. Hier haben sich Einflüsse skandinavischer Architektur niedergeschlagen, vor allem aus dem nahegelegenen Dänemark, wo sich die gleiche Behandlung von Baukörper und Dach, von Form und Material findet. Die Veränderung erfolgte 1956 mit dem Haus Sandforth in Braunschweig, einem ausgefachten Skelettbau mit großzügiger Verbindung von innen und außen, aber mit der gleichen sorgfältigen Behandlung von Raum und Material.

Was damals in den fünfziger Jahren vom Büro entworfen und gebaut wurde, ist für jüngere Architekten heute bereits Geschichte, für diejenigen aber, die nach dem II. Weltkrieg ihr Studium aufnahmen und in den fünfziger Jahren ihre ersten tastenden Schritte als Architekten unternahmen, ist es erlebte Vergangenheit; – für sie waren diese Bauten vorbildlich, und das gilt insbesondere für das Verwaltungsgebäude der Unterharzer Berg- und Hüttenwerke in Goslar, aber ebenso für die Handelsschule in Heidelberg, die Werkstattgebäude von Rolleiflex oder die Volkswagengroßhandlung Max Voets in Braunschweig.

Wie sehr das Büro seiner Zeit voraus war, zeigen auch die zu Vorbildern gewordenen Ansätze der Erhaltung und Erneuerung vorhandener Bausubstanz, lange bevor dieses Thema im allgemeinen Bewußtsein akut wurde. Das Gewandhaus mit der Gestaltung des Altstadtmarktes (1948) in Braunschweig ist zu nennen, die Herzog August Bibliothek in Wolfenbüttel, das Lessinghaus und das dortige Zeughaus, ein Komplex, an dem das Büro erhaltend und erneuernd ohne geschmäcklerische Anpassung zwei Jahrzehnte tätig war.

Der größte Teil des Buches und sicher das interessanteste Kapitel ist dem Büro- und Verwaltungsbau gewidmet. Auf diesem Gebiet hat das Büro nicht nur bauend sondern auch forschend wichtige Beiträge geliefert. Über die Bauten hinaus ist dieses Kapitel ein Abbild der Entwicklung auf diesem Gebiet, es zeigt den Weg von der zwei- und dreibündigen Anlage mit Zellenbüros zum Großraum auf, zur Bürolandschaft und von dort zu Bauten mit reversibler Nutzung sowohl als Zellen- wie als Großraumbüros und schließlich zum Bürogruppenraum.

Hier liegt nicht nur ein Schwerpunkt der Arbeit des Büros sondern zugleich seiner Leistungsfähigkeit. Das Gebäude der Hauptverwaltung der DKV Köln zeigt, welche Gestaltungsmöglichkeiten das Prinzip Großraum enthält durch sinnvolle Gliederung der Grundrisse, durch Trennung von Büro- und Servicegeschossen, durch Wechsel von geschlossenen und offenen, bündig liegenden und eingezogenen Fassadenteilen. Von den Bauten der letzten Jahre ist das Verwaltungsgebäude GEW in Köln zu nennen, ein vielfach gegliederter Bau mit kleinteiliger Bürolandschaft, aufgelockert durch Innenhöfe und in den Maßnahmen zur Energieeinsparung vorbildlich. Allen Bauten gemeinsam ist das Bemühen um eine Einheit von Form und Funktion als menschengerechte Hülle und die

Entwicklung einer glaubwürdigen technischen Sprache zu ihrer
Verwirklichung. Die konstruktiven Antworten auf die gestellten funktionalen und gestalterischen Fragen wurden jeweils neu gesucht und entwickelt.
Neben Solitärbauten mehren sich in den siebziger Jahren innerstädtische Aufgaben, eingebunden in die Maßstäblichkeit der gewachsenen Umgebung, häufig Altbauten oder Altbaufassaden einbeziehend. Bei der Neu- und Umgestaltung der Deutschen Bank an der Düsseldorfer Königsallee wurde aus einem Straßenkarree mit 12 Einzelparzellen eine Gesamtform entwickelt, bei der sich restaurierte Gründerzeitpalais', ein neues, den kleinteiligen Fassen angepaßtes Eingangsbauwerk, moderne Büroneubauten und übriger Altbaubestand um zwei Gartenhöfe gruppieren. Bei der benachbarten Dresdner Bank entsteht aus dem glasüberdachten Innenhof zwischen Altbauten und Neubauanlagen eine lichtdurchflutete Kassenhalle, in die der Kundentresor eingebettet ist.
Die Kölner Kreishausgalerie, eine Wohn- und Geschäftsanlage in einem Innenstadtviertel, belastet von der benachbarten Hochhausscheibe des Interconti-Hotels, nutzt die Fassade des alten Kreishauses, einem Bau des geometrischen Jugendstils, als Eingang zu einer neuen Glaspassage.
Allen Bauten gemeinsam ist die Absicht, für individuelle Bauherren, aus unterschiedlichen Aufgabenstellungen und aus den jeweilig verschiedenen Umgebungen eine eigenständige Lösung zu finden, eine Lösung, die nicht nur die praktischen Bedürfnisse erfüllt sondern auch hohen gestalterischen Ansprüchen gerecht wird.

Jürgen Joedicke

A comment on the work of the architects Kraemer Sieverts and Partners

The contents of this book provide a survey of five decades of an architect's life. The practice was founded in 1935 by Friedrich Wilhelm Kraemer, and since 1960 it has been run in partnership with colleagues of many years' standing. The book is an account of the designs and buildings the office has created over these decades.
At the same time this survey provides an insight into the various periods of post-war architecture, beginning with the work of reconstruction and the closing of the gaps left in the building fabric by the war. This phase was followed by the first commissions from public authorities, (e.g. a broadcasting house, schools and university buildings), and in the 60s by projects that reflected the needs of an expanding economy and the dynamics of the »economic miracle«, (administrative buildings for insurance firms, banks and industry); and finally, a turning to a greater sense of restraint, empathy and compliance towards the existing environment, to a greater degree of identification with the object itself and its location.
The history of the office began with Kraemer setting up on his own in private practice at the age of 28, having completed his studies and his activities as assistant lecturer at the Technische Hochschule in Brunswick. The initial projects were for single-family houses, simple built forms with tightly fitting steep-pitched roofs, carefully detailed and with clear spatial configurations, in which one can recognize the influences of Bonatz and Schmitthenner. This line of development was continued in the houses designed after 1945, and if there is any difference from the earlier buildings, it is in the plan layout and the interpenetration of the elements of the building with nature. The influences of Scandinavian architecture are evident here, and in particular those of neighbouring Denmark, where one can find the same handling of built volume and roof, form an materials. The change occurred in 1956 with the Sandforth House in Brunswick, a skeleton frame structure with infill panels, affording a generous link between indoors and outdoors, but still exhibiting the same careful treatment of space and materials.

The projects designed and built by the office in the 50s have already become part of history for the younger generation of architects today. But for those who began their studies in the aftermath of the Second World War and took their first tentative steps as architects in the 50s, it is a piece of the past they themselves have experienced. These buildings were models for them, and that applies in particular to the administrative building for the Unterharzer Berg- und Hüttenwerke in Goslar, but also to the Commercial College in Heidelberg, the factory buildings for Rolleiflex, or the complex for the Volkswagen wholesale dealers Max Voets in Brunswick.
Just how much the office was ahead of its time can also be seen from the model early schemes involving the conservation and restoration of existing building fabric, long before this area had established itself in the general awareness. The Gewandhaus building, together with plans for the old city market in Brunswick (1948), can be cited in this context, as well as the Herzog August Library, the Lessing House and the Zeughaus in Wolfenbüttel, a complex of schemes in which for two decades the practice was to play an active role in the realm of conservation and restoration, without resorting to mere polite conformity.
The largest section of the book, and without doubt the most interesting chapter, is devoted to office and administrative buildings. In this realm the practice has made a number of significant contributions, not merely in respect of construction, but in the sphere of research as well. Apart from the actual buildings depicted, this chapter provides a reflection of the general developments that have occurred in this field. It traces the path from the two or three-bay layout with individual offices to the open-plan office apace and to the landscape office; from there the path leads to buildings having a »reversible« or flexible use, with both individual office spaces and open-plan offices, and finally to the group office.
In this realm lies a focal point, not merely of the actual work of the office, but of its capabilities. The DKV administrative headquarters in

Cologne show what design scope the open-plan office principle can yield, with a sensible articulation of layout plans, the separation of office working and servicing storeys, and alternations from closed to open, from flush to inset façade elements. Amongst the projects of recent years one should mention the GEW administrative building in Cologne, a strongly articulated building with small-area office landscapes, punctuated by internal courtyards. It is also a model scheme in terms of energy-saving measures. Common to all the buildings are the efforts to achieve a unity of form and function in the creation of a shelter for the needs of man, plus the development of a credible technical language in the realization of these objectives. The structural solutions to the problems posed by functional and design constraints are sought and developed anew each time.

In addition to free-standing buildings, urban projects necessitating an integration into the scale of the existing fabric begin to manifest themselves more and more in the 70s –, frequently involving treatment to older buildings or their façades. In the re-design and alterations to the Deutsche Bank in the Königsallee, Düsseldorf, an overall form was developed for an entire street block comprising some 12 individual plots of land. The project included the restoration of two palais dating from the turn of the century, a new entrance structure to fit in with the small-scale articulation of the existing façades, plus new modern office buildings and existing structures, all grouped around two landscaped courtyards. In the neighbouring Dresdner Bank scheme the glass-roofed courtyard between the existing buildings and the new complex was turned into a banking hall suffused with light, in which the customers' safe deposit is embedded. The Kreishaus Gallery in Cologne, a housing and commercial complex in a city centre location overtowered by the neighbouring high-rise slab of the Interconti Hotel, uses the façade of the old Kreishaus, a building of geometric art nouveau design, as the entrance to a new glass-roofed arcade.

The aim behind all the buildings was to find individual solutions for individual clients, solutions that meet the requirements of different briefs and reflect the special constraints of each different location, and that not merely comply with practical requirements, but also fulfil more demanding design criteria.

Jürgen Joedicke

Bauten der Denkmalpflege / Historic buildings and conservation

Aufgaben der Denkmalpflege können oft nur eingeschränkt, größere Vorhaben nur über längere Zeiträume verwirklicht werden, weil die Bereitstellung öffentlicher Mittel jeweils abgewartet werden muß. Eine zügige Durchführung dagegen ist gewährleistet, wenn mit Wiederherstellung und Instandsetzung eine aktuelle Verwendung verbunden werden kann, für die ein – öffentlicher oder privater – Bauherr die Mittel bereitstellt. In solchem Fall verlangt die neue Nutzung an manchen Stellen Eingriffe in die historische Substanz, was Kompromisse zwischen den Wünschen der Denkmalpflege und der Planung des Architekten nötig macht. Wenn hierzu die bestellten Denkmalhüter verständlicherweise weniger geneigt sind, so zeigen doch viele Beispiele, daß mit – pfleglichen und einfühlsamen – Veränderungen für den heutigen Gebrauch ein historisches Bauwerk an Bedeutung dergestalt zunimmt, daß es über seinen Anspruch als historisch-künstlerisches Objekt (»nur« an-)gesehen zu werden hinaus die Bereicherung erfährt, durch seine praktische Einbeziehung dem zeitgenössisch tätigen Leben zurückgewonnen zu sein und ihm so in doppelter Wertschätzung dienen zu können.

In many instances the aims of conservation can be achieved only partially, larger scale schemes realized only over a longer period of time, because one has to await the allocation of public funds in each particular case. A swifter execution may be expected, however, where reconstruction and rehabilitation can be combined with an acute need, which either a public or a private building client is prepared to finance. In such cases the new use may well impinge at certain points on the historic substance, something that in turn will necessitate compromises between the wishes of the conservationists and the plans of the architect. Although the conservationists responsible are, understandably enough, less inclined to enter into such a compromise, there are numerous examples to show that an historic building can gain enormously in importance when adapted to present day usage. With sensitive and well-considered alterations it can transcend its claim to interest as a purely historic-artistic object, merely to be looked at, and undergo such enrichment that, through its practical integration, it can be restored to modern, active life and in serving this purpose enjoy double the esteem.

Gewandhaus Braunschweig

Das im Krieg bis auf die Außenmauern zerstörte Baudenkmal wurde 1946 bis 1954 wieder aufgebaut. Der teilweise eingestürzte Renaissance-Ostgiebel konnte nach Trümmerresten und Fotos rekonstruiert werden. Die früher durch vorgebaute Bürgerhäuser verdeckte Nordseite bildet nach deren Zerstörung nun eine Platzwand des Altstadtmarktes; als Erinnerung an die ursprüngliche Situation wurde ein baufälliges Zollhaus von 1638 vor den Toren Braunschweigs abgebrochen und in die städtebauliche »Lücke« zwischen Gewandhaus und Martini-Kirche eingefügt.
Im Innern wird das 20 m x 60 m große Volumen in 7 Ebenen für Repräsentationsräume der Stadt Braunschweig, der Industrie- und Handelskammer und für Restaurationsräume – mit Einbeziehung der historischen Kellerräume – genutzt.

This architectural monument, which was destroyed down to the outer walls in the war, was rebuilt between 1946 and 1954. With the help of ruined fragments and photographs it proved possible to reconstruct the Renaissance east gable, which had in part collapsed.
The north face, which had previously been concealed by old town-houses, now forms a closing wall to the open space of the old city market after the destruction of these houses. As a reminder of the original state of affairs, a dilapidated customs house outside the gates of Brunswick and dating from 1638 was demolished and inserted in the gap between the Gewandhaus (the old cloth merchants' hall) and the Martini Church. The interior of the building, 20 m x 60 m on plan and rising over 7 storeys, is used for representative purposes by the City of Brunswick, the Chamber of Commerce, and for restaurant and refreshment space, including the use of the historic cellar rooms.

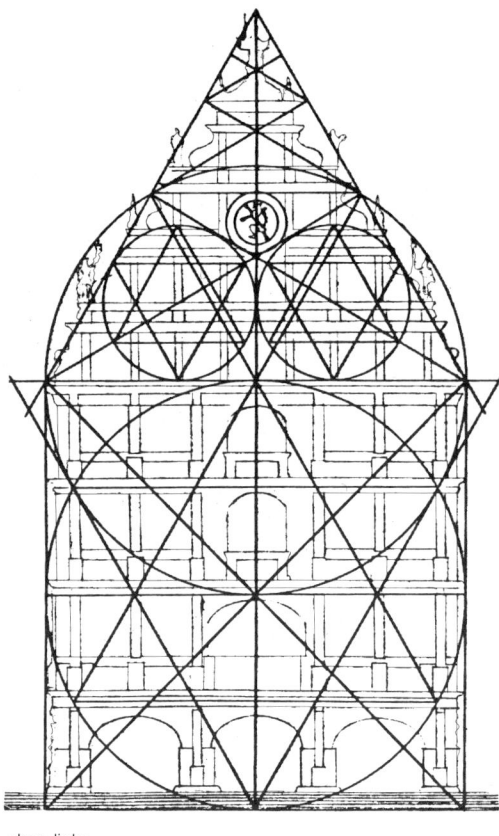

oben links
Im Krieg zerstörter Renaissance-Ostgiebel
oben Mitte
Rekonstruierter Ostgiebel
oben rechts
Proportionsstudien
unten links
Nordwand mit vorgebauten Bürgerhäusern vor dem Krieg
unten rechts
Wiederaufgebaute Nordwand mit altem Zollhaus

top left
Renaissance east gable destroyed in war
top middle
Reconstructed east gable
top right
Studies in proportions
bottom left
North face with town houses in front before the war
bottom right
Restored north face with customs house

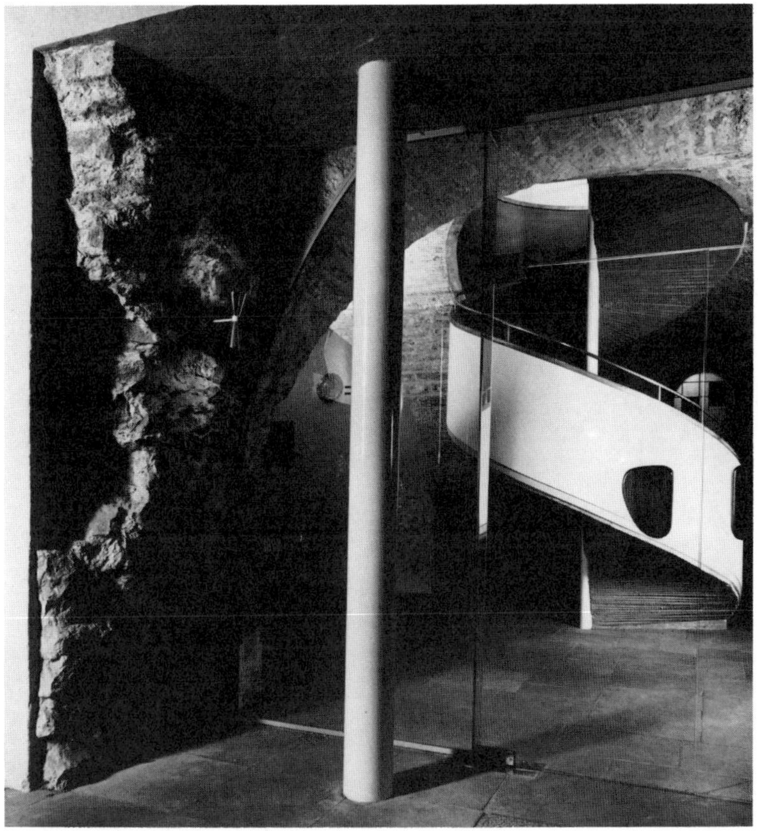

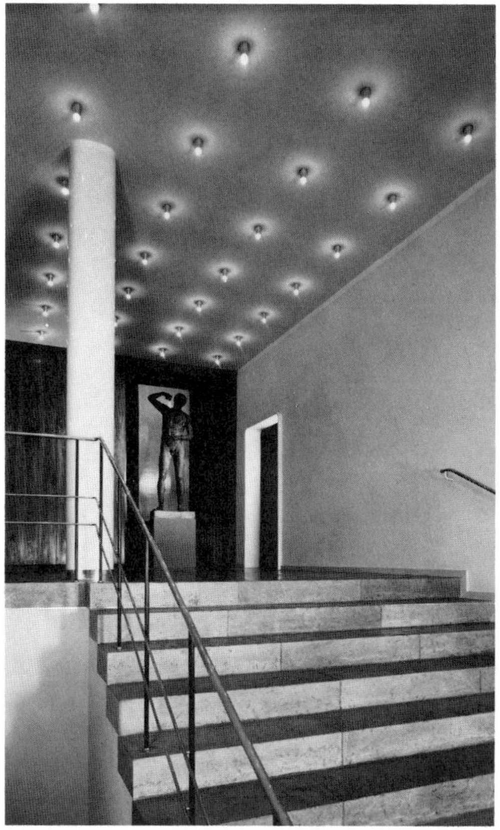

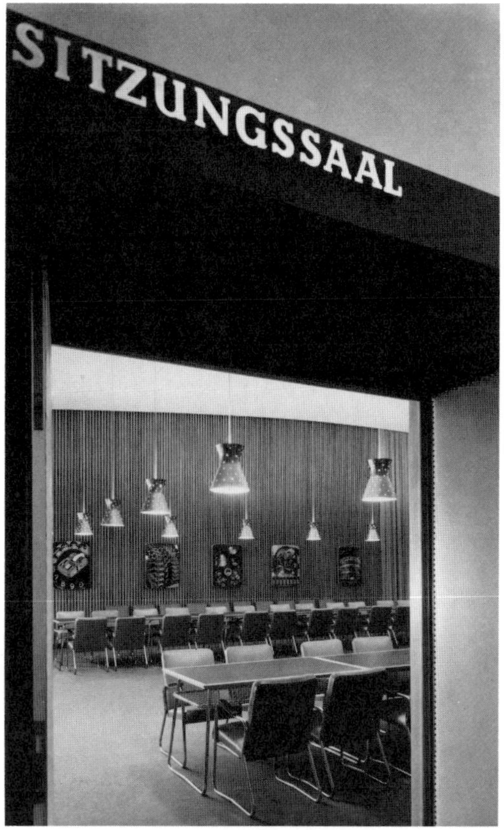
SITZUNGSSAAL

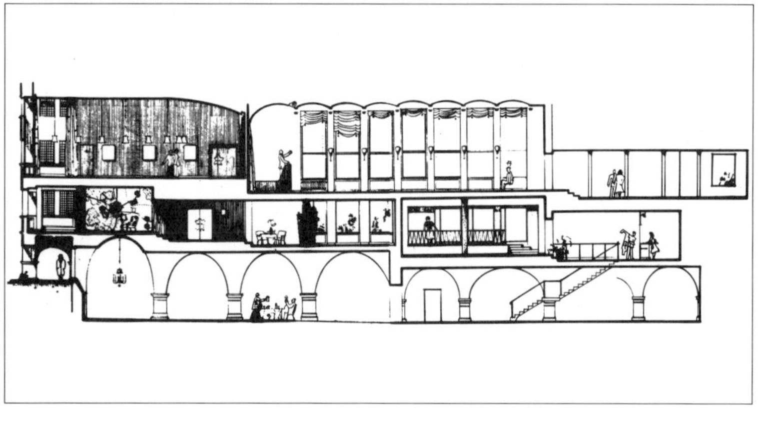

Herzog August Bibliothek Wolfenbüttel

Der Umbau des 1887 erbauten Bibliotheksgebäudes markiert den Anfang der Schaffung eines baulichen Quartiers für die Herzog August Bibliothek in der Barockzeit, eine der bedeutendsten Bibliotheken des Abendlandes. In 20 Planungs- und Baujahren seit 1961 wurden die Bibliothek, das Lessinghaus und das Zeughaus für die Zwecke der Bibliothek hergerichtet. Zentrum des Umbaus des alten Bibliotheksgebäudes ist die Augusteerhalle – ein ehemals ungenutzter Repräsentationsraum –, an deren Wänden jetzt in drei Geschossen die Bibliotheca aurea aufgestellt ist, und die für Konzerte, Vorträge und Ausstellungseröffnungen 300 Hörern Platz bietet. Mit dem BDA-Preis Niedersachsen 1976 ausgezeichnet.

The conversion of the library building erected in 1887 marks the beginning of the creation of a home for the Herzog August Library, one of the most important libraries of the western world during the Baroque age. Over a period of 20 years of planning and construction work since 1961, the library building, the Lessing House and the Armoury have been adapted to the needs of the Library.
The centre of the conversion work on the old library building is the Augusteer Hall, which was at one time an unused space reserved for representative purposes. Along the walls of this hall and extending over three floors the bibliotheca aurea is housed; the hall also affords space for 300 people at concerts, lectures and exhibition openings. Awarded the BDA Prize of Lower Saxony in 1976. (BDA = Bund Deutscher Architekten, Federation of German Architects).

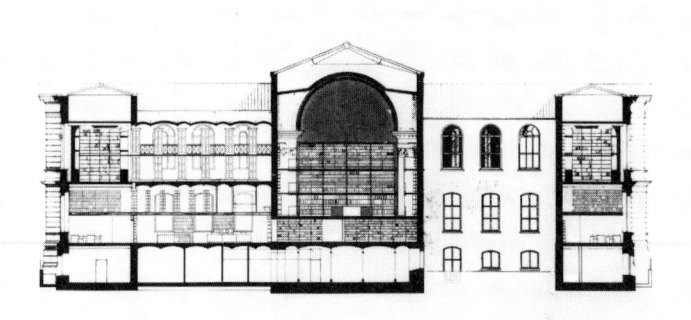

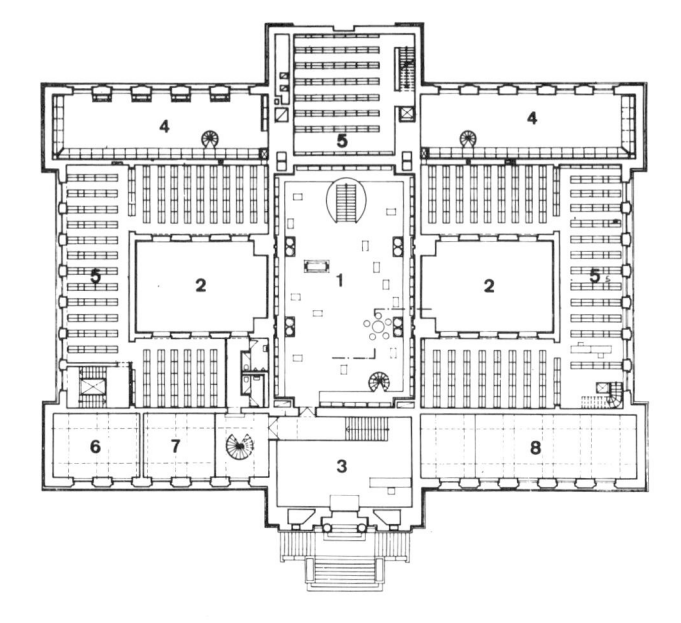

2. Geschoß / 2nd Floor
1 Schauhalle / Display hall
2 Lichthof / Glass-roofed courtyard
3 Luftraum Vestibül / Void over vestibule
4 Galerien / Galleries
5 Magazine / Stores
6 Luftraum Handschriften-Lesesaal / Void over manuscript room
7 Luftraum Sekretariat / Void over secretariat
8 Luftraum Lesesaal / Void over reading room

oben Globussaal
rechts Schauhalle

above Globe room
right Hall

Lessinghaus Wolfenbüttel

Das von Lessing von 1777 bis 1781 während seiner Amtszeit als Bibliotheksdirektor bewohnte Fachwerkhaus wurde von 1975 bis 1978 gründlich renoviert und enthält nun das Lessing Museum.

The timber framed house in which Lessing resided from 1777 to 1781, during his period of office as library curator, underwent a thorough renovation between 1975 and 1978 and now houses the Lessing Museum.

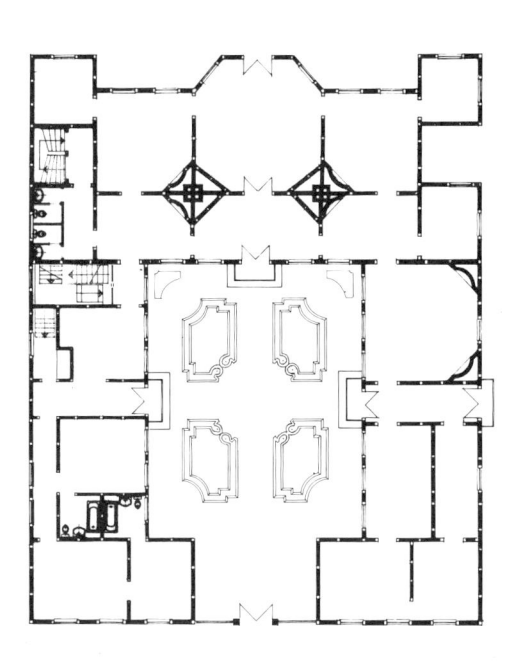

Zeughaus Wolfenbüttel

Als Waffenarsenal der Wolfenbütteler Herzöge von Paul Francke 1619 errichtet, diente es von 1753–1945 als Kaserne. Durch Einbau von Wänden, Treppen und Schornsteinen für Mannschaftsstuben etc. verlor das Bauwerk seine großzügige Renaissance-Räumlichkeit. Im Zusammenhang mit großen Aufwendungen der erhaltenden Denkmalpflege wurde das den Schloßplatz mitbestimmende Renaissancegebäude – wie die Herzog August Bibliothek, S. 12 – zu einer Forschungsstätte der europäischen Kultur- und Geistesgeschichte der frühen Neuzeit von 1979–81 umgebaut. Im Erdgeschoß wurde die dreischiffige Gewölbehalle (20 m x 60 m) wiederhergestellt, genutzt als Schauraum, Büchermagazin und mit Emporeneinbau als Forschungsbibliothek. In zwei Obergeschossen sind Katalogisierungsräume, weitere Arbeitsräume, Handbibliotheken, Seminarräume, sowie ein großer Lesesaal und eine Cafeteria untergebracht. Mit dem BDA-Preis Niedersachsen 1982 ausgezeichnet.

Erected by Paul Francke in 1619 as the Armoury of the Dukes of Wolfenbüttel, the building was used from 1753 to 1945 as barracks. Through the insertion of dividing walls, stairs and chimneys for soldiers' quarters, etc. the structure was divested of its generous Renaissance spatial character.
Like the Herzog August Library (p. 12), and with the help of large-scale financial support on the part of conservation bodies this Renaissance building, one of the dominant structures of the Schloßplatz (Palace Square) was converted between 1979 and 1981 to house a research establishment devoted to European cultural history and the history of ideas of the early modern age. The three-bay vaulted hall (20 m x 60 m) on the ground floor was restored for use as display space and book store, with a research library situated on specially inserted side galleries. Two upper floors house cataloguing rooms, additional working rooms, reference libraries, seminar rooms, a large reading room and a cafeteria. Awarded the BDA Prize of Lower Saxony, 1982.

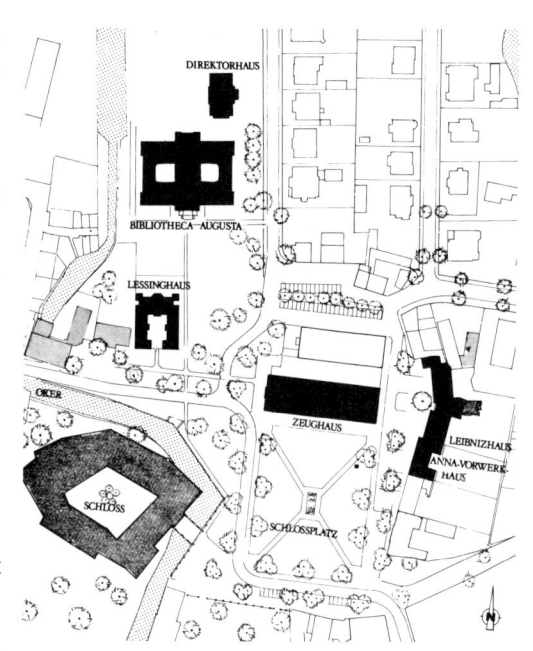

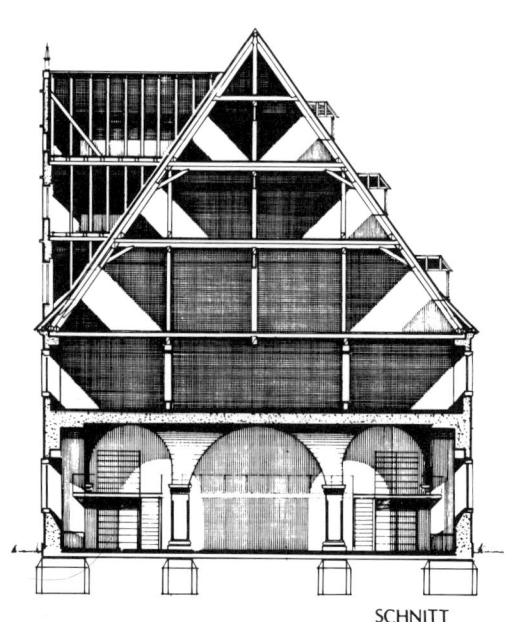

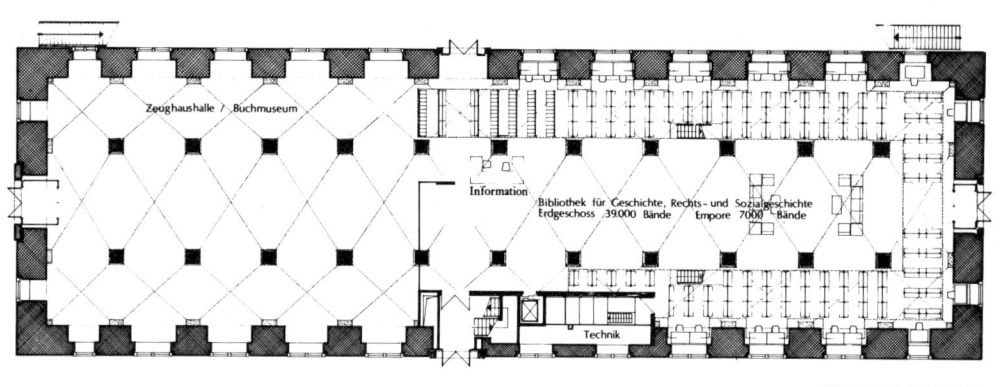

SCHNITT

ERDGESCHOSS MIT EMPORE

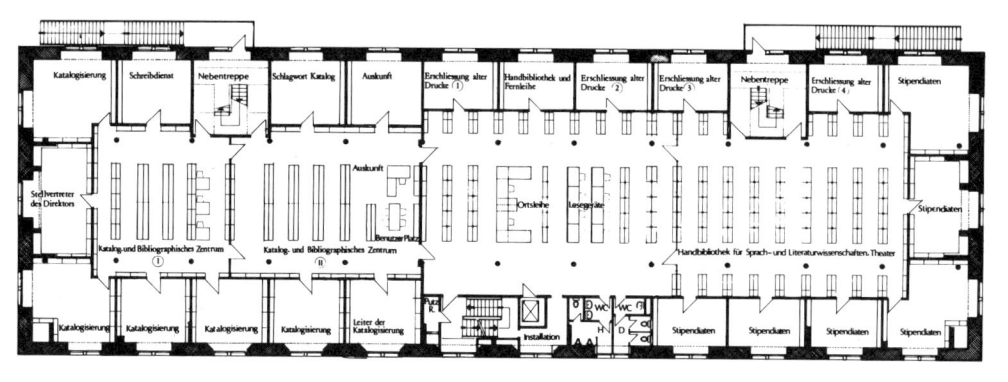

GRUNDRISS I. OBERGESCHOSS

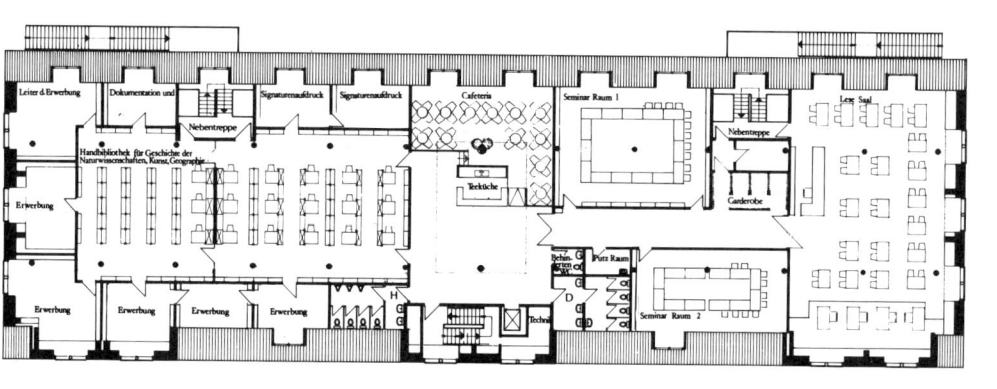

GRUNDRISS II. OBERGESCHOSS

Das Bild unten zeigt, wie das Innere des bedeutenden Renaissancebaus durch Einbauten entstellt war, nach deren Entfernung die räumliche Mächtigkeit der dreischiffigen Gewölbehalle, 20 m x 60 m, wiederhergestellt werden konnte.

The picture below shows how the interior of this important Renaissance structure was marred by later additions, the removal of which enabled the restoration of the three-bay vaulted hall (20 m x 60 m) to its old spatial grandeur.

Büro- und Wohnhaus Am Römerturm 3 Köln

Das im Krieg zerstörte klassizistische Stadthaus enthält 1974 nach Wiederherstellung und Atriumanbau die Räume des Kölner Büros KSP und im Dachgeschoß eine Wohnung. Das zweischiffige romanische Kellergewölbe von 11 m x 20 m dient kulturellen Veranstaltungen. Mit dem BDA-Preis Köln 1975 ausgezeichnet.

This classicistic town house, which was destroyed in the war, now contains, after its restoration and courtyard extension, the Cologne offices of KSP and a top storey flat. The two-bay Romanesque vaulted cellar, 11 m x 20 m in size, is used for cultural events. Awarded the BDA Prize of the City of Cologne in 1975.

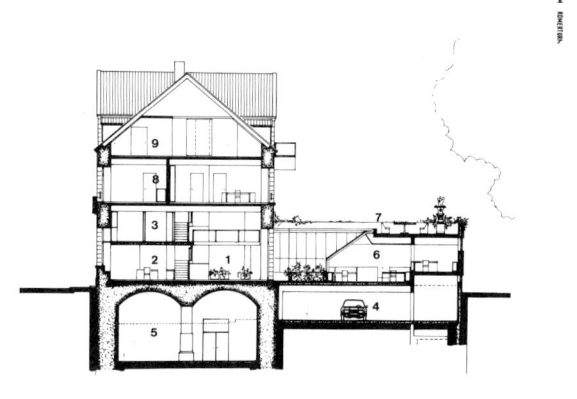

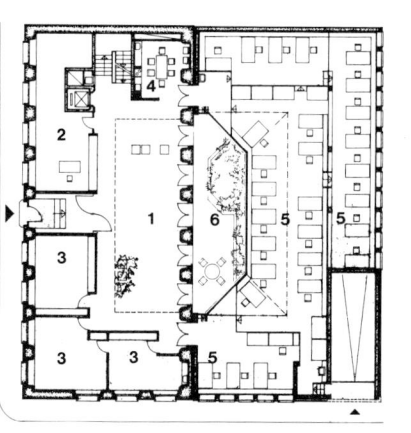

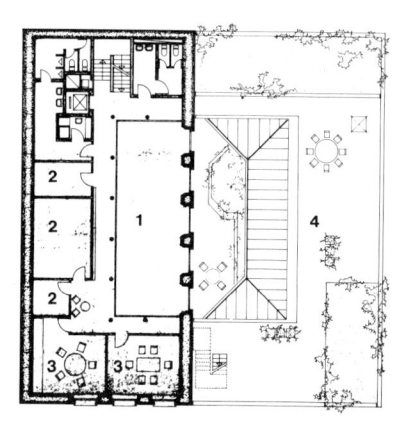

oben links Schnitt / top left Section
1 Halle / Hall
2 Sekretariat / Secretariat
3 Archiv und Besprechung / Archives and conference
4 Tiefgarage / Basement garage
5 Kellergewölbe St. Clara / Vaulted basement, St. Clara
6 Großraumbüro / Open-plan office
7 Dachterrasse / Roof garden
8 Mietbüro / Rented office
9 Wohnung / Flat

oben Mitte Erdgeschoß / top middle Ground floor
1 Halle / Hall
2 Sekretariat / Secretariat
3 Einzelbüro / Individual office
4 Pausenraum / Rest room
5 Großraumbüro / Open-plan office
6 Innenhof / Courtyard

oben rechts Zwischengeschoß / top right Mezzanine level
1 Luftraum Halle / Void over hall
2 Nebenräume / Ancillary rooms
3 Besprechung / Conference
4 Dachterrasse / Roof garden

links
Blick in den Hof zwischen Altbau und Büroanbau

rechts
Der romanische Gewölbekeller aus dem 13. Jahrhundert

left
View into courtyard between existing building and office extension

right
13th Century Romanesque vaulted cellar

Deutsche Bank Düsseldorf (Königsallee 49/51)

Zwei ehemalige Stadtpalais, erbaut 1905 und 1906 von Gabriel v. Seidl und Otto Engler, wurden im Rahmen der Neu- und Umgestaltung des Gesamtblocks der Deutschen Bank (S. 196) 1979–1981 umgebaut, dabei mit einem neuen Erschließungskern und einer neuen Haustechnik versehen. Die wertvollen Innenausbauten wurden denkmalpflegerisch sorgfältig restauriert. Als Innenarchitekt war Klaus J. Ehrensberg tätig. Unter Eingliederung in den – rechts und links inzwischen höher bebauten – Kontext wurden die ehemals ungenutzten und im Krieg zerstörten Dachböden durch zwei vollwertige kupfergedeckte Geschosse ersetzt, womit u. a. ein Saal für 200 Personen, ein festliches Foyer und zugehörige Nebenräume gewonnen wurden.

Two buildings that were originally town palais, built in 1905 and 1906 by Gabriel v. Seidl and Otto Engler, were converted between 1979 and 1981 within an overall programme of new construction and alterations to the entire Deutsche Bank block (p. 196). A new access core and new mechanical services were installed in the process. The valuable interior design elements were restored with conservational care (in co-operation with Klaus J. Ehrensberg). The attic storeys, which had not been used before and which were destroyed in the war, were replaced by two full storeys with copper cladding, as part of the overall integration of the buildings into the existing context to left and right, which had been raised in height in the meantime. As a result of this it was possible to accommodate, amongst other things, a hall for 200 persons, a festive foyer and ancillary rooms.

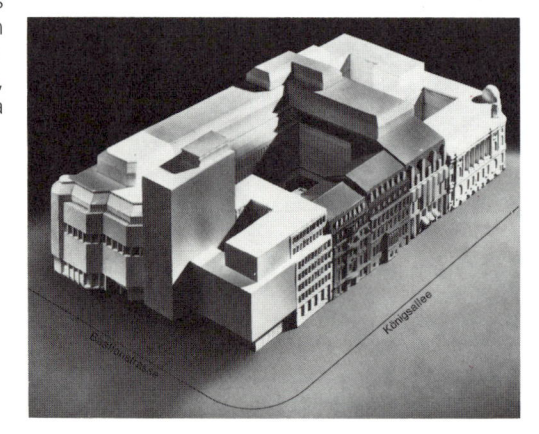

oben links Hofansicht / top left Courtyard
oben rechts Direktionsfoyer / top right Foyer to directors' room
unten links Modell: Die beiden mittleren Gebäude sind die wiederhergestellten Altbauten / bottom left Model: In the middle are the two rehabilitated historic buildings

oben links Neuer Saal im Dachgeschoß / top left New hall in mansard storey
oben Mitte Treppenaufgang / top middle Staircase
oben rechts Durchblick zum überdachten Innenhof / top right View into covered courtyard
unten rechts Zwei der restaurierten Decken / bottom right Two of the restored ceilings

Hörfunkzentrale Westdeutscher Rundfunk Köln

Der Bau des historischen Café Reichard, das dem Dom direkt gegenüberliegt, wird ausgekernt und restauriert. Nach der Instandsetzung wird das Erdgeschoß wieder das traditionsreiche Café aufnehmen, alle anderen Geschosse werden für die vier Hörfunkprogramme des Westdeutschen Rundfunks genutzt. Planung nach Erfolg im Entwurfsgutachten 1976; Baubeginn 1981.

The building in which the historic Café Reichard was housed, directly opposite the cathedral, is being gutted and restored. After restoration the ground floor will accommodate the famous coffee house again, and the other floors will serve for the four radio programmes of West German Broadcasting (WDR). Planning commenced after successful design study in 1976. Start of construction work, 1981.

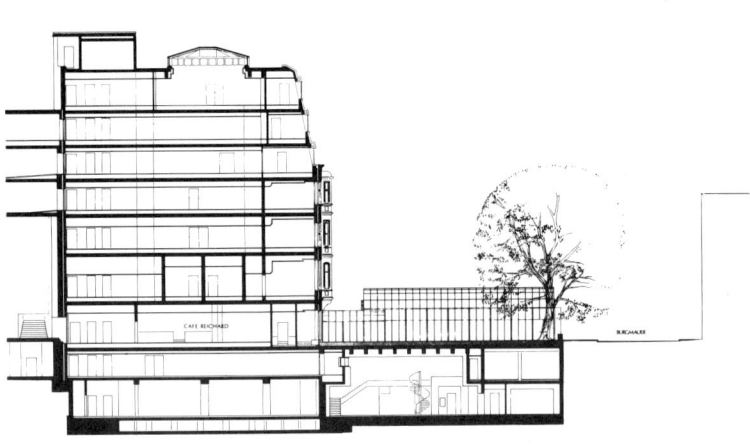

Zustand des Reichardhauses um die Jahrhundertwende

Reichard House at the turn of the century

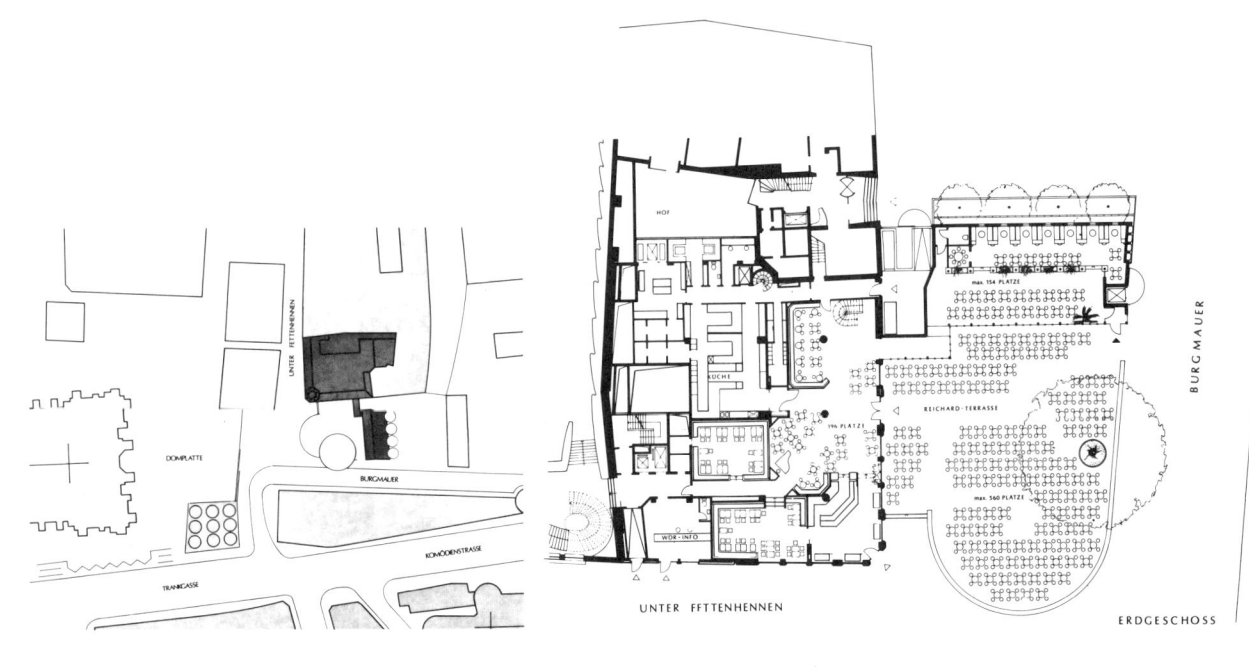

Provisorium Reichardhaus nach dem Krieg

The Reichard House post-war interim state

Blick aus dem Café-Pavillon auf den Dom

View from café pavilion to cathedral

**Wohnungsbauten, Heime, Hotels/
Housing, homes, hotels**

Haus Wolff-Limper Braunschweig

Ein Beispiel für die zahlreichen Einfamilienhäuser, die vor dem Kriege, vor allem in Braunschweig, entstanden. Gemeinsam ist allen die sorgsame Durcharbeitung von Raum und Detail.

An example of the many single-family houses built before the war, especially in Brunswick. Common to them all is the careful through-planning of space and detail.

Haus Hoeck Braunschweig

Haus eines Malers. Das durch zwei Geschosse reichende Atelier ist im Erdgeschoß mit dem Wohnbereich durch eine räumlich überleitende Kaminecke verknüpft.

The house of a painter. The studio, which extends over two floors, is linked to the living area on the ground floor by the spatial transition of a chimney corner.

»Unter den Eichen« Bad Harzburg

Gaststätte und Ladenzeile, vorwiegend für den Fremdenverkehr, am Rande des Kurparks in der Nähe einer Seilbahnstation. Baujahr 1938/39.

A restaurant and row of shops, mainly for tourism, on the edge of the spa park and close to a cable car station. Construction date 1938-39.

Haus Hess Braunschweig

Fertiggestellt 1950. Typisches Beispiel für zahlreiche weitere Einfamilienhäuser, die in den fünfziger Jahren in Braunschweig gebaut wurden.

Completed 1950. A typical example of many other single-family houses built in Brunswick in the 1950s.

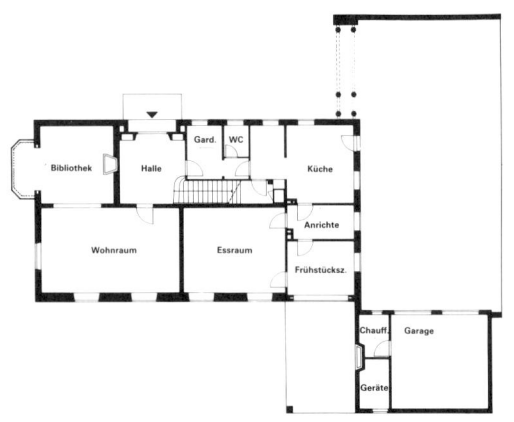

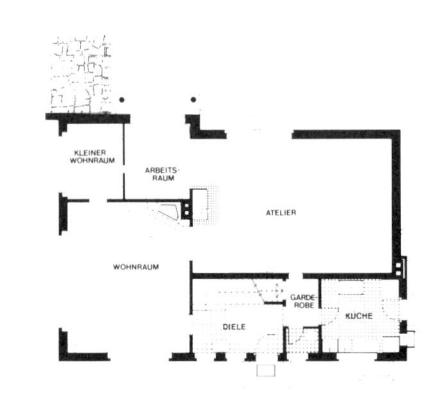

Haus Flebbe Braunschweig

Viele Wohnhäuser haben ähnliche aus Erfahrung sinnvolle Grundrißdispositionen, wie hier: der Wohntrakt, mit den Garagen, Wirtschafts- und Schläflügel gewinkelt verbunden, trennt Eingangsvorplatz und Wohngarten.

Many houses have similar layout plans to this, and they are, as experience shows, sensible ones; here the living quarters are connected at an angle to the garages, utility and sleeping wing, separated by entrance forecourt and living garden.

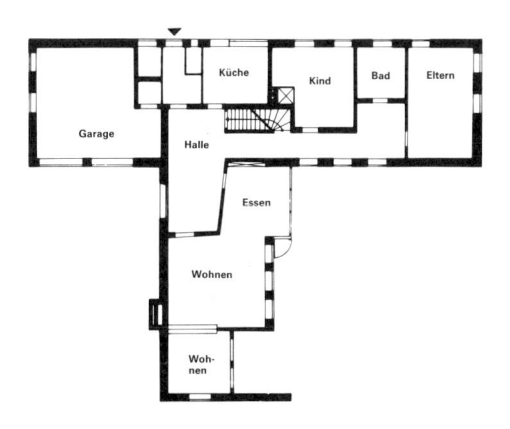

Haus Luther Braunschweig

Nach dem Kriege setzt sich die Reihe der Einfamilienhäuser fort – insgesamt sind es mehr als vierzig. Bewährtes wird immer wieder angewendet: z.B. geschlämmtes Sichtmauerwerk und die Eindeckung mit historischen Kremp-Ziegeln.

After the war the series of single-family houses was continued; in all there are more than forty of them. Well-tried features recur, for example, slurried facing brickwork and the roofing with historic Kremp tiles, (cf. Roman tiling).

Kaserne Nienburg-Langendamm

Fertigstellung 1957. Der weitläufige, in einen Wald eingebettete, Kasernen-Komplex umfaßt Unterkünfte, Kfz-Hallen, Kantine, Verwaltung, Werkstätten, Kammer- und Nebengebäude.

Completed 1957. This extensive complex of military barracks embedded in a forest comprises accommodation, motor vehicle halls, a canteen, administration, workshops, stores and ancillary buildings.

Haus Sandforth Braunschweig

Baujahr 1956. Neue Baukonstruktionen und -materialien verändern das Gesicht der Einfamilienhäuser: Flachdach und sichtbare Stahlskelettkonstruktion. Unverändert bleibt das Bemühen, den individuellen Bedürfnissen der Bauherrn die angemessene innere und äußere räumliche und landschaftliche Wohnumgebung zu schaffen.

Construction date, 1956. New forms of construction and materials change the face of single-family houses: flat roof and an exposed steel skeleton frame. What is unchanged is the effort to create the appropriate internal and external spatial and landscape habitat for the individual needs of the client.

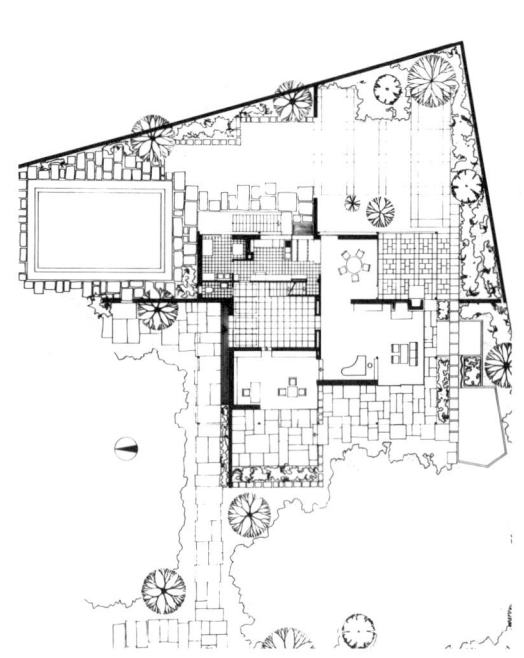

oben Erdgeschoß / top Ground floor
unten 1. Obergeschoß / bottom 1st Floor

Haus Munte Braunschweig

Fertigstellung 1965. Ein Haus ohne Flure, dessen Reiz im fließenden Übergang der Räume vom Wohnzimmer über das an einem kleinen Patio gelegene Eßzimmer zum Kinderspielraum liegt.

Completed 1965. A house without halls or corridors, whose attraction lies in the flowing transitions between rooms, – from the living room via the dining room, situated next to a small patio, to the children's play area.

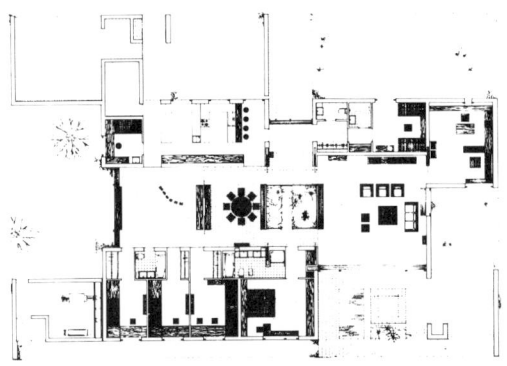

Haus Roedenbeck Stöckheim

Das Wohnhaus eines Gartenarchitekten, fertiggestellt 1965, mit seinem unkonventionellen Grundriß (Erschließung Kindertrakt), verbindet sich in vielfältigen Verzahnungen (Höfe, Pergolen, Mauern, Palisaden) mit der Landschaft.

This house, completed in 1965 and belonging to a landscape architect, with its unconventional layout, (children's realm access), creates numerous interlocking links (courtyards, pergolas, walls, palisades) with the landscape.

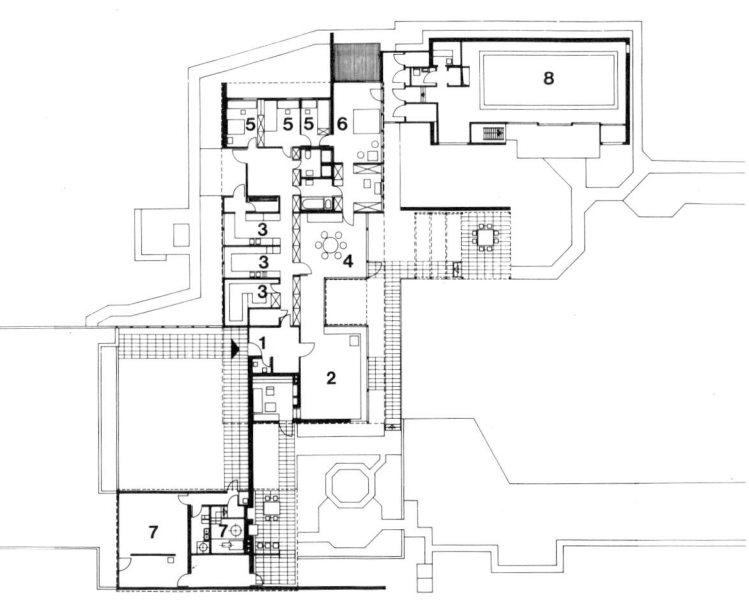

1 Halle / Hall
2 Wohnen / Living
3 Wirtschaftsräume / Kitchen + utilities
4 Essen / Dining
5 Kinder / Children
6 Eltern / Parents
7 Garage + Heizung / Garage + heating
8 Schwimmbad / Swimming pool

Haus Kraemer 1 Braunschweig **Haus Kraemer 2 Braunschweig**

Das 1937 fertiggestellte, erste Haus von Friedrich Wilhelm Kraemer enthält Büro und Wohnung des Architekten, sowie einen Konzertsaal.

Friedrich Wilhelm Kraemer's first house, completed in 1937, contains the architect's office and residence as well as a concert hall.

Nach nur 3 Monaten Bauzeit 1955 fertiggestelltes Wohnhaus einer exakten Vorstellung vom individuellen Wohnen als Verwirklichung der Erfahrung aus vielen vorhergehenden Wohnhausprojekten. Der Wohnbereich öffnet sich nach Süden zum weiten Garten und nach Westen zu einem intimen Höfchen.

Completed after a mere three month period of construction (1955), the house represents a precise concept of individual habitation as the sum of experiences gained from the numerous preceding house projects. The living realm opens out to a broad garden to the south and to a small intimate courtyard to the west.

Studentenwohnheime Berlin

Von 1967 bis 1969 entstanden in der Bitscherstraße und in der Clayallee ähnliche Studentenwohn-Anlagen, bestehend aus kreuzflügeligen Einheiten, die mit sparsamstem Verkehrsflächenaufwand 8 Studentenappartments (mit Dusche, WC und Kochnische) um ein zentrales Treppenhaus, jeweils um ein $1/4$ Geschoß versetzt, gruppieren. In der Mollwitzstraße wird dieses Thema mit der Kombination von zwei Kreuzeinheiten variiert.

Between 1967 and 1969 two similar complexes of student housing were built in the Bitscherstraße and the Clayallee. They consist of cross-wing units that are most economical in terms of access space and contain 8 student flats (with shower, WC and kitchen recess), grouped around a central staircase, and each rising a $1/4$ storey. In the Mollwitzstraße this theme is varied, using a combination of two cross units.

Mitte
Schnitt, Kreuzgrundriß und drei Wohnhäuser in der Clay-Allee
rechts
Addierter Kreuzgrundriß in der Mollwitzstraße

middle
Section, cross-form plan and three blocks in Clay-Allee
right
Additive cross-form plan in Mollwitzstraße

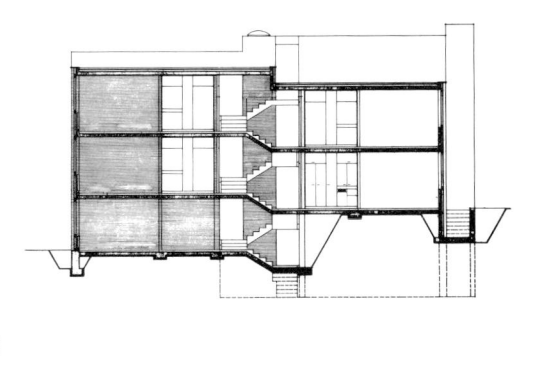

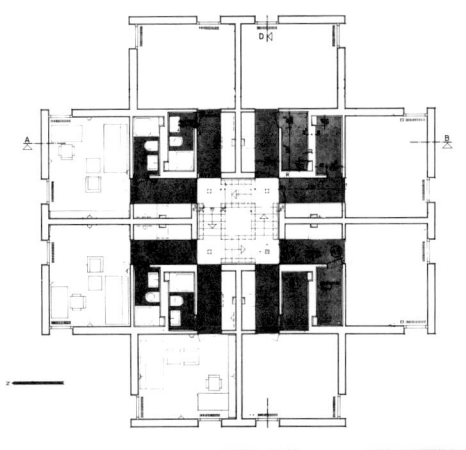

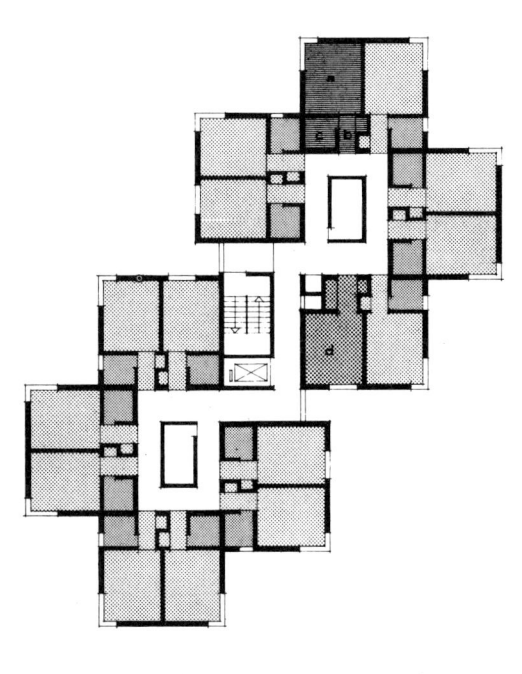

Atriumhotel Braunschweig

Fertiggestellt 1966. Das Hotel bildet den Endpunkt eines umfangreichen Wohn- und Geschäftshauskomplexes. Grundidee war, die aus Kostengründen nicht klimatisierten Zimmer vom Verkehrslärm der umgebenden Straßen abzuwenden. Sie liegen mit Ausnahme einer Front, die auf einen schönen Park blickt, alle zum Atriumhof. Unter den drei Zimmergeschossen befinden sich im Erdgeschoß und 1. Obergeschoß Eingangshalle, Empfang, Verwaltung, Restaurants, Bar und Gesellschaftsräume. Zentrum des Hotels ist der reizvolle, bepflanzte Atriumhof, dessen plätschernder Brunnen die Atmosphäre entspannender Ruhe verbreitet. Den Brunnen krönt ein Kapitell des leider abgerissenen Braunschweiger Schlosses.

Completed 1966. The hotel forms the final point of an extensive housing and commercial building complex. The basic idea behind this project was to orientate the rooms, which were for cost reasons not air conditioned, away from the traffic noise of the surrounding streets. With the exception of one face, which has an attractive park as aspect, all the rooms are situated facing a closed courtyard. Beneath the three floors of hotel rooms and situated on the ground and first floors are the entrance hall, reception, administration, restaurants, bar, lounges and other public rooms. The heart of the hotel is formed by the attractive, planted courtyard, the plashing fountain of which radiates an atmosphere of relaxation and peace. The fountain is crowned by a column capital from Brunswick Palace, which has unfortunately been demolished.

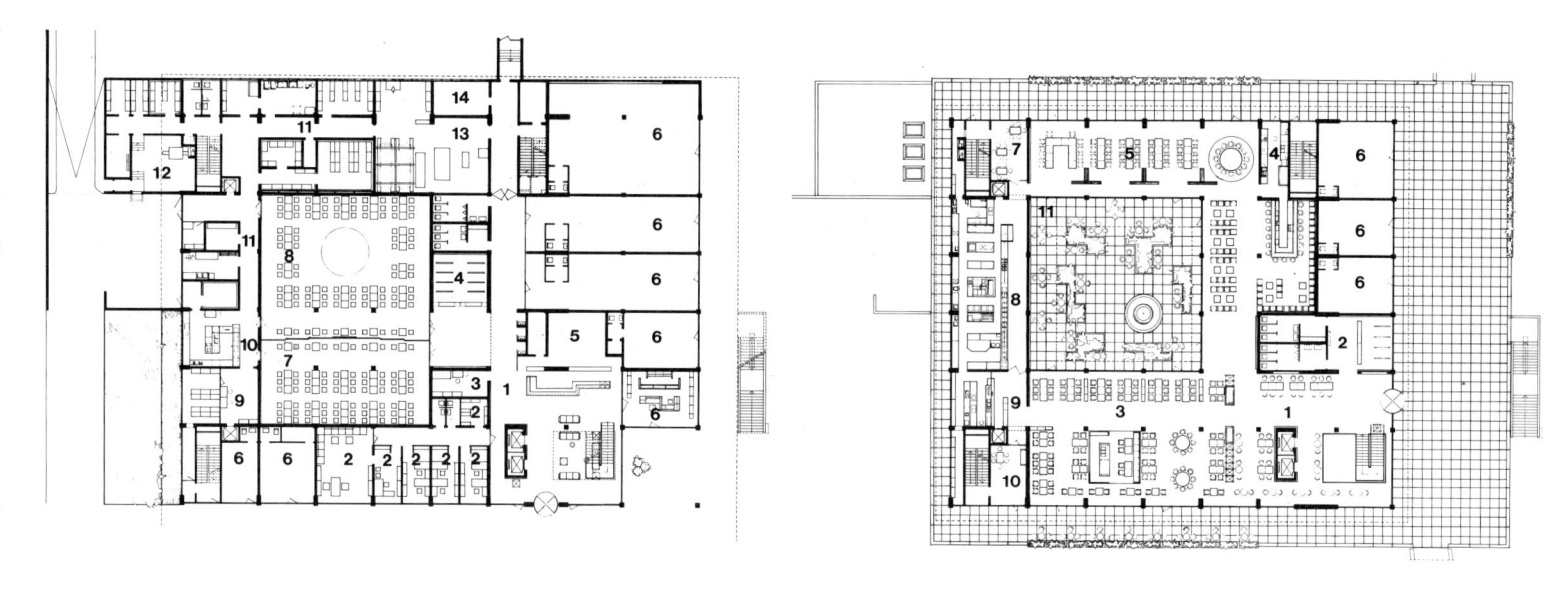

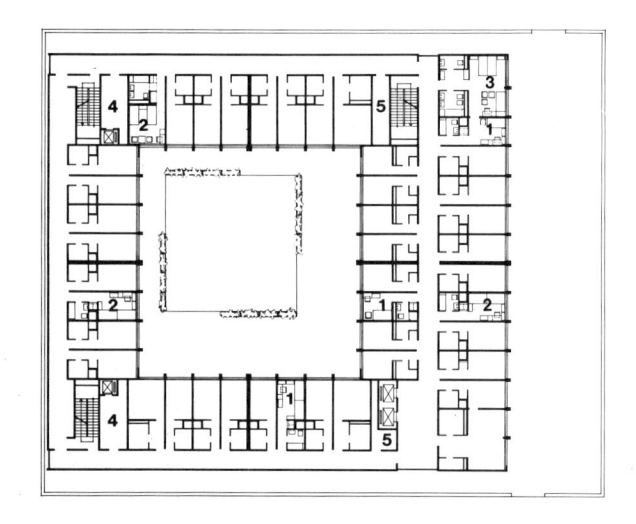

oben links Erdgeschoß /
top left Ground floor

1 Hotelhalle / Hotel hall
2 Verwaltung / Administration
3 Kofferraum / Luggage store
4 Garderobe / Cloakroom
5 Empfangschef / Head receptionist
6 Laden / Shop
7 Kleiner Saal / Small hall
8 Großer Saal / Large hall
9 Wäscherei / Laundry
10 Anrichte + Ausgabe / Kitchen
11 Lagerung + Vorbereitung / Food storage + preparation
12 Heizung / Heating
13 Lüftung + Warmwasser / Ventilation + warm water
14 Stuhllager / Chair store

oben rechts Obergeschoß /
top right Upper floor

1 Café / Café
2 Garderobe / Cloakroom
3 Restaurant / Restaurant
4 Barraum mit Barküche / Bar and bar kitchen
5 Konferenzräume / Conference rooms
6 Laden / Shop
7 Personalspeiseraum / Staff dining room
8 Küche / Kitchen
9 Frühstücksküche / Breakfast kitchen
10 Kellner Office / Waiters' pantry
11 Atrium / Courtyard

unten Bettengeschoß /
bottom Bedroom floor

1 Einbettzimmer / Single bedroom
2 Zweibettzimmer / Double bedroom
3 Dreibettzimmer / Three-bed-room
4 Wäscheräume / Linen room
5 Installationsraum / Mechanical services

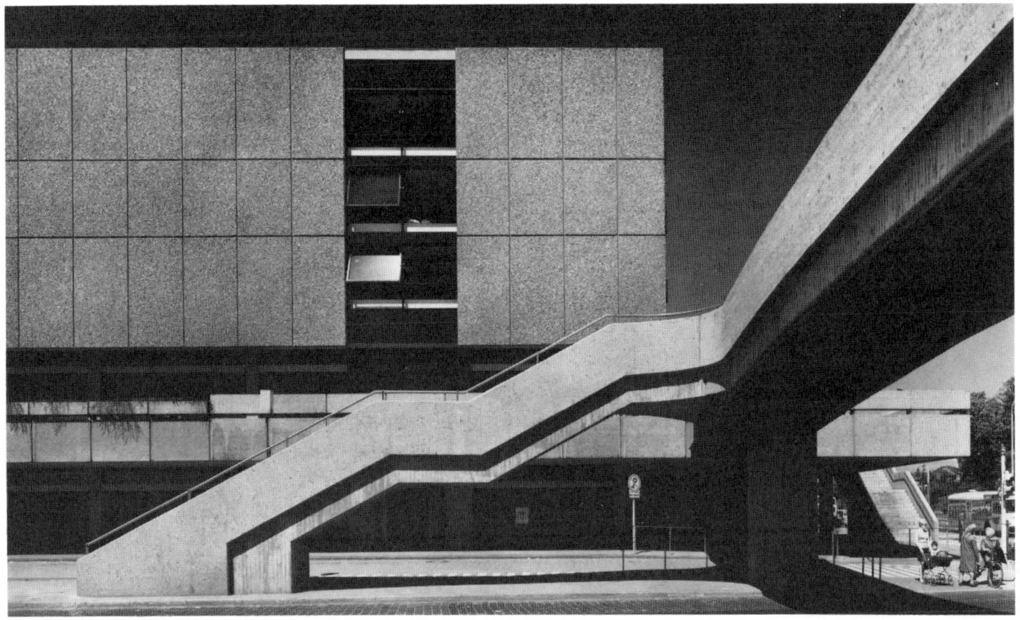

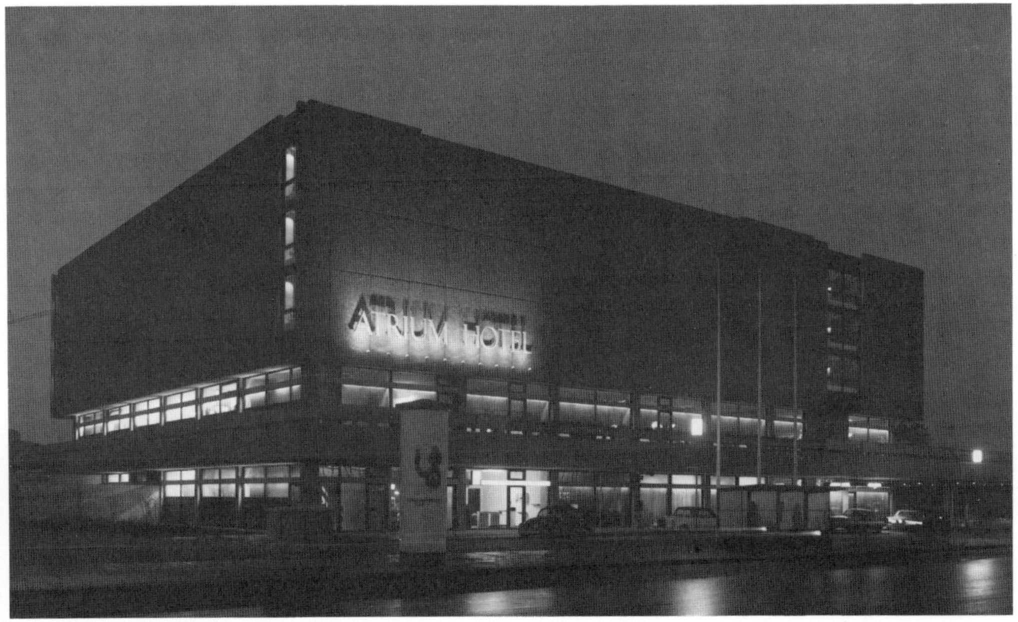
ATRIUM HOTEL

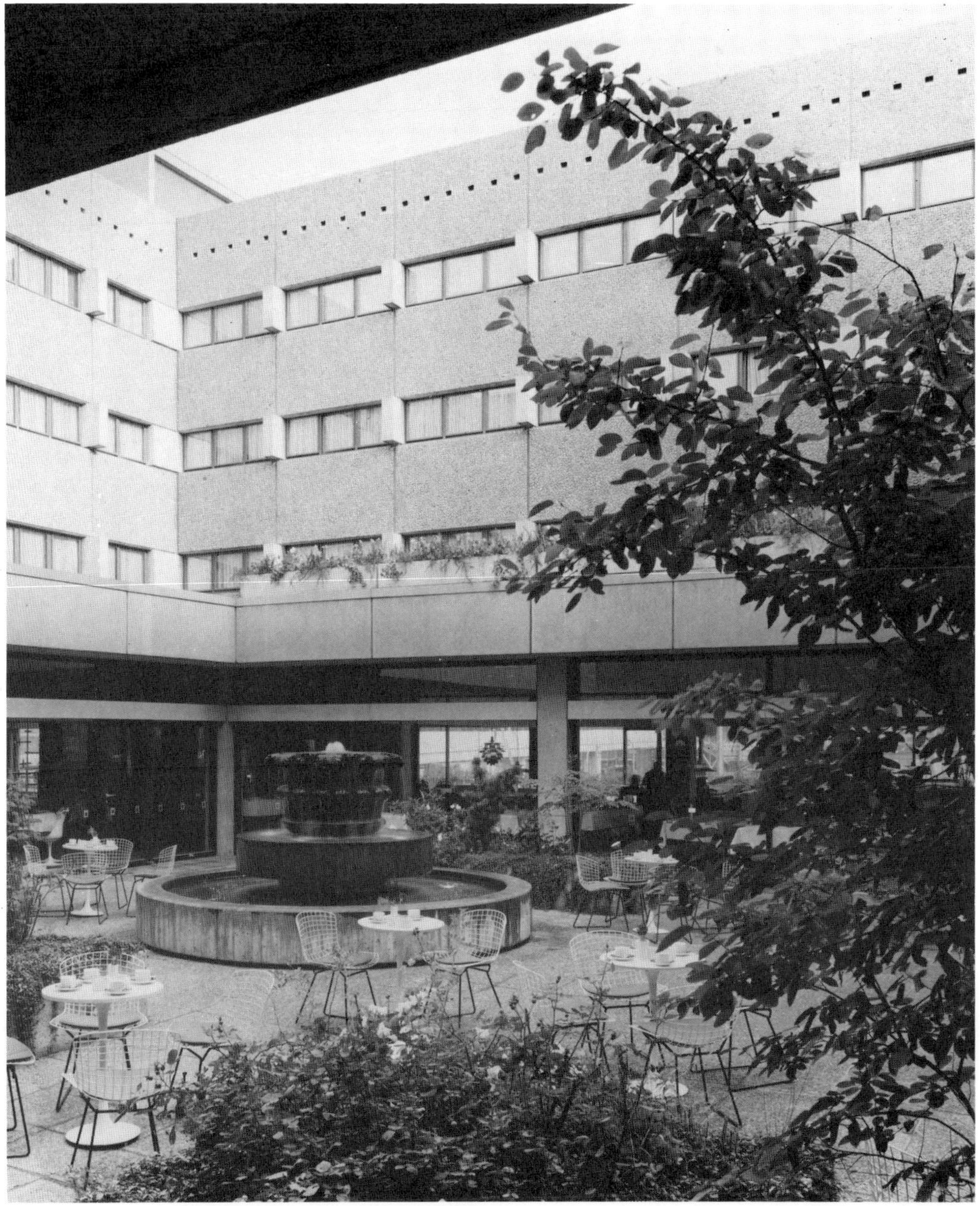

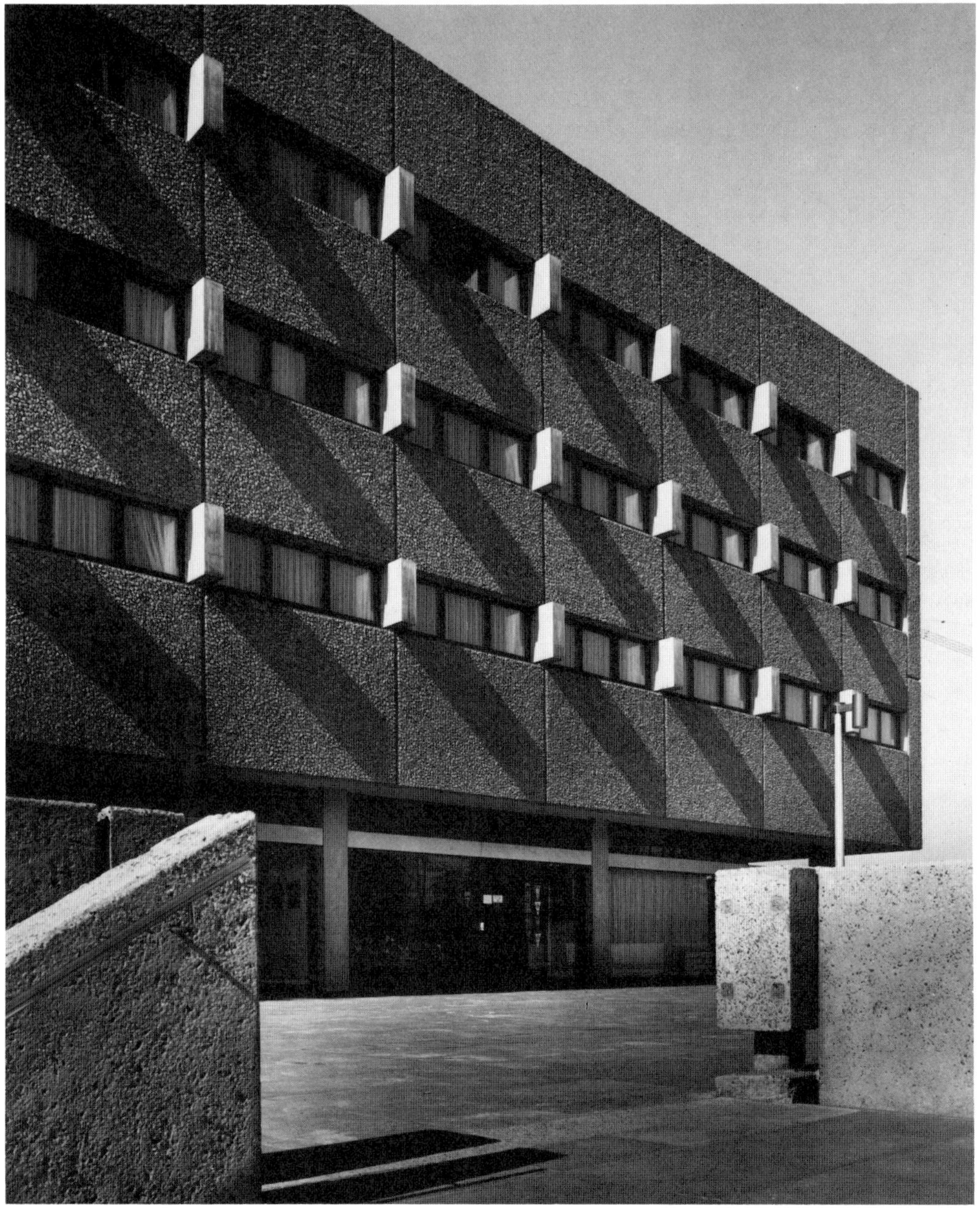

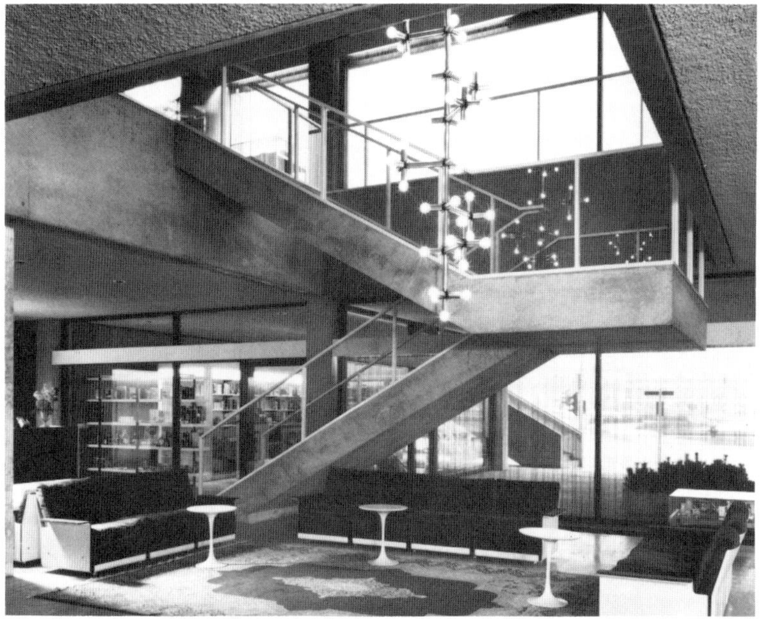

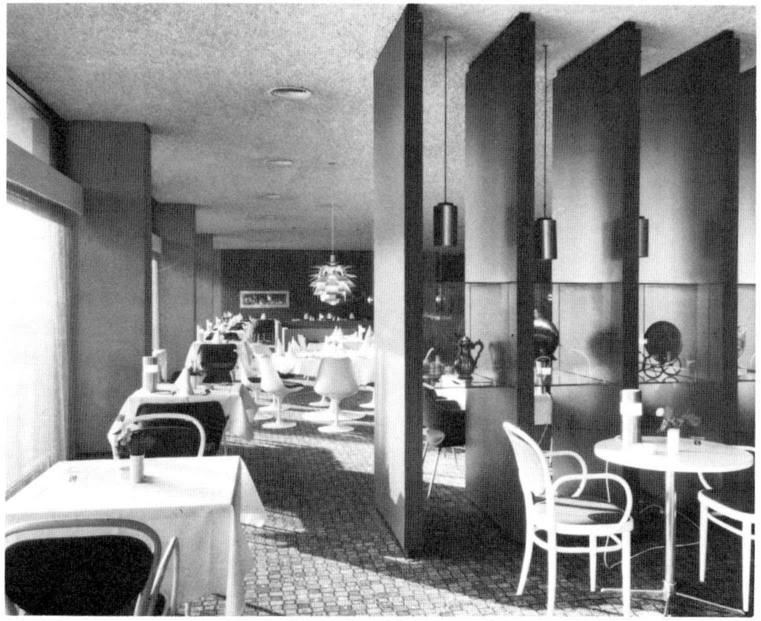

Wohnbebauung am Alsterufer Hamburg

1. Preis im Wettbewerb 1968. Die Wohnungen sind so angeordnet, daß alle Anteil an dem schönen Ausblick auf die Alster haben. Ihre Loggienwände sollen an Segel erinnern.

1st Prize in competition, 1968. The dwellings are laid out so that each of them shares a beautiful view to the Alster. The walls to the loggias are meant to remind one of sails.

Hotel Holiday-Inn Wolfsburg

Fertiggestellt 1970 als erster Teil eines innerstädtischen Zentrums. Die Schwierigkeit lag darin, die Standardvorstellungen des Hotelkonzerns mit den städtebaulichen und baurechtlichen Notwendigkeiten in Einklang zu bringen.

Completed 1970 as the first part of an inner-city centre. The difficulty of the scheme lay in reconciling the standard concepts of the hotel concern with the constraints of urban planning and building regulations.

1 Parkpalette / Parking
2 Vorfahrt / Arrivals
3 Eingangshalle / Entrance hall
4 Kiosk / Shop
5 Aufzugshalle / Lift hall
6 Personal- + Lagerräume / Staff rooms + stores
7 Gästezimmer / Guest rooms
8 Anlieferung / Deliveries
9 Schwimmbad / Swimming pool
10 Restaurant / Restaurant
11 Bar / Bar
12 Küchenbereich / Kitchen area
13 Café / Café
14 Gesellschaftsräume / Lounge

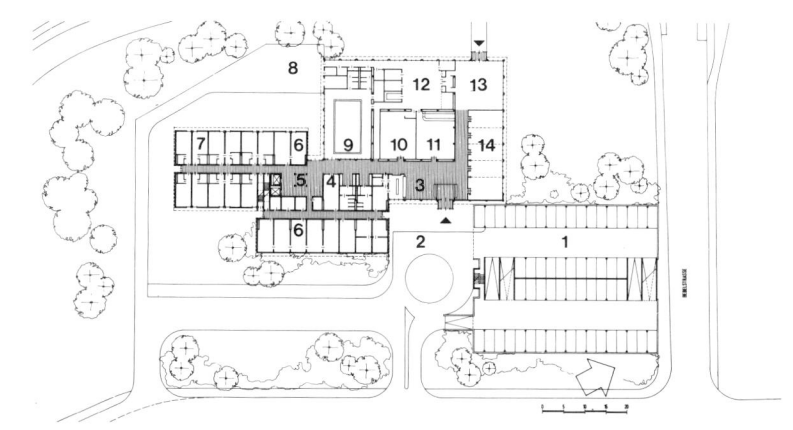

Erdgeschoß / Ground floor

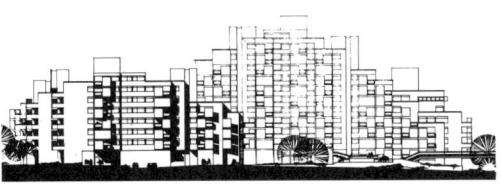

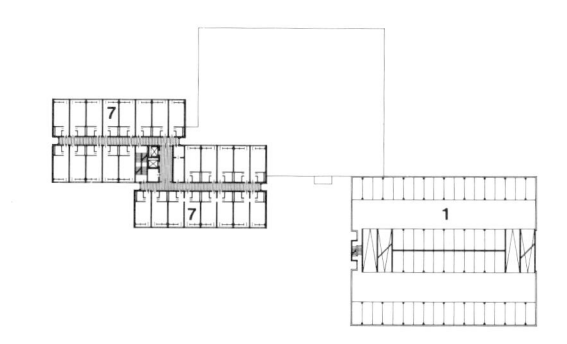

Normalgeschoß / Typical floor

33

Eifelhöhenklinik Marmagen

Das Konzept dieses Rehabilitationszentrum besteht darin, die Funktionen einer modernen Spezialklinik für Innere Medizin, Orthopädie und Neurologie mit dem Komfort eines Hotels zu verbinden. Über drei am Hang liegende Sockelgeschosse mit den medizinischen Einrichtungen, den Schwimmbädern und den Club- und Speiseräumen erheben sich sechs Bettengeschosse mit maximal 476 Betten sowie ein Terrassengeschoß als Aussichtscafé.

The concept underlying this rehabilitation centre comprises the combining of those functions specific to a modern specialist clinic for internal medicine, orthopaedics and neurology with the comfort of an hotel. Above a three-storey plinth structure set on the slope of a hill and housing medical facilities, the swimming pools, club and dining rooms, rise six floors of bedrooms, providing space for a maximum of 476 beds, plus a terrace storey with café and panorama view.

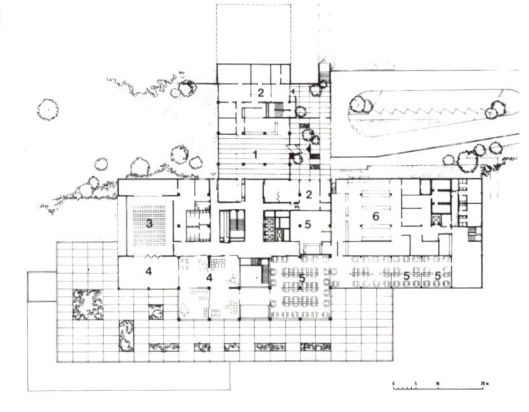

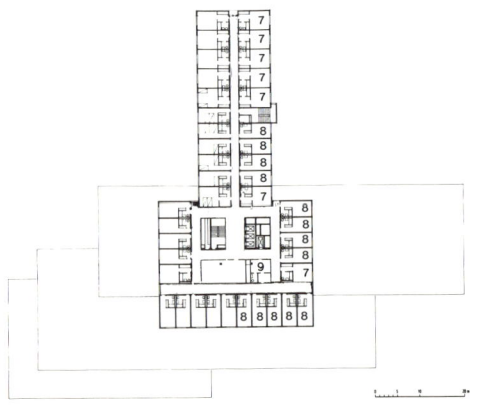

Erdgeschoß + Bettengeschoß / Ground floor + bedroom floor
1 Eingangshalle / Entrance hall
2 Verwaltung / Administration
3 Mehrzweckraum / Multi-purpose space
4 Clubräume / Club rooms
5 Speisesäle / Dining halls
6 Küche / Kitchen
7 Einzelzimmer / Single room
8 Doppelzimmer / Double room
9 Geschoßservice / Floor service

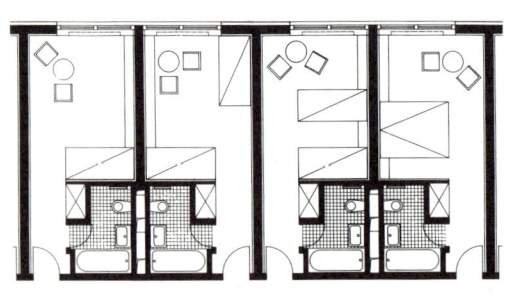

Studentenwohnheim Berlin-Schlachtensee

Eines der ersten Gruppenwohnheime, die im Neubau die in Altbauten beliebte Wohnform der Wohngemeinschaft anbieten. Fünf bis sieben Schlaf- und Arbeitszimmer (Privatzone) werden über den gemeinsamen Wohnraum erschlossen; Küche und Sanitärbereich werden ebenfalls gemeinsam genutzt. Die Wohnungen sind so kombinierbar, daß die Gruppengrößen variiert werden können.

One of the first student group-housing schemes to provide in a new building the popular communal form of living found in older housing. Access to between five and seven bed-sitting rooms (private zone) is via the communal living room. The kitchen and sanitary area are also used communally. The dwellings can be combined in various ways, allowing a variation of group sizes.

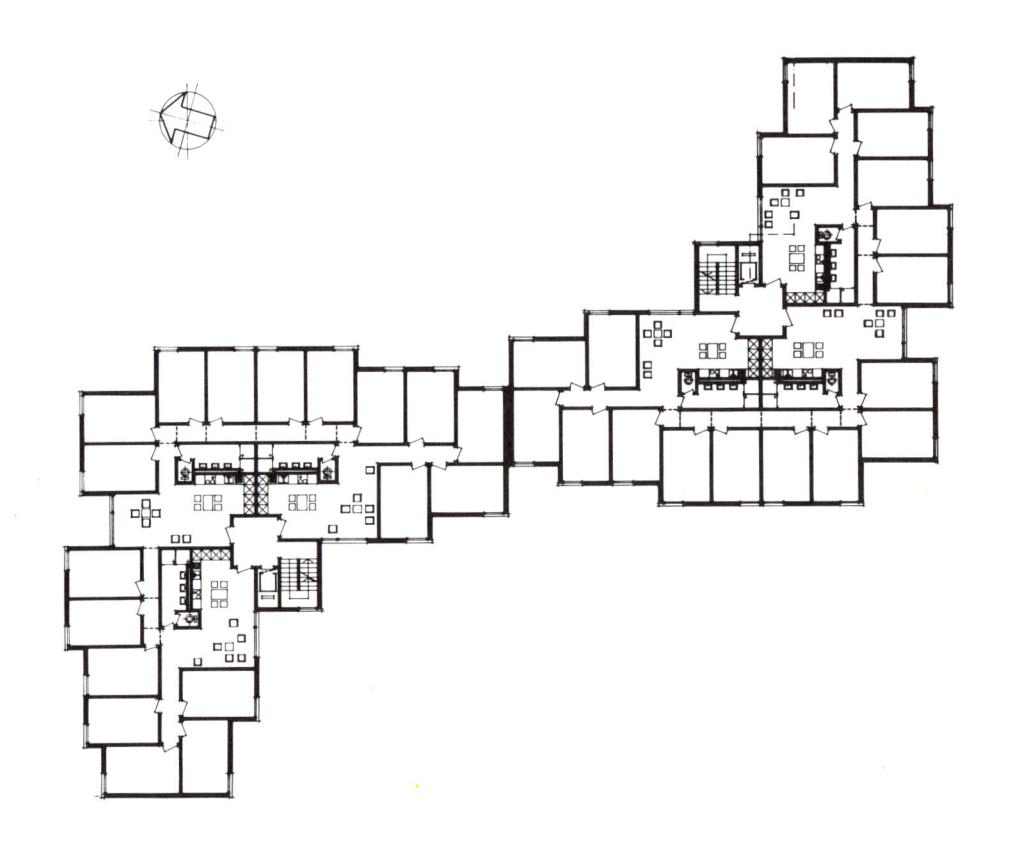

Studentenwohnheim Würzburg-Keesburg

Fortentwicklung des Berliner Typs der Appartmentswohnheime (S. 29), die wegen der Möglichkeit individueller Möblierungsanordnung und der größeren Ungestörtheit immer beliebter wurden.

A development of the Berlin-type apartment hostel for students (p. 29), that came to enjoy ever greater popularity on account of the individual furnishing arrangements it permitted and the greater degree of privacy.

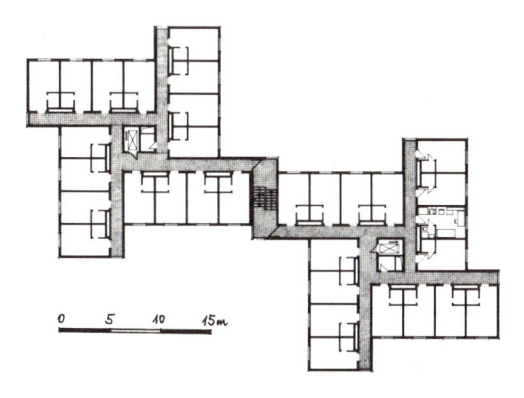

Studentenwohnheim Bamberg

Konstruktive und wirtschaftliche Weiterentwicklung des schon vorher in Berlin und Würzburg angewandten Systems kreuzförmig versetzter Einbundtrakte um einen zentralen Erschließungskern.

Further structural and economic development of a system of student hostels previously employed in Berlin and Würzburg and consisting of cross-form staggered tracts situated about a central access core.

Studentisches Wohnen

Bundesoffener Wettbewerb 1973, bei dem am Beispiel der Standorte Oldenburg, Nürnberg und Krefeld wirtschaftliche und zukunftsweisende Lösungen gefunden werden sollten, ein 2. Preis, zwei 5. Preise.

A second prize and two fifth prizes for student housing in a competition held in 1973, open to the entire area of the Federal Republic of Germany. Economical, forward-looking solutions were required based on examples in Oldenburg, Nuremberg and Krefeld.

Studentenwohnheim Würzburg Zweierweg

Durch Zusammenlegung von zwei oder drei Studentenappartements können Zwei- oder Drei-Zimmerwohnungen gebildet werden, falls das Wohnheim nicht voll ausgenutzt sein sollte, (siehe Nutzungsvarianten S. 37). Baubeginn 1981.

By combining two or three one-room student flats, two- or three-room dwellings can be formed in the event of the home not being fully used, (see Alternative layouts p. 37). Start of construction, 1981.

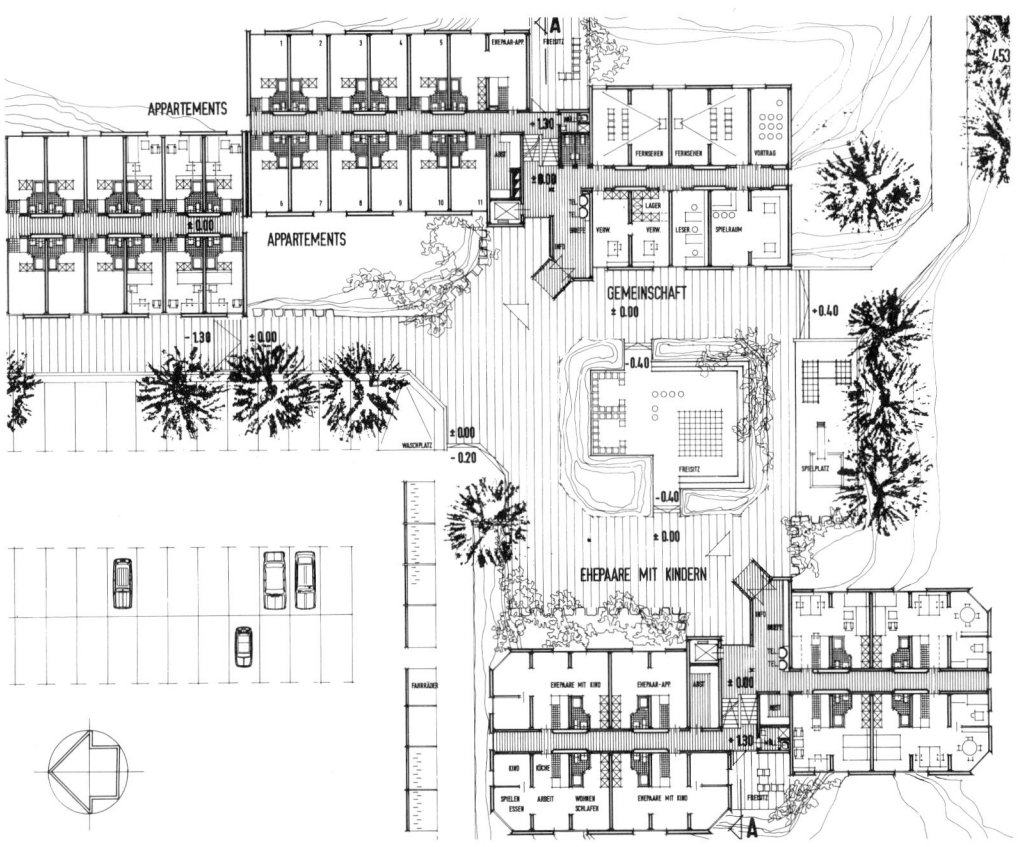

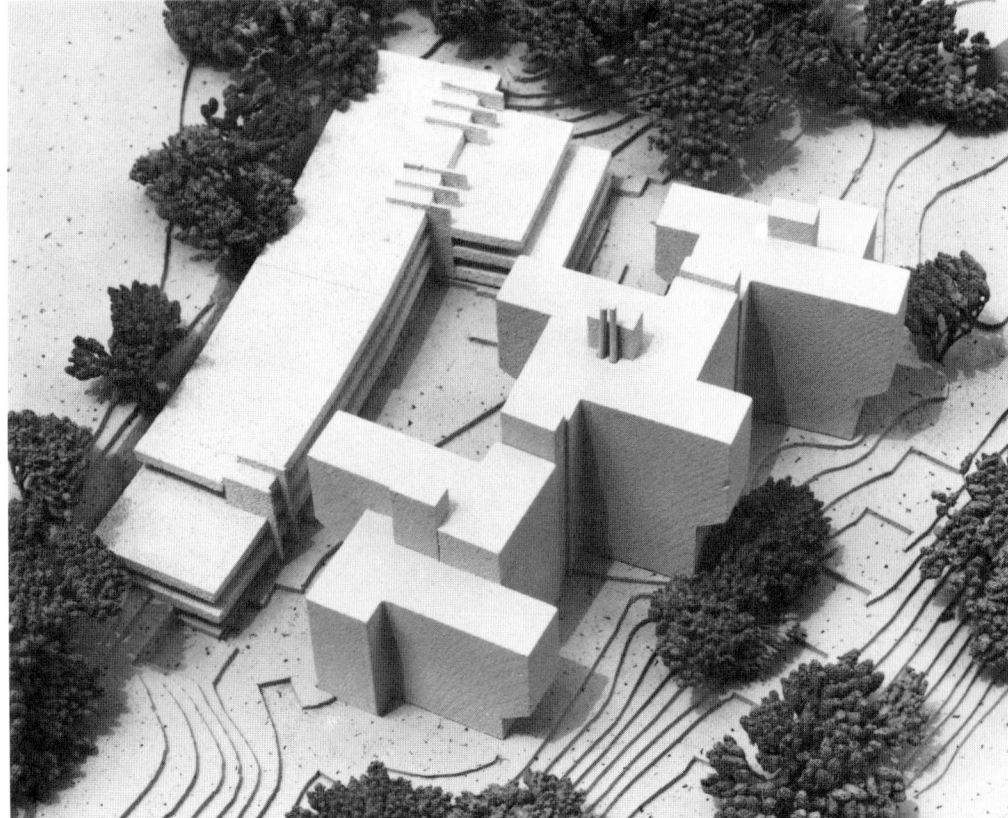

oben links Erdgeschoß /
top left Ground floor

Erdgeschoß / Ground floor
1 Eingangshalle / Entrance hall
2 Studentenappartment (17 m²) / Student apartments
3 Hausmeisterwohnung (85 m²) / Caretaker's flat
4 Kinderspielplatz / Children's play area
5 Gemeinschaftshaus / Community house
6 Fahrradstand / Bicycle stand
7 Traforaum / Transformer station
8 PKW-Garagenplätze / Car garages

unten links 6. + 7. OG /
bottom left 6th + 7th Floor

oben rechts Nutzungs-
varianten /
top right Alternative layouts
1 Einzelappartement (17 m²) / Single-room flat
2 Doppelappartement (35 m²) / 2-room-flat
3 Appartement für ein Ehepaar mit Kind (43 m²) / Flat for couple with one child
4 4-Zimmer-Wohnung (65 m²) / 4-room flat
5 4-Zimmer-Wohnung (85 m²) / 4-room flat

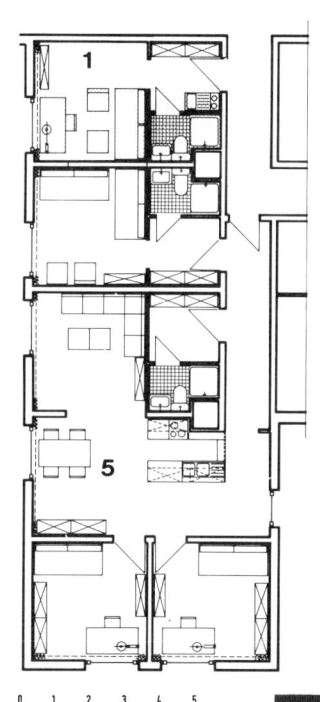

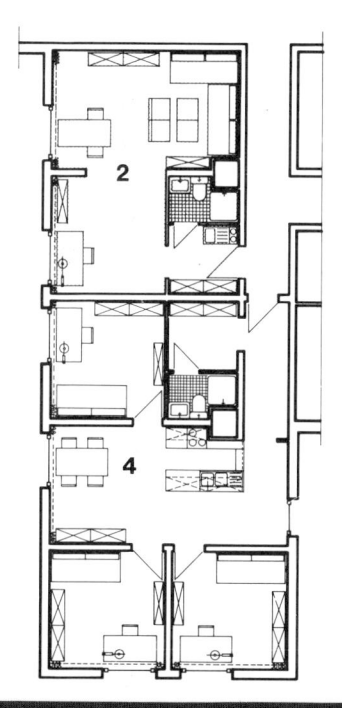

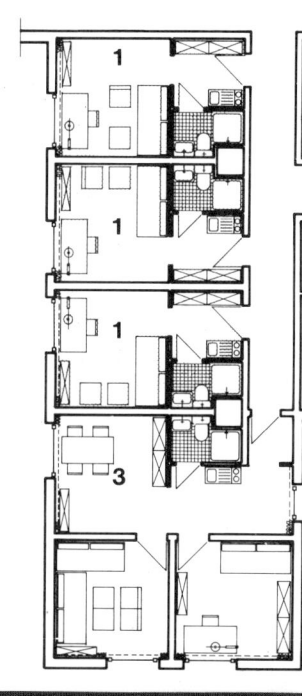

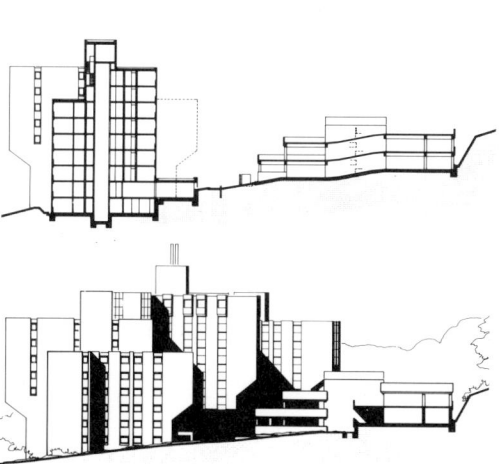

**Wohn- und Geschäftshaus
Am Römerturm 2 Köln**

Innerstädtisches Sanierungsprojekt mit Läden im Erdgeschoß, Wohnungen und Büros in den Obergeschossen. Planungsbeginn 1974, Fertigstellung 1983.

An inner-city rehabilitation project with shops on the ground floor and housing and offices on the upper floors. Commencement of planning, 1974, Completion 1983.

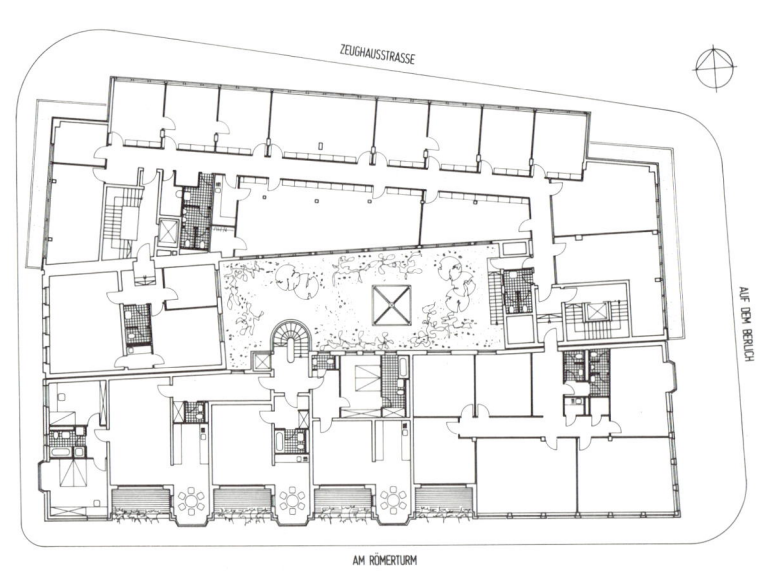

Musikerhaus in Monte Leon bei Maspalomas Gran Canaria

Fertiggestellt 1971. Um einen Patio gruppieren sich die Wohnungen der Musiker, ein Konzertraum, zwei Gästewohnungen und die Wohnung des Hausmeisters.

Completed 1971. The musicians' dwellings, a concert room, two flats for guests and the caretaker's flat are grouped about a patio.

Altenheim St. Vinzenz Köln

Wettbewerb 1979, 2. Preis, Einbeziehung eines alten Verwaltungsgebäudes in eine umfangreiche Altenwohnanlage.

Competition entry 1979 for St. Vinzenz Old People's Home, Cologne; 2nd prize. Incorporation of an existing administrative building into an extensive old people's housing complex.

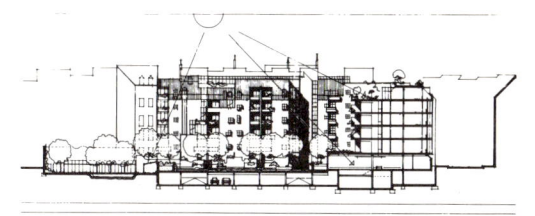

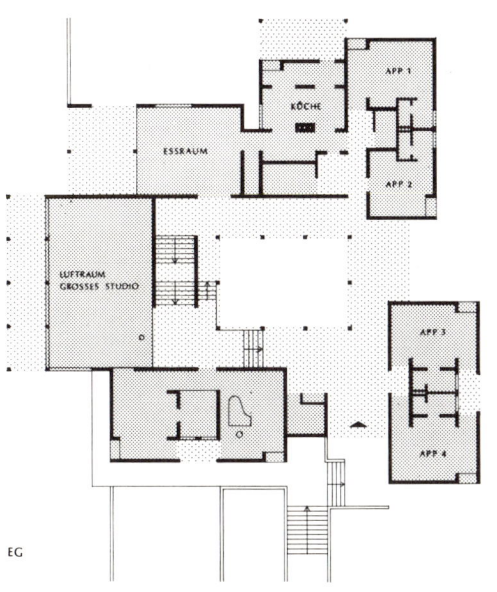

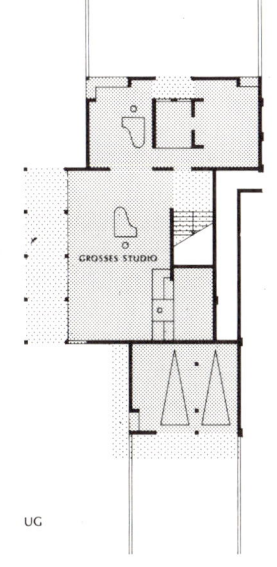

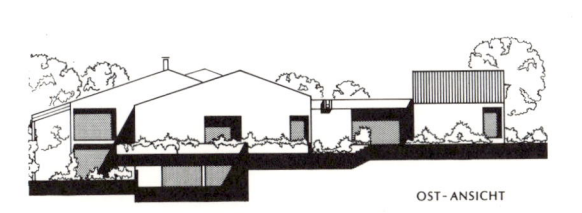

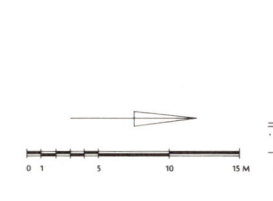

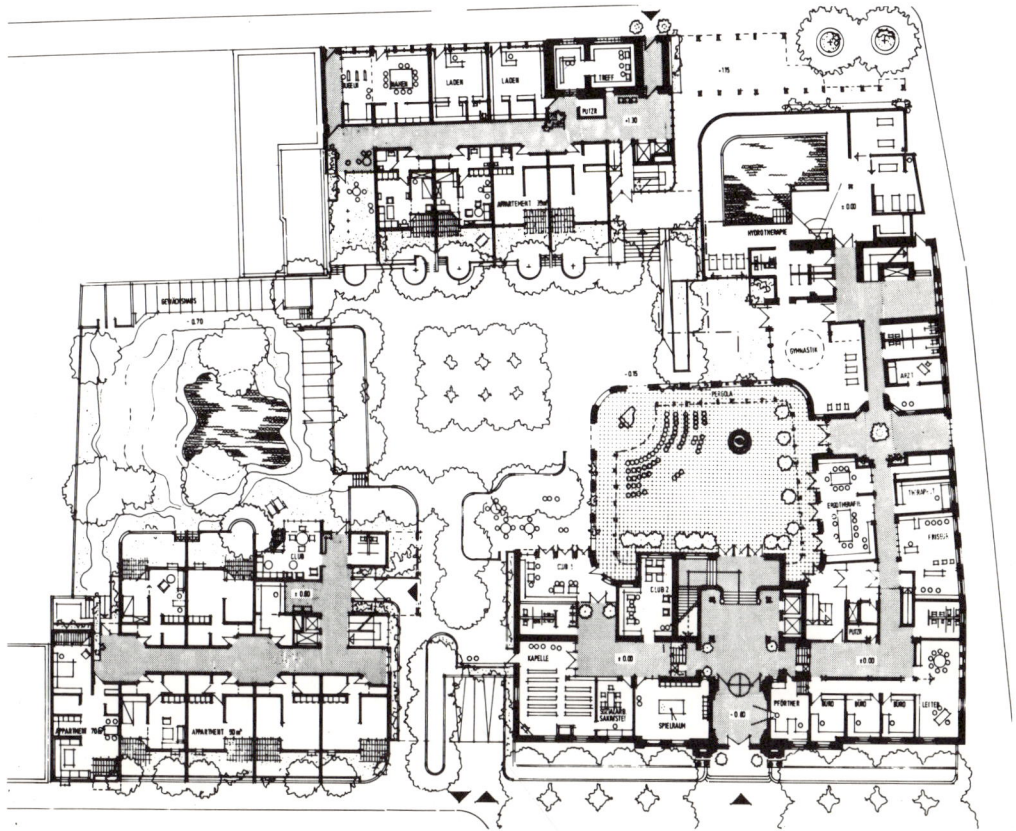

**Schul- und Hochschulbauten/
School and university buildings**

Oberschule Wolfsburg

Aufbau- und Abendgymnasium Dortmund

1. Preis im Wettbewerb 1950. Errichtung in mehreren Bauabschnitten. Ein Entwurf, der die skandinavischen Vorbilder der damaligen Zeit spüren läßt.

1st Prize in a competition, 1950, for a secondary school in Wolfsburg. Erected in several stages. A design in which there are clear traces of the Scandinavian models of that time.

2. Preis im Wettbewerb 1954, fertiggestellt 1959.

2nd Prize in a competition in 1954 for an evening college and college for further secondary education in Dortmund. Completed in 1959.

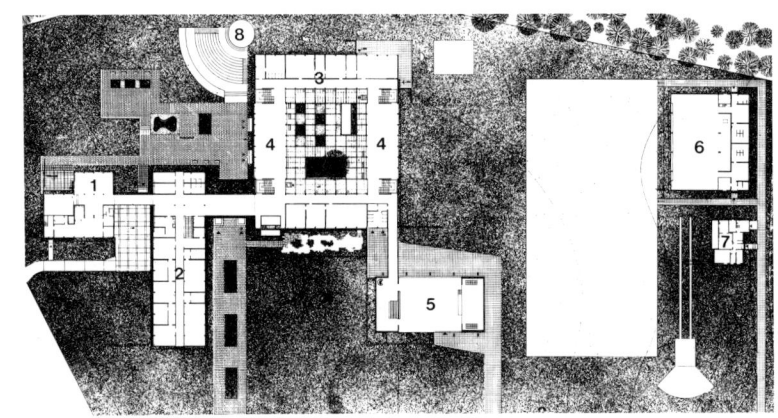

Erdgeschoß / Ground floor
1 Mensa / Dining hall
2 Sonderklassentrakt / Special classrooms tract
3 Normalklassen / Normal classrooms
4 Pausenhallen / Recreation halls
5 Aula / Assembly hall
6 Turnhalle / Gymnasium
7 Hausmeister / Caretaker
8 Freilichtbühne / Open air theatre

Mittelschule Peine

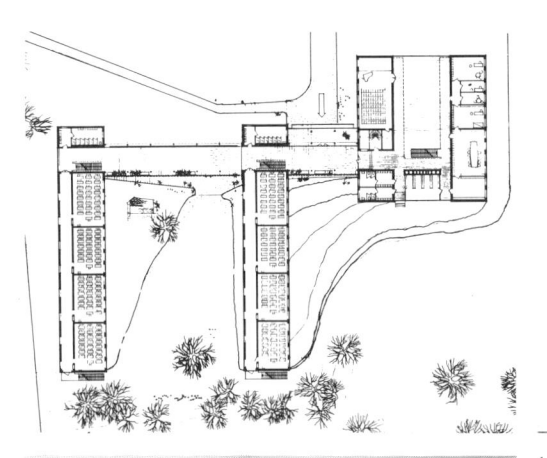

Handelsschule Heidelberg

1. Preis im Wettbewerb 1952, fertiggestellt 1954.

1st Prize in a competition in 1952 for a secondary school (up to O-level) in Peine. Completed in 1954.

1. Preis im Wettbewerb 1953, fertiggestellt 1957.

1st Prize in a competition in 1953 for a commercial college in Heidelberg. Completed in 1957.

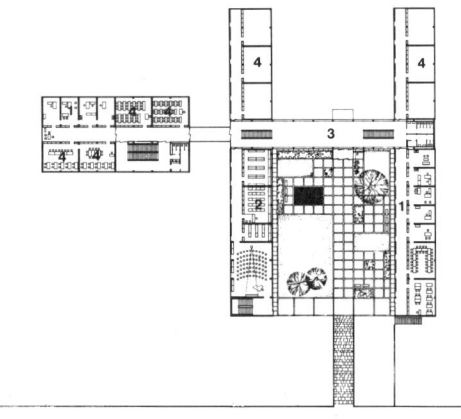

1 Verwaltung + Lehrerzimmer / Administration + teachers' room
2 Sonderklassentrakt / Special classrooms tract
3 Pausenhalle / Recreation hall
4 Normalklassen / Normal classrooms

Auditorium Maximum TH Braunschweig

Als erster Abschnitt des seit 1958 errichteten Hochschulforums entstand das Auditorium maximum (1000 Plätze) mit großem Physik-Hörsaal (600 Plätze) im Untergeschoß. Der kristallinen Form des Beton- und Glaskubus im Äußeren entspricht die strenge Ordnung der Bauglieder im Inneren in wiederkehrenden Proportionen.

The first stage of the university forum, under construction from 1958 onwards, was the main auditorium for 1000 persons, with a large physics lecture hall (600 places) in the basement. The external crystalline form of this cube of concrete and glass corresponds to the strict ordering of the building elements on the interior in its repeating proportions.

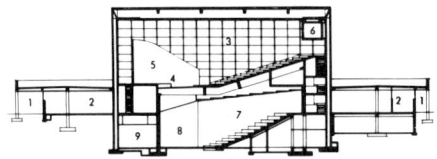

Schnitt West-Ost / Section West-East
1 Arkade / Arcades
2 Garderobe / Cloakroom
3 Auditorium / Main lecture hall
4 Podium / Podium
5 Schallwand / Acoustic screen
6 Vorführkabine / Projection cabin
7 Physiksall / Physics hall
8 Demonstration / Demonstration area
9 Vorbereitung / Preparation area

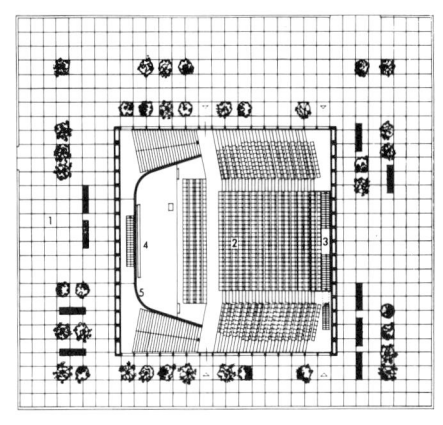

Terrassengeschoß / 1st floor roof level
1 Terrasse / Roof terrace
2 Auditorium / Main lecture hall
3 Vorführkabine / Projection cabin
4 Podium / Podium
5 Schallwand / Acoustic screen

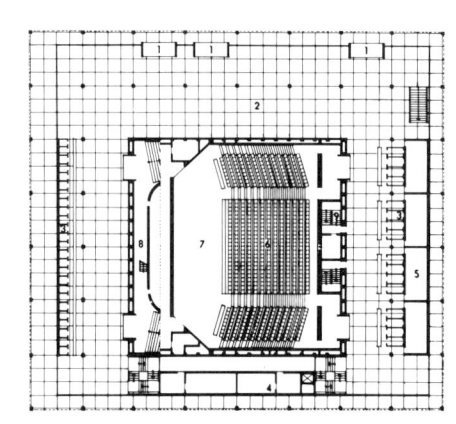

Foyergeschoß mit Physiksaal / Foyer level with physics hall
1 Fingänge / Entrances
2 Foyer / Foyer
3 Garderoben / Cloakrooms
4 Toiletten / Toilets
5 Dozenten / Lecturers
6 Physiksaal / Physics hall
7 Demonstration / Demonstration area
8 Vorbereitung / Preparation area
9 Treppe zum Auditorium / Stairs to lecture hall

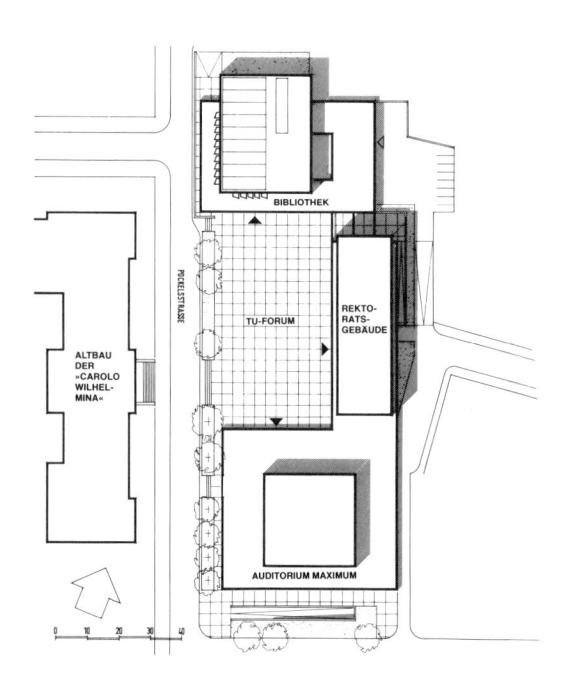

Rektorat und Fakultät 1 TH Braunschweig

Der horizontal gestreckte Mittelbau des Hochschulforums ermöglicht in seinem dreibündigen Grundrißsystem mit variabler Fluranordnung die Einrichtung verschieden tiefer Räume entsprechend dem unterschiedlichen Bedarf.

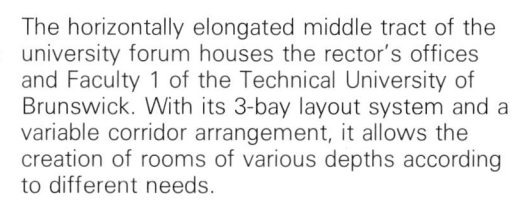

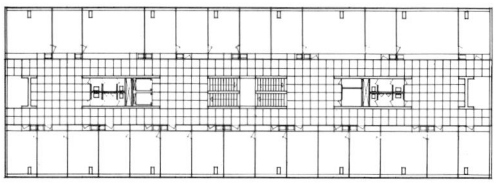

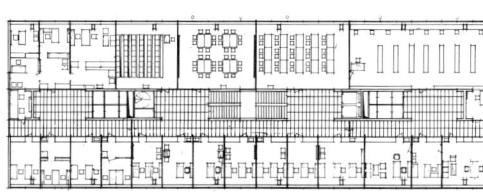

The horizontally elongated middle tract of the university forum houses the rector's offices and Faculty 1 of the Technical University of Brunswick. With its 3-bay layout system and a variable corridor arrangement, it allows the creation of rooms of various depths according to different needs.

Die signumartige Aluminiumplastik an der Westwand stammt von Hans Arp.

The emblematic aluminium sculpture on the west wall is by Hans Arp.

Auditorium maximum, Rektorat und die später angefügte Bibliothek (S. 46) umschließen einen gemeinsamen Vorplatz.

The main lecture hall and auditorium, rector's offices and the subsequently added library extension (p. 46) are grouped about a common forecourt.

Bibliothek TH Braunschweig

In vier räumlich miteinander verbundenen Geschossen sind Lesesäle, Klausurzellen, Präsenzbibliothek, Ausleihe und Verwaltung untergebracht. Der magazinierte Buchbestand befindet sich in zwei Tiefgeschossen.

This library building for the Technical University of Brunswick, extending over 4 spatially interconnected storeys, houses reading rooms, individual cells, reference library, lending department and the administration. The book collection, which is kept in stores, is situated on two basement floors.

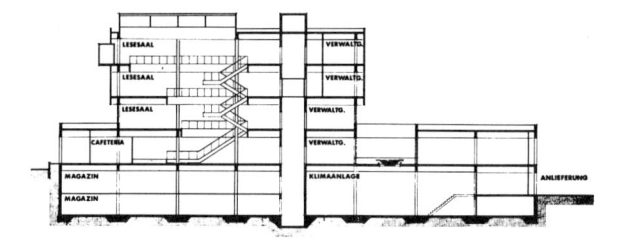

top Section east-west
middle left 1st Basement level
middle right 1st Floor
bottom left Forum
bottom right 3rd Floor

oben Schnitt Ost-West
Mitte links 1. Untergeschoß
Mitte rechts 1. Obergeschoß
unten links Forum
unten rechts 3. Obergeschoß

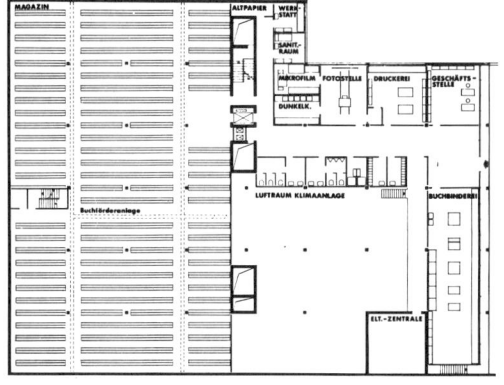

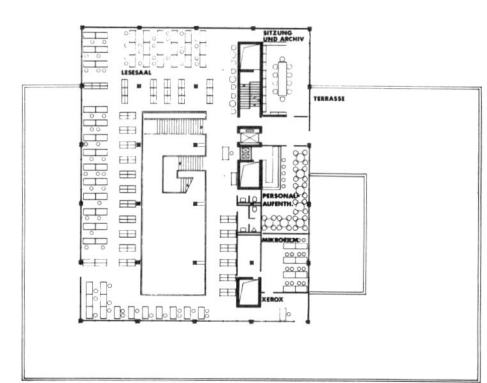

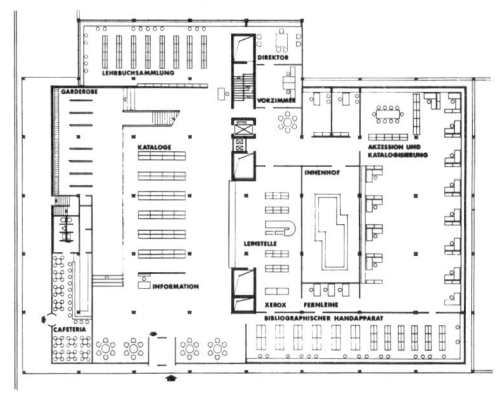

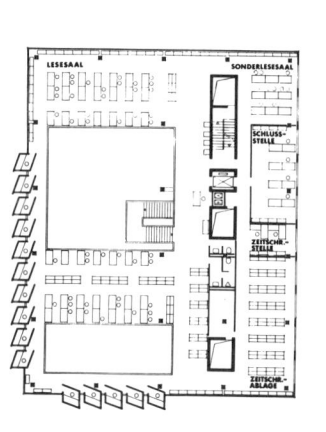

Die Südwand zeigt fünf der im 3. Obergeschoß eingefügten fünfzehn Klausurzellen.

In the south wall one can see five of the fifteen study cabins inserted on the 3rd floor.

Elektrotechnische Institute TH Braunschweig

Labors, Büro- und Lehrräume für elektrotechnische Institute, sowie Hörsaal und Seminarraum im Dachgeschoß. Fassade aus geschliffenen Betonwerksteinfertigteilen.

Laboratories, offices and teaching space for the electro-technical institutes of the Technical University of Brunswick. On the top floor are a lecture hall and seminar room. The façade is of polished precast reconstructed stone elements.

oben Normalgeschoß/
top Typical floor
1 Echofreier Raum/Acoustic room
2 Assistenten/Assistants
3 Oberingenieur/Chief engineer
4 Schreibkräfte/Typing pool
5 Institutsdirektor/Director of institute
6 Bücherei/Library

unten Dachgeschoß/
bottom Attic storey
1 Dachterrasse/Roof garden
2 Seminarraum/Seminar room
3 Vorbereitung/Preparation area
4 Garderobe/Cloakroom
5 Hörsaal/Lecture hall

Volksschule Dortmund-Rahm

Fertiggestellt 1960.

This primary and part secondary school was completed in 1960.

1 Verwaltung/Administration
2 Normalklassentrakte/Normal classrooms tract
3 Eingangs- + Pausenhalle/Entrance + recreation hall
4 Sonderklassentrakt/Special classrooms tract
5 Schulhof/Playground
6 Turnhalle/Gymnasium
7 Hausmeister/Caretaker

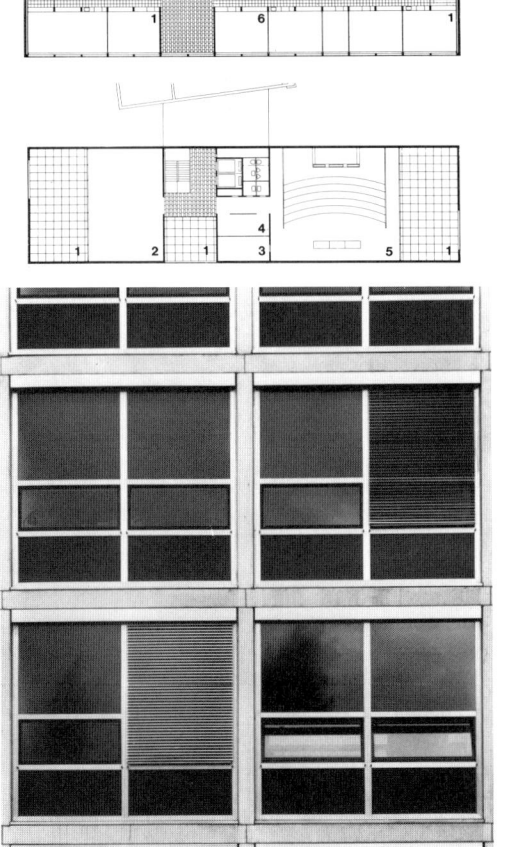

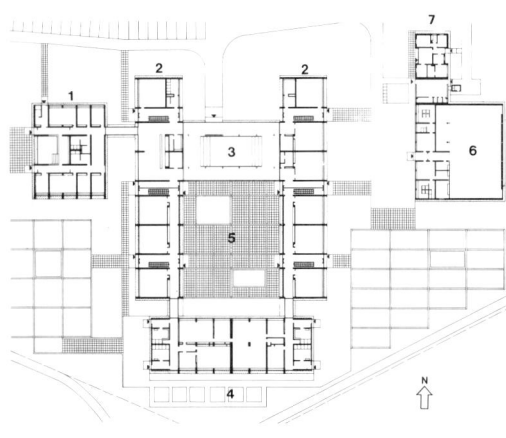

Hörsaalgebäude Universität Münster

Fertiggestellt 1966. Das Bauwerk enthält mehrere unterschiedlich große Hörsäle und die dazu gehörenden Nebenflächen.

Completed 1966. This lecture hall building for the University of Münster contains a number of lecture halls of various sizes together with their respective ancillary rooms.

Fakultät III TH Braunschweig

Für die Institute der Fakultät III wurde 1963/64 auf dem beengten Grundstück zwischen Altbauten und einem Flußlauf ein Hochhaus projektiert, dessen Grundriß sich aus drei ineinander geschobenen Kreissegmenten zusammensetzt.

A tower block was projected in 1963–64 for the various institutes comprising Faculty III of the Technical University of Brunswick. It was designed for a restricted site between older buildings and a river. The layout plan is composed of three intersecting segments of a circle.

Universität Bremen

Wettbewerb 1967.

Competition in 1967 for the University of Bremen.

Universität Bielefeld

Wettbewerb 1969.

Competition in 1969 for the University of Bielefeld.

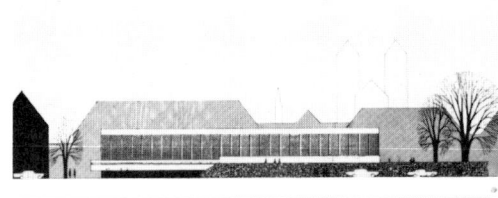

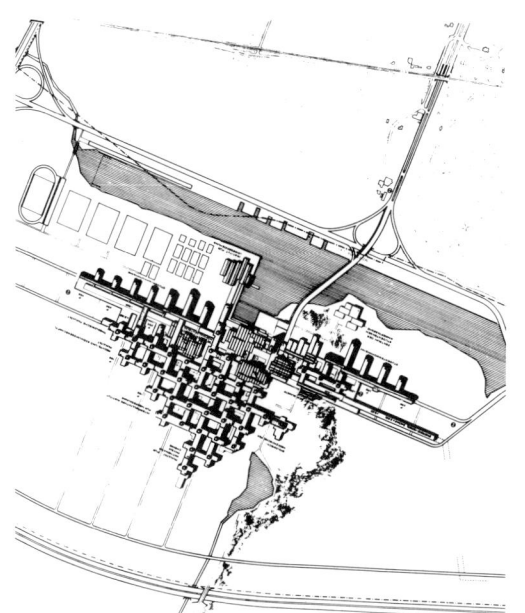

Mensa und Studentenhaus Universität Kiel

1. Preis im Wettbewerb 1960, fertiggestellt 1966. Den von allen Seiten erreichbaren Atriumhof umgeben zweigeschossige Baukörper. Sie enthalten Mensa, Küche, Dozentenspeisesaal, Cafeteria, Räume des Studentenwerks, der Verwaltung, Studentenarzt, Freizeit- und Arbeitsgruppenräume. Eine Studiobühne mit den dazugehörigen Nebenräumen ist in einem solitären Baukörper untergebracht (S. 209).

1st Prize in a competition in 1960 for the dining halls for the University of Kiel. Completed in 1966. Two-storey buildings about a courtyard that is accessible from all sides. They contain the dining halls, kitchen, lecturers' dining hall, cafeteria, student union rooms, rooms for the administration and students' doctor, leisure rooms and rooms for working groups. A studio theatre with ancillary rooms is housed in a separate building, (p. 209).

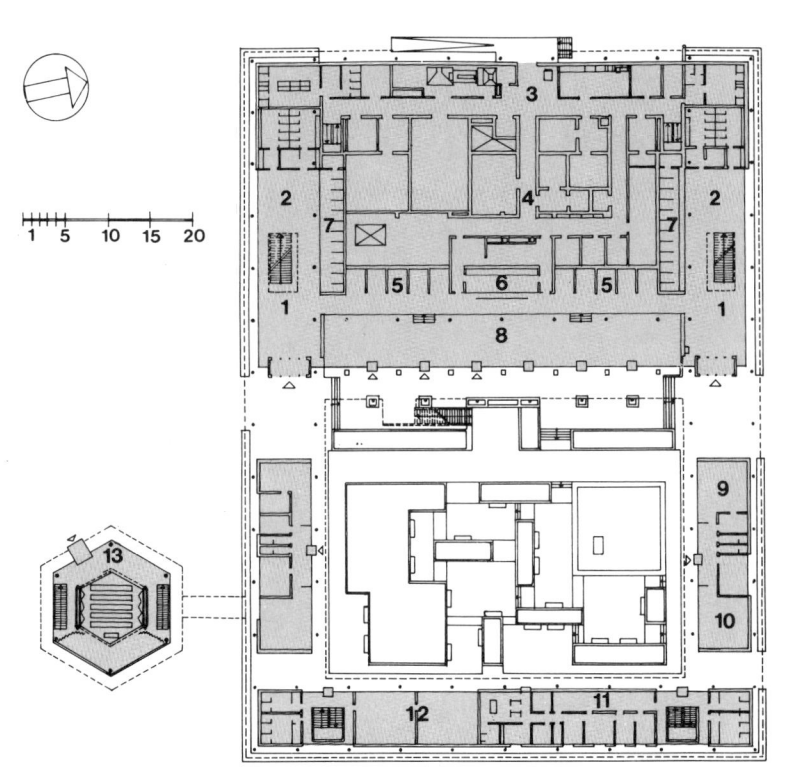

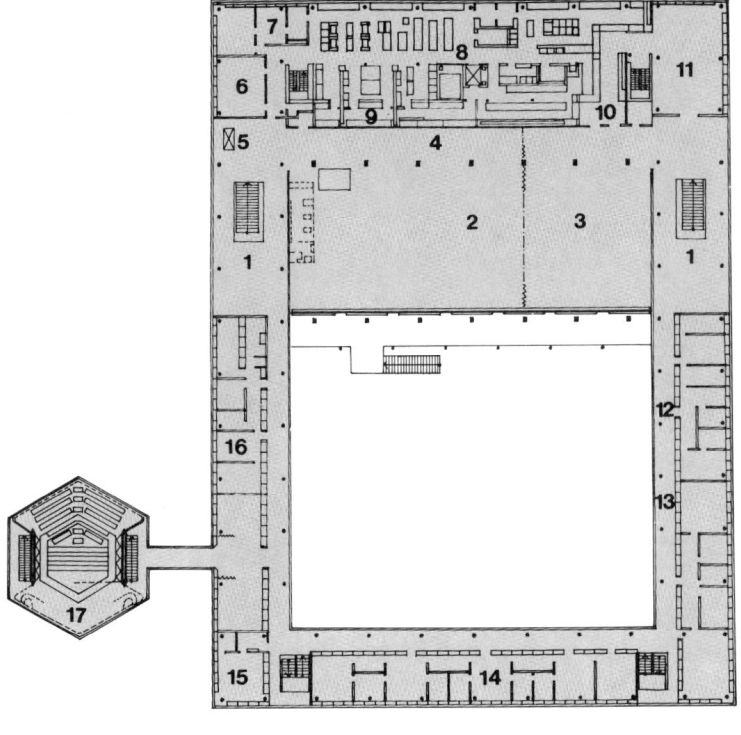

Erdgeschoß / Ground floor
1. Eingangshalle / Entrance hall
2. Bonautomaten / Meal voucher machines
3. Anlieferung / Deliveries
4. Vorräte + Kühlräume / Stores + cold stores
5. Bierklause / Beer alcoves
6. Selbstbedienungsausgabe / Self-service counter
7. Garderobe / Cloakroom
8. Aufenthaltshalle + Cafeteria / Recreation hall + cafeteria
9. Diskussion / Discussions
10. Ausländer / Foreign students
11. Verwaltung / Administration
12. Bücherei + Leseraum / Library + reading room
13. Studiobühne / Studio theatre

Obergeschoß / Upper floor
1. Treppenhalle / Staircase hall
2. Großer Speisesaal (Stammessen) / Large dining room (table d'hôte)
3. Kleiner Speisesaal (à la carte) / Small dining room (à la carte)
4. Abholgang / Meals collection
5. Kartenausgabe / Voucher issue
6. Personalspeiseraum / Staff dining room
7. Verwaltung / Administration
8. Küche / Kitchen
9. Ausgabe / Meals counter
10. Kellnerausgabe / Waiters' counter
11. Dozentenspeiseraum / Lecturers' dining room
12. ASTA / Students' union
13. Pfarr-Räume / Church rooms
14. Verwaltung / Administration
15. Fernsehraum / TV room
16. Arbeitsgemeinschaften / Working groups
17. Studiobühne / Studio theatre

Sportforum Universität Kiel

2. Preis im Wettbewerb 1966.

2nd Prize in a competition in 1966 for the design of a sports forum for the University of Kiel.

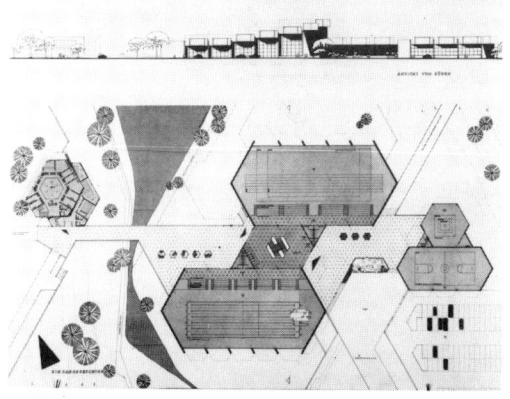

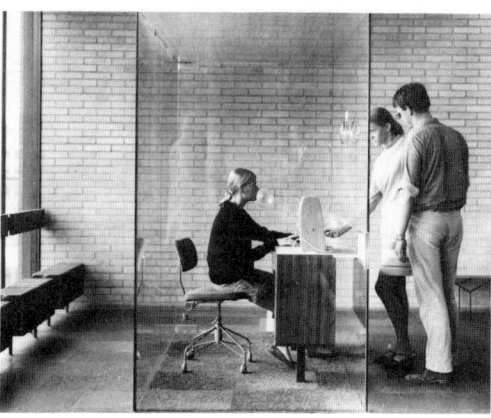

Ingenieurschule Gelsenkirchen

Nach Planungen auf verschiedenen Grundstücken Baubeginn 1967. Fertigstellung 1969. Die Baukörperanordnung brauchte keine städtebaulichen Rücksichten zu nehmen. Sie widerspiegelt die funktionalen Zusammenhänge: im Zentralbau sind Auditorium maximum, Mensa, Hörsäle und Verwaltung untergebracht. Zwei flankierende Turmbauten enthalten Seminarräume, Zeichensäle und Dozentenzimmer, ein Werkstättentrakt ist über einen Gang angeschlossen.

Construction of the Engineering School in Gelsenkirchen started in 1967, following a number of planning proposals made for various sites. Completed, 1969. There were no urban planning constraints to dictate the layout of the buildings. The layout reflects the functional interrelationships involved: in the central structure are the main auditorium, the dining halls, lecture halls and administration. Seminar rooms, drawing studios and lecturers' rooms are housed in two flanking tower structures. The workshop tract is connected via a corridor.

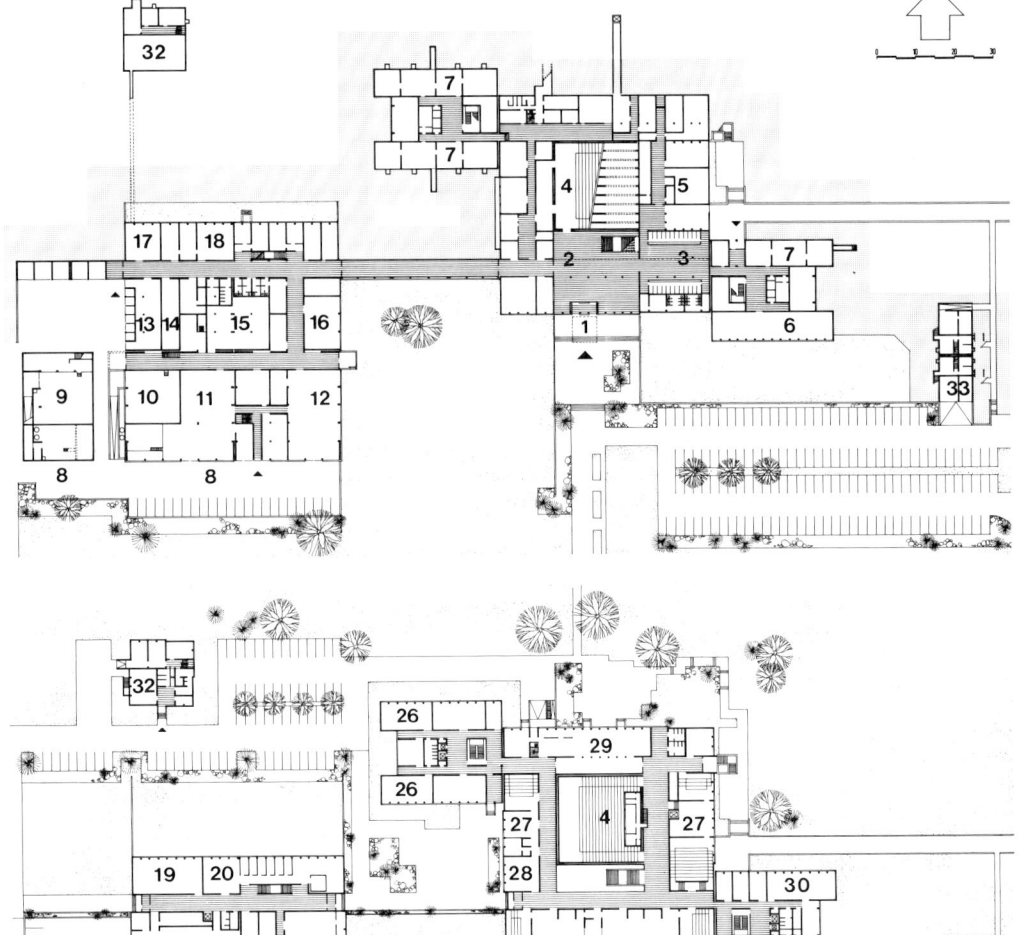

Erdgeschoß + 1. Obergeschoß / Ground floor + 1st floor
1 Eingang / Entrance
2 Eingangshalle / Entrance hall
3 Garderobe / Cloakrooms
4 Großer Experimentiersaal / Large hall for experiments
5 Heizung / Heating
6 Keller / Basement
7 Schutzraum / Shelter
8 Hochspannungslabor Erdgeschoß und Obergeschoß / High-voltage lab, ground floor and upper level
9 Hochspannung / High-voltage room
10 Hochspannung / High voltage room
11 Kraft- und Arbeitsmaschinen / Machine room
12 Werkzeugmaschinen / Machine tools
13 Hochspannung / High-voltage room
14 Umformerstation / Converter station
15 Heizung, Lüftung / Heating, ventilation
16 Schweißerei / Welding shop
17 Tischlerei / Joinery shop
18 Meßtechnik / Measurement technique
19 Regelungstechnik / Control engineering
20 Drahtnachrichtentechnik / Telegraphic communications
21 Elektrische Maschinen, Antriebstechnik / Electrical motors, propulsion technology
22 Werkstoffkunde / Materials technology
23 Luftraum Hochspannung / Void over high-voltage room
24 Luftraum Kraft- und Arbeitsmaschinen / Void over machine room
25 Luftraum Werkzeugmaschinen / Void over machine tools room
26 Semesterraum / Study room
27 Sammlung und Vorbereitung / Materials collection and preparatory work
28 Labor Chemie / Chemistry lab
29 Mensa / Dining hall
30 Konferenzzimmer / Conference room
31 Verwaltung / Administration
32 Eingeschossiges Kernphysiklaboratorium / Single-storey nuclear physics lab
33 Doppelhaus für zwei Hausmeister / Semi-detached houses for two caretakers

53

Bildungsstätte Nümbrecht

Ausbildungsort für eine Berufsgenossenschaft als internatsartige Anlage. Die Funktionsbereiche für Lehre, Beköstigung, Freizeit, Sport und Verwaltung sind in einem zweigeschossigen, stark gegliederten Flachbaukörper konzentriert, darüber der Wohnbereich, Fertigstellung 1977.

Training college for a trade co-operative organisation, in the form of a boarding institution. The functional realms of training, dining, leisure, sport and administration are concentrated in a clearly articulated two-storey building, above which is the living realm. Completion, 1977.

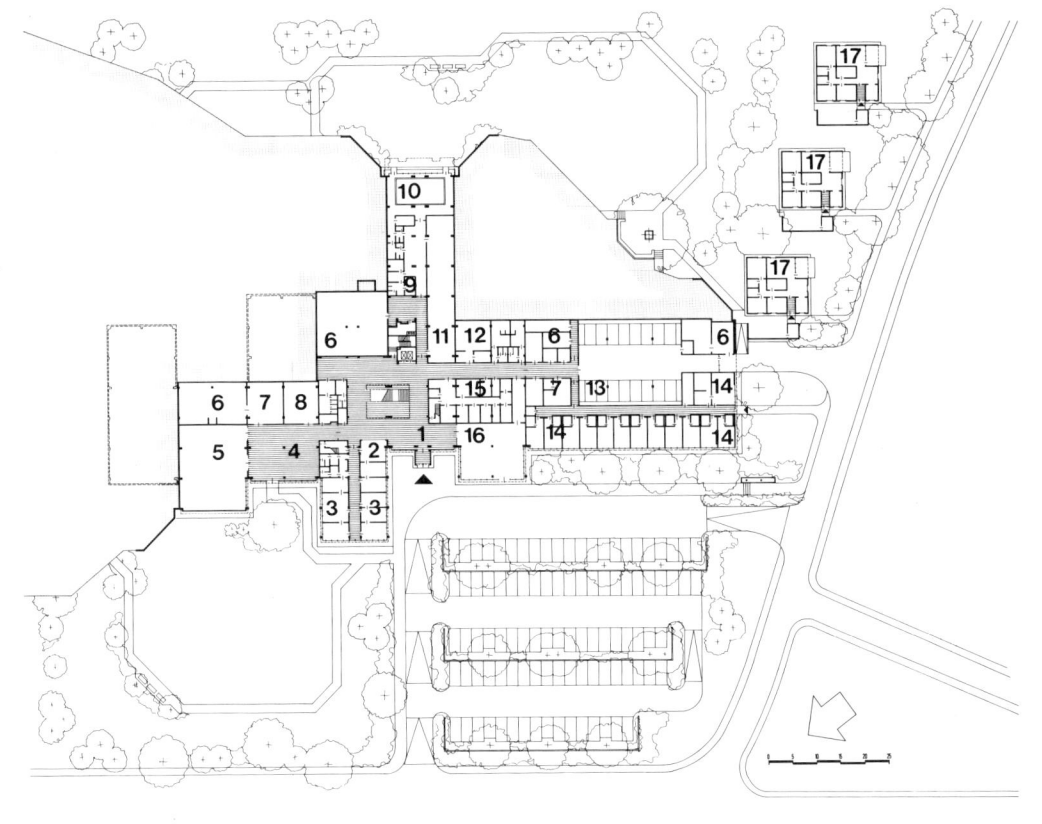

Untergeschoß / Lower ground floor

1 Halle / Hall
2 Empfang / Reception
3 Verwaltung / Administration
4 Ausstellungsfoyer / Exhibition foyer
5 Mehrzwecksaal / Multi-purpose hall
6 Technik / Mechanical services
7 Lager / Store
8 Archiv / Archives
9 Sauna / Sauna
10 Schwimmbad / Swimming pool
11 Kegelbahn / Bowling alley
12 Wäscherei / Laundry
13 Garage + Anlieferung / Garages + deliveries
14 Personalwohnbereich / Staff accommodation
15 Küchenlager / Kitchen store
16 Demonstrationsraum / Demonstration area
17 Wohnhäuser / House accommodation

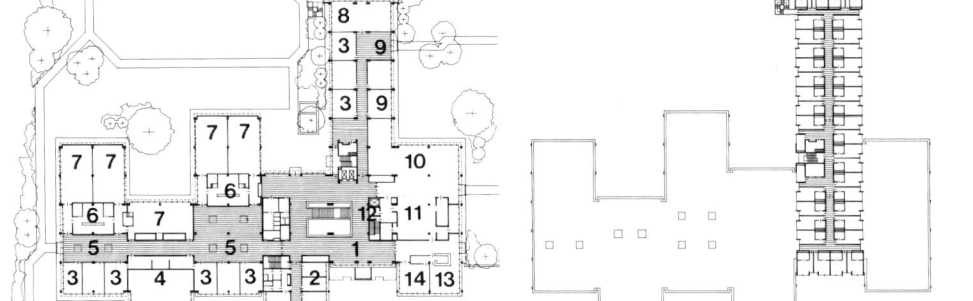

links Erdgeschoß / left Ground floor

1 Halle / Hall
2 Dozentenbereich / Lecturers' area
3 Gruppenraum / Group rooms
4 Luftraum Mehrzwecksaal / Void over multi-purpose hall
5 Pausenraum / Recreation area
6 Vorbereitung / Preparation area
7 Seminarraum / Seminar room
8 Mehrzweckraum / Multi-purpose room
9 Freizeitraum / Leisure activities
10 Casino / Club
11 Küche / Kitchen
12 Kiosk / Kiosk
13 Cafeteria / Cafeteria
14 Gästespeiseraum / Visitors' dining room

rechts 1.–4. Obergeschoß / right 1st–4th Floor

36 Einzelzimmer je Geschoß / 36 Single rooms per floor

Materialverwendung und Detailausbildung zielen auf solide Dauerhaftigkeit.

The choice of materials and the detailing were aimed at achieving soundness and durability.

Schulzentrum Gifhorn

1. Preis im Wettbewerb. Fertigstellung 1976 nach sehr kurzer Planungs- und Ausführungszeit von insgesamt nur 18 Monaten durch Anwendung von weitgehend vorgefertigten Elementen bei Einhaltung der niedrigen, vorgegebenen Baukosten (ca. 230 DM/m^3) und hohem Ausbaustandard (Ausführung in Arbeitsgemeinschaft mit A + I, Wolfsburg).

1st Prize in a competition for the design of a schools centre in Gifhorn. Completed in 1976 after a very short period of planning and construction, (a mere 18 months in all), achieved largely by the extensive use of pre-fabricated elements. The low cost estimate was also adhered to, (approx. DM 230/m^3), and a high standard of finishings was possible; (executed in co-partnership with A + I, Wolfsburg).

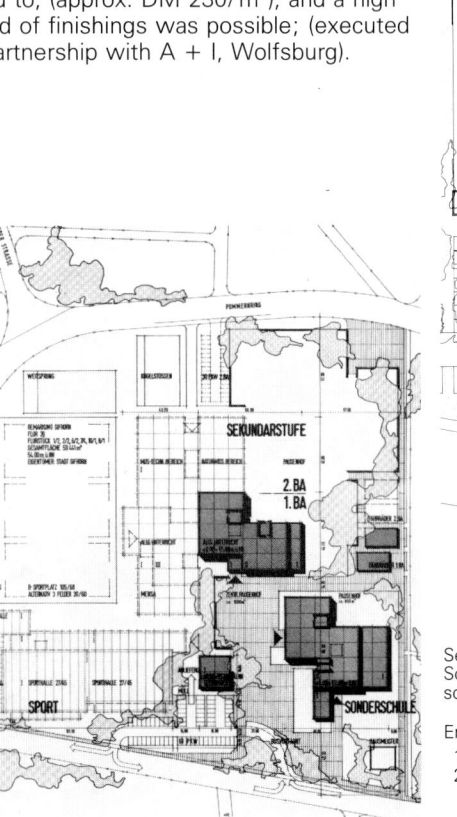

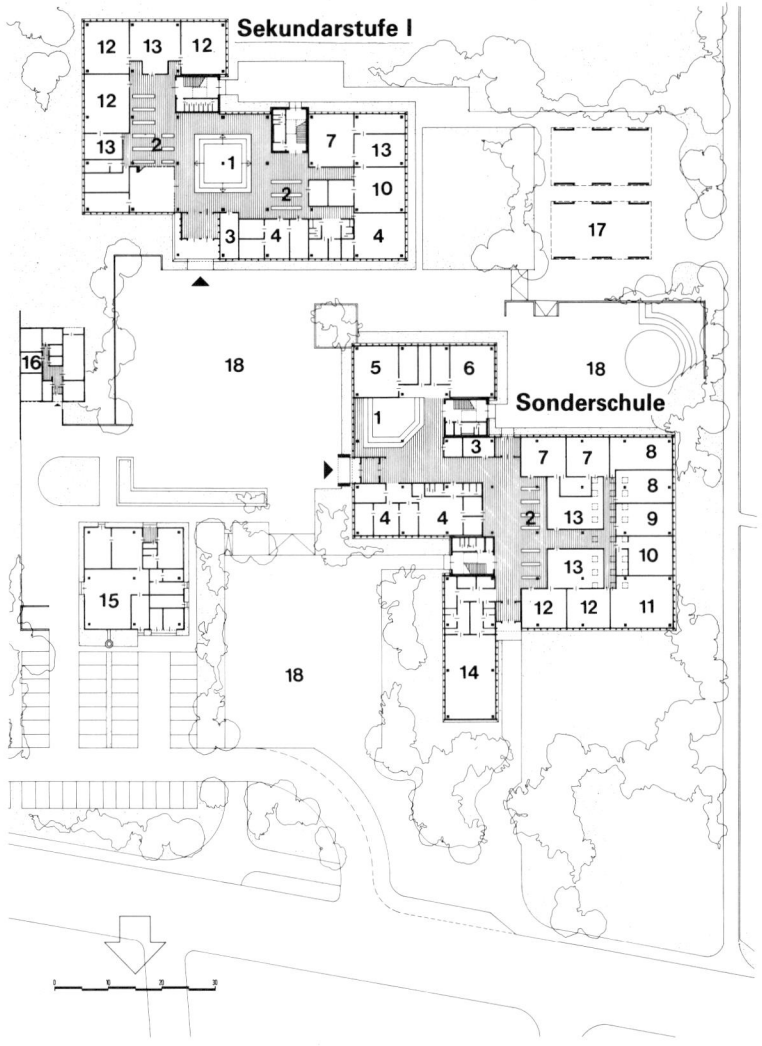

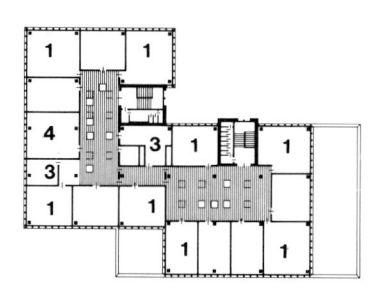

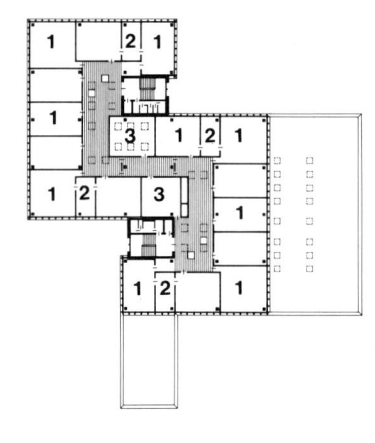

Sekundarstufe 1 und Sonderschule / Secondary school and special school

Erdgeschoß / Ground floor
1 Forum / Forum
2 Garderoben + Schließfächer / Cloakrooms + lockers
3 Hausmeister / Caretaker
4 Verwaltungs- + Lehrbereich / Administration + teachers' area
5 Musik / Music
6 Bibliothek / Library
7 Werken / Workshop
8 Textiles Werken / Textile workshop
9 Sprachtherapie / Speech therapy
10 Kunsterziehung / Art
11 Lehrküche / Teaching kitchen
12 Naturwissenschaften / Natural sciences
13 Sammlung / Materials, teaching supplies
14 Gymnastik / Gymnasium
15 Technikgebäude / Technical services
16 Hausmeisterwohnung / Caretaker's dwelling
17 Fahrradstände / Bicycle stands
18 Schulhof / Playground

Obergeschoß / Upper floor
1 Allgemeiner Unterrichtsraum / General classrooms
2 Gruppenraum / Group rooms
3 Lehrbereich, Lehrmittel / Teachers, teaching supplies
4 Sprachlabor / Language laboratory

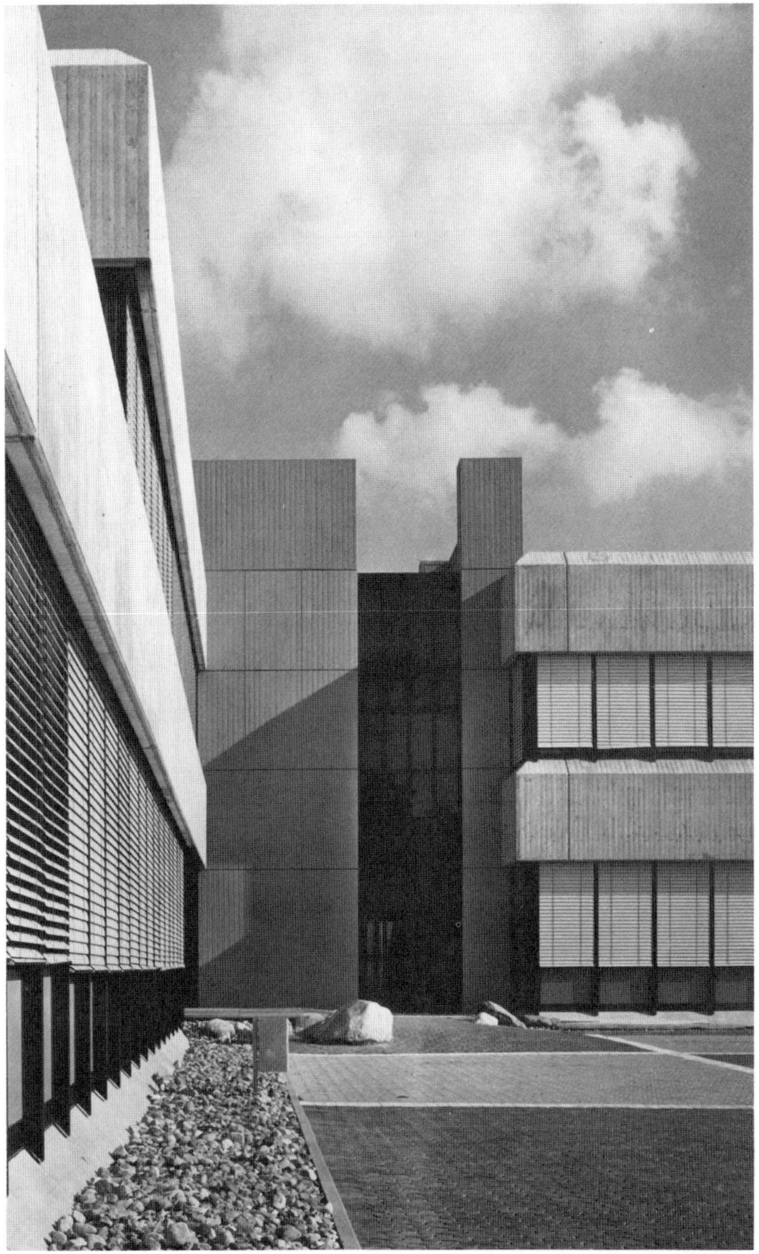

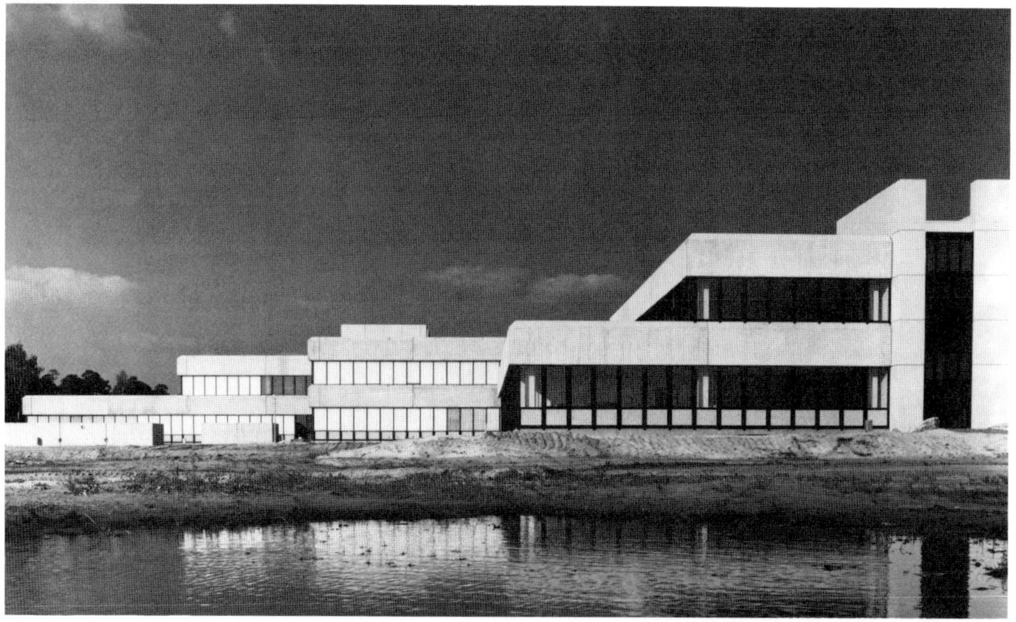

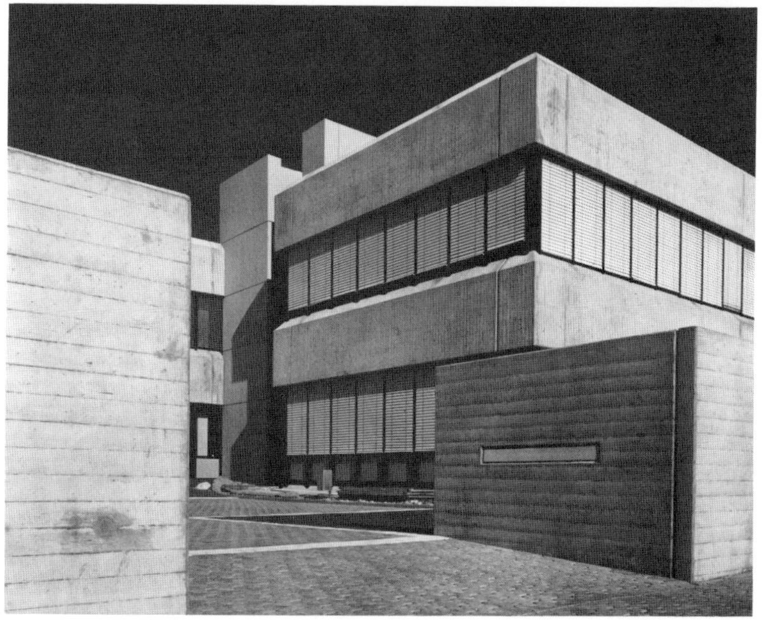

Bildungszentrum Südwest Karlsruhe

Regionales Schulzentrum für 2500 Schüler. Fertigstellung des dritten Bauabschnittes 1980. Starke Baukörpergliederung und geringe Bauhöhe fügen die große Anlage in die Waldumgebung ein. Außenwandverkleidung aus horizontal verlegten Wellasbestplatten.

Regional school centre for 2500 pupils. Third stage of building completed in 1980. The bold articulation of the building volume and the low height help to integrate this extensive complex into the wooded surroundings. External wall cladding of corrugated asbestos sheeting fixed horizontally.

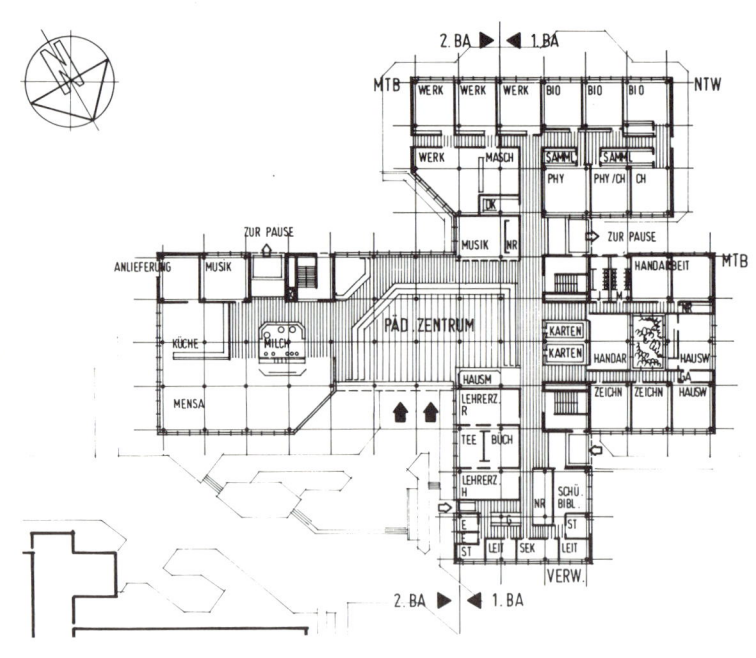

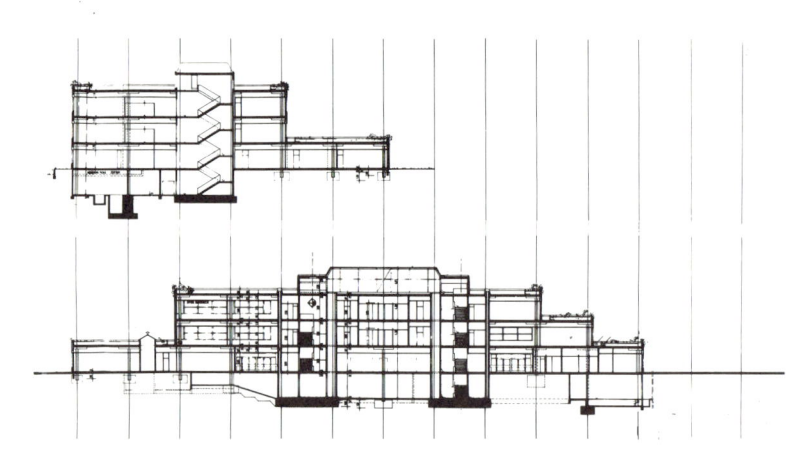

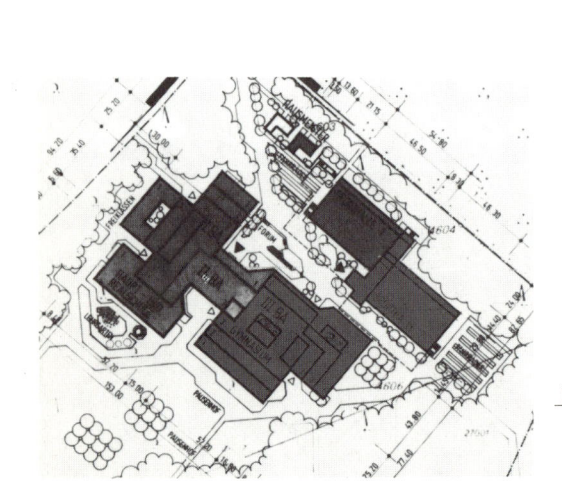

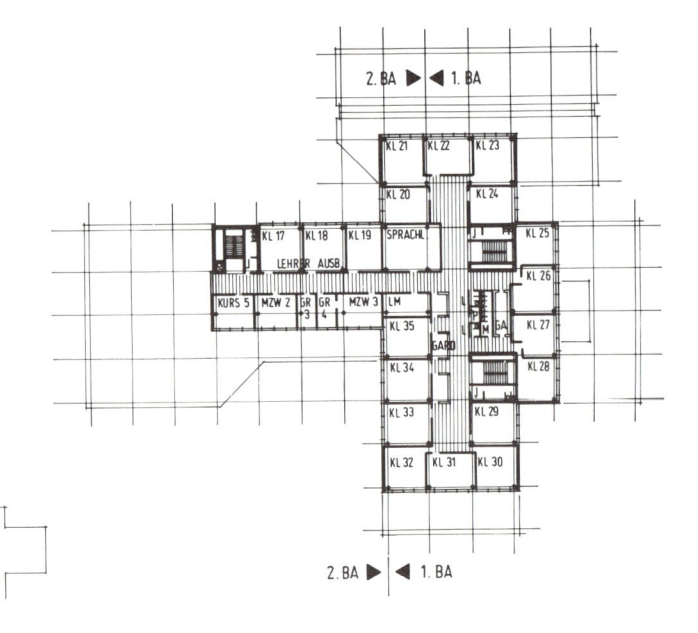

Sparsamkeit, Einfachheit und Robustheit kennzeichnen die Details dieser Schulanlage.

The details of this school complex are characterized by economy of means, simplicity and robustness.

**Internal Security Forces College Riyadh
Saudi-Arabien**

Entwurfsgutachten 1977. Der Entwurf gliedert die sehr große Baumasse durch ein hierarchisch geordnetes System äußerer Architekturräume mit dem Vorteil einfacher Orientierung.

Design study, 1977. The design breaks up the very large building volume by means of a system of external architectural spaces that is hierarchically ordered and has the advantage of clear orientation.

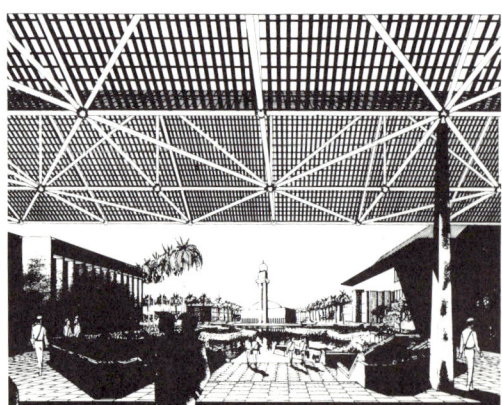

Ein großes Schattendach überspannt den Zentralbereich zwischen den Lehrgebäuden, dem Auditorium Maximum und den zwei Klausurhallen für je 1000 Prüflinge.

A large shade-giving roof structure spans the central area between the teaching tracts, the main assembly hall and the two examiniation halls, each accommodating 1000 examinees.

60

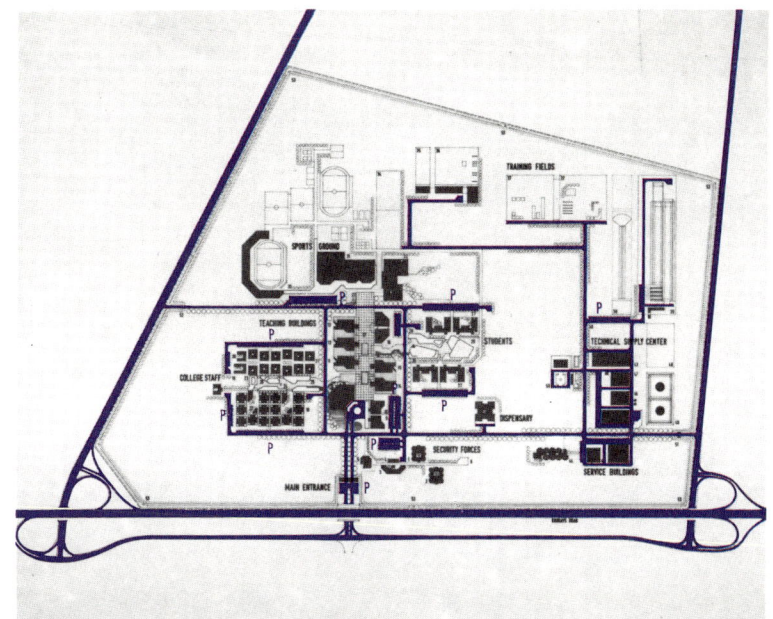

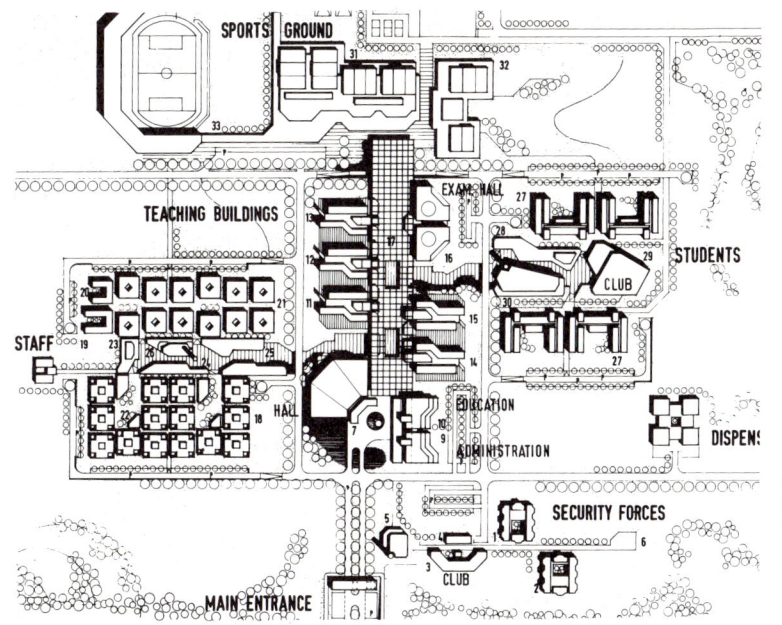

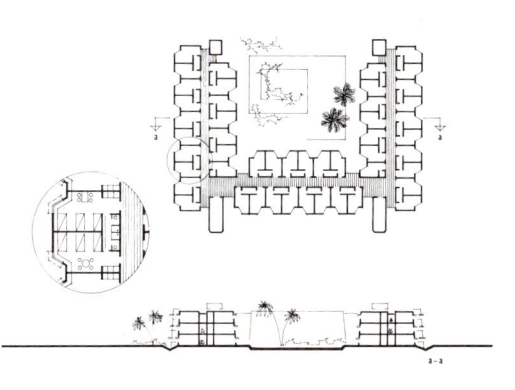

oben links Fahrverkehr
unten links Fußgängerwege
oben Mitte Zentralbereich
unten Mitte Lehrgebäude
oben rechts Unterkünfte

top left Vehicular traffic
bottom left Pedestrian routes
top middle Central area
bottom middle Teaching tract
top right Accommodation

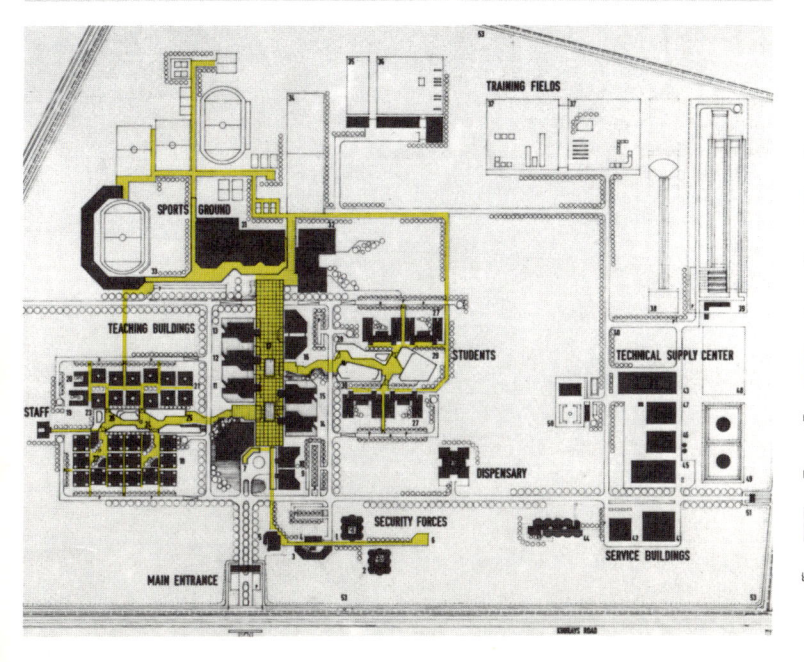

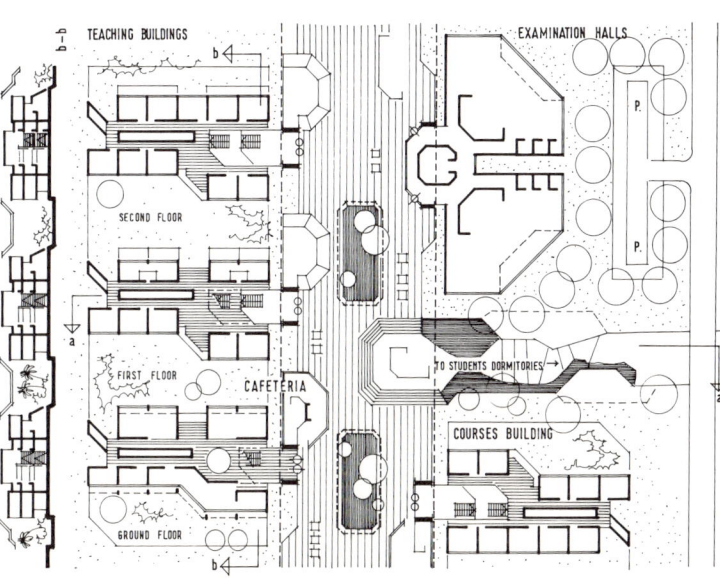

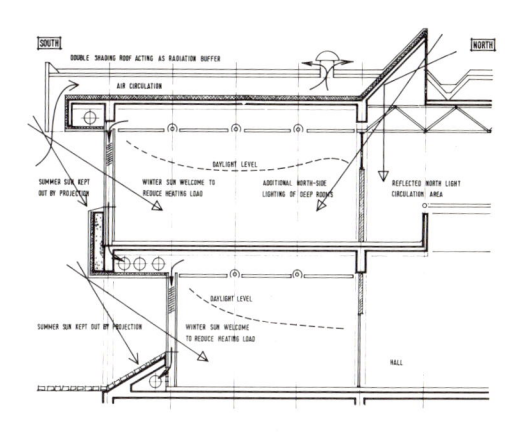

Die Detailausbildung der Baukörper (Schnitt oben) folgt aus den klimatischen Bedingungen: durchlüftetes Doppeldach, Dachüberstände, die die Sommersonne abwehren und die Wintersonne einlassen.

The detailing of the structure (cross section above) is based on constraints imposed by climate control: a ventilated double-layer roof, cantilevered out, affording solar protection in summer and allowing the winter sun access.

WDR College Köln-Bocklemünd

Auf dem Außengelände des Westdeutschen Rundfunks war ein College für Radio- und Fernsehmitarbeiter aus Entwicklungsländern geplant. Die nicht verwirklichte Anlage umfaßt als konzentrierter Kampus Bereiche für Lehre, Wohnen, Kommunikation, Verpflegung, Freizeit und Sport.

A college for radio and television personnel from developing countries was planned for a non-central site belonging to West German Broadcasting (WDR). The complex, which was never realized, includes realms for training, housing, communications, dining, leisure and sport in the form of a concentrated campus.

Schulzentrum Hankensbüttel

1. Preis im Wettbewerb 1973. Den Bauauftrag erhielt der zweite Preisträger.

1st Prize in a competition for a schools centre in Hankensbüttel in 1973. The commission was awarded to the second prizewinner.

Bundesakademien Brühl

Wettbewerb 1977.

Competition for the Federal Academies in Brühl, 1977.

Paul Ehrlich Institut Langen

Wettbewerb 1977, 4. Preis. Das Institut enthält Labors, Büros, Lehrräume, Räume für Tierhaltung und Sonderflächen. Die sehr komplizierten funktionellen Zusammenhänge (Sicherheitsvorkehrungen gegen Infektionen) ergaben die Netzstruktur der Baukörperfügung.

4th Prize in competition, 1977. The institute building contains laboratories, offices, teaching rooms, rooms for keeping animals, and other special areas. The extremely complicated functional interrelationships, (safety precautions against infection), led to this network structure in the disposition of the building volumes.

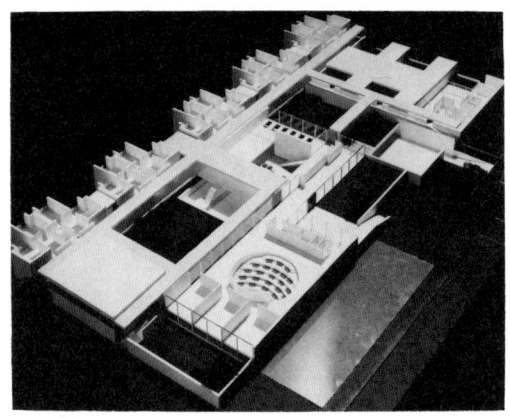

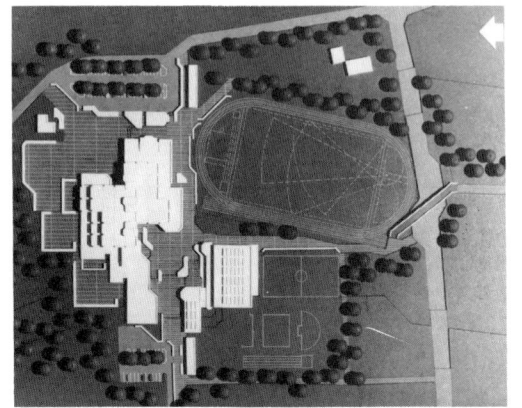

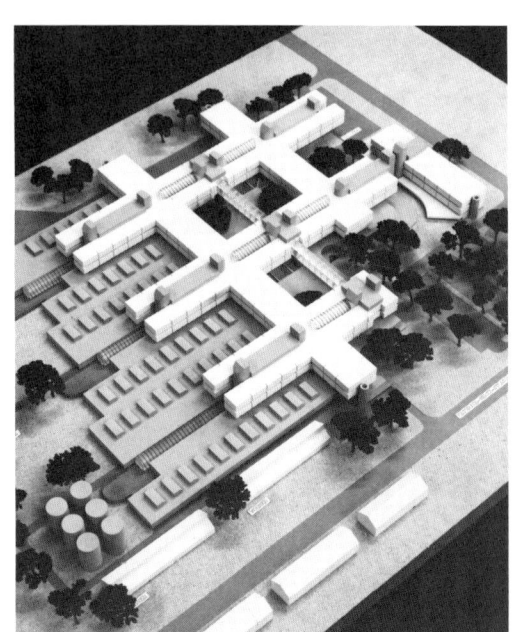

Civil Defence Institute Riyadh Saudi-Arabien

1. Rang im internationalen Entwurfsgutachten 1976, Ausführungsplanung fertiggestellt 1980. Bearbeitung im Rahmen von AGC (Associated German Consultants). Das Institut enthält auf einem Areal von 2 km x 2 km Gebäude für Verwaltung, Ausbildung, Bibliothek, Mensa, Studentenwohnheime, Sport- und Schwimmhallen, Klinik, Moschee, Trainings-Center, Technisches Zentrum, ein Sportstadion mit 5000 gedeckten Sitzplätzen sowie Gäste- und Dozentenwohnungen. Bausumme umgerechnet ca. 1 Mrd. DM. – Der Zentralbereich soll in der flachen Wüstenlandschaft ein markantes tektonisches Zeichen setzen. Dazu wurde die Anlage mit der langen Fassadenfront des siebengeschossigen Verwaltungsbaues genau nach Süden ausgerichtet. Von der Dachkante bis zum Erdboden spannt sich ein mächtiger Schattenrost, unter dem eine Oasenlandschaft mit Bäumen und Wasserflächen gedeihen kann.

1st Place in an international design study, 1976. Detail planning completed in 1980. Development of project within the framework of AGC (Associated German Consultants). The institute, covering an area 2 km x 2 km in extent, comprises buildings for administration, training, a library, dining hall, student hostels, sports and swimming halls, a clinic, a mosque, a training centre, a technical centre, a sports stadium with covered seating for 5000 persons, and flats for guests and lecturers. The construction costs, (converted to DM) were approx. DM 1000 million. The central realm is intended to set a striking tectonic sign in the flat desert landscape. In addition, the 7-storey administrative complex with its long front was orientated due south. From the edge of the roof to the ground a mighty shadow grid is spanned, beneath which an oasis landscape with trees and areas of water flourishes.

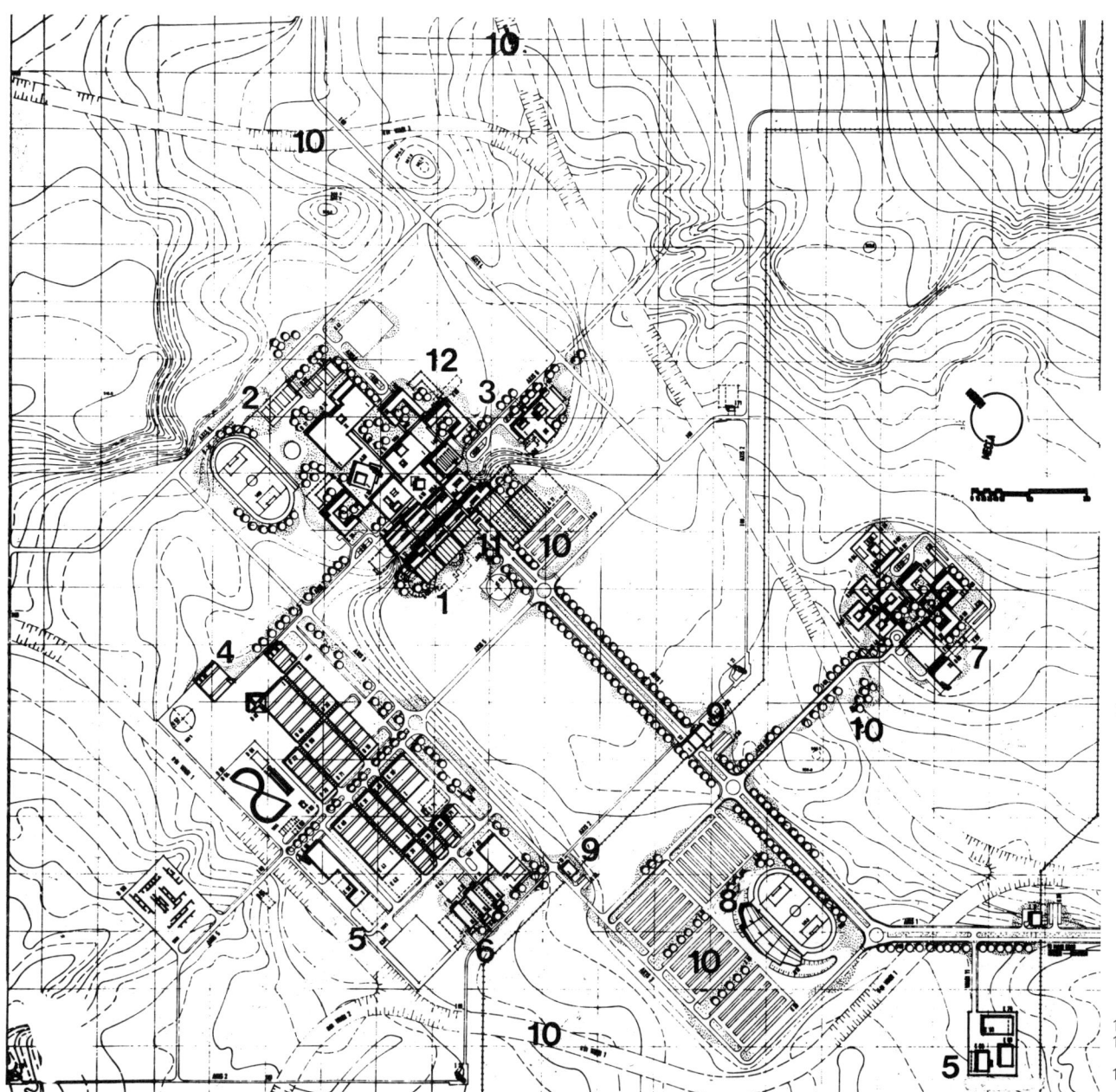

Lageplan / Site plan
1 Zentralbereich / Central area
2 Sportbereich / Sports area
3 Studentenunterkünfte / Student housing
4 Übungsbereich / Training services
5 Technischer Versorgungsbereich / Technical services
6 Soldatenunterkünfte / Soldiers' housing
7 Personalwohnbereich / Staff housing
8 Stadion / Stadium
9 Sonderbauten / Special constructions
10 Verkehrsanlagen / Traffic
11 Kommando Bunker / Operations room
12 Bunker / Underground shelters

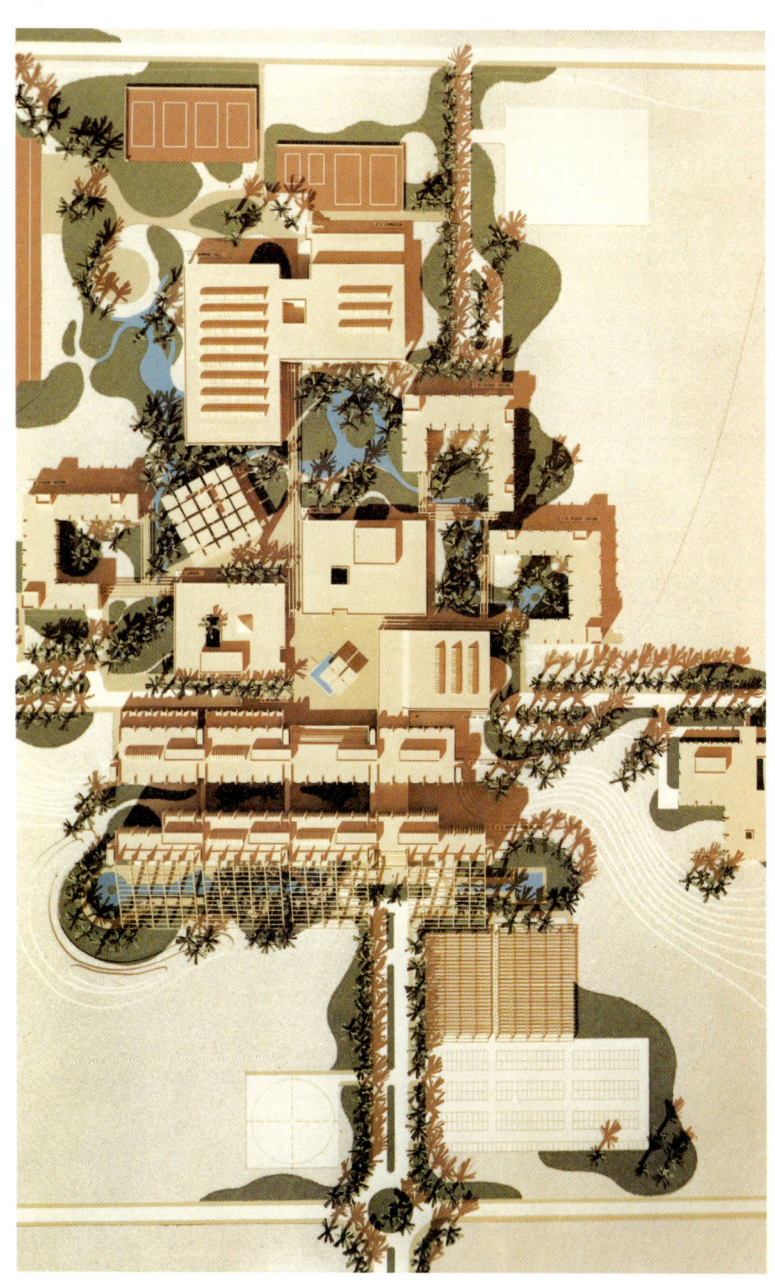

Verwaltungs- und
Schulungsgebäude
obere Eingangsebene /
Administrative and teaching
buildings, upper entrance
level

1 Eingang vom Zentralhof /
 Entrance from central
 courtyard
2 Obere Eingangshalle /
 Upper entrance hall
3 Ausstellungshalle /
 Exhibition hall
4 Gebäudehohe Innenhöfe / Courtyards, full height
 of building
5 Büroräume / Offices
6 Technische Labors /
 Technical laboratories
7 Dozentenräume / Lecturers' rooms
8 Aufenthaltsräume /
 Meeting rooms
9 Auditorien / Lecture
 halls
10 Zentralhof / Central
 courtyard
11 Bibliothek / Library
12 Mensa / Dining hall

Untere Eingangsebene /
Lower entrance level

1 Vorfahrt / Arrivals
2 Untere Eingangshalle /
 Lower entrance hall
3 Ausstellungshallen /
 Exhibition halls
4 Gebäudehohe Innenhöfe / Courtyards, full
 height of building
5 Büroräume / Offices
6 Übungsräume / Training
 areas
7 Anlieferung / Deliveries
8 Beschatteter Palmengarten / Shaded palm
 garden

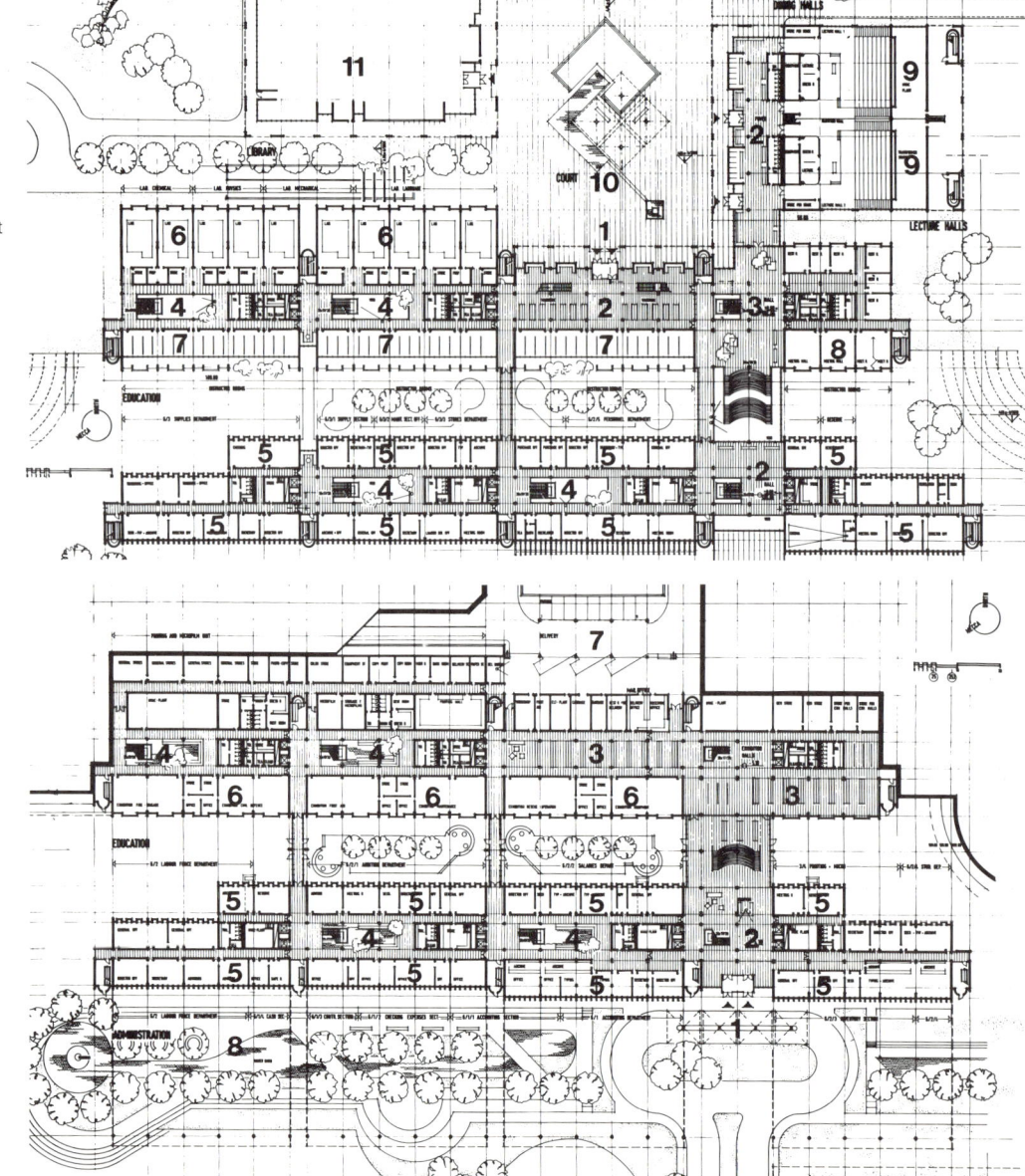

65

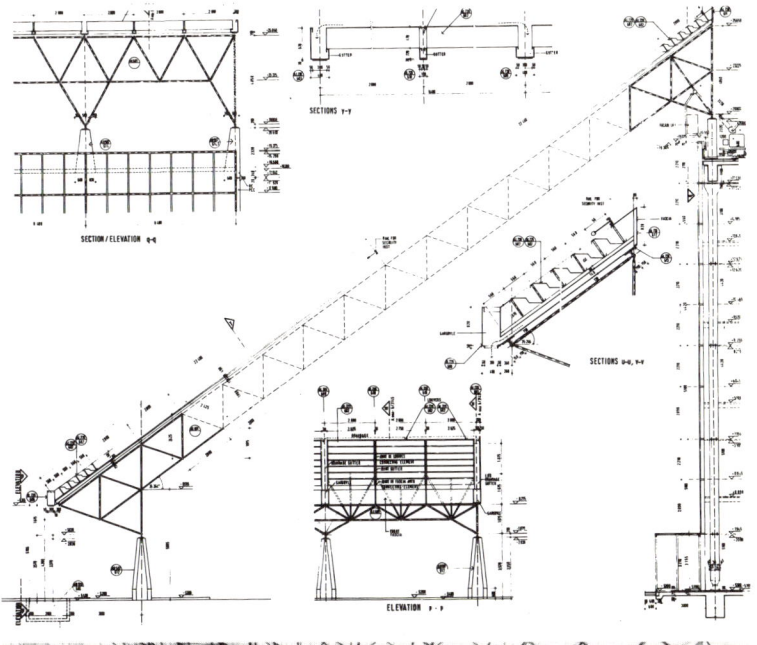

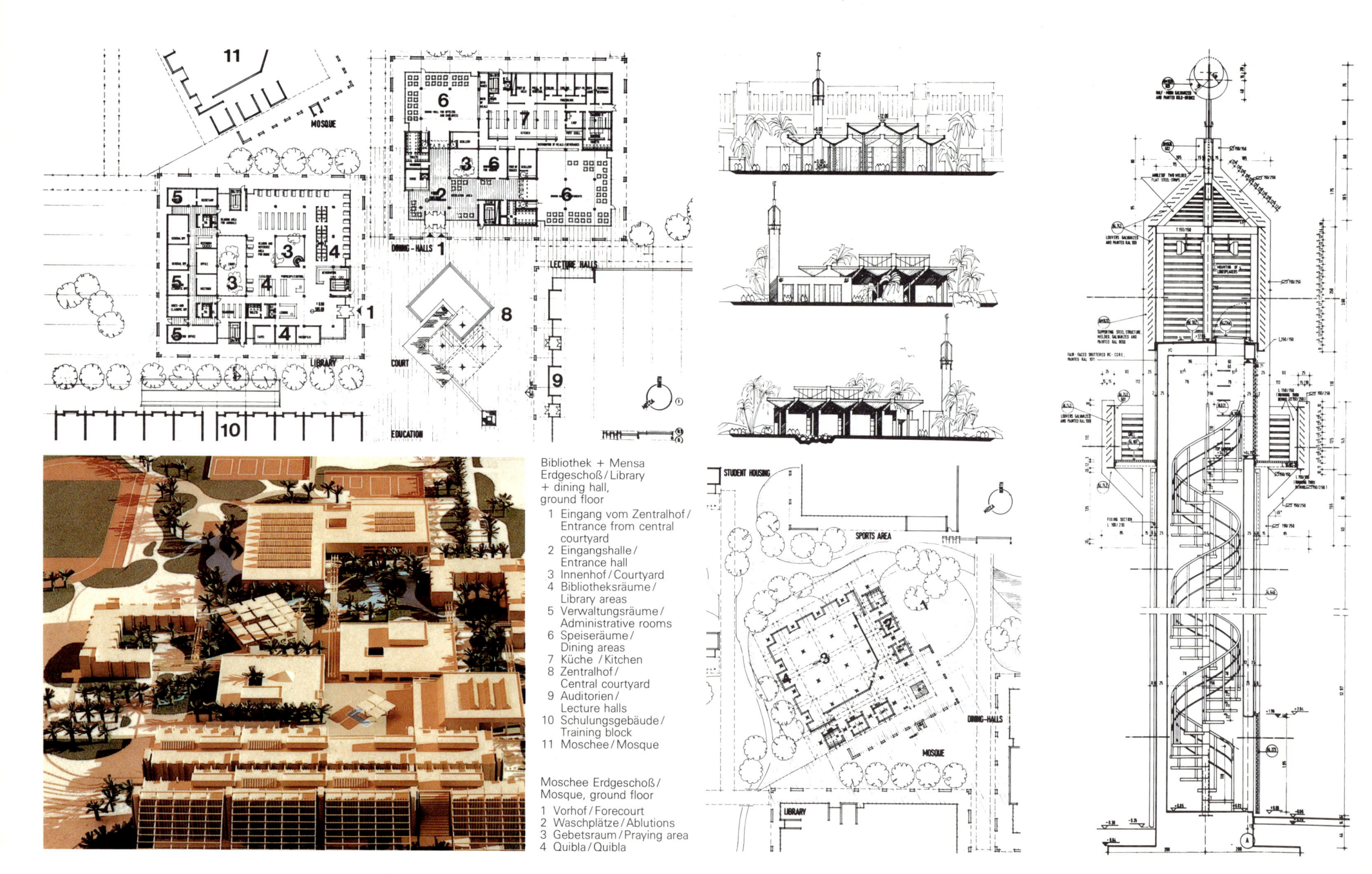

Bibliothek + Mensa
Erdgeschoß / Library
+ dining hall,
ground floor
1 Eingang vom Zentralhof /
  Entrance from central
  courtyard
2 Eingangshalle /
  Entrance hall
3 Innenhof / Courtyard
4 Bibliotheksräume /
  Library areas
5 Verwaltungsräume /
  Administrative rooms
6 Speiseräume /
  Dining areas
7 Küche / Kitchen
8 Zentralhof /
  Central courtyard
9 Auditorien /
  Lecture halls
10 Schulungsgebäude /
   Training block
11 Moschee / Mosque

Moschee Erdgeschoß /
Mosque, ground floor
1 Vorhof / Forecourt
2 Waschplätze / Ablutions
3 Gebetsraum / Praying area
4 Quibla / Quibla

Personalwohnungen
Erdgeschoß / Staff
accommodation,
ground floor
1 Zentralhof / Central
  courtyard
2 Zugang / Arrivals
3 Hof / Courtyard
4 Wohnräume / Living
  rooms
5 Küche / Kitchen

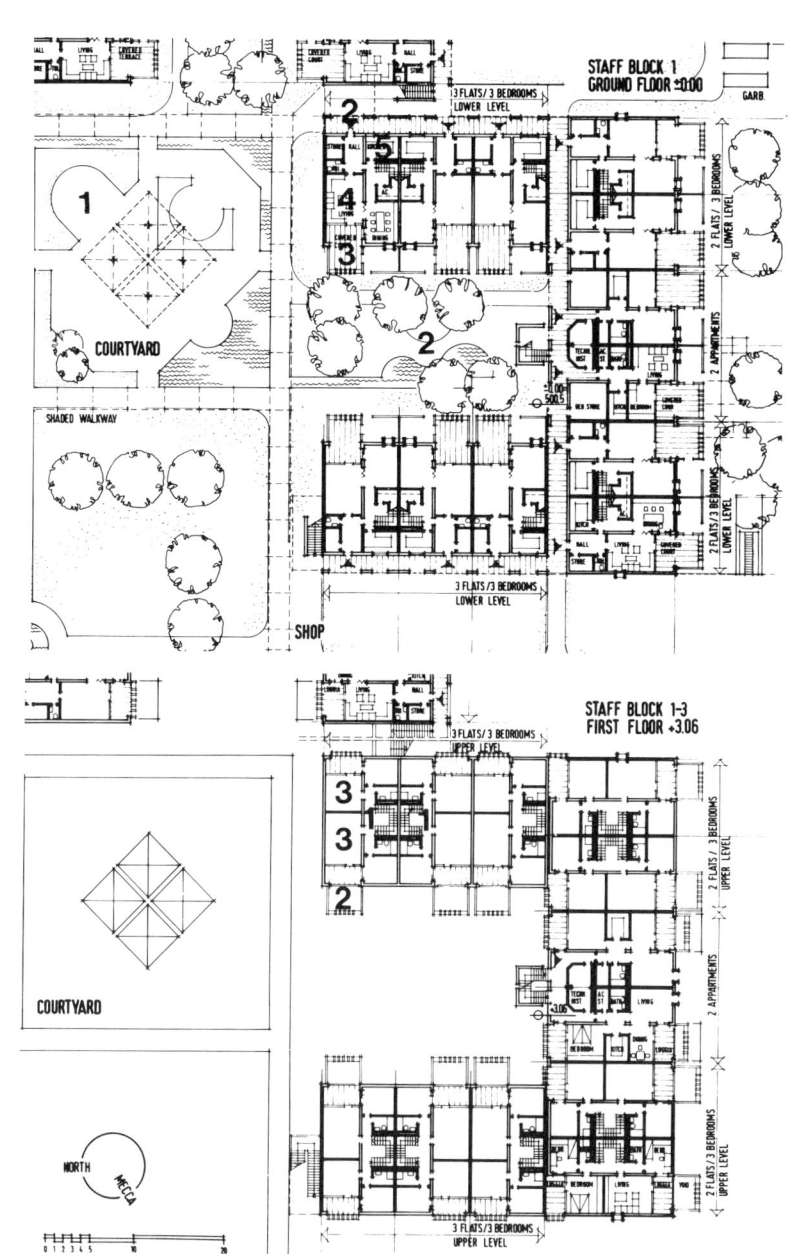

Personalvillen
Erdgeschoß /
Staff villas,
ground floor
1 Zentralhof / Central
  courtyard
2 Zugang / Access
3 Innenhof / Internal
  courtyard
4 Wohnräume / Living
  rooms
5 Schlafräume / Bedrooms
6 Wirtschaftsräume /
  Kitchen + utility

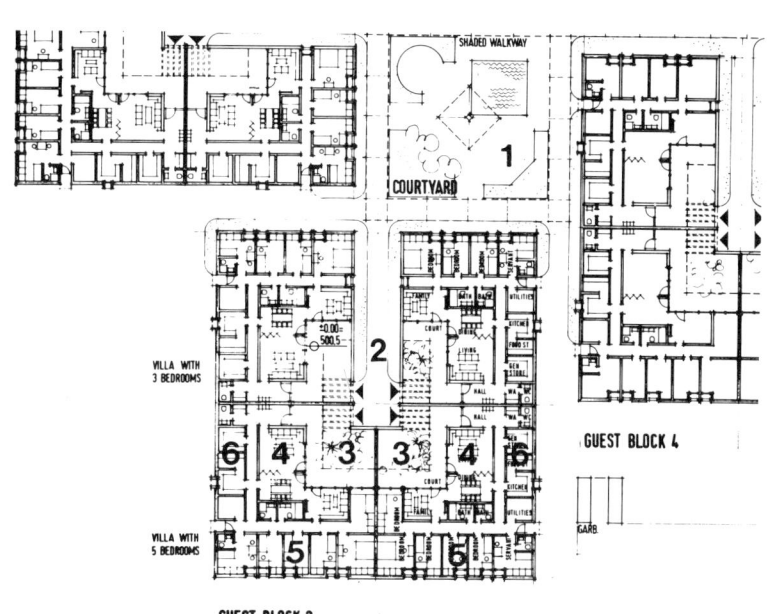

Obergeschoß / Upper floor
1 Treppe / Staircase
2 Hof, Balkon / Courtyard,
  balcony
3 Schlafräume / Bedrooms

Pharmazeutische Institute der TU Braunschweig

1. Preis im Wettbewerbsverfahren nach funktionaler Leistungsbeschreibung 1979 mit Strabag-Bau. Laborgebäude für Lehre und Forschung mit Hörsälen und angegliedertem Tierversuchstrakt und Gewächshaus. Vier pharmazeutische Institute sind in einem H-förmigen Baukörper angeordnet, dessen Form der Erschließung und der haustechnischen Versorgung in horizontaler und vertikaler Richtung entspricht. Fertigstellung 1981.

1st Prize under competition conditions (1979), based on a specification of functions for the pharmaceutical institutes of the Technical University of Brunswick, in collaboration with the Strabag building concern. Laboratory building for teaching and research with lecture halls, and an adjacent tract for animal experiments and a greenhouse. Four pharmaceutical institutes are situated in an H-shaped building, whose form corresponds to the access routes and mechanical services both horizontally and vertically. Completed 1981.

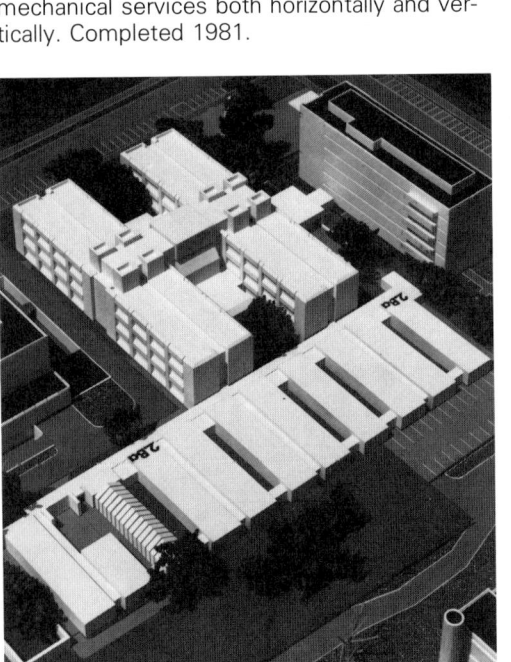

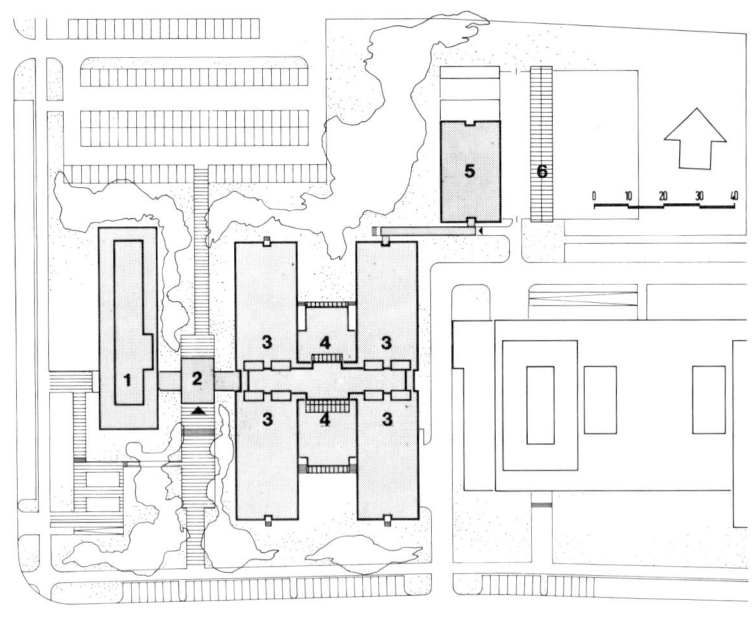

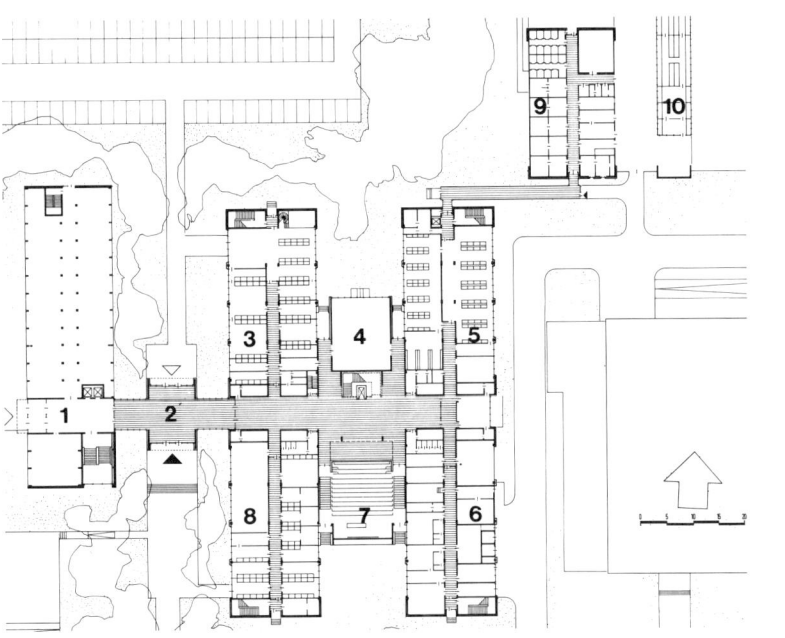

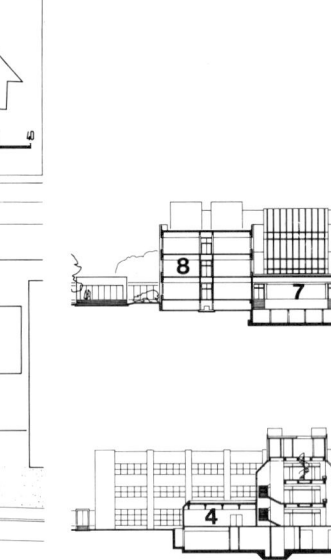

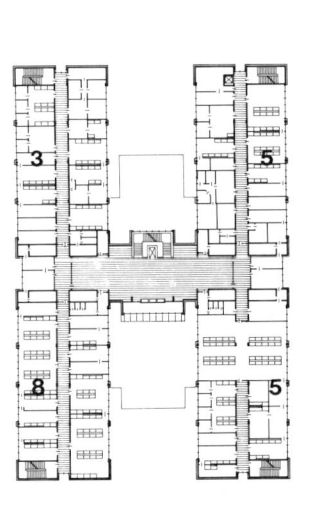

Lageplan / Site plan
1 Altbau / Existing building
2 Eingangshalle / Entrance hall
3 Institutstrakte / Institute buildings
4 Hörsäle / Lecture halls
5 Tierhaltung / Animal compound
6 Gewächshaus / Greenhouse

oben rechts Querschnitt / top right Cross section
Mitte rechts Längsschnitt / middle right Longitudinal section
unten links Erdgeschoß / bottom left Ground floor
unten rechts 1. Obergeschoß / bottom right 1st Floor

1 Pharmazeutische Chemie, Altbau / Pharmaceutical chemistry, existing building
2 Eingangshalle / Entrance hall
3 Institut für pharmazeutische Technologie / Institute for pharmaceutical technology
4 Hörsaal 2 / Lecture hall 2
5 Institut für pharmazeutische Biologie / Institute for pharmaceutical biology
6 Institut für Pharmakologie / Institute for pharmacology
7 Hörsaal 1 / Lecture hall 1
8 Institut für pharmazeutische Chemie / Institute for pharmaceutical chemistry
9 Tierhaltung Pharmakologie / Animal compound for pharmacology
10 Gewächshaus pharmazeutische Biologie / Greenhouse for pharmaceutical biology

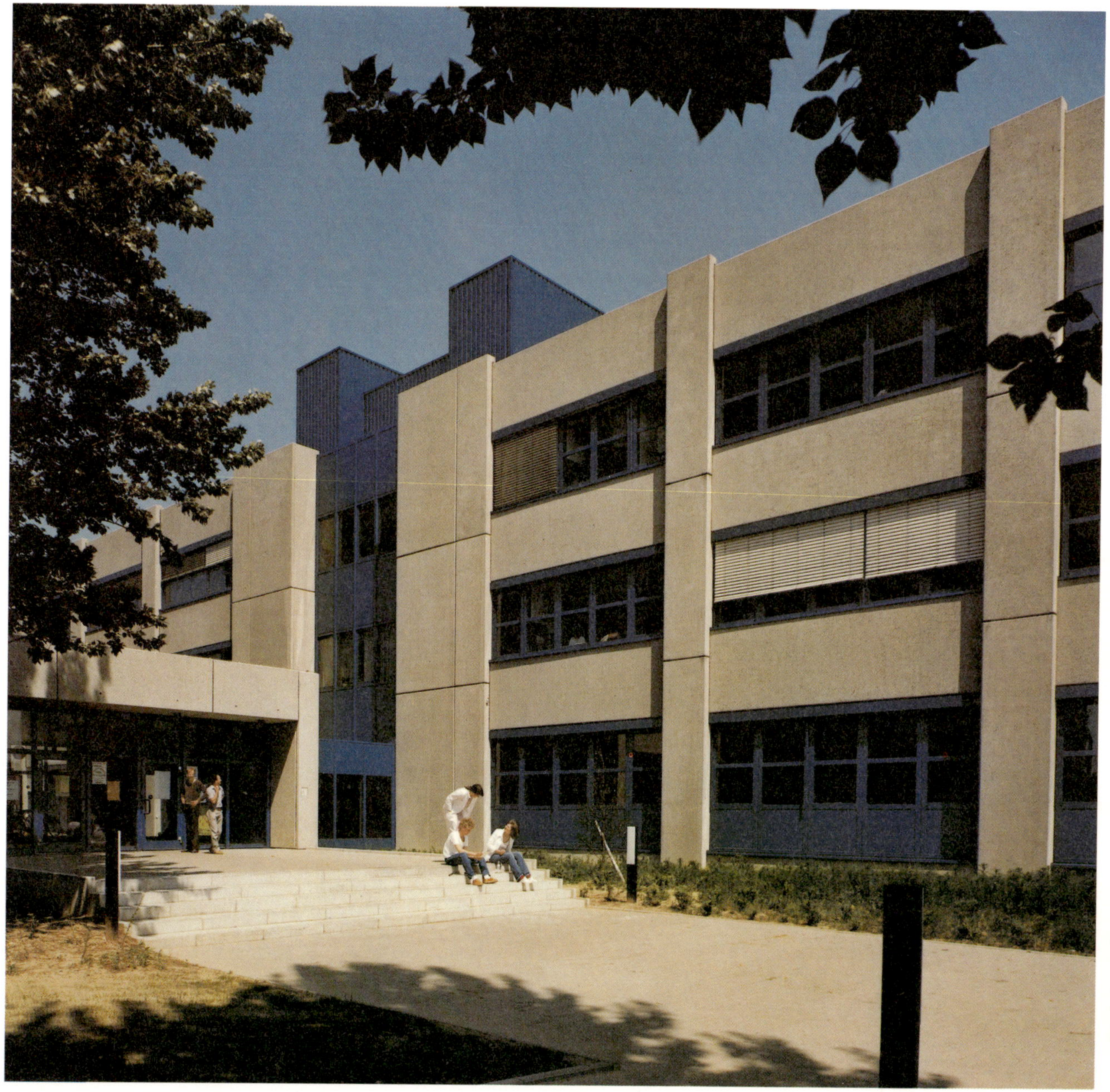
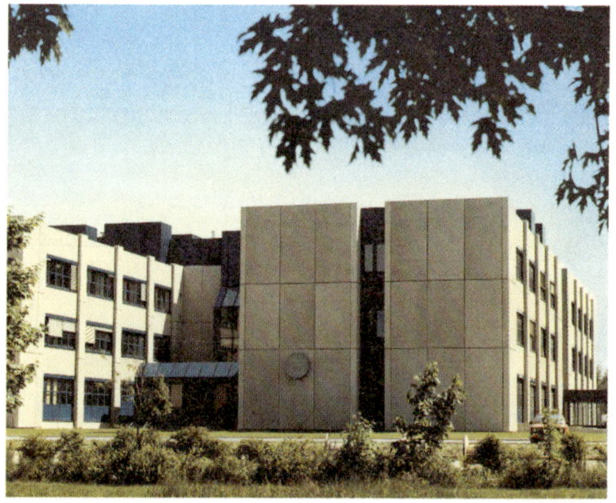
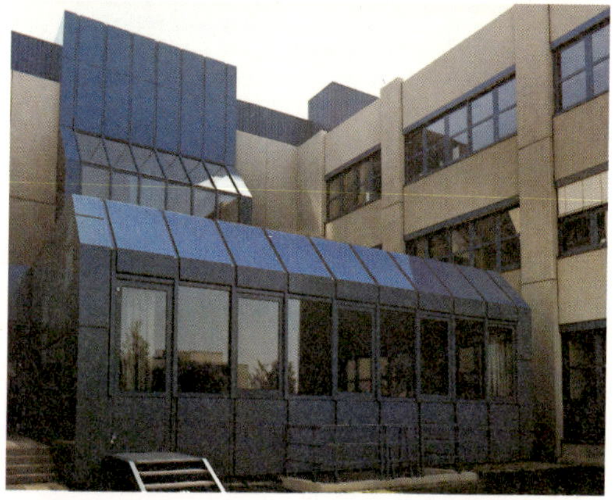
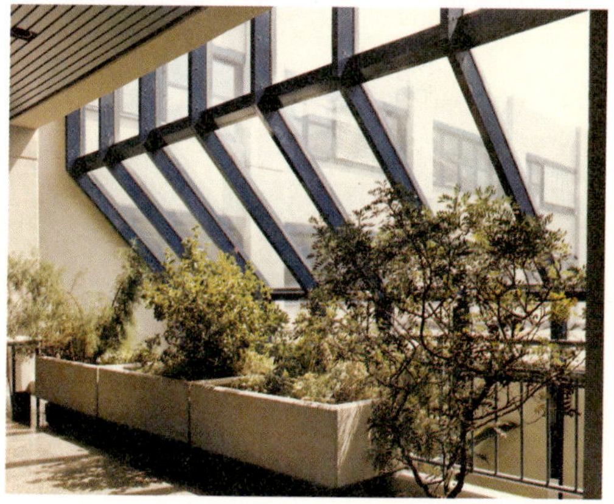

Forschungsgebäude Leibnizhaus Wolfenbüttel

Der Neubau, fertiggestellt 1981, Teil des Bibliotheksquartiers, hatten sich städtebaulich und detailentsprechend (siehe Herzog August Bibliothek S. 12, Zeughaus S. 14 und Lessinghaus S. 13) in eine Baulücke am Schloßplatz östlich vom Zeughaus einzuordnen. Das Leibnizhaus bietet Arbeitsräume für ständige oder vorübergehende forschende Wissenschaftler, dazu Cafeteria und Restaurant für alle Mitarbeiter der Bibliothek, abends auch für die Öffentlichkeit.

For the new building, completed in 1981 and part of the library complex, (see Herzog August Library, p. 12, Zeughaus, p. 14 and Lessinghaus, p. 13), a building site was available in the Schloßplatz to the east of the Armoury building. The Leibniz House provides working space for temporary and permanent research scientists, plus a cafeteria and restaurant for the library staff that are open in the evening to the public as well.

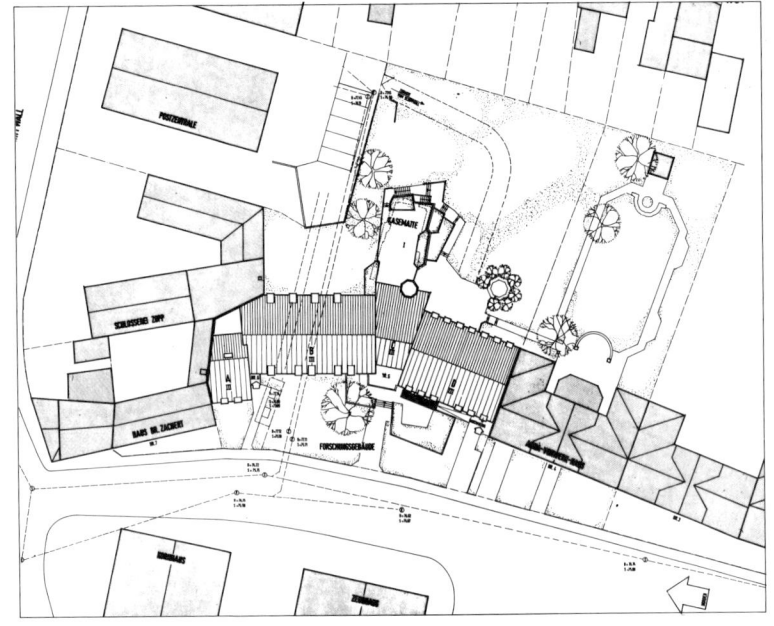

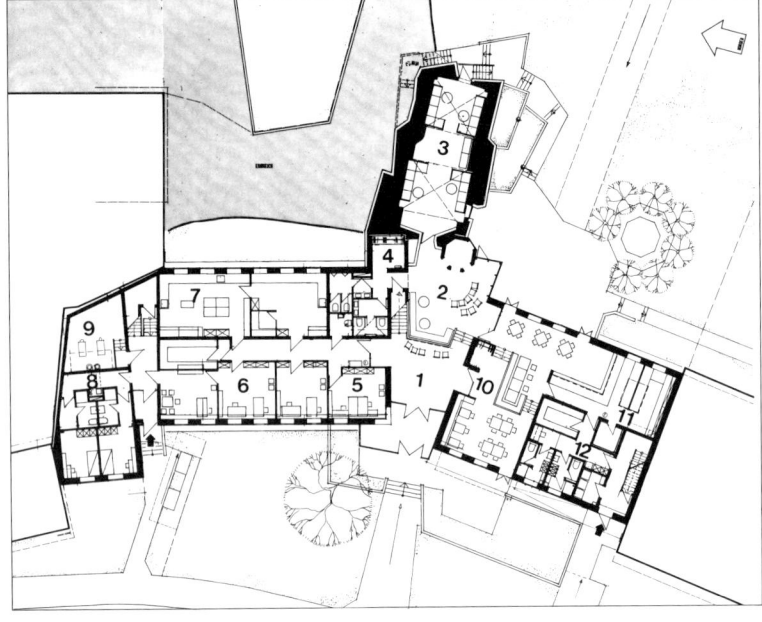

oben rechts Erdgeschoß /
top right Ground floor

1 Eingangshalle / Entrance hall
2 Versammlungshalle / Assembly hall
3 Klubraum / Clubroom
4 Garderobe / Cloakroom
5 Schreibzimmer / Office
6 Chemiker / Chemists
7 Nassraumlabor / Laboratory wet area
8 Zwei Gastappartements / Two guest apartments
9 Heizung / Heating
10 Cafeteria / Cafeteria
11 Küche / Kitchen
12 Nebenräume / Ancillary rooms

unten rechts Dachgeschoß /
bottom right Attic storey

1 Hausmeisterwohnung / Caretaker's flat
2 Wissenschaftler / Scientists' rooms
3 Resident fellow / Resident fellow
4 Halle / Hall
5 Luftraum Halle / Void over hall
6 Besprechung / Conference room
7 Dozent / Lecturer

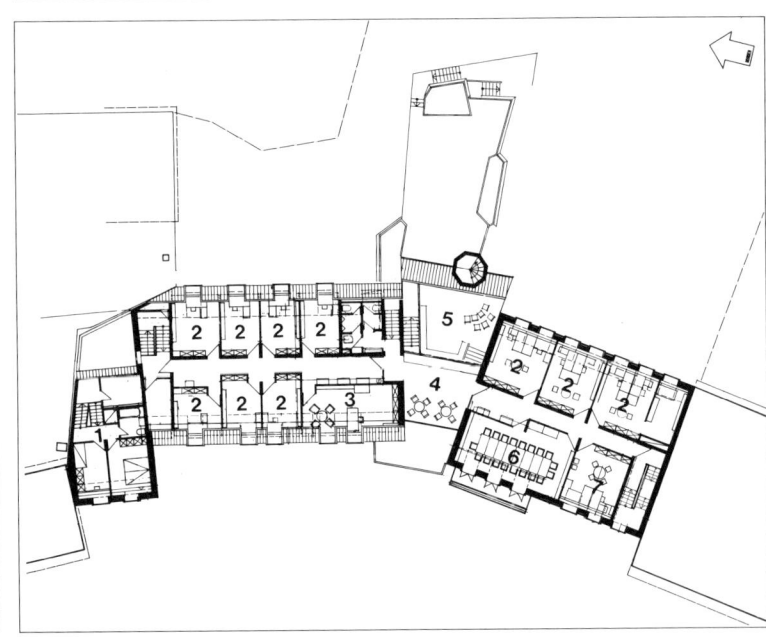

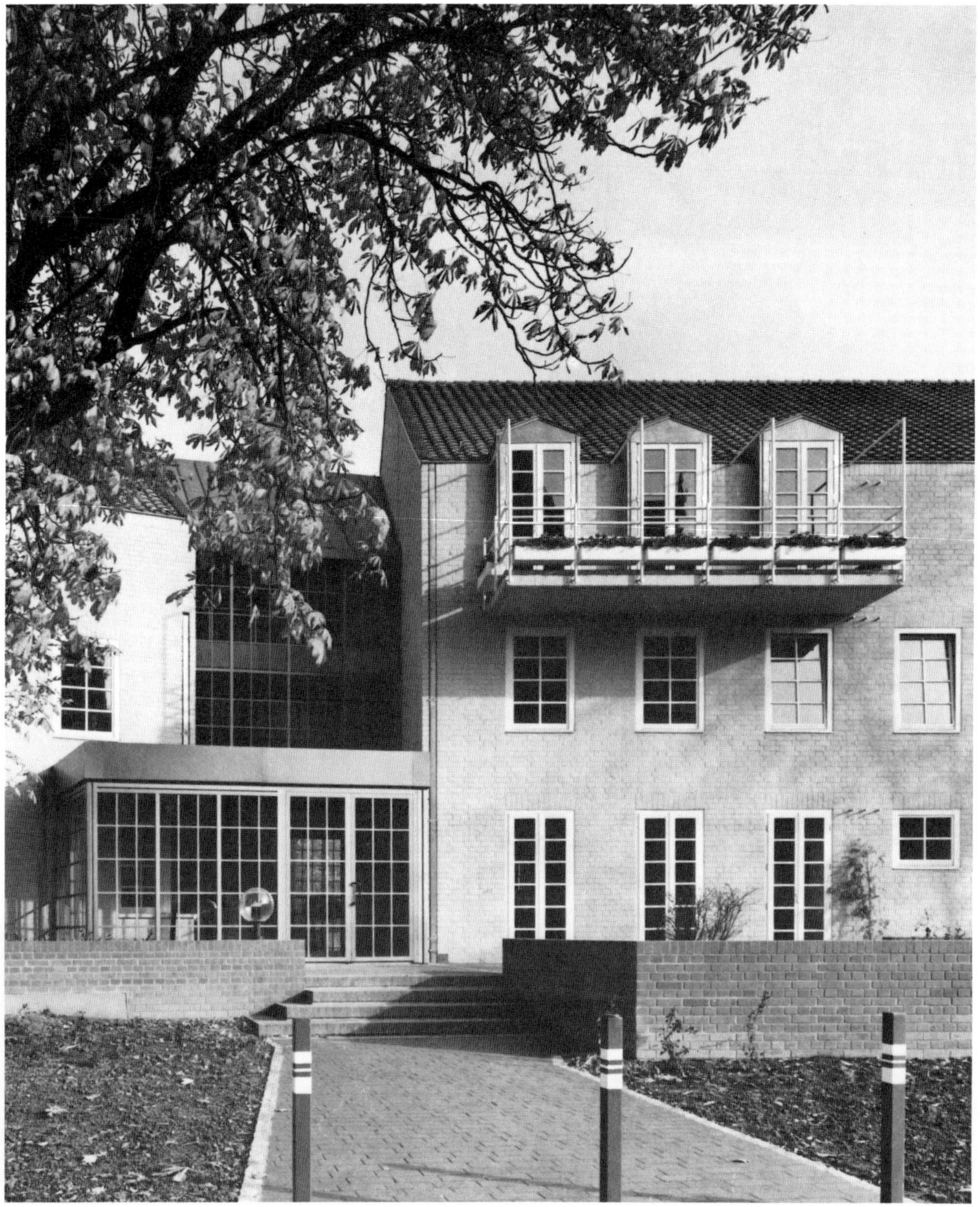

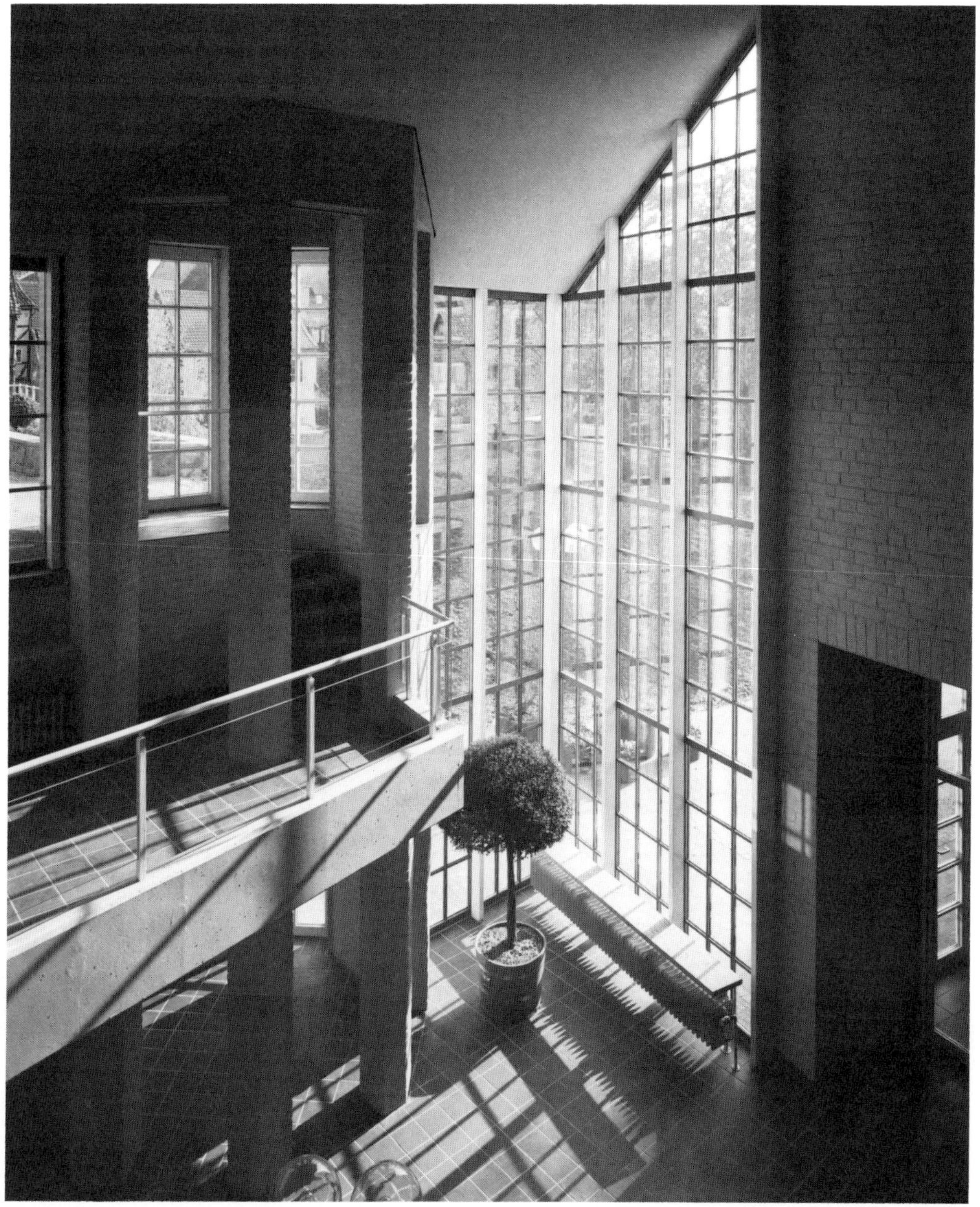

Hochschule für Bildende Künste
Braunschweig

1. Preis im Wettbewerb 1980. Erweiterung des vorhandenen Hochschulkomplexes durch ein Gebäude mit Ateliers für die darstellenden Künste, Filmstudios und Ausstellungsflächen, sowie durch eine Mensa mit Cafeteria. Fertigstellung 1983

1st Prize in competition, 1980. Extension of the existing complex of the University for Visual Arts, Brunswick, with a building containing studios for the visual arts, film studios and exhibition space, plus a dining hall with cafeteria. Completion date, 1983.

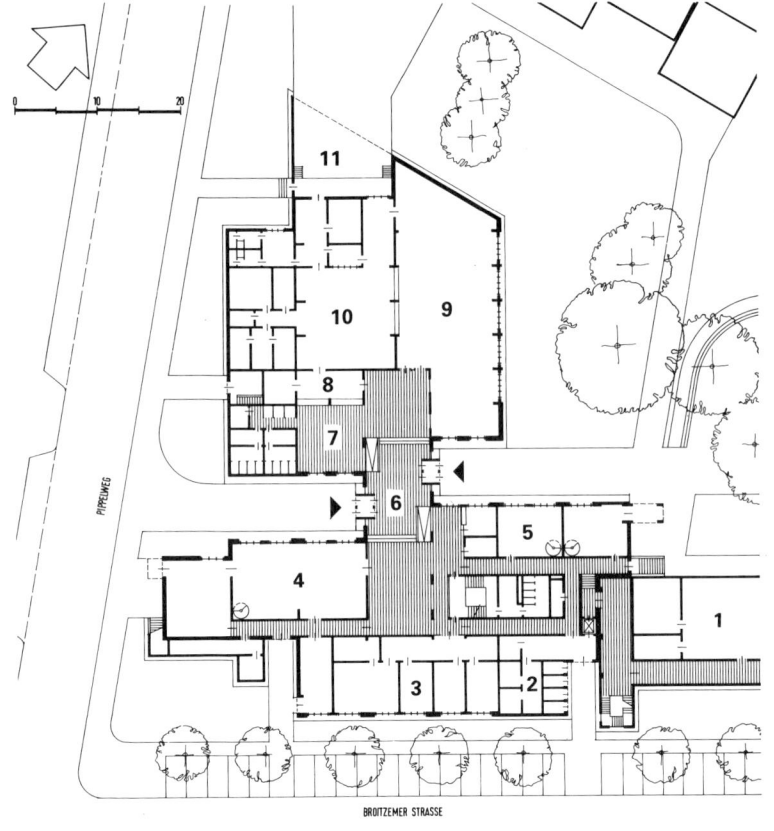

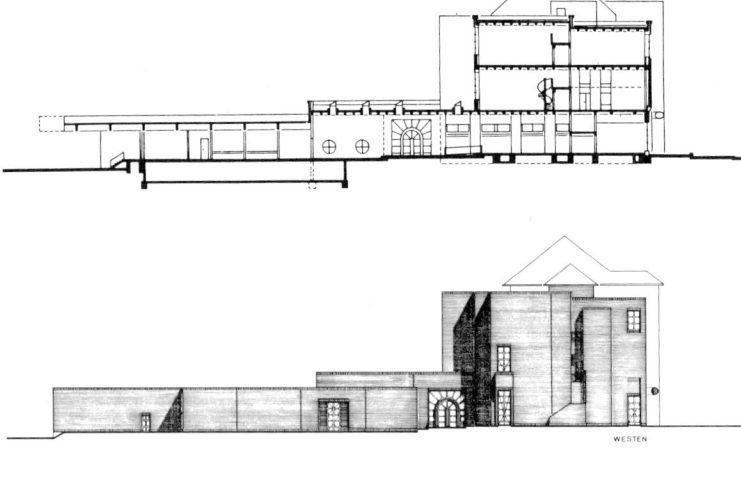

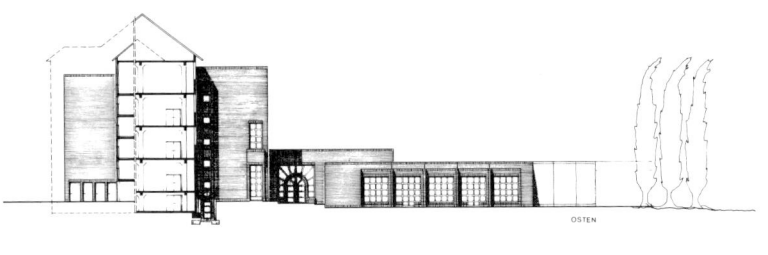

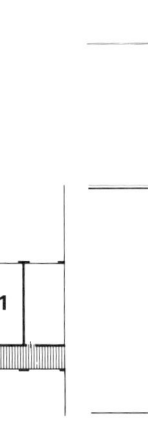

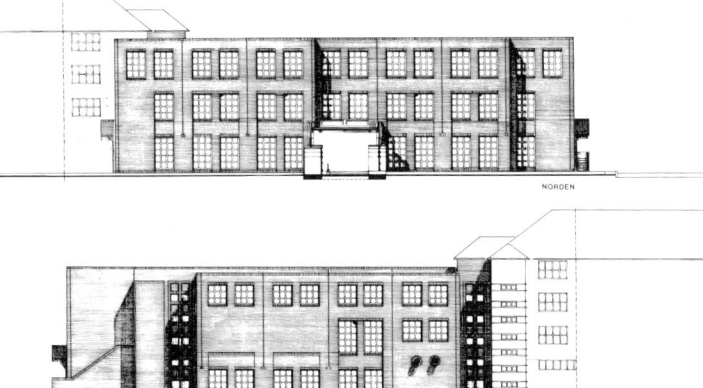

oben Erdgeschoß /
top Ground floor

1 Altbau / Existing building
2 Haustechnikzentrale / Mechanical services centre
3 Verwaltung / Administration
4 Maltechnik- + Malersaal / Painting technique + artists' studio
5 Dozentenräume / Lecturers' rooms
6 Eingangshalle / Entrance hall
7 Lounge / Lounge
8 Kiosk / Kiosk
9 Speisesaal / Dining hall
10 Küchenbereich / Kitchen area
11 Anlieferung / Deliveries

unten 1. Obergeschoß /
bottom 1st Floor

1 Altbau / Existing building
2 Projektgruppenraum / Group project room
3 Dozentenräume / Lecturers' rooms
4 Plenum / Assembly room
5 Ateliers / Studios

Die äußere Erscheinung wird bestimmt durch das sorgfältig detaillierte Kalksandsteinsichtmauerwerk.

The external appearance is governed by the carefully detailed sand lime brick facings.

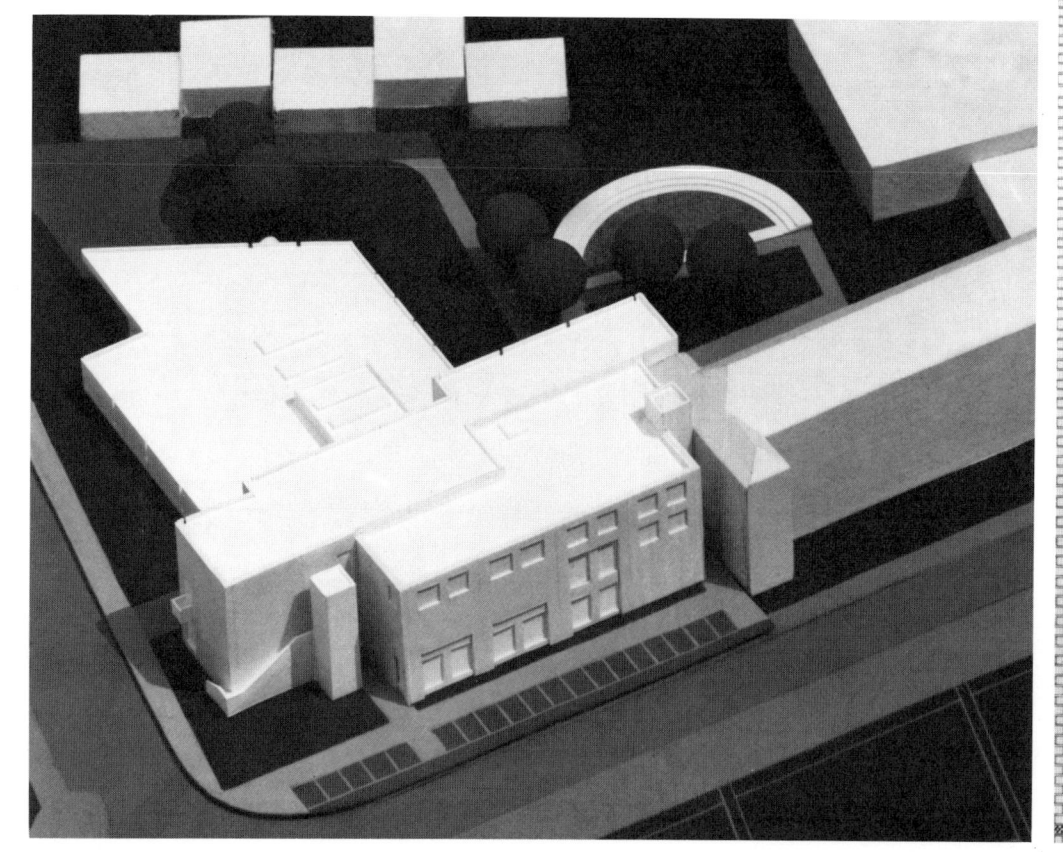

Imam Mohammad Bin Saud Islamic University Riyadh Saudi Arabien

Wettbewerb 1977. Campus-Universität mit Lehrgebäuden und Wohnheimen für 15000 Studenten und Wohnungen für weitere 10000 Mitglieder des Lehrkörpers und deren Angehörige mit allen Folgeeinrichtungen (Schulen, Läden, Klinik, etc.)

Competition, 1977. A campus-type university with faculty buildings and hostels for 15000 students, as well as housing for a further 10000 members of the faculty staff and their families, together with all ancillary facilities – (schools, shops, clinic, etc.)

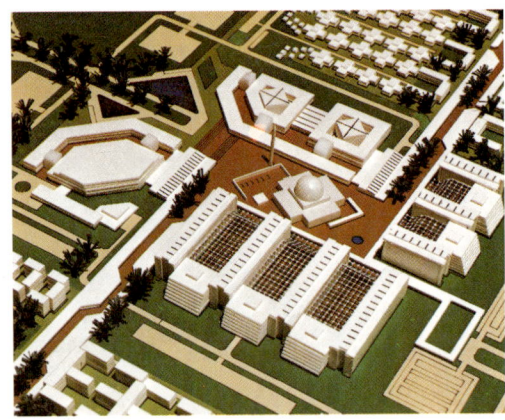

Technische Universität Hamburg-Harburg

Wettbewerb 1981.

Competition for the Technical University, Hamburg-Harburg, 1981.

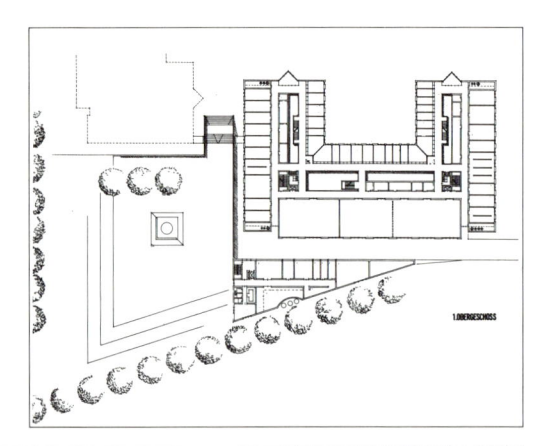

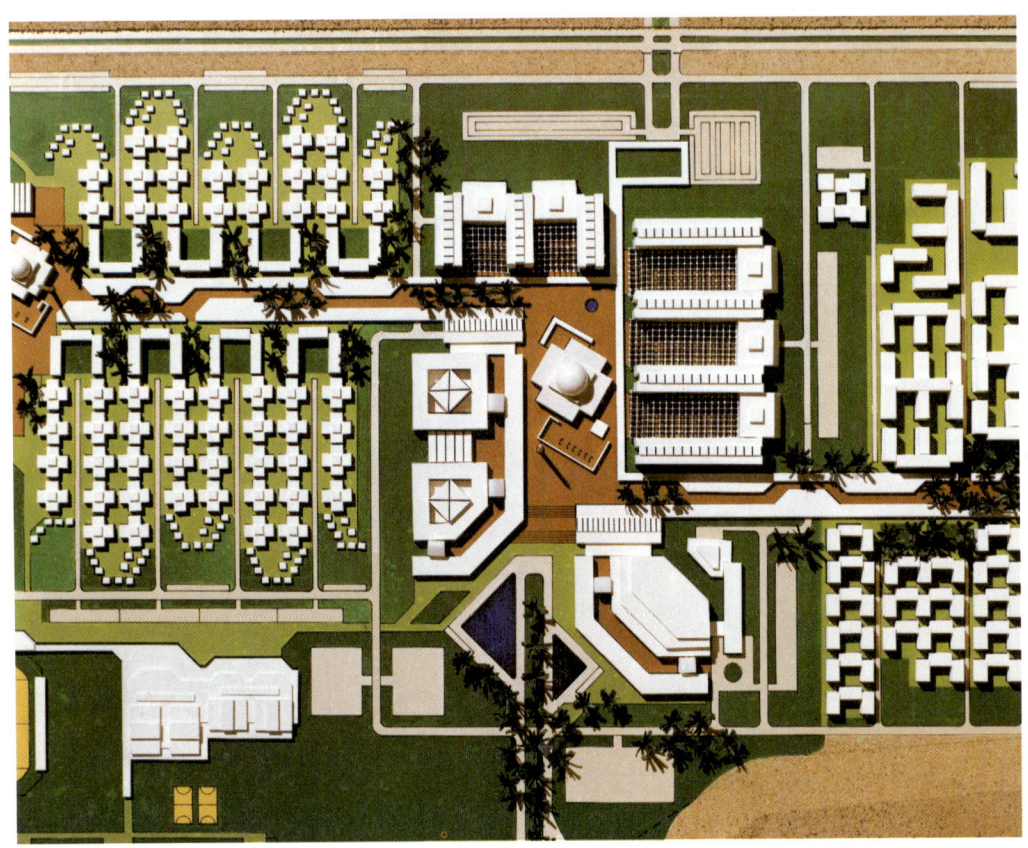

Girls' College Riyadh Saudi-Arabien

Wettbewerb 1982. Die von einer Mauer umgebene Anlage, die sich um ein vorhandenes Palmenwäldchen gruppiert, enthält die Fakultäten, Bibliothek, Hörsaalgebäude, Students' centre, Verwaltung, Sporteinrichtungen, Dormitorien für 3000 Studentinnen und Wohnungen mit Folgeeinrichtungen für Hochschulbedienstete.

Competition, 1982. The complex, surrounded by a wall and grouped around a small existing palm wood, contains the various faculties, a library, a lecture hall building, a students' centre, administration, sports facilities, dormitories for 3000 female students and housing with various ancillary facilities for the university staff.

unten Mitte links Erdgeschoß /
bottom middle left Ground floor
unten Mitte rechts Obergeschoß /
bottom middle right Upper floor

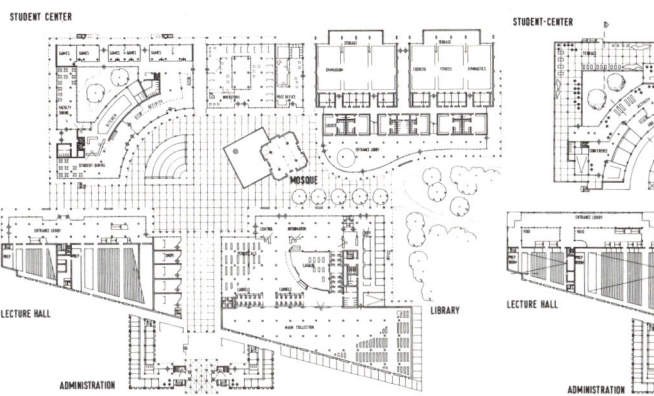

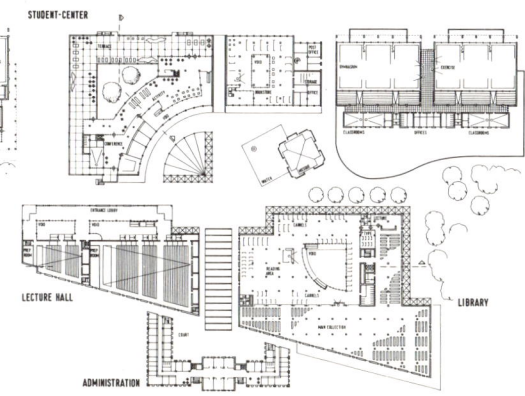

Innerstädtische Zentren / Urban centres

Iduna-Zentrum Braunschweig

Das 1972 fertiggestellte Sanierungsprojekt umfaßt ein 200-Betten-Hotel, ca. 400 Wohnungen in drei bis 19 Geschosse hohen Türmen, ein Einkaufszentrum mit ca. 4000 m² Verkaufsfläche und ca. 400 Einstellplätze in einer Tiefgarage. Zusammen mit dem Atrium-Hotel (S. 30) verbindet das Iduna-Zentrum, gegenüber dem Vieweg-Park gelegen, die Innenstadt mit neu erbautem Hauptbahnhof. Die Plastik im Vordergrund schuf Fritz Koenig.

This rehabilitation scheme, completed in 1972, comprises a 200-bed hotel, approximately 400 dwellings in three tower blocks rising up to 19 storeys in height, a shopping centre with approximately 4000 m² sales area and roughly 400 parking spaces in a basement garage. Together with the courtyard hotel, (p. 30), the Iduna Centre, situated opposite the Vieweg Park in Brunswick, links the city centre with the new main station building. The sculpture in the foreground is by Fritz Koenig.

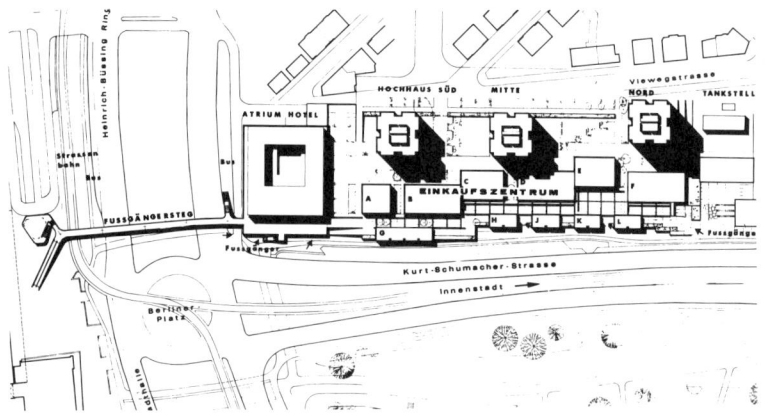

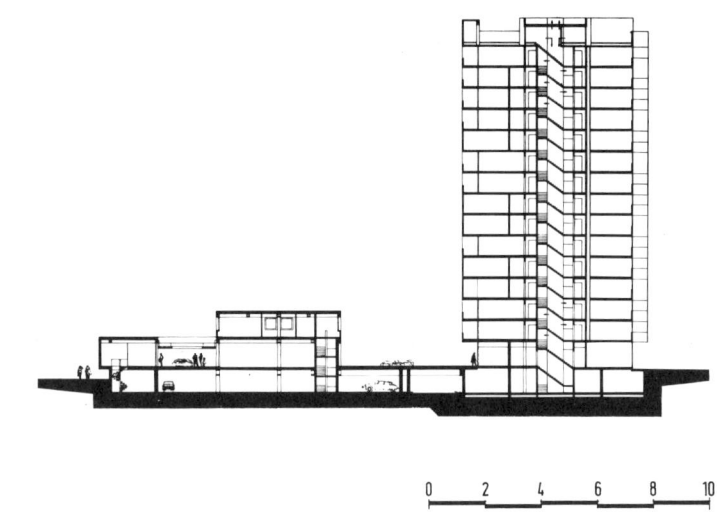

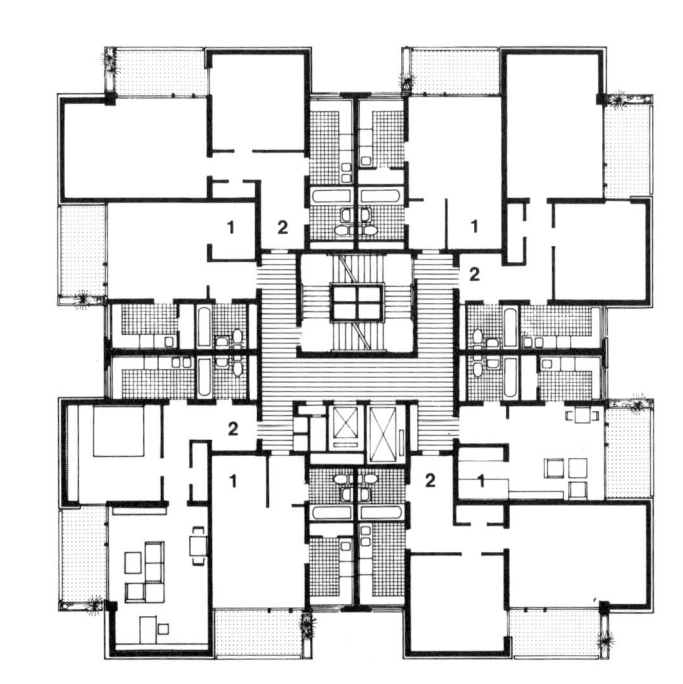

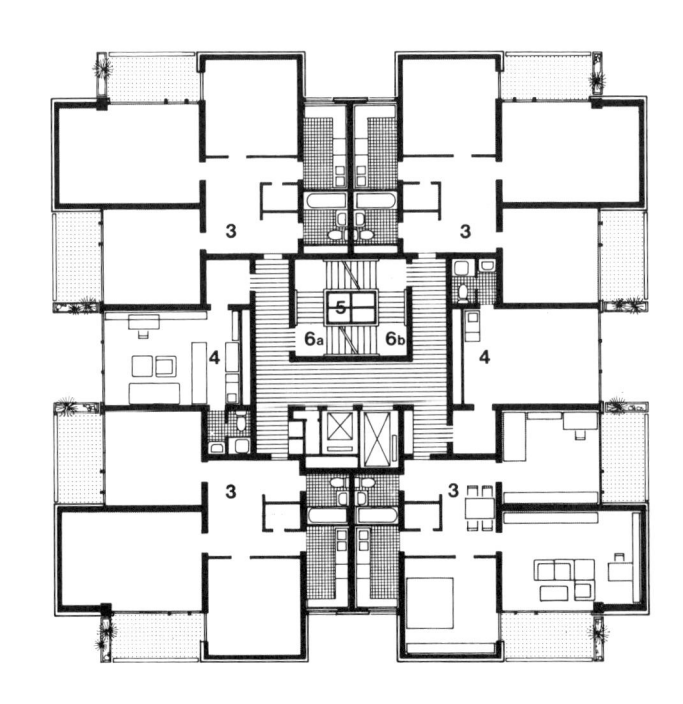

Wohnungsgrundrisse verschiedener Geschosse / Housing plans of various floors
links Wohngeschoß 1, rechts Wohngeschoß 2 / left Residential floor 1, right Residential floor 2
1 Ein-Zimmer-Wohnung 34 m² / One-room-flat 34 m²
2 Zwei-Zimmer-Wohnung 60 m² / Two-room-flat 60 m²
3 Drei-Zimmer-Wohnung 80 m² / Three-room-flat 80 m²
4 Appartement 26 m² / Apartment 26 m²
5 Lüftung / Ventilation
6a + 6b Treppen / Stairs

**Fußgängerbrücke Berliner Platz
Braunschweig**

Die 140 m lange Brücke führt die Fußgänger vom Bahnhofsvorplatz mittels Rollrampe über den Fahrverkehr hinweg zur Innenstadt. Sie wurde in zwei Fertigteilen ohne Unterbrechung des Verkehrs errichtet.

The 140 m long bridge conveys pedestrians from the station forecourt via a moving ramp over the vehicular traffic to the city centre. It is constructed of two pre-fabricated elements and was erected without interrupting the traffic.

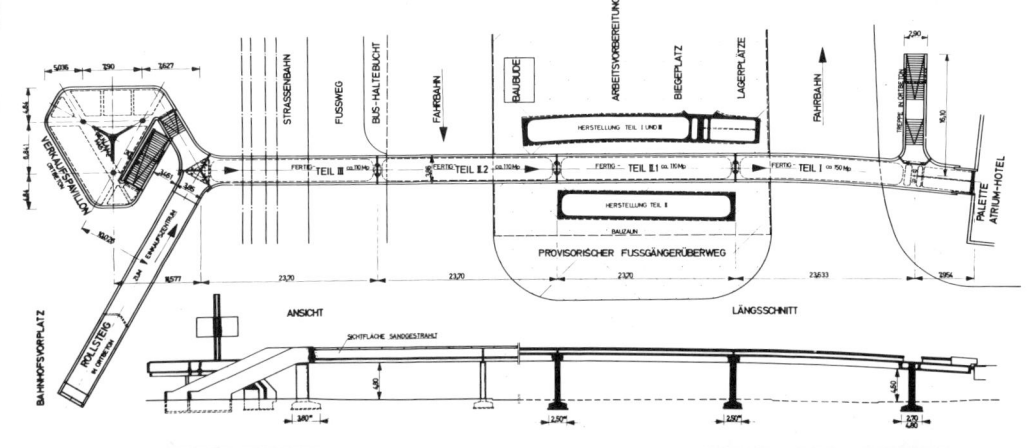

Altstadtsanierung Karlsruhe

Planung 1969. Nicht ausgeführt. Das gleiche Gebiet war später Gegenstand eines internationalen Wettbewerbs.

Rehabilitation scheme, 1969, for the old part of Karlsruhe. Not implemented. The same area of the city became later the subject of an international competition.

Wohnbebauung Fontenay Hamburg

Wettbewerb 1978 um die Bebauung eines schon weitgehend mit »Villen« vorstrukturierten, anspruchsvollen Wohnbereichs an der Alster mit hoher Ausnutzung. Versuch, das charakteristische Gesamtbild trotz der großen zusätzlichen Baumasse mit weiteren villenähnlichen Baukörpern zu erhalten.

Competition, 1978, for higher density housing in an existing, much sought after residential area on the Alster, with a primarily »villa«-type of structure. An attempt to retain the characteristic overall picture, with villa-like buildings, despite the much greater additional building volume.

**Innerstädtisches Zentrum
Neustadt/Weinstraße**

Fertiggestellt 1977. Flächensanierung, deren (privat)-wirtschaftlicher Erfolg von sehr hoher Ausnutzung des Grundstücks abhing: über mehreren Garagentiefgeschossen nimmt gewerbliche Nutzung das Erdgeschoß und 1. Obergeschoß ein. Darüber sind in mehreren Geschossen Wohnungen um einen Gartenhof auf Höhe des 2. Obergeschosses untergebracht. Aufnahme des Maßstabes der Nachbarschaft durch entsprechende Baukörpergliederung.

Town centre, completed 1977. Large-scale redevelopment, the (private) economic viability of which depended on a very intensive exploitation of the site. The ground and first floors, set above a number of basement garage storeys, are reserved for commercial uses. Above these are several storeys of flats arranged about a garden courtyard, whose ground level is at 2nd floor level. Adoption of the scale of the surrounding fabric by means of the articulation of the building.

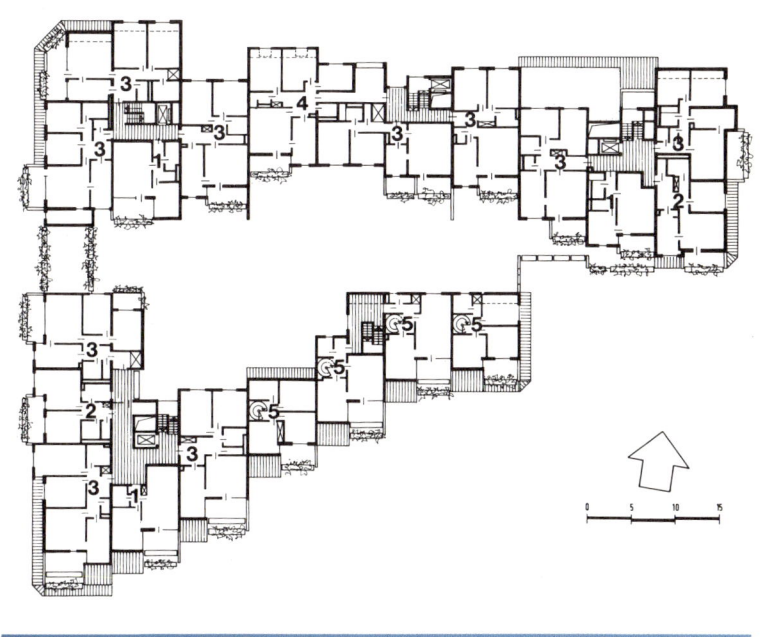

links Erdgeschoß/left Ground floor
1 Passageneingang/Arcade entrance
2 Anlieferung/Deliveries
3 Terrasse/Terrace
4 Einfahrt/Access
5 Ausfahrt/Exit
6 Aufgang zum 1.OG/Stairs to 1st floor
7 Laden/Shop
8 Zweigeschossiger Laden/Two-storey shop

rechts Normalgeschoß/right Typical floor
1 Ein-Zimmer-Wohnung/One-room flat
2 Zwei-Zimmer-Wohnung/Two-room flat
3 Drei-Zimmer-Wohnung/Three-room flat
4 Vier-Zimmer-Wohnung/Four-room flat
5 Fünf-Zimmer-Maisonette-Wohnung/Five-room maisonette

Research and Study Centres Saudi Arabien

In den Städten Riyadh, Taif, Tabuk, Jeddah, Dammam und Abha wurden für das Innenministerium kombinierte Büro- und Wohnanlagen geplant, die durch unterschiedliche Größe und Umgebungsbedingungen der jeweiligen Grundstücke aus stets unterschiedlichen Kombinationen der Grundeinheiten Bürogebäude (mit wechselnder Geschoßzahl) und der Wohnungsbauelemente zusammengesetzt wurden.

In the cities of Riyadh, Taif, Tabuk, Jeddah, Dammam and Abha, combined office and housing estates were planned for the Ministry of the Interior. They were formed using various changing permutations of the basic units of office building, (with different numbers of storeys), and housing elements, to fit the different building sites with their various sizes and surrounding conditions.

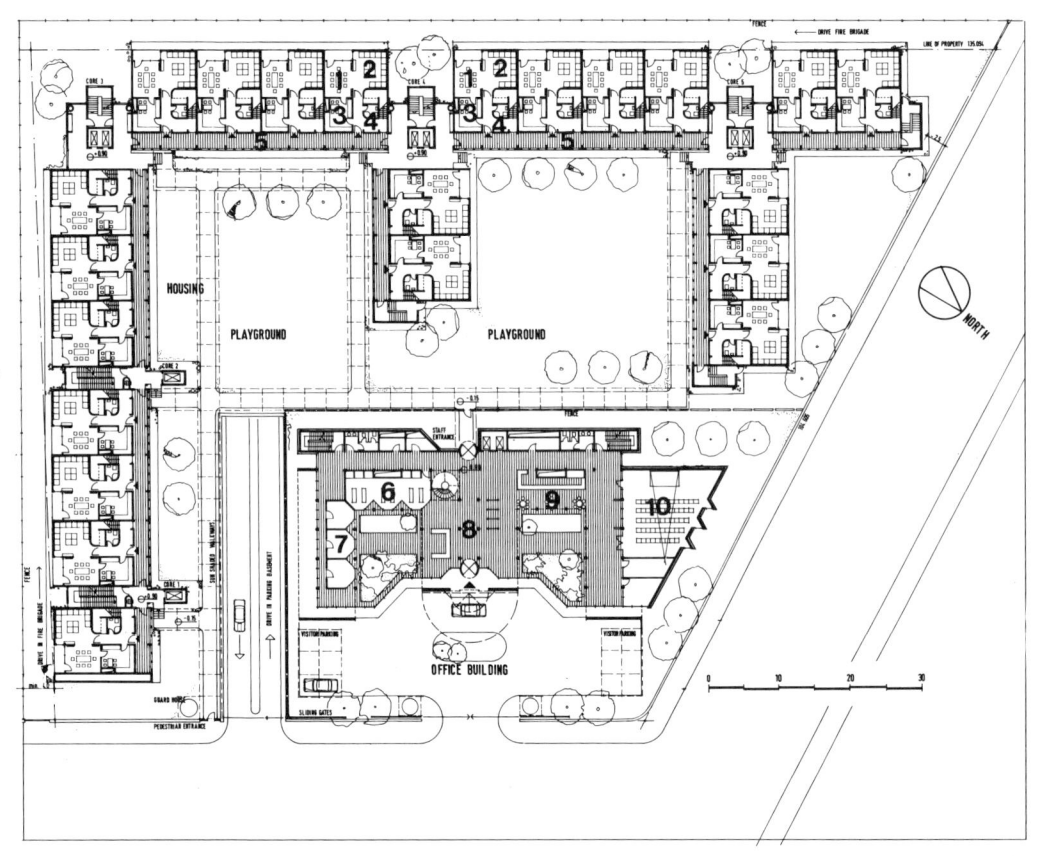

Büro- und Wohnanlage / Office and housing estatees

Erdgeschoß / Ground floor
1 Essen / Dining room
2 Wohnen / Living room
3 Küche / Kitchen
4 Eingangsflur / Lobby
5 Laubengang / Covered access
6 Bücherei / Library
7 Post- + Telefonzentrale / Mail + Telephones
8 Eingangshalle / Entrance hall
9 Cafeteria / Cafeteria
10 Vortragssaal / Lecture hall

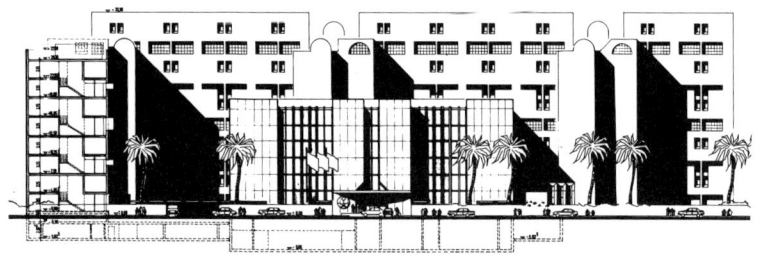

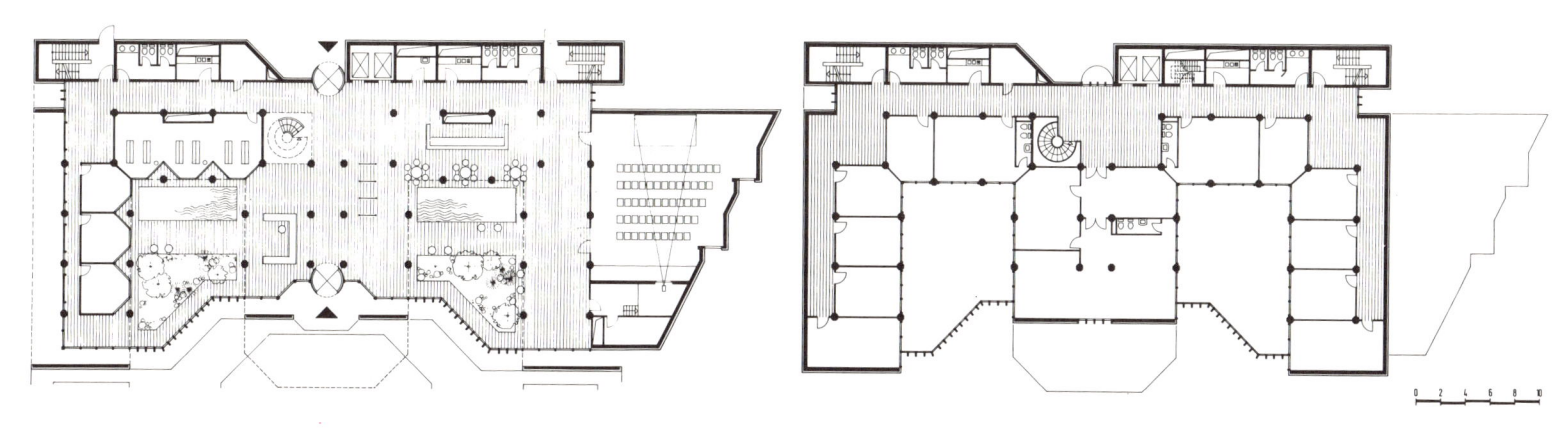

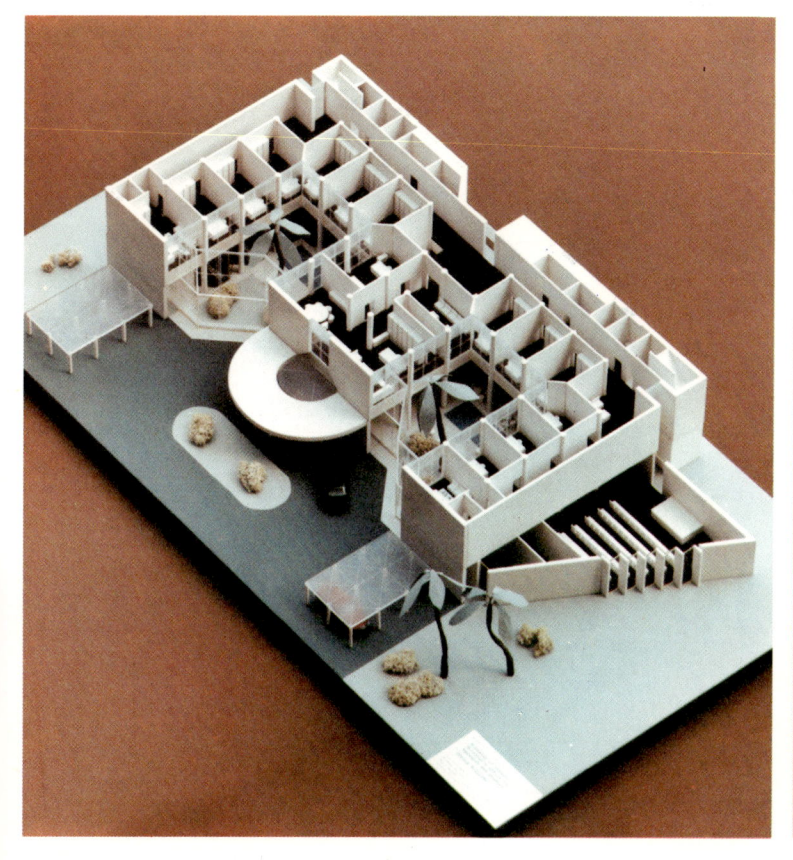

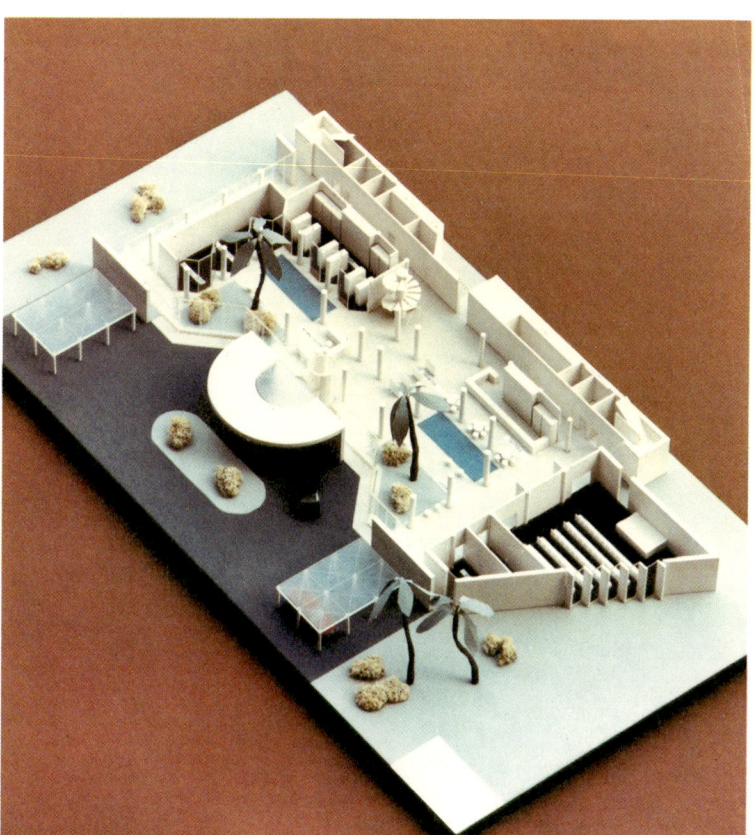

Alle Büroräume und Sonderflächen orientieren sich zu zwei glasüberdeckten Innenhallen mit Palmen.

All office spaces and special areas are orientated to two glass-roofed internal halls with palm trees.

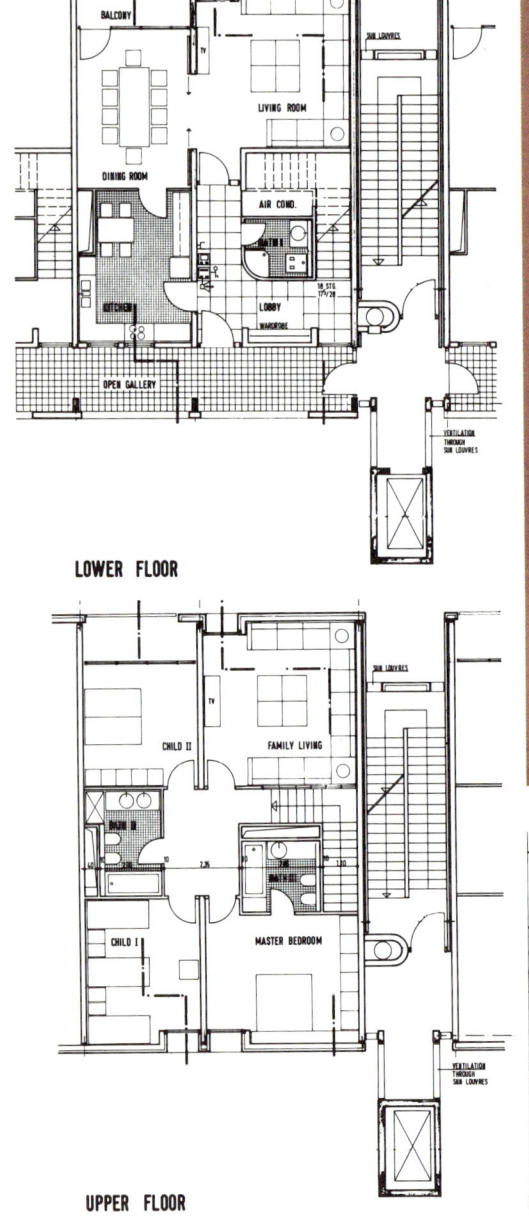

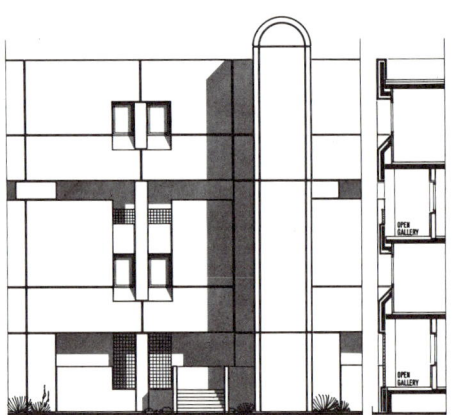

Die Grundrisse der zweigeschossigen Wohnungen nehmen Rücksicht auf die Lebensweise der Bewohner: die obere Ebene ist der Familie allein vorbehalten.
links Grundrisse der zwei Wohngeschosse, Ansicht, Schnitt
oben links Modelle der Wohnblockgeschosse
oben rechts Modell der Villen für die Leiter der Zentren

The layout of the two-storey dwellings reflects the living patterns of the occupants. The upper level is the exclusive realm of the family.
left Floor plans, view, section
top left Models of the floors in housing blocks
top right Model of the villas for the directors of the centres

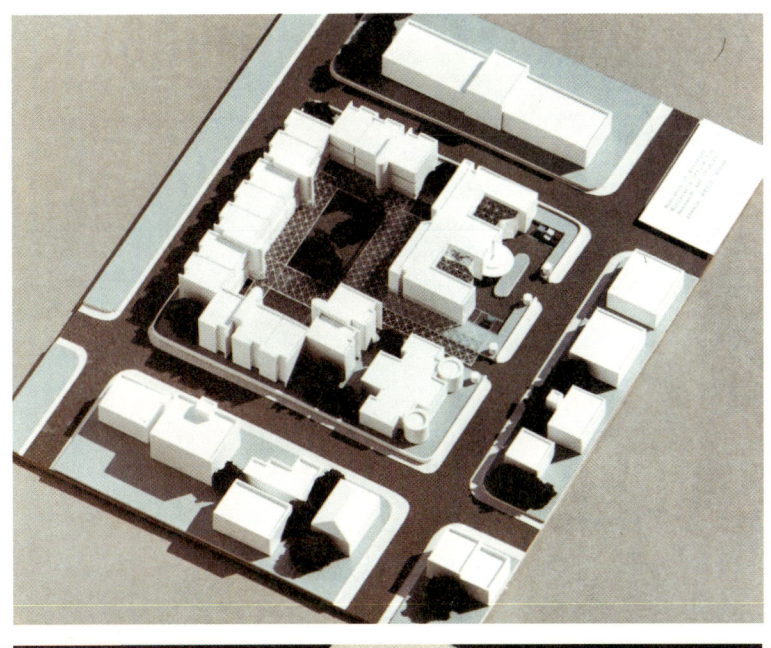

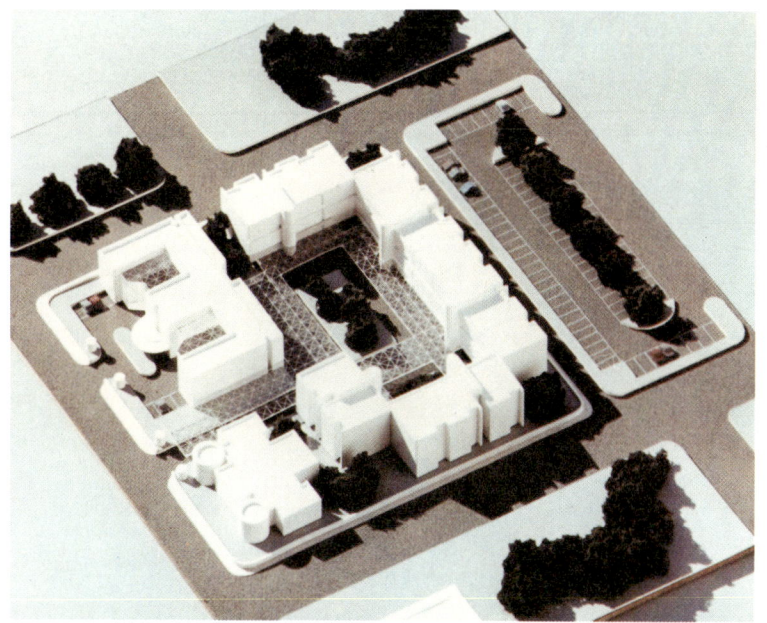

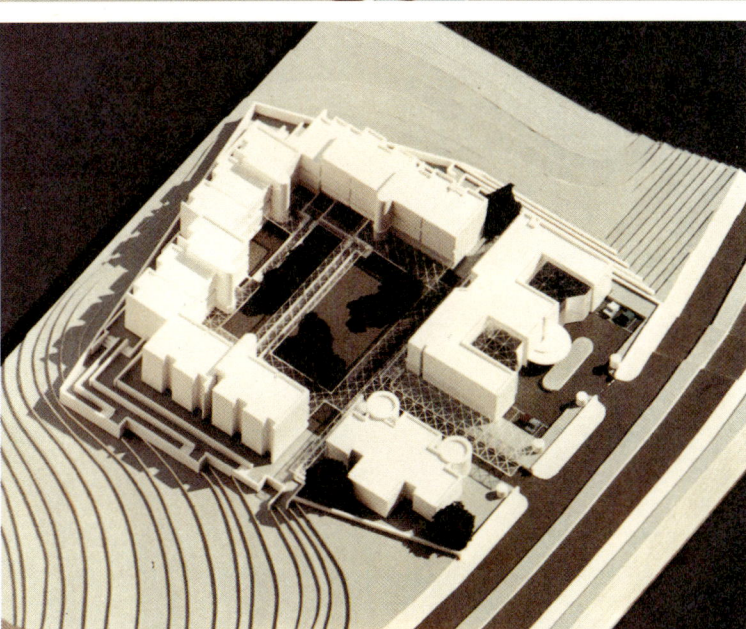

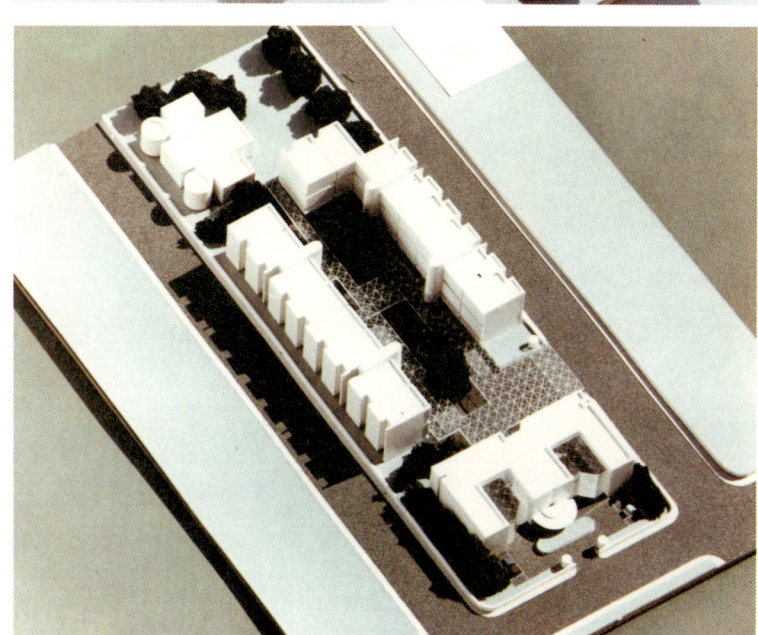

Die Modellfotos zeigen wie je nach der besonderen Situation der verschiedenen Grundstücke die Anordnung der Bausteine: Bürohaus, Wohnblocks, Villen variiert wurde.

The model photos show how the disposition of the individual building elements –, office and housing blocks and villas –, was varied according to the specific situation of the different sites.

Wohn- und Geschäftszentrum Kreishaus-Galerie St. Apern Straße Köln

Bauherr: Allianz Lebensversicherung Stuttgart. 70 Wohnungen, Läden und Büroflächen gruppieren sich in wertvoller innerstädtischer Lage um einen ruhigen Hof, dessen Zentrum eine große, unter Naturschutz stehende Kastanie bildet. Einbeziehung der historischen Fassade des ehemaligen Kreishauses (Architekt Moritz 1906), dessen Eingang eine glasüberdachte Ladenpassage erschließt. Durch Bildung von »Hauseinheiten« mit Mansarddächern Aufnahme des Maßstabs der Umgebung. Fertigstellung 1982.

Client: Allianz Lebensversicherung (life insurance) Stuttgart. 70 Dwellings, shops and office space in a valuable city centre location are grouped round a quiet courtyard, at the centre of which stands a chestnut tree (under preservation order). Integration of the historic façade of the earlier Kreishaus, (by the architect Moritz, 1906), the entrance to which is via a glass-roofed shopping arcade. Adoption of the scale of the surroundings by the creation of »house units« with mansard roofs. Completion, 1982.

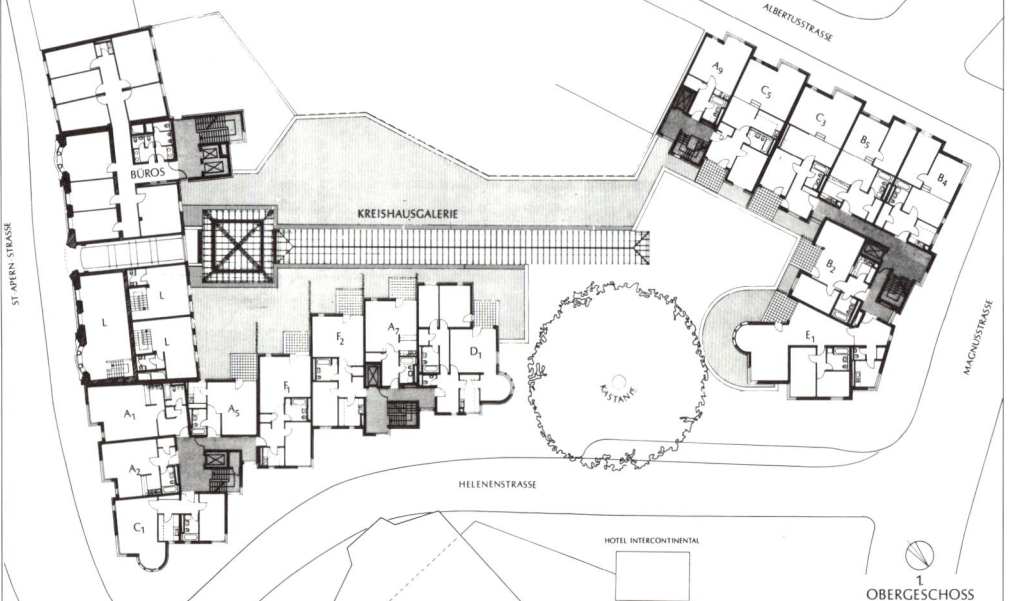

Erdgeschoß
Die in Lage und Größe stark variierenden Läden sind mit 1 bis 30 bezeichnet.

1. Obergeschoß
Die Buchstaben – Zahlenkombinationen in den Wohnungsgrundrissen zeigen die Vielfalt der unterschiedlichen Wohnungstypen und deren Abwandlungen.

Ground floor
The shops, varying considerably in size and situation, are numbered 1–30.

1st Floor
The letter-numeral reference codes in the housing layout plans reveal the variety of dwelling types and the possible variations.

87

Wadi Saqra Circle Projekt Amman Jordanien

Internationaler Wettbewerb 1980. Am Rande von Amman waren auf einem reizvollen Hanggrundstück 10 000 m² Büros, Läden, Mehrzwecksaal, Kino und 1000 Einstellplätze unterzubringen.

International competition, 1980. The project was for the erection of 10 000 m² of office space, shops, a multi-purpose hall, cinema and 1000 car parking spaces on an attractive sloping site on the outskirts of Amman.

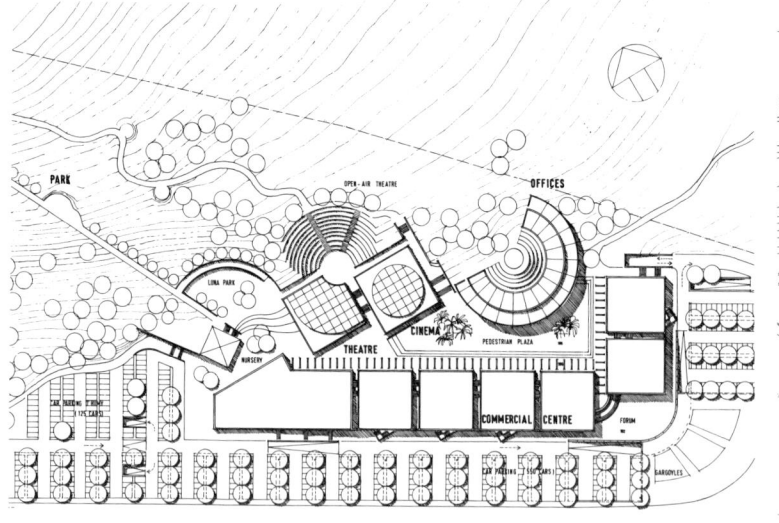

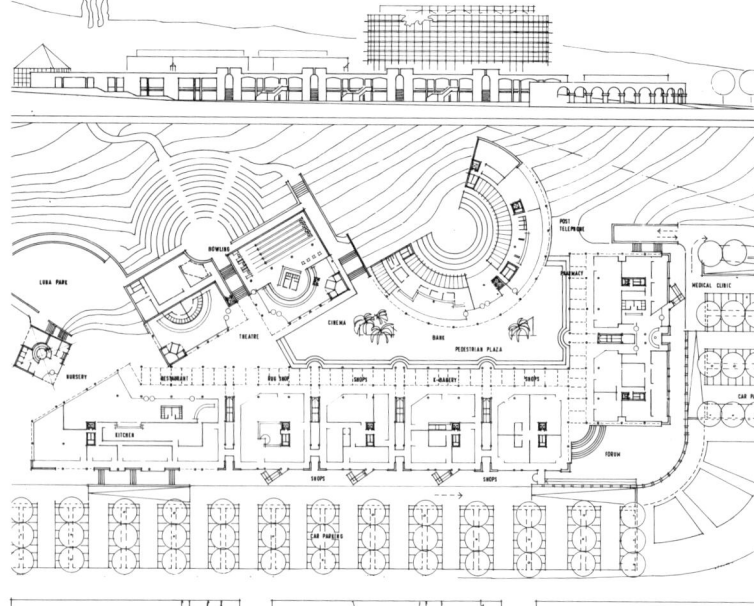

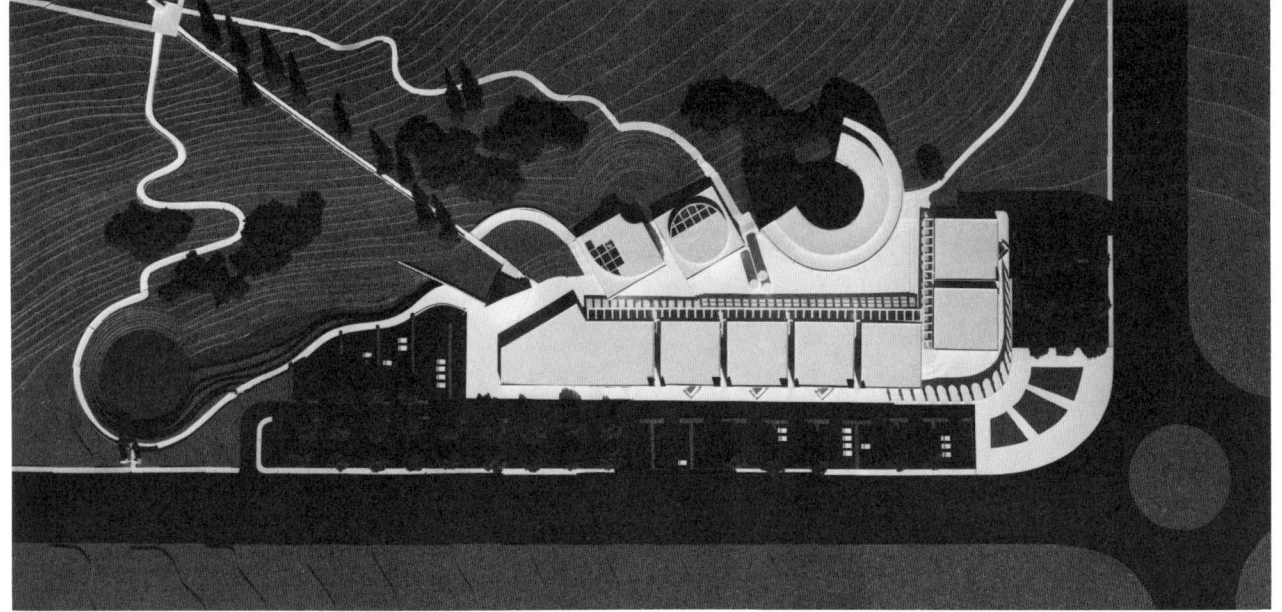

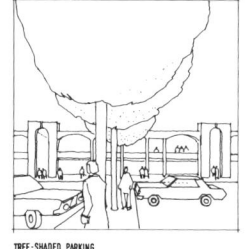

89

Berliner Platz Mülheim/Ruhr

1. Preis im bundesoffenen städtebaulichen Wettbewerb 1981.

1st Prize in urban planning competition, 1981, open to the whole of Federal Germany.

ISOMETRIE

unten links
Stadträume
1 Berliner Platz interpretiert als stadträumliches Bindeglied City + Ruhrpark, neue Platzwand im Süden ermöglicht eindeutige Begrenzung und bauliche Überleitung zum Park.
 Die Hauptfußwegbeziehung City – Ruhrpark wird zusätzlich erreicht durch
2 die Baumallee und
3 den »grünen« Vorplatz an der Ruhraue.
4 Durch die Neubauten am Berliner Platz entsteht im Süden ein maßstäblicher Raum um das Fachwerkhaus, die Kastanie und den Geschäftsbau.
5 Dieser neue Platz ist mit dem Berliner Platz durch eine Quergasse verbunden.

unten Mitte
Grün
1 Die Grünraumplanung unterstützt die räumliche Verbindung Innenstadt – Ruhraue durch Baumpflanzungen bis hin zum Berliner Platz.
2 Die Bäume auf dem Berliner Platz stellen ein sichtbares Zeichen der Wegeverbindung zur Ruhraue dar: Aufforderungscharakter.
3 Der Innenhof des Baublocks Sparkasse – Dresdner Bank wird mit einer üppigen Vegetation (begrünte Dachterrassen, Bäume) lebendig gestaltet.

unten rechts
Nutzung/Variante
1 Sparkasse als U-förmige Anlage konzipiert, eindeutig zum Berliner Platz orientiert.
2 Wohn-, Dienstleistungs- und Gewerbeflächen in Ergänzung der Blockbebauung und in der südlichen Platzrandbebauung angesiedelt.
3 EG-Zonen durch Geschäfte belebt
4 Hotel als Kopfbau in exponierter Lage
5 Alternativer Vorschlag: Abriß des mittleren Gebäudes an der Ruhrstraße, dadurch optische Einbeziehung der historischen Bauzeile in den grünen Innenhof des Gebäudekomplexes.

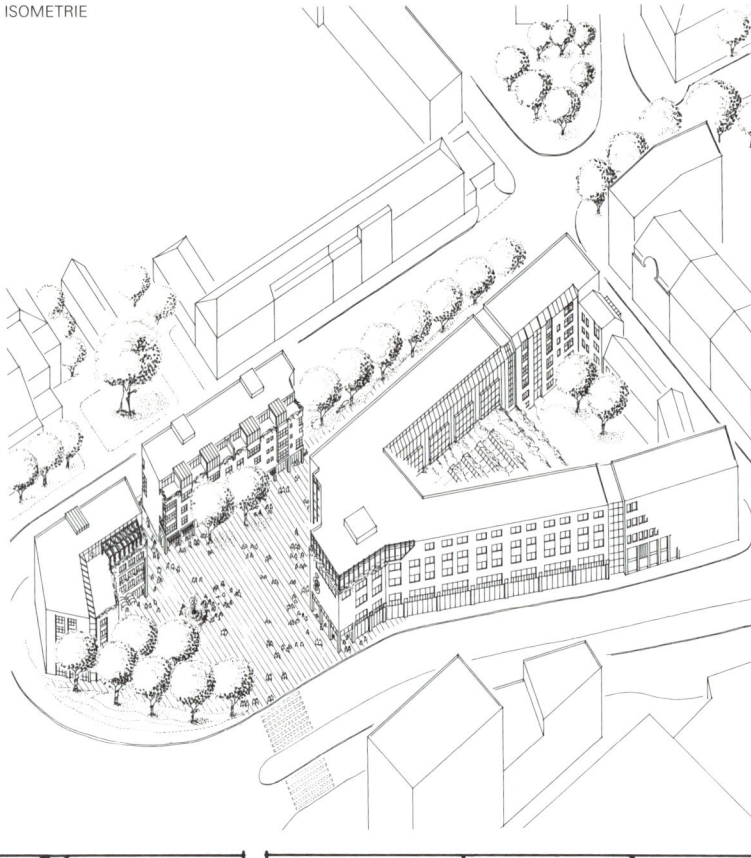

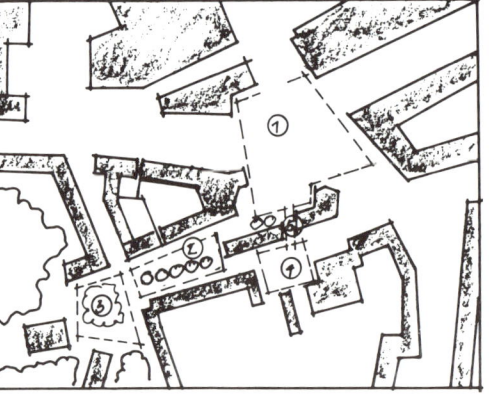

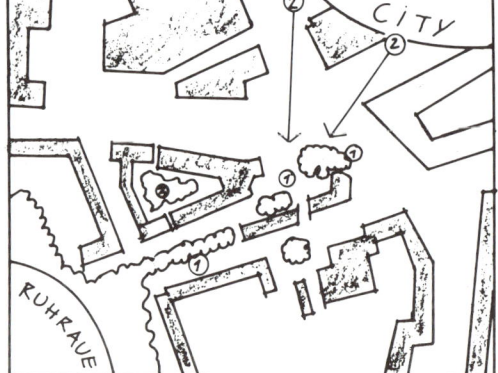

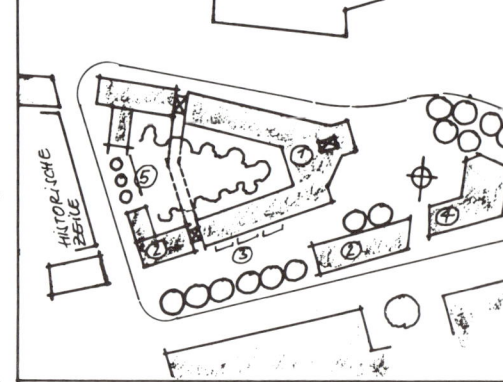

Kleiner Schloßplatz Stuttgart

Zusammen mit Meyer-Hakala, Braunschweig, 6. Preis im für Baden-Württemberg offenen Wettbewerb mit weiteren 12 Einladungen.

6th Prize, together with Meyer-Hakala, Brunswick, in a competition open to all offices in Baden-Württemberg and to 12 additionally invited outstanding architects for the redesign of the Kleiner Schloßplatz (Lesser Palace Courtyard) in Stuttgart.

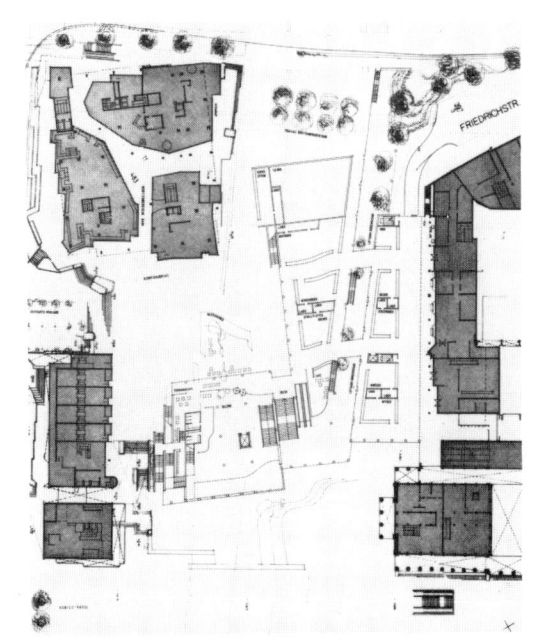

Gürzenich I und II Köln

Gürzenich I

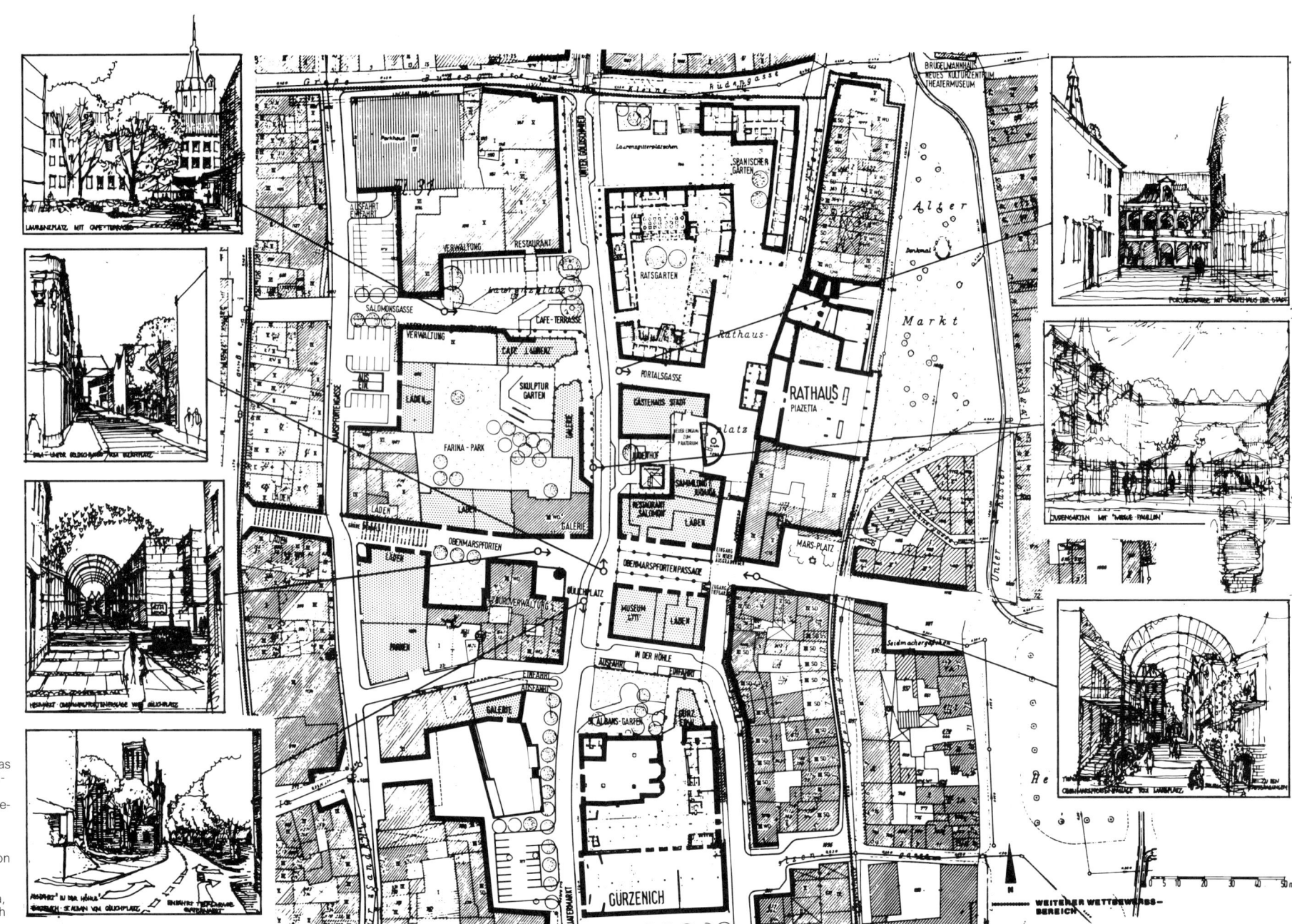

Wettbewerb 1. Stufe für das Areal zwischen dem historischen Kölner Rathaus mit der berühmten Renaissancelaube und dem mittelalterlichen Gürzenich

1st Stage of the competition for the area between the historic city hall with its famous Renaissance loggia, and the medieval Gürzenich building

In einem zweistufigen Ideenwettbewerb sollte die Neugliederung des Areals zwischen dem historischen Rathaus mit der berühmten Renaissancelaube und dem mittelalterlichen Gürzenich geklärt werden. In der 1. Stufe erhielt der Vorschlag, die gewachsenen Stadtstrukturen durch eine Folge von Straßen-, Platz- und Grünräumen fortzusetzen, den 3. Preis. Obwohl in der 1. Stufe fast alle Preisträger die historischen Baugrenzen wiederherstellten, sollte in der 2. Stufe vor dem Rathaus ein neuer Platz entstehen. Der Kompromiß, diese Baugrenzen durch Baumreihen nachzubilden und die Fläche vor dem Rathaus zunächst von Bebauung freizuhalten, bekam den 2. Preis.

The brief of the two-stage ideas competition required the rearticulation of the area between the historic city hall, with its famous Renaissance loggia, and the medieval Gürzenich building. In the 1st stage of the competition the proposal to extend the existing living urban tissue with a sequence of street spaces, squares and planted open spaces was awarded 3rd prize. Although in the 1st stage nearly all the prizewinners reinstated the historic building lines, one of the conditions of the 2nd stage was the creation of a new open space in front of the city hall. The compromise solution of marking these building lines with lines of trees and leaving the space in front of the city hall free for the time being won 2nd prize.

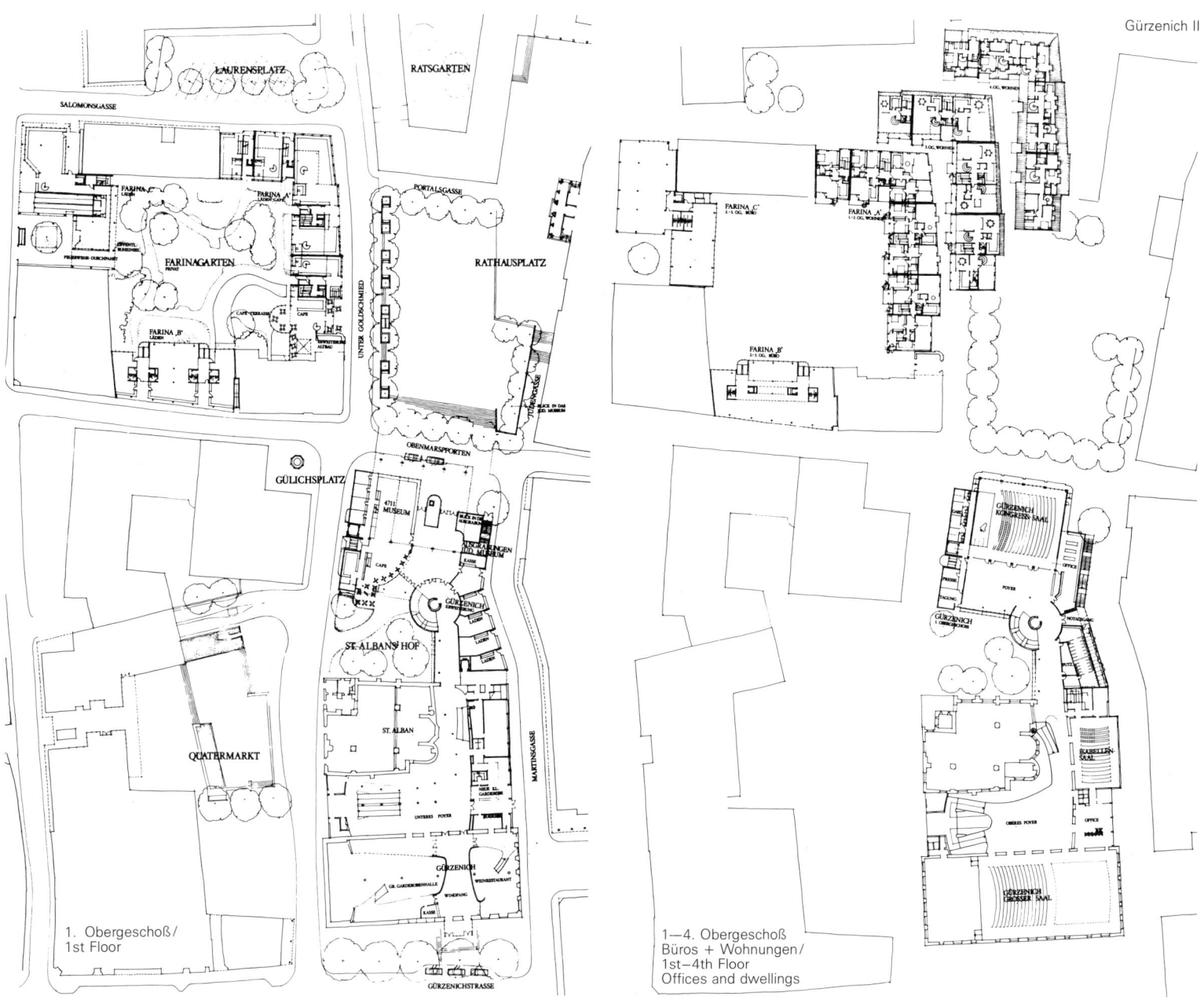

Industriebauten/Industrial buildings

Unger und Sohn Braunschweig

Wiederaufbau einer im Krieg zerstörten Fabrikanlage mit einfachsten Mitteln unter Verwendung der erhaltenen Außenmauern.

Reconstruction of a factory plant destroyed in the war, using the simplest of means and incorporating the remaining outer walls.

Rolleiflex Werkstattgebäude VII Braunschweig

Erster Abschnitt der Vergrößerung der Werksanlagen der Rolleiflex-Kamerafabrik. Mehrgeschossiges Fabrikationsgebäude mit unterzugslosen Decken. Glasbausteinfenster dienen der Lichtlenkung und Heizkosteneinsparung.

First stage of the extension of the works of the Rolleiflex camera factory. Multi-storey manufacturing building with flat plate floor slabs. Glass block windows serve to direct light into the interior and reduce heating costs.

Sozialgebäude Büssing Braunschweig

Durch knappen Grundstückszuschnitt mußten die großen Speiseraumflächen in mehreren Geschossen gestapelt werden. Der Grundriß erhielt seine Besonderheit durch ihre Zugangs- und Versorgungsnotwendigkeiten.

Due to the restricted site area, the large dining areas in the Büssing social welfare building in Brunswick had to be stacked on top of each other and spread over a number of storeys. The peculiarities of the layout plan are attributable to the constraints of access and services.

NSM Spielautomatenfabrik Bingen

Die kammartig angeordneten Geschoßbauten für die Produktion von Spielautomaten sind durch eine Verkehrsspange untereinander und mit dem Verwaltungskopfbau verbunden. Bezugsjahr 1955.

The multi-storey blocks of this factory producing gaming machines are laid out in tooth-comb fashion and linked to each other and to the administrative head building by a communications strip. Year of occupation, 1955.

Max Voets Braunschweig

Fertiggestellt 1956. Die Gesamtanlage der Volkswagengroßhandlung umfaßt Reparatur- und Wartungshallen, Ersatzteillager, Kundendiensträume und Verwaltung. Der erste unverkleidete Stahlskelettbau in Deutschland. Die anthrazit gestrichene Stahlkonstruktion wurde mit leichten, starkfarbigen Sandwichelementen oder grau-weißen Keramikplatten ausgefacht.

Completed in 1956. The entire plant of the Volkswagen wholesale distributor comprises repair and servicing halls, spare-parts stores, customer service rooms and administrative areas. The first unclad steel skeleton frame structure in Germany. The infill panels to the anthracite painted steel structure are lightweight boldly coloured sandwich elements or greywhite ceramic slabs.

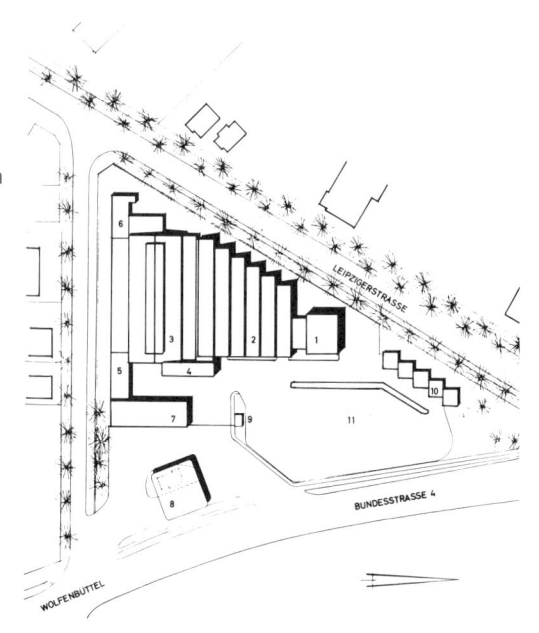

Lageplan/Site plan
1 Verwaltung/Administration
2 Schneller Dienst, Ersatzteillager/Quick service, spare parts store
3 Schwerreparatur/Major repairs
4 Reparaturannahme/Repairs reception
5 Gewährleistungsabteilung/Guarantee department
6 Lackiererei/Spray shop
7 Pflegedienst/Cleaning + servicing
8 Tankstelle/Petrol pumps
9 Pförtner/Gatekeeper
10 Fahrradständer/Bicycle stands
11 Parkplatz/Parking

Rolleiflex Werkstattgebäude VIII
Braunschweig

Flachbauhalle für die Aufnahme schwerer und Schwingungen erzeugender Werkzeugmaschinen für die Kamerafertigung. Zeiss-Dywidag-Schalenshedkonstruktion. Baujahr 1955.

A low-rise hall structure for heavy machine tools and plant causing oscillations, necessary for the manufacture of cameras. Zeiss-Dywidag north-light shell structure. Construction date, 1955.

Rolleiflex Werkstattgebäude IX
Braunschweig

Das Produktionsgebäude wurde 1956 fertiggestellt. Es enthält Fertigungsräume für die Herstellung von Präzisionskameras. Seine für die damalige Zeit besonderen Neuerungen waren: Sichtbetonskelett, weitgespannte, balkenlose Rö-Bau-Decken in Gebäudequerrichtung, deren Röhrenhohlräume zugleich der Zuluftführung des vollklimatisierten Gebäudes dienen. Flexibilität der Flächennutzung durch Verwendung von Montagetrennwänden.

This production building was completed in 1956. It contains production space for the manufacture of precision cameras. The particular innovations of the time were the exposed reinforced concrete skeleton frame, large-span tubular section structural floor slabs, without beams, spanning the width of the building, the tubular voids of which also served to conduct the fresh air supply of this fully air conditioned building. Flexibility in the use of floor areas is obtained by using lightweight partitions.

Konstruktions- und Installationsschema /
Diagram of structural system and services

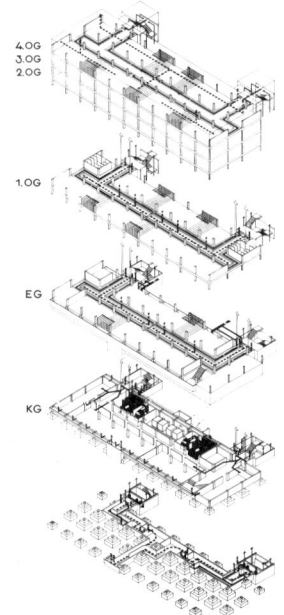

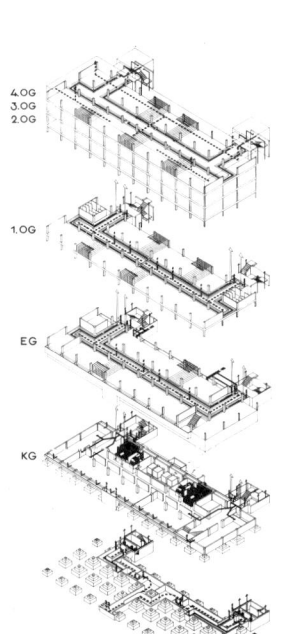

Maschinenfabrik Wohlenberg Hannover

Aus Anlaß des notwendigen Neubaus einer Produktionshalle und einer Heizzentrale wurde eine Gesamtwerkplanung mit Lagezuweisungen für die Bereiche Produktion, Lager, Sozialflächen und Verwaltung in Abhängigkeit vom Ver- und Entsorgungssystem entwickelt.

Out of what was initially a need for a new machine making production hall and a central heating plant developed an overall works plan with locational decisions affecting the realms of production, storage, social welfare, and administration, relating them to the services system.

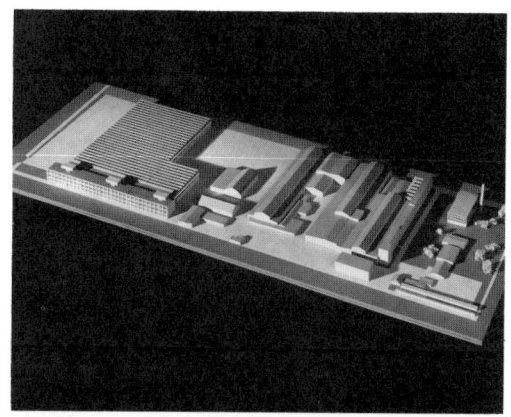

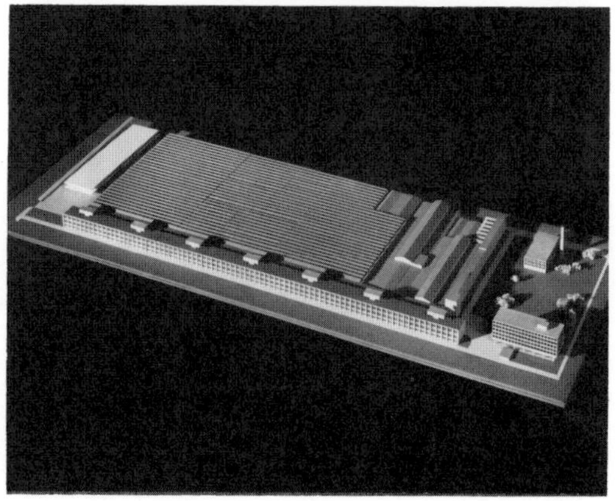

Prüflabor Rheinisch-Westfälische Kalkwerke Dornap

Wegen Korrosionsgefahr besteht die Außenwand aus leichten Holzrahmenelementen, deren, jeweils nach verschiedener Raumfunktion, unterschiedliche Flächeneinteilung vom Gleichmaß der außenliegenden Konstruktion überspielt wird.

In view of the dangers of corrosion, the external walls of the laboratory building for the limestone works in Dornap were built of lightweight timber framed elements, the various area divisions of which reflect the different spatial functions; the whole is counterpointed by the regularity of the load-bearing structure set outside the building.

Gemeinschaftshaus Aluminium-Walzwerke Singen

1. Preis im Wettbewerb 1959. Sichtbetonskelettkonstruktion und Ausbau unter bevorzugter Verwendung eigener Aluminiumprodukte sind auf Einfachheit und Durabilität angelegt.

1st Prize in competition 1959, for the community centre of the Aluminium Works in Singen. The choice of an exposed concrete skeleton frame structure and the firm's own aluminium products as far as possible for finishings is based on criteria of simplicity and durability.

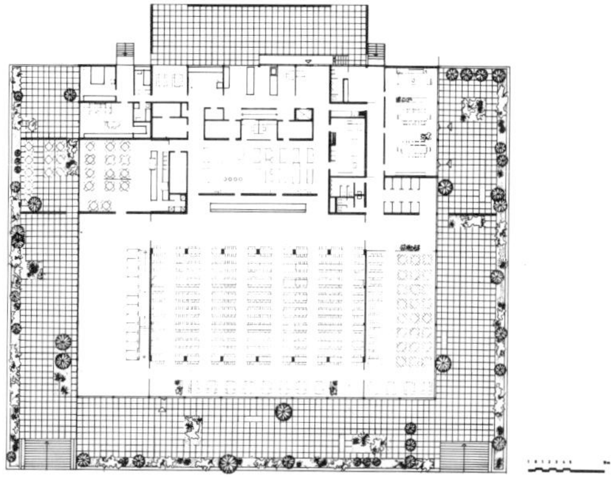

Kantine Veba Chemie Gelsenkirchen-Buer

Wettbewerbserfolg, fertiggestellt 1972 als erster Abschnitt einer umfangreicheren Gesamtplanung (S. 128). Das Gebäude enthält neben der Hauptküche, die auch Nebenkantinen beliefert und ca. 3000 Essen täglich produziert, die Zentralkantine, eine Cafeteria, sowie Speiseräume für den Vorstand und Gäste. Die Verkehrsführung vermeidet Kreuzungen zwischen Ausgabe und Geschirrückgabe. Gebäudeaußenhaut aus großformatigen Keramikplatten.

A successful competition entry, completed in 1972 as the first stage of a comprehensive overall plan (p. 128). As well as the main kitchen, which supplies ancillary kitchens and serves some 3000 meals a day, the canteen building contains the central canteen area, a cafeteria and dining rooms for the management and for guests. The organisation of the flow of traffic avoids any crossing of routes between the issue of food and the return of crockery. The outer skin of the building is of large ceramic slabs.

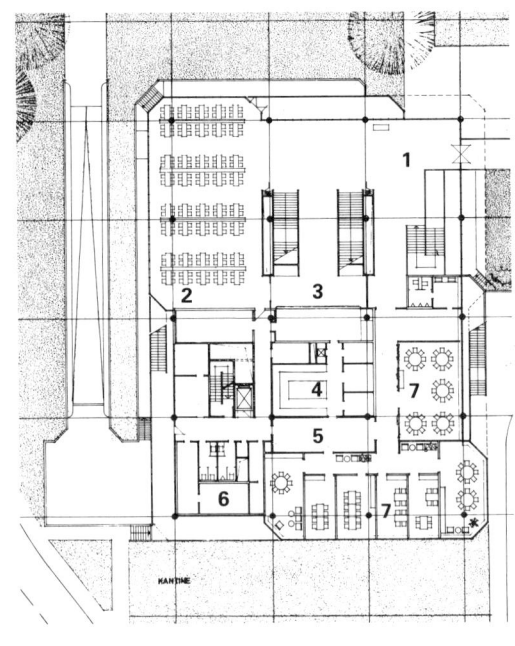

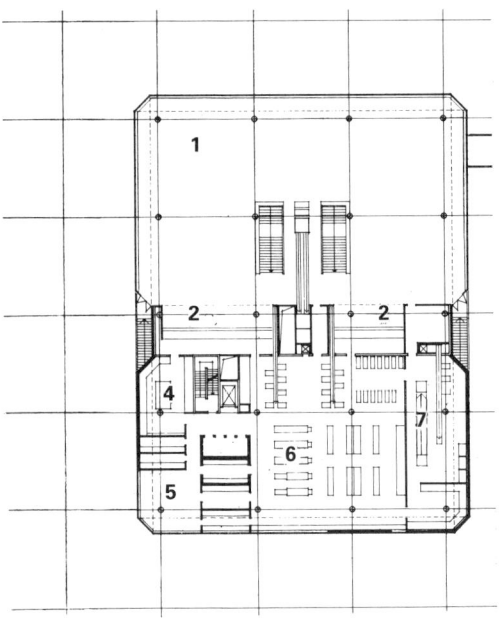

oben Erdgeschoß / top Ground floor
1 Eingangshalle / Entrance hall
2 Cafeteria / Cafeteria
3 Ausgabe / Food counter
4 Küche / Kitchen
5 Anrichte / Food preparation
6 Waschraum / Toilets
7 Speisesäle Direktion / Management dining rooms

unten 1. Obergeschoß / bottom 1st Floor
1 Speisesaal / Dining hall
2 Ausgabe / Meals counter
3 Abgabe / Crockery return
4 Kalte Küche / Cold meals kitchen
5 Personal / Staff
6 Hauptküche / Main kitchen
7 Geschirrspüle / Dish washing

Heidelberger Druckmaschinenfabrik
Heidelberg

Wettbewerbsbeitrag 1978. Auf beengtem Grundstück waren in städtebaulich bedeutsamer Situation ein neues Hauptverwaltungsgebäude, ein Kasino und eine Vorführdruckerei in die vorhandene Altbausubstanz einzufügen.

Competition entry in 1978. The brief required the integration of a new building for the administrative headquarters, club rooms and a demonstration printing shop into an existing fabric of older buildings on a restricted site in an important urban situation.

Erdgeschoß / Ground floor

Normalgeschoß / Typical floor

Fernmeldeturm Düsseldorf

Entwurf im Rahmen eines Bauträgerwettbewerbs für die Bundespost 1978.

Design for a telephone service tower as part of a developers' competition for the Post Office in 1978.

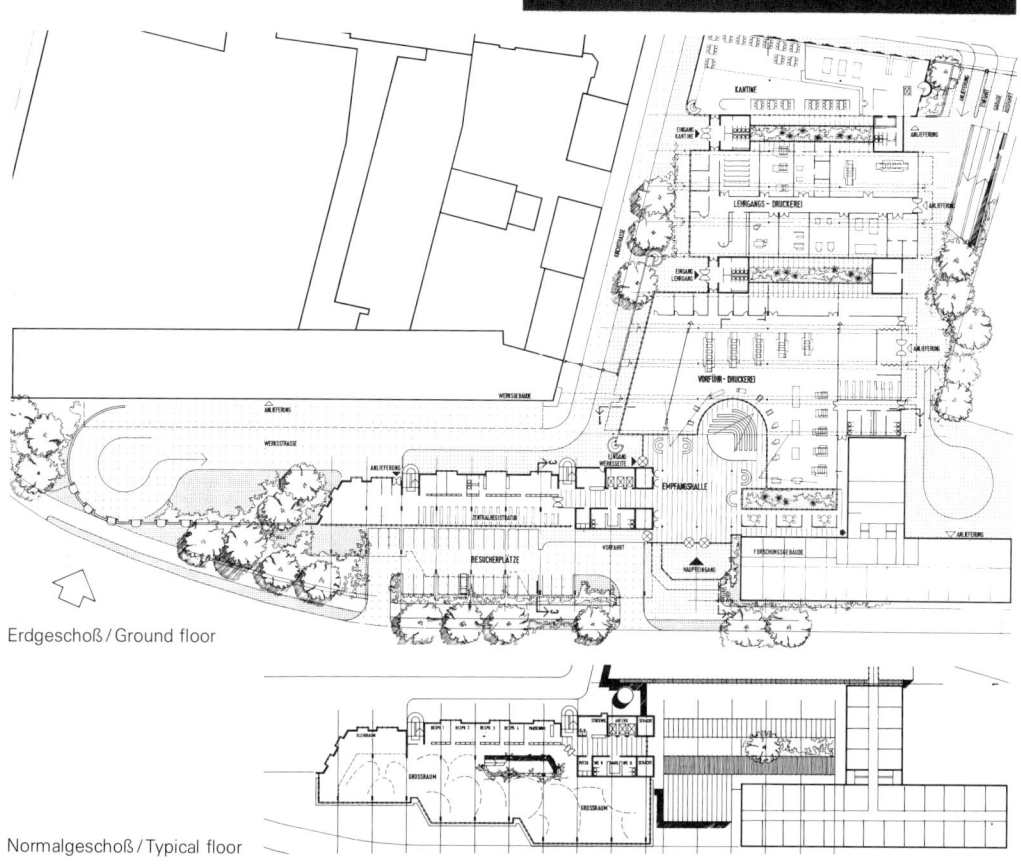

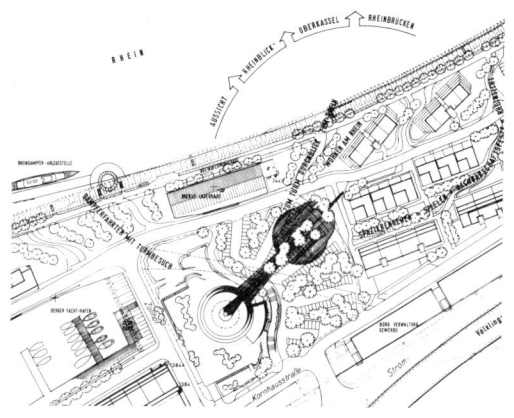

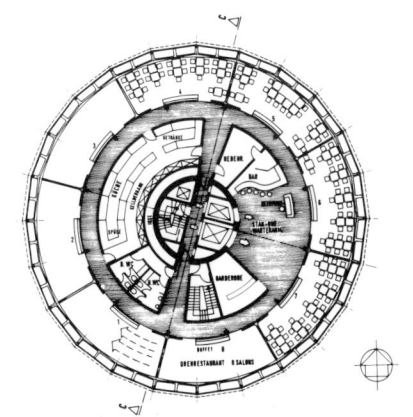

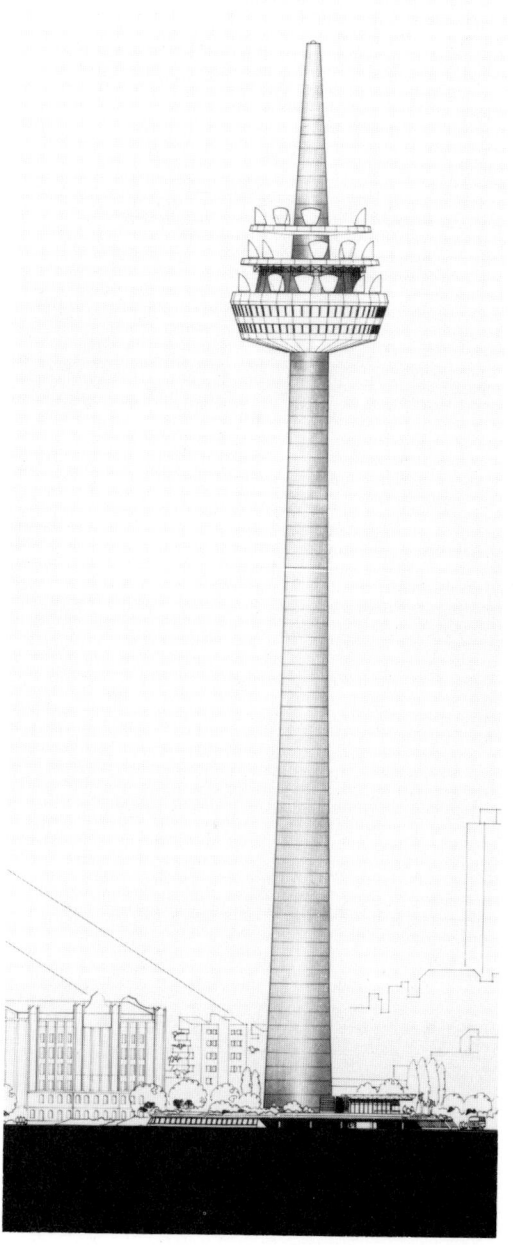

Braunschweiger Zeitung Braunschweig

Erster Rang in einem Entwurfsgutachten. Die Gesamtanlage umfaßt in einem Bürohaus Räume für Verlag, Verwaltung und Redaktionen, in einem Produktionsgebäude die elektronische Satzherstellung, Flach- und Rotationsdruck, Lager und Expedition. Eine gläserne Verkehrsspange verbindet diese Gebäude mit entgegengesetzt liegenden Eingängen für Mitarbeiter und Besucher und dem Sozialgebäude. Fertigstellung 1981.

First place in a design study. The overall complex comprises an office building with rooms for the newspaper publishing house and space for the administration and editorial staff; and a production building for electronic type-setting, flat plate relief printing and rotary press printing, stores and dispatch. A glass communications link connects the two buildings, with their separate entrances for employees and visitors, and the social building. Completed 1981.

oben links Lageplan /
top left Site plan
1 Besucherparkplätze / Visitors' parking
2 Verbindungsspange / Connecting strip
3 Verwaltung / Administration
4 Erweiterung / Space for extension
5 Kantine / Canteen
6 Anlieferung / Deliveries
7 Druckerei / Printing shop
8 Versand / Dispatch
9 KFZ-Service / Van servicing
10 Tankstelle / Petrol station
11 Garagen / Garages
12 Werkstätten / Workshops
13 Pförtner / Gatekeeper
14 Parkplätze für Angestellte / Employers' parking

oben rechts Schnitt /
top right Section
1 Verwaltung / Administration
2 Verbindungsspange / Connecting strip
3 Anlieferung / Deliveries
4 Rollenlager / Reel store
5 Tageslager / Day store
6 Klimazentrale / Air conditioning plant
7 Rotation / Rotary printing
8 Verarbeitung Zeitung / Newspaper processing
9 Versandstraße / Dispatch road

unten links Produktionsgebäude Sockelgeschoß /
bottom left Production building, plinth storey
1 Anlieferstraße / Delivery road
2 Rollenlager / Reel store
3 Tageslager / Day store
4 Rotation / Rotary printing
5 Verarbeitung Zeitung / Newspaper processing
6 Versandstraße / Dispatch road
7 Versand / Dispatch
8 Verarbeitung Bogen / Sheet processing
9 Bogendruck / Sheet printing
10 Bogenlager / Sheet paper store

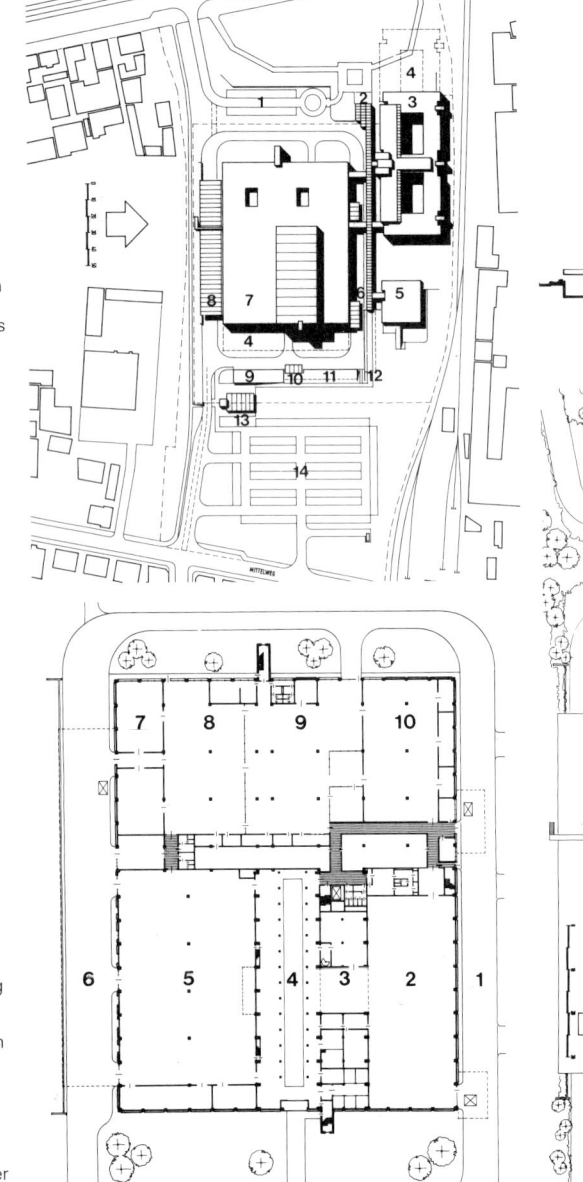

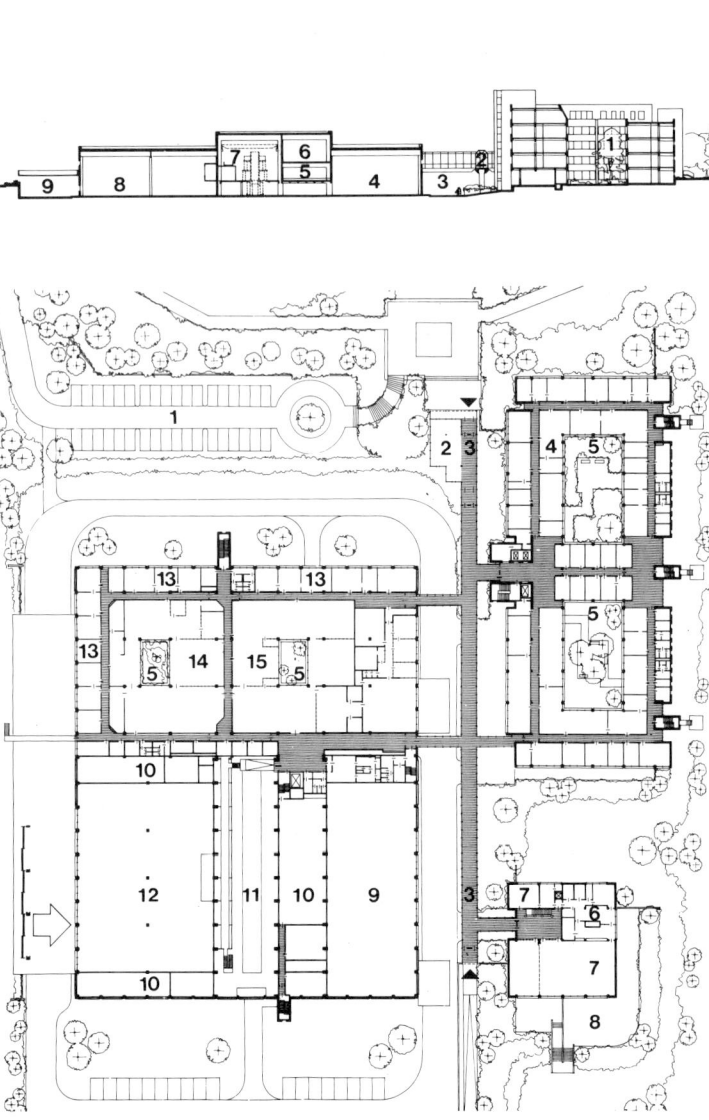

unten rechts Erdgeschoß /
bottom right Ground floor
1 Besucherparkplätze / Visitors' parking
2 Anzeigenannahme / Small-ad desk
3 Verbindungsspange / Connecting strip
4 Verwaltungsgebäude / Administrative building
5 Innenhöfe / Courtyards
6 Küche / Kitchen
7 Speiseräume / Dining rooms
8 Terrassen / Terrace area
9 Luftraum Rollenlager / Void over reel store
10 Klimatechnik / Air conditioning plant
11 Luftraum Rotation / Void over rotary printing room
12 Luftraum Verarbeitung Zeitung / Void over newspaper processing
13 Druckereiverwaltung / Printing administration
14 Druckformherstellung: Film- + Plattenherstellung / Printing processes: film + plate
15 Druckformherstellung: Erfassung + Montage / Printing processes: Compilation + montage

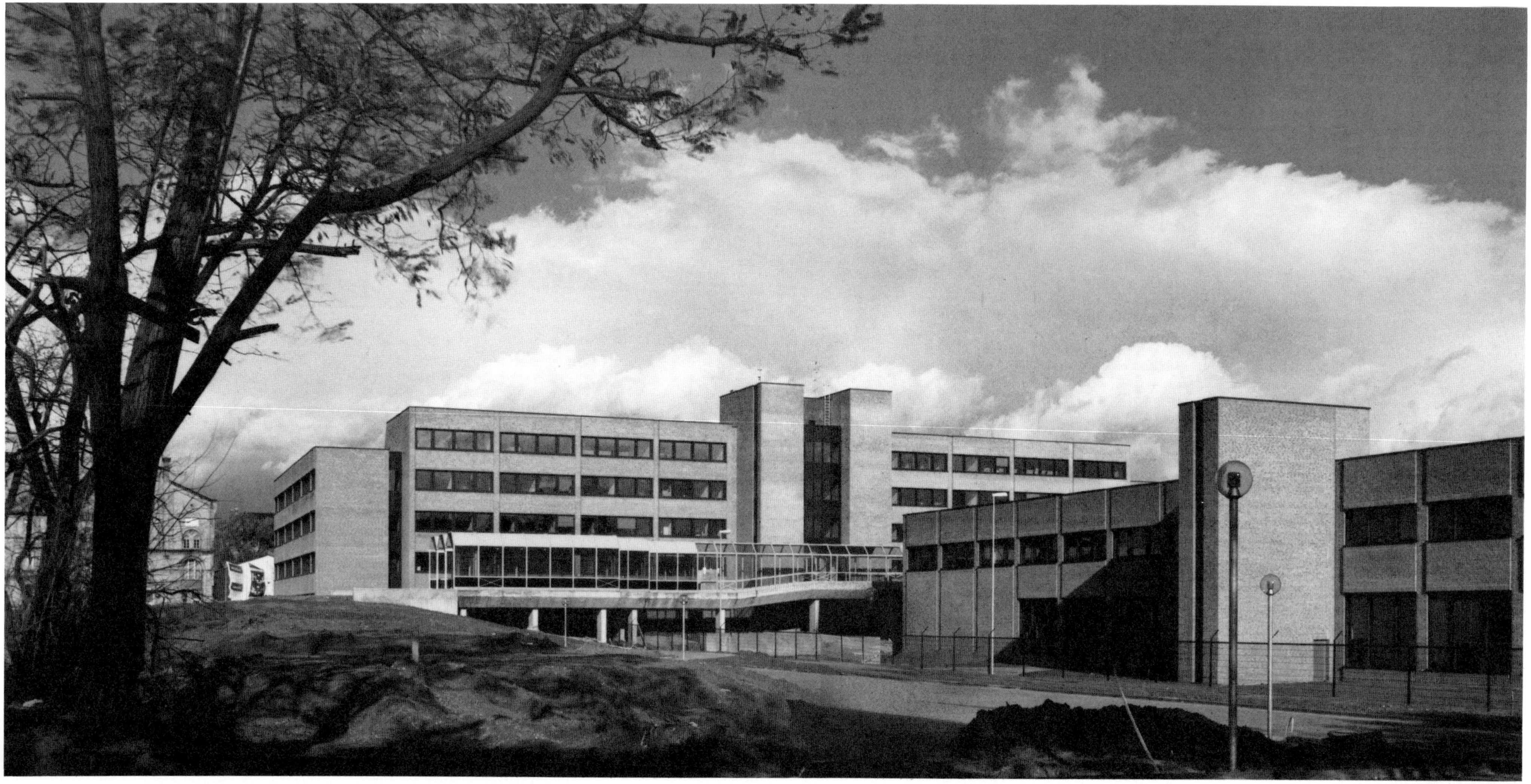

Die Baugruppe lebt vom Kontrast zwischen den massiven Mauerwerkskuben und der transparenten Verkehrsspange.

The building complex is enlivened by the contrast between the massive volumes of brickwork and the transparent access route.

Holländische Vormauersteine mit grobsandiger Fuge geben den massiven Wandflächen eine rauhe Oberfläche.

Dutch facing brickwork with coarse sand pointing lends the large wall areas a rough textured appearance.

Büro- und Geschäftshäuser / Office and commercial buildings

Wenn wir die Bauepochen der Vergangenheit überschauen, erkennen wir jeweils vorherrschende Bauaufgaben, die den anderen Zeitaufgaben an Bedeutung vorangehen und in der Rückschau zu den charakteristischen Zeugnissen eines bestimmten Zeitalters geworden sind: griechische Tempel, römische Foren, mittelalterliche Dome, Paläste der Renaissance, Schlösser mit Gartenparks in der Barockzeit, Bahnhof- und Ausstellungshallen im 19. Jahrhundert. Für unsere Zeit müssen wir leider als Charakteristikum eine simplere Chiffre erkennen: der vielgeschossige Großbau, der aus Räumen gleichartiger Kategorie zellenartig zusammenwächst und seine unumgängliche Ausprägung im Bürohaus darstellt.
Diese – gemessen an den einstigen Zwecken gewiß nicht stolze – Feststellung schränkt jedoch die andere nicht ein, daß entsprechend der Bedeutung des Bürohauses in unserem Wirtschaftsleben an seiner Verbesserung und Vervollkommnung in Forschung und Praxis unentwegt gearbeitet wird. Unser Büro, in diesem Aufgabengebiet besonders engagiert, hat an der ständigen Entwicklung in Forschung (z. B. im Arbeitskreis der deutschen Versicherungswirtschaft an der Entwicklung des Gruppenbüros) und Praxis intensiv teilgenommen und zu manchen Veränderungen aktiv beigetragen. Wir verminderten die Störquellen in Arbeitsräumen durch Erschließungen über Service-Geschosse, wandten frühzeitig Veränderungen in der Haustechnik an (in der Klimatechnik die Luftführung von unten nach oben, in der Lichttechnik die energiesparende Kombination von Allgemein- und Arbeitsplatzbeleuchtung in Großräumen, in der Akustik die Entwicklung von Unterdecken mit Schwerauflagen), wir planten und bauten das erste reversible Bürohaus und entwickelten Richtwertsätze für Kosten von Bruttogeschoßflächen.
Die Früchte unserer Spezialbeschäftigung zeigen die folgenden Seiten, die also nicht zufällig das umfangreichste Kapitel unseres Berichtes ergeben haben.

If one examines the various periods of building of the past, one can identify in each case certain dominant objectives that take precedence over the other goals of the age and that, in retrospect, have become the characteristic statements of that particular age: the Greek temple, the Roman forum, the cathedral of the Middle Ages, the Renaissance palace, the castles and palaces of the Baroque age with their landscaped parks and gardens, and the railway and exhibition halls of the 19th century. With our own age we must, unfortunately, identify a simpler building type –, that of the multi-storey large-scale building complex, a conglomeration of almost identical cell-like rooms of a single category, which finds its inevitable manifestation in the office block.
This conclusion, (which, when measured against the models of the past, is certainly not one to arouse pride), nevertheless does not invalidate the fact that, as some reflection of its importance in our economic life, constant efforts are being made in research and practice to improve and perfect the office building. Our practice, which has shown a particular commitment in this realm, has played an extremely active role in the continuing process of development, both in research, (e.g. in the development of group offices within the German insurance economy's working group), and in practice, and has made an active contribution to a number of changes that have taken place. We reduced the sources of disturbance in working spaces by providing access via service storeys; applied changes in services technology at an early date, (e.g. in climate control, the direction of fresh air flow from floor to ceiling; in lighting, an energysaving combination of general and specific lighting over work places in open plan offices; in acoustics, the development of suspended ceilings with heavy bearings); we designed and built the first »reversible« office building, and have developed a system of standard guideline rates for assessing the costs of gross floor areas. The fruits of our specialist activities are to be seen on the following pages, and it is no coincidence that they represent the largest section of our report.

Flebbe Braunschweig

Auf einem Trümmergrundstück wurde 1950 zunächst ein eingeschossiger Ladenbau errichtet, auf dem 1958 die übrigen Geschosse aufgebaut wurden. Die Maßordnung der Fassadenteilungen, horizontal und vertikal ergibt, in rhythmisch geordneter Wiederkehr, ein strenges Proportionssystem.

On a bomb site a single-storey shop structure was initially erected in 1950, on top of which the remaining storeys of commercial and administrative space were built in 1958. The dimensional co-ordination of the elevational divisions, both horizontally and vertically, creates a strict proportional system within a rhythmically ordered repetitive pattern.

Vereinigte Leben Bremen

Das Mietbürohaus – mit Läden im Erdgeschoß – füllt eine Baulücke am »Wall«, gegenüber der alten Windmühle. Die frei vor der Fassade stehenden Außenstützen sind geschliffene Betonwerksteinfertigteile. Bezug 1957.

A block containing rented office space with shops on the ground floor that fills a building gap along the »Wall« opposite the old windmill. The external columns, set freely in front of the facade, are of polished pre-fabricated reconstructed stone elements. Building taken into occupation in 1957.

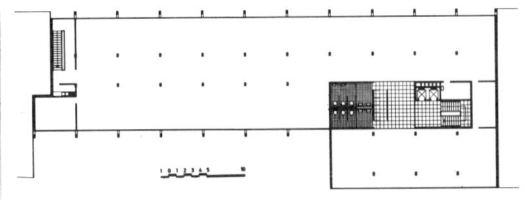

Hamburg Mannheimer Versicherung Hannover Friedrichswall

Das in eine Baulücke einzupassende Bürohaus sucht durch filigrane Teilungen der Glasfront sich zwischen den Nachbarbauten einzufügen. Dabei sollen die bedacht gewählten Proportionen die selbständige Erscheinung festigen. Baujahr 1959.

By means of filigree divisions of the glass face of this insurance office block, an attempt is made to fit it into an infill space between adjoining buildings. The deliberate choice of proportions is nevertheless intended to assert its independent appearance. Construction date, 1959.

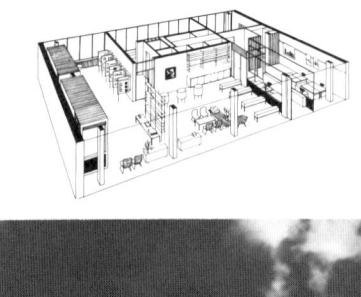

Staatskanzlei Hannover

Weiterbearbeitung eines Entwurfs, der 1960 bei einem beschränkten Wettbewerb mit dem 1. Preis ausgezeichnet wurde. Der Zentralbau war in einem kleinen, an der Leine gelegenen Park zwischen Waterlooplatz und Friederikenplatz geplant.

The further development of a design awarded first prize in a limited competition in 1960. The centrally planned state chancellory building was to be set in a small park on the River Leine between Waterlooplatz and Friederikenplatz.

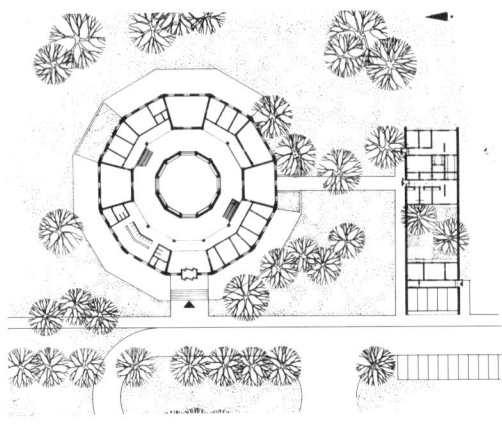

Pfeiffer & Schmidt Braunschweig

Der alsbald nach der Währungsreform konzipierte Bau war nur unter äußerster Sparsamkeit zu verwirklichen, wozu die Verwendung der z. T. mittelalterlichen Fundamente gehörte. Mit dem Peter-Joseph-Krahe-Preis der Stadt Braunschweig 1955 ausgezeichnet.

This commercial building, conceived immediately after the currency reform, could only be realized with extreme economy. Included in these measures was the re-use of foundations dating in part from the Middle Ages. Awarded the Peter-Joseph-Krahe Prize of the City of Brunswick in 1955.

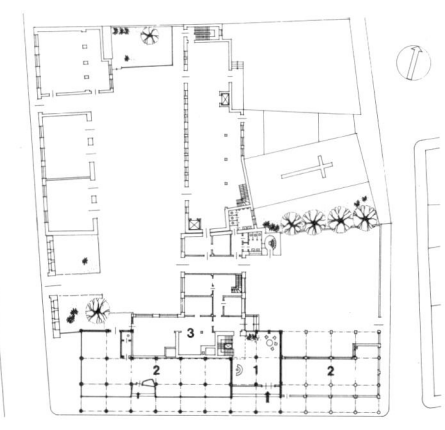

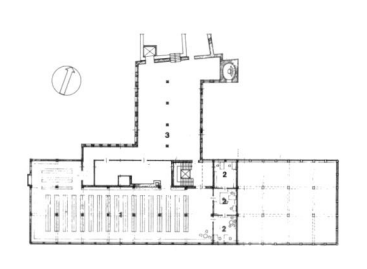

oben Erdgeschoß / top Ground floor
1 Eingangshalle Büro- + Lagerhaus / Entrance hall offices + stores
2 Läden / Shops
3 In den Neubau einbezogener Rest des sonst zerstörten Altbaus / Part of existing building not destroyed, integrated into new structure

unten Obergeschoß / bottom Upper floor
1 Lagerfläche / Storage area
2 Büros / Offices
3 Erhaltener Altbau / Existing building retained

Wasser- und Schiffahrtsdirektion und Kataster- und Vermessungsamt Bremen

Das auf der Weserinsel zwischen Altstadt und Neustadt errichtete Behördenhaus ist das Ergebnis eines Wettbewerbs 1952. Der Backsteinbau wurde 1974 mit dem BDA-Preis der Stadt Bremen ausgezeichnet.

This public authority building, erected on the island in the River Weser between the old and new parts of the city, is the result of a competition held in 1952. The brick building was awarded the BDA Prize of the City of Bremen in 1974.

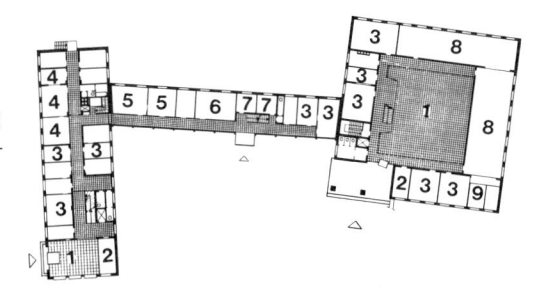

Wasser- + Schiffahrtsdirektion   Kataster- + Vermessungsamt

Erdgeschoß / Ground floor
1 Halle / Hall
2 Pförtner / Janitor
3 Büroräume / Offices
4 Dienstwohnung / Official dwelling
5 Technisches Büro / Technical office
6 Registratur / Records office
7 Verwaltungsbüro / Administration office
8 Plankammer / Plan room
9 Kasse / Cashier

Unterharzer Berg- und Hüttenwerke Goslar

Ausgewählt als 1. Preis in einem zweistufigen Wettbewerb unter 8 Professoren von Entwurfslehrstühlen, steht der Verwaltungsbau vor einem nach Goslar sich öffnenden Harztal. An das deswegen aufgeständerte Erdgeschoß mit Eingangshalle ist ein Atriumbau für Vorstandsräume angeschlossen. Das dreibündige Bürogebäude (Treppen, Aufzüge, WC, Garderoben im Mittelbund) gehört zu den ersten dieser Art. Die Betonwerksteinstützen sind als geschliffene Fertigteile hergestellt. Baujahr: 1958/59.

Selected as 1st prizewinner in a two-stage competition amongst 8 professors for design. This administrative building stands at the entrance to one of the valleys in the Harz Mountains that opens on to the town of Goslar. The ground floor with entrance hall is raised for this reason and is linked to a courtyard building housing rooms for the management. The three-bay office building, (staircases, lifts, WCs, cloakrooms in the middle bay), is one of the first of its kind. The columns of reconstructed stone are prefabricated and polished. Construction date, 1958-59.

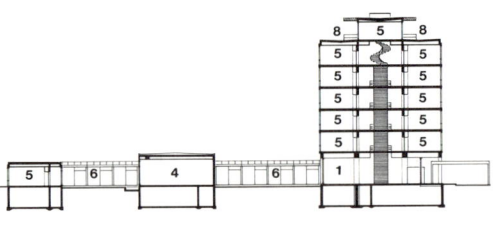

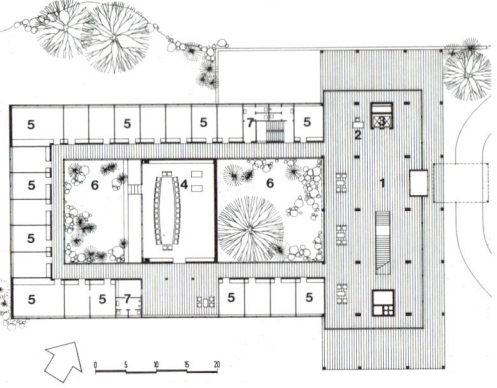

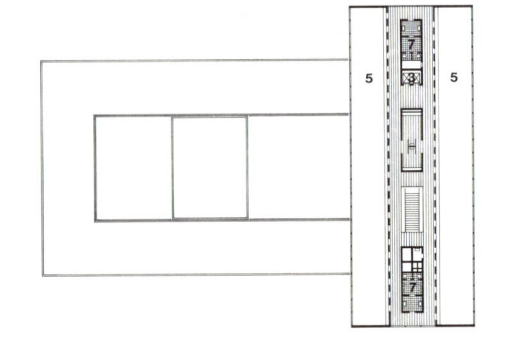

Schnitt, Erdgeschoß, Normalgeschoß /
Section, Ground floor, Typical floor
1 Eingangshalle / Entrance hall
2 Anmeldung / Reception
3 Personalaufzug / Staff lift
4 Sitzungsraum / Conference room
5 Büroräume / Offices
6 Innenhof / Courtyard
7 WC- + Waschräume / Toilets
8 Dachterrasse / Roof terrace

111

Wullbrandt und Seele Braunschweig

Büro- und Geschäftshaus des ältesten deutschen Großhandelshauses mit Ausstellungs- und Verkaufsräumen im Erdgeschoß und Zellenbüros in zweibündiger Anordnung in den Obergeschossen. Das oberste Bürogeschoß ist stützenfrei und beliebig aufteilbar. Ungewöhnlich ist die Zweizonenfensterlüftung mit Kipp- und Klappflügeln hinter feststehenden Lamellen im Brüstungsbereich und zwischen Konstruktion und abgehängter Decke. Außenliegende Lamellenstoren. Fertigstellung 1962.

The office and commercial building of the oldest German wholesale merchants, with exhibition space and sales area on the ground floor and office cells in two-bay divisions on the upper floors. The topmost floor of offices is free of columns and can be divided up as required. What is unusual is the two-zone window ventilation with top and bottom hung flaps behind fixed louvres in the balustrade area and between the structure and the suspended soffit. Externally hung louvred blinds. Completed 1962.

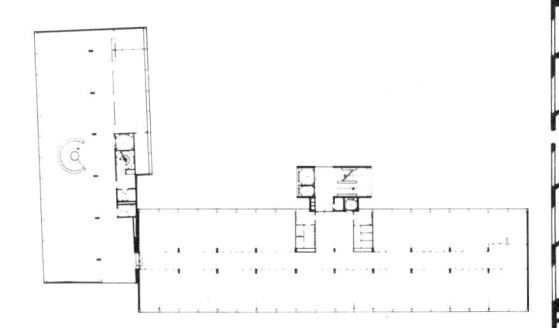

Fassadenschnitt / Section through façade
1 L-Stahl / Metal angle
2 Hartschaumplatte / Expanded foam plastic sheet
3 Asbestzementplatte / Asbestos cement sheet
4 Be- + Entlüftungsklappe / Ventilation shutter
5 Gummiprofil / Rubber profile
6 Profilleiste / Bead
7 Isolierverglasung / Insulated double glazing
8 Lüftungslamellen / Ventilation louvres
9 Blech / Metal sheet
10 Dauerplastischer Kitt / Non-hardening mastic

Iduna Braunschweig

Innerstädtisches Renditeobjekt mit Mietbüros in den Obergeschossen und Läden, die sich, auf Straßenhöhe betretbar, über vier versetzte Halbgeschosse erstrecken. Von 1962 bis 1967 Sitz unseres Büros.

A city centre speculative object with rented office space on the upper floors above shops that are accessible at street level and rise over four half-storey split levels. Our office from 1962 to 1967.

Iduna Osnabrück

Mietbürohaus mit Läden im Erdgeschoß. Knapper Zentralkern. Die tragende Stahlkonstruktion der Außenwände blieb, nur von innen feuergeschützt, unverkleidet sichtbar. Fertigstellung 1960.

Block with rented office space and ground floor shops. Tight central core. The load bearing steel structure of the external walls remained unclad and exposed, with fire protection only internally. Completed 1960.

Iduna Münster

Mietbürohaus mit Läden im Erdgeschoß und einem freistehenden zweigeschossigen Pavillon. Ein Bauwerk, das seine kubische Einfachheit gegen den Reiz des umgebenden Parks in bevorzugter städtebaulicher Lage ausspielt.

Block with rented office space, ground floor shops and a free-standing two-storey pavilion. A building whose cubic simplicity is set off against the attractions of the surrounding park in a much favoured urban situation.

Iduna Essen

Ein weiteres der zahlreichen, damals für die Iduna-Versicherung errichteten Anlageobjekte. Hochhaus mit ca. 9000 m² Bürofläche, großen Läden in einem zweigeschossigen Flachbau und einem Parkhaus.

Another of the many investment objects erected at this time for the Iduna Insurance concern. A high-rise block with approximately 9000 m² office space, large shop units in a two-storey flat building, together with a garage block.

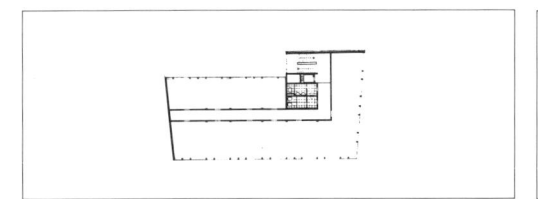

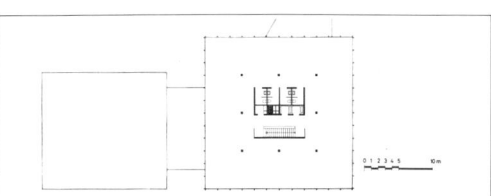

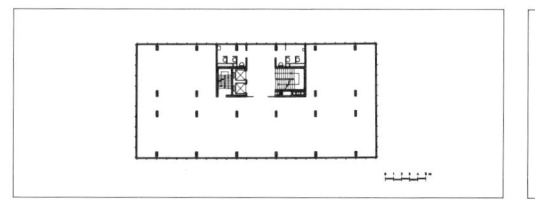

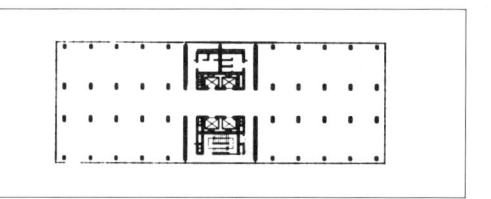

Perschmann Braunschweig

Ausstellungs-, Verkaufs-, Lager- und Bürohaus einer Eisenwaren- und Werkzeuggroßhandlung. Fertiggestellt 1960. In die geschliffenen Betonwerksteinsprossen der Fassade sind die hohen Brüstungselemente rahmenlos eingesetzt.

Exhibition, sales, store and office building of a wholesale firm for ironmongery and tools. Completed 1960. The high infill elements are inserted unframed between the polished reconstructed stone dividing members of the façade.

Iduna Schweinfurt

Das Mietbüro-Hochhaus, im Grünbereich des Wall-Ringes gelegen, markiert den Eingang zur Innenstadt. Unverkleidete Sichtbetonkonstruktion. Ein kleines Hotel mit Restaurant bildet einen eigenen Baukörper. Fertiggestellt 1966.

This high-rise block of rented office space, situated in the green-planted section of the old defence ring, marks the entrance to the city centre. Unclad exposed concrete structure. A small hotel with restaurant forms a building volume of its own. Completed 1966.

Erweiterungsbau Preussag Hannover

Kurze Bauzeit und geringe Baukosten waren die Planungsvorgaben dieses Verwaltungsbaus. Konstruktion: unterzugsfreies Mauerwerksskelett. Alu-Schiebefenster mit äußerem Sonnenschutz. Fertigstellung 1964.

A short period of construction and low construction costs were the main points of the brief. The structure of this administrative building consists of a brick skeleton frame with flat slab floors (beamless) and sliding windows with external solar protection. Completed 1964.

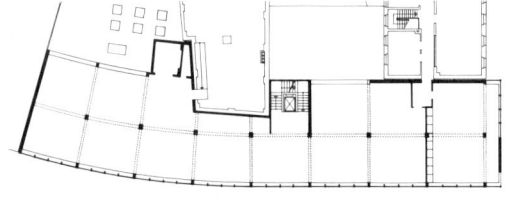

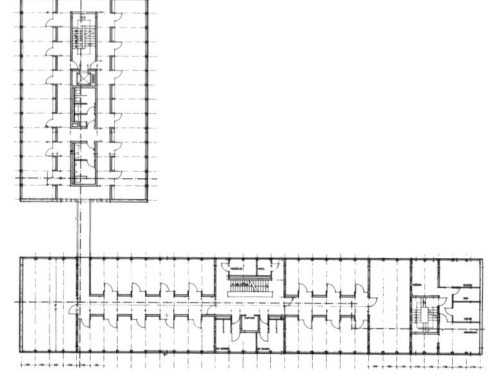

Rechenzentrum eines Chemiekonzerns

Mit der kubusstrengen Form wurde ein adäquater Ausdruck für das in diesem Hause geforderte exakte Gedankenwerk angestrebt. Vier umlaufende Bürogeschosse entsprechen im Inneren zwei Rechensaalgeschossen von 20 m x 30 m Fläche, für deren freigespannte Decken und begehbare Installationsgeschosse die entsprechenden Konstruktionshöhen so zur Verfügung standen.

The strictly cubical form was an attempt to find an adequate expression for the precise way of thinking required in this computing centre. Four peripheral floors of offices correspond on the interior to two floors of calculating halls, 20 m x 30 m in area, thus providing sufficient structural depth for the clear-span floor slabs and for accessible service storeys.

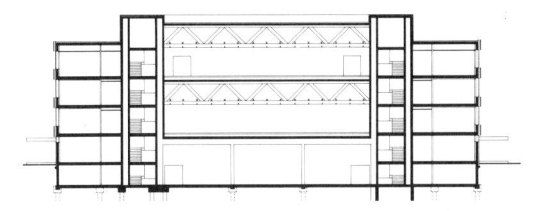

Grundrisse
oben Erdgeschoß
Mitte 2. Obergeschoß
unten 3. Obergeschoß

Plans
top Ground floor
middle 2nd Floor
bottom 3rd Floor

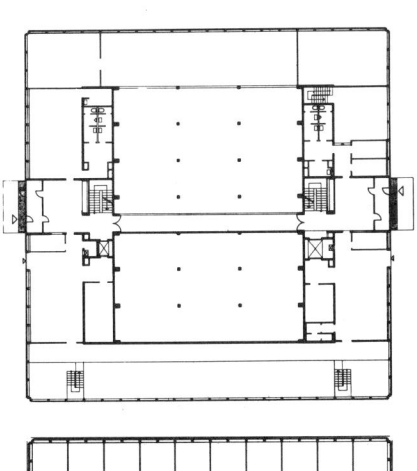

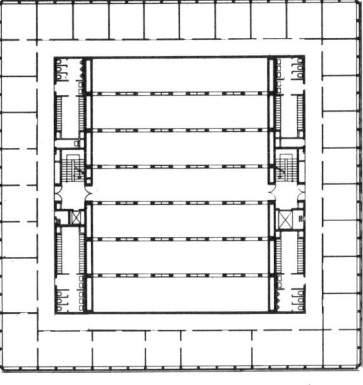

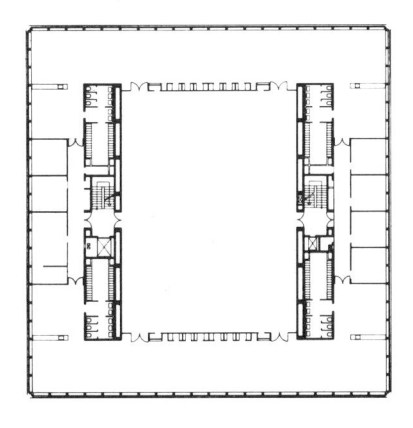

115

Rathaus Essen

Die systemstrenge Planung mit geordneten Baukörpern aus gleichen Modulabschnitten errang im Wettbewerb 1964 den 2. Preis, (wozu uns Egon Eiermann telegraphisch gratulierte). Mit dem parlamentarisch-festlichen Rathaussaal im Mittelpunkt und städtebaulich prägnant großzügigen Platzanlagen versuchten wir den repräsentativen Anspruch der Stadtmitte im Kern einer gewachsenen Großstadt zu erfüllen.

The strict systems planning with regular built volumes of the same modular divisions won 2nd prize in a competition in 1964, (on which Egon Eiermann cabled his congratulations). By making the parliamentary-ceremonial hall the centre piece of the town hall complex and by setting an urban accent with generously pro-portioned open spaces, we attempted to meet the representative demands of an urban centre at the heart of the living tissue of a city.

Mitte
oben Längsschnitt
Mitte Querschnitte
unten Kellergeschoß

middle
top Longitudinal section
middle Cross-sections
bottom Basement

rechts
oben Eingangsgeschoß Fußgänger
Mitte Eingangsgeschoß Fahrverkehr
unten 1. Obergeschoß

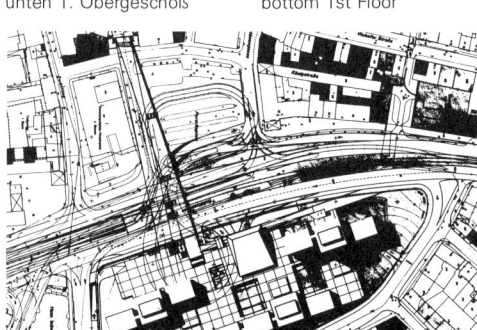

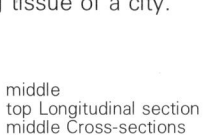

right
top Entrance level for pedestrians
middle Entrance level for vehicles
bottom 1st Floor

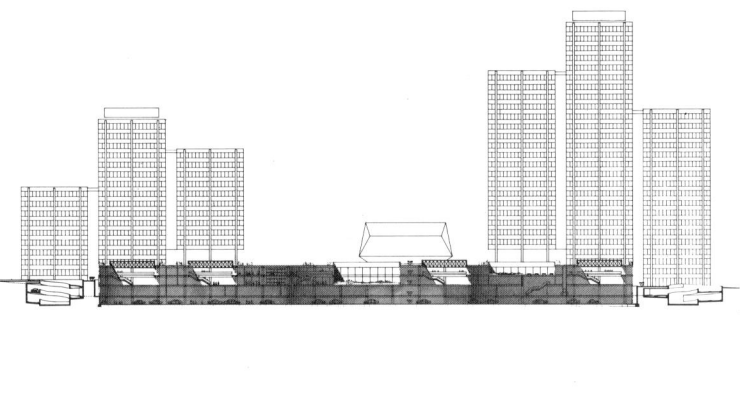

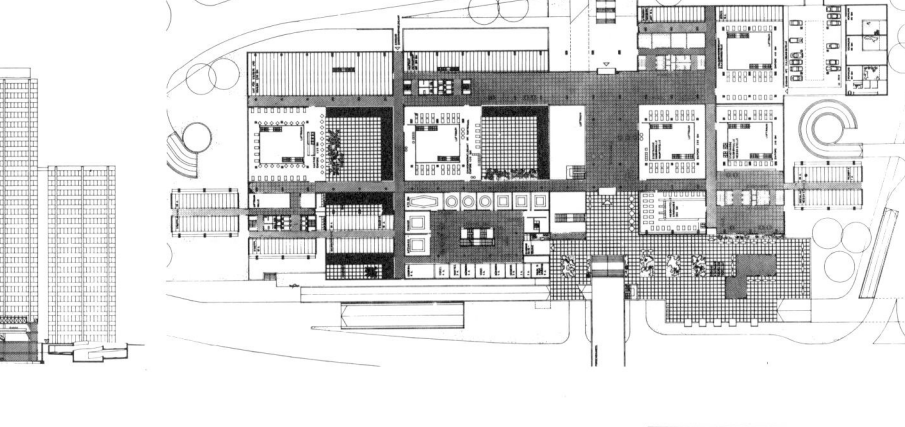

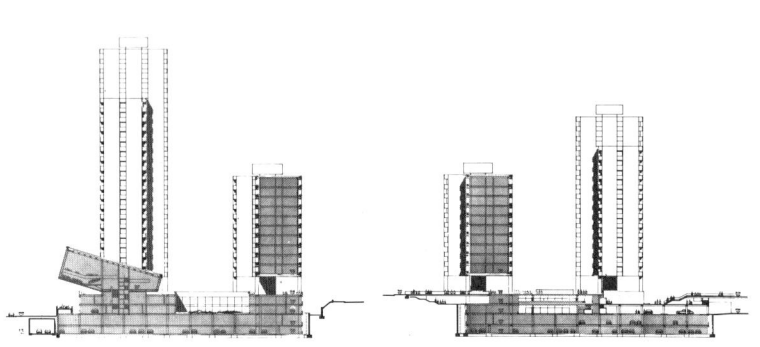

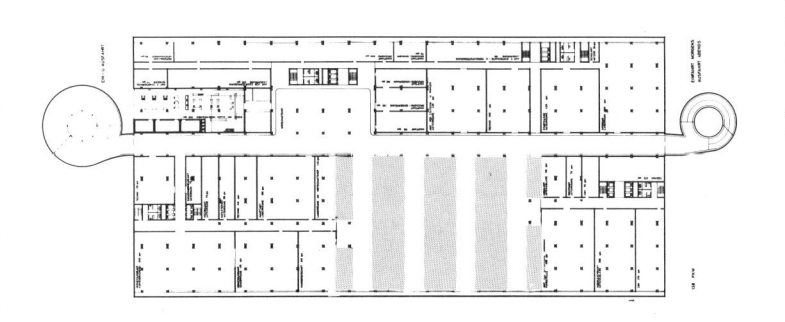

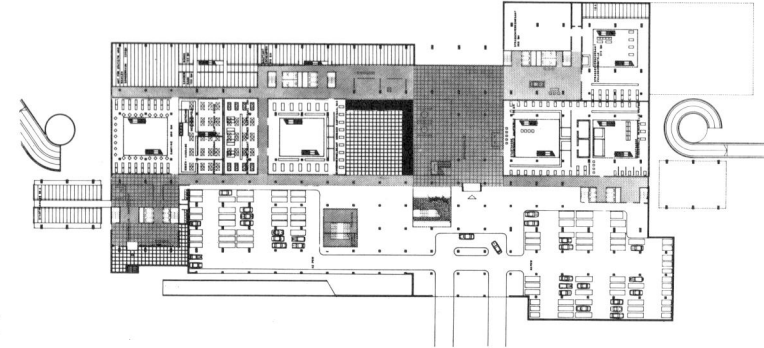

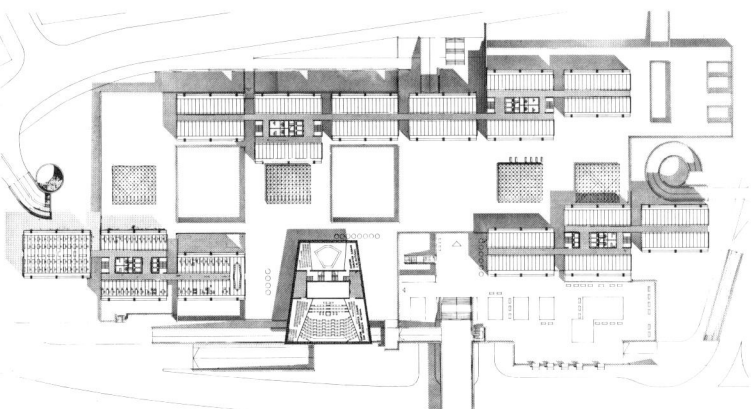

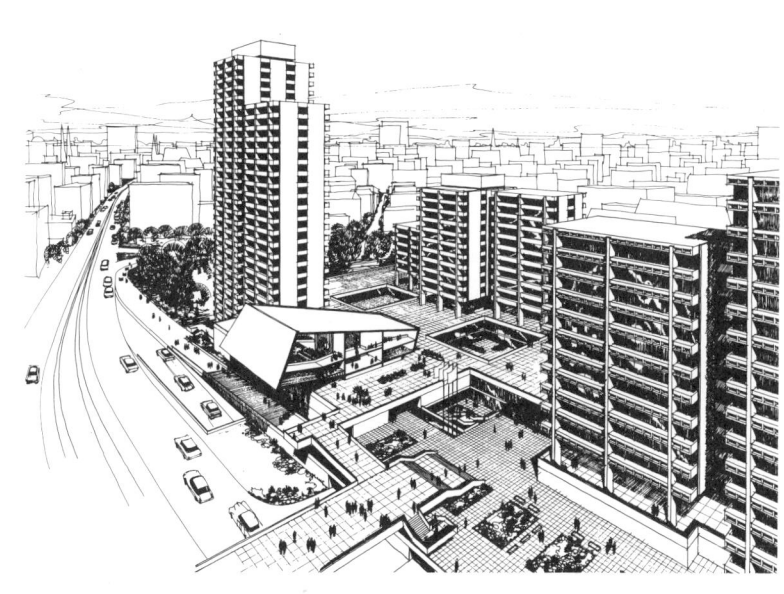

Die vielen verlangten Bauabschnitte führten zur Entwicklung eines wachstumsfähigen Systems, einer vermehrungsfähigen »Baukörperfamilie« (dargestellt jeweils vom gleichen Standpunkt).

The many phases of building required in the brief led to the development of an incremental system, an extendible »family of built units«, (depicted in each case from the same viewpoint).

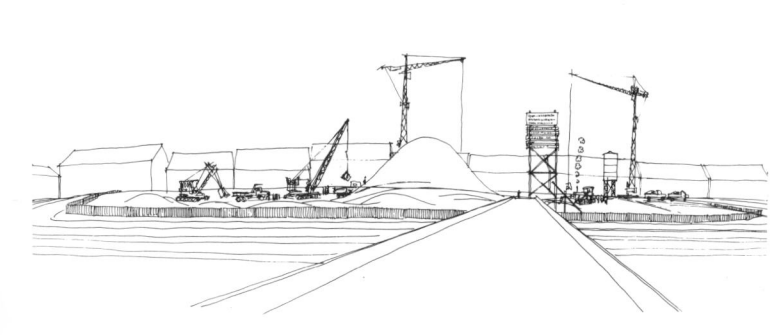

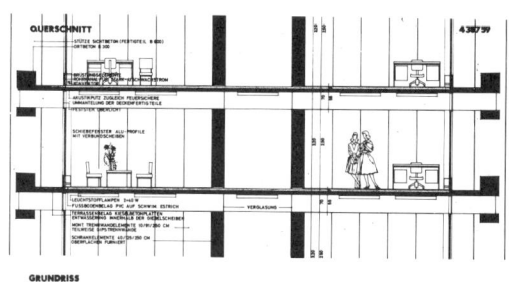

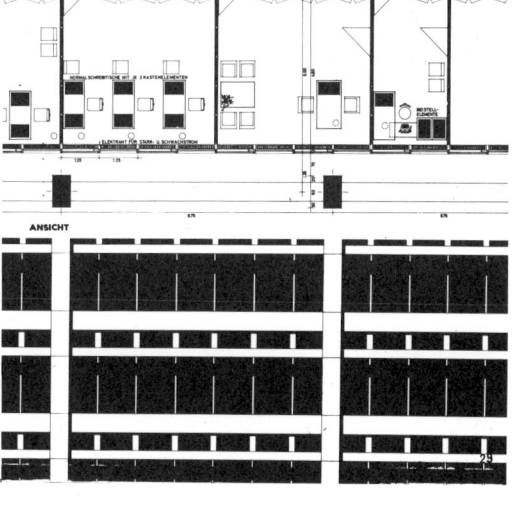

Konstruktion
Aufgabe: Variabler Grundriß und montable Ausbaustücke für Zellen- und Großraumbüros
Lösung: Vorgespannte Plattenbalkenelemente auf Doppellängsbalken in Ortbeton, nach Fugenverguß statisch steife Platte ohne Innenstützen, Stützen aus Fertigteilen vor der Fassade, so gesamte Geschoßfläche frei aufteilbar mit verschiedenen Ausbauelementen.

Construction
Brief: flexible layout and assembly of finishings elements to create individual office units and open-plan office areas.
Solution: prestressed T-beam slab elements on double longitudinal beams in insitu concrete. After grouting of joints, – structurally stable slab without internal columns. Prefabricated column elements set in front of facade: entire floor area can be freely laid out, using various partition and finishings elements.

Hauptverwaltung BP Hamburg

Das Großraumbürohaus für insgesamt ca. 2500 Mitarbeiter wurde 1971 bezogen. Es ist das Ergebnis erster Preise in zwei aufeinanderfolgenden Wettbewerben. Jedes Normalgeschoß enthält vier sechseckige Großraumbüroeinheiten von je 1000 m², die sich um einen zentralen Sechseckkern ordnen, der die vertikalen Verkehrseinrichtungen, Sozial- und Pausenräume, Garderoben, Besprechungszimmer und einige Zellenbüros enthält. Das Erdgeschoß nimmt Kantine, Küche, Expedition, Lagerräume, EDV, Schulung, Konferenz, Arzträume und die Eingangshalle auf.

This open-plan office block for approximately 2500 employees was taken into use in 1971. It is the outcome of first prizes in two successive competitions. Each typical floor level contains four hexagonal open-plan office units with an area of 1000 m² each, arranged about a central hexagonal core, housing vertical communications, rooms for social purposes, rest rooms, cloakrooms, conference rooms and a number of office cells. On the ground floor are the canteen, kitchen, dispatch, storage space, data processing, training, conference and medical rooms and the entrance hall.

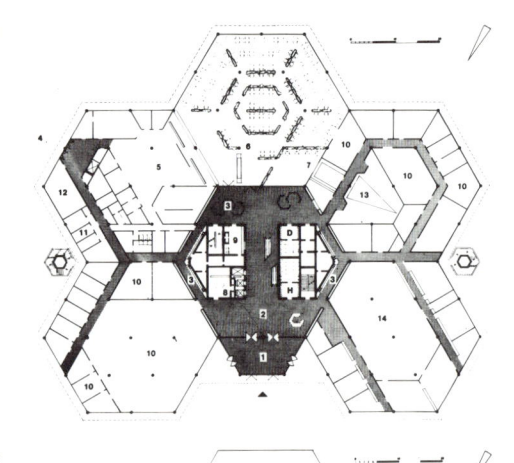

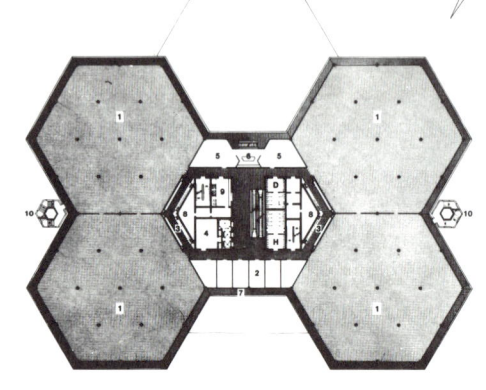

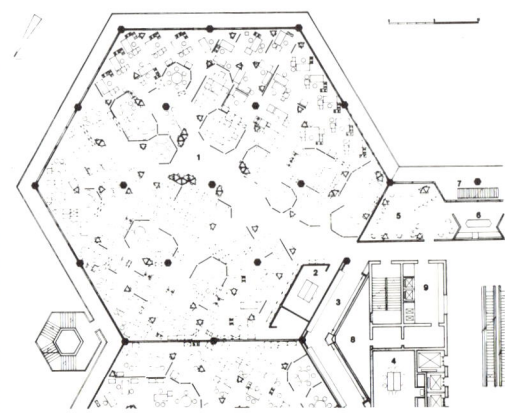

Erdgeschoß / Ground floor
1. Windfang / Draught excluding lobby
2. Eingangshalle / Entrance hall
3. Garderobe / Cloakroom
4. Anlieferung / Deliveries
5. Küche / Kitchen
6. Speiseraum / Dining area
7. Cafeteria / Cafeteria
8. Technische Überwachungszentrale / Technical control centre
9. Stockwerksdienst / Storey services
10. Büro- + Sonderräume / Offices + special rooms
11. Erste Hilfe / First aid
12. Poststelle / Mail room
13. Vortrags- + Filmraum / Lecture hall + cinema
14. Elektronische Datenverarbeitung / Computer area

Normalgeschoß / Typical floor
1. Bürogroßraum je 1000 m² / Open-plan office space each 1000 m²
2. Einzelräume / Single rooms
3. Garderobe / Cloakroom
4. Konferenzraum / Conference room
5. Pausenraum / Recreation room
6. Pantry / Pantry
7. Umlaufender Balkon / Peripheral balcony
8. Installationsschacht / Services shaft
9. Stockwerksdienst / Storey services
10. Nottreppen / Emergency stairs

Großraummöblierung / Open-plan office furnishing
1. Bürogroßraum / Open-plan office
2. Einzel- + Besprechungsräume / Individual + discussion rooms
3. Garderobe / Cloakroom
4. Konferenzraum / Conference room
5. Pausenraum / Recreation room
6. Pantry / Pantry
7. Pausenbalkon / Recreation balcony
8. Installationsschacht / Services shaft
9. Stockwerksdienst / Storey services

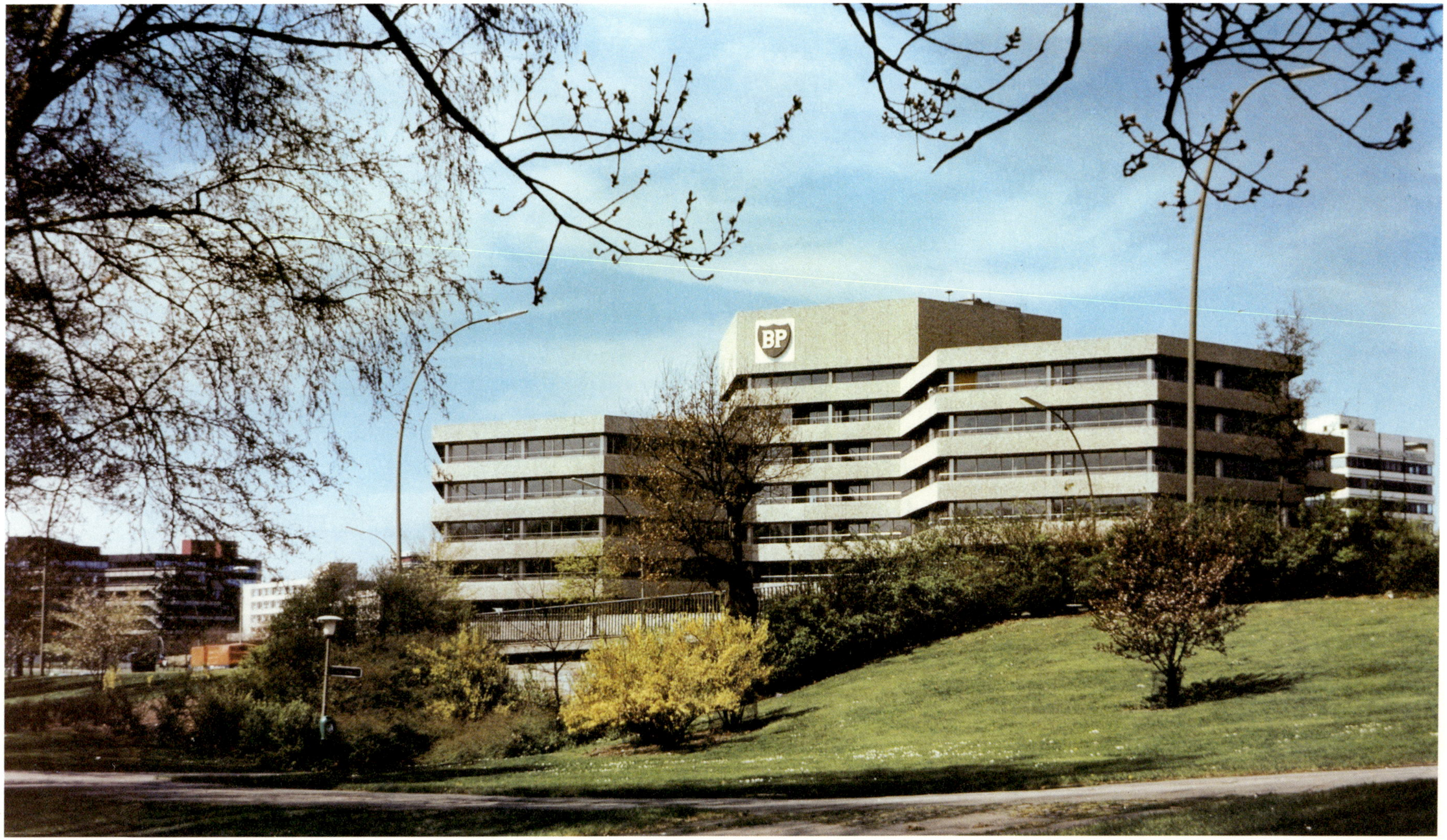
BP

Bayer Verkaufsabteilungen Leverkusen

Entwurfsgutachten 1969. Eine der ersten Aufgabenstellungen, bei denen der Bauherr »Reversibilität«, d.h. totale Umwandelbarkeit der Bürogeschoßflächen von Zellenbüros in Großräume (und umgekehrt) verlangte. Der gewählte versetzt kreuzförmige Grundrißzuschnitt erfüllt diese Forderung durch großen Außenwandanteil. Erschließung über Sonder-(Service-)Geschosse mit Garderoben, WC, Pausenräumen und konstanten Zellenbüros, die jeweils zwischen zwei völlig nebenraumfreien Normalgeschossen liegen.

Design study, 1969. One of the first briefs in which the client demanded »reversibility«; i.e. the possibility of total convertibility of the office storey areas, from individual office cells or unit offices to open-plan spaces and vice versa. The form chosen, that of staggered cross-shaped layout plans, meets this requirement by means of the high proportion of external walls. Access is via special service storeys, containing cloakrooms, WCs, rest rooms and permanent office cells and situated between two typical storeys, which are thus completely free of ancillary spaces.

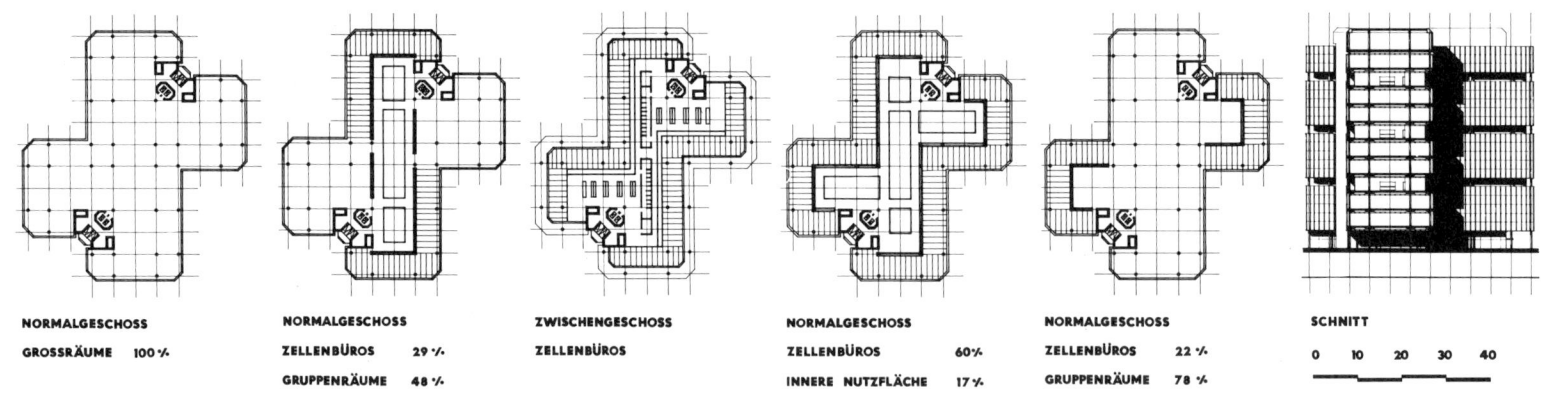

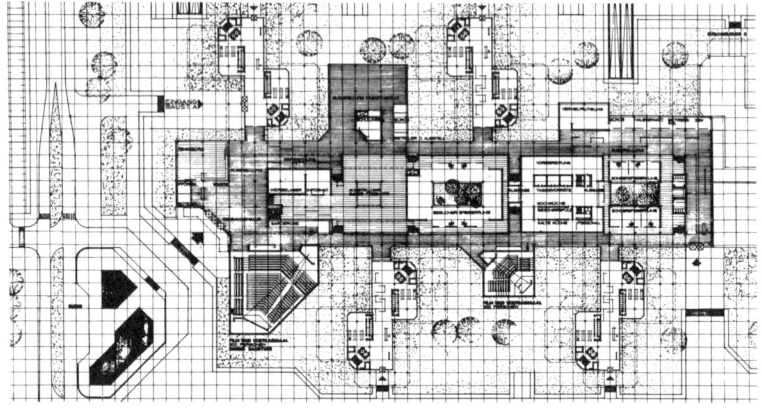

NORMALGESCHOSS	NORMALGESCHOSS	ZWISCHENGESCHOSS	NORMALGESCHOSS	NORMALGESCHOSS	SCHNITT
GROSSRÄUME 100%	ZELLENBÜROS 29%	ZELLENBÜROS	ZELLENBÜROS 60%	ZELLENBÜROS 22%	
	GRUPPENRÄUME 48%		INNERE NUTZFLÄCHE 17%	GRUPPENRÄUME 78%	

Preussag Berlin

Die Entwurfsidee dieses Verwaltungsbaus entstand aus der Notwendigkeit abschnittsweiser Errichtung. Die Baukörper sind jeweils durch ein Gelenk miteinander verbunden, das die Funktion der Vertikalerschließung übernimmt. Fertigstellung 1965.

The design idea behind this administrative building was derived from the need to erect the building in a number of stages. The individual built volumes are connected to each other by linking members that assume the functions of vertical access. Completed 1965.

Stadthaus Bonn

Wettbewerb 1969, 2. Preis. Im Gegensatz zum ausgeführten ersten Preis versucht der Entwurf die Baumasse aus Rücksicht auf die Nachbarschaft niedrig zu halten. Daraus ergab sich der ungewöhnliche Querschnitt der Gebäudetrakte.

2nd Prize in a competition in 1969. In contrast to the first prize-winning scheme, which was actually built, this design attempts to keep the building volume of the civic centre in Bonn at a low height in consideration for the immediate environment. This is the reason for the unusual cross-section of the building tracts.

Iduna Gelsenkirchen

Mietbüro- und Geschäftshaus in prominenter innerstädtischer Lage mit zwei Tiefgaragengeschossen unter dem flachen Ladentrakt. Unverkleidete Stahlbetonkonstruktion, Brüstungsplatten aus Gussaluminium.

Block containing rented office space and business premises in a prominent town centre situation with two basement levels of garaging beneath the low-rise shop tract. Unclad reinforced concrete structure. Balustrade panels of cast aluminium.

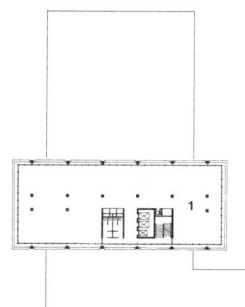

1. – 10. Obergeschoß Bürogebäude, 1. Obergeschoß Ladengebäude/
1st – 10th Floors office block, 1st Floor shopping building
1 Frei aufteilbare Bürofläche/Flexible office space
2 Laden/Shop
3 Turnsaal/Gymnasium
4 Sauna/Sauna

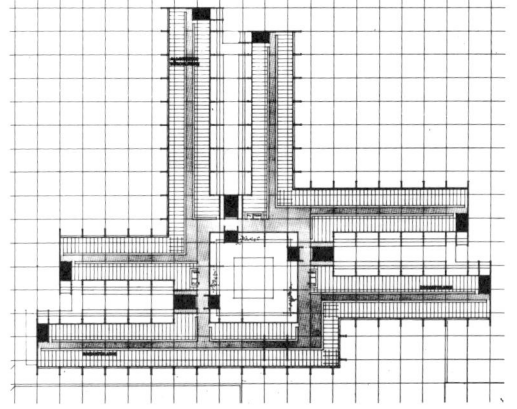

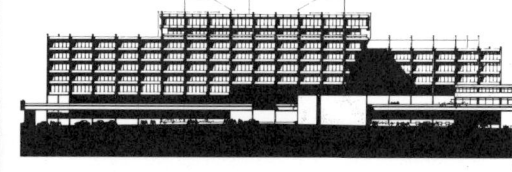

Hauptverwaltung DKV Köln

1. Preis im beschränkten Wettbewerb der Hauptverwaltung der Deutschen Krankenversicherung 1966. Auf 18 000 m² Grundstücksfläche waren in zwei Bauabschnitten 40 000 m² Bürofläche als Großraumbüro zu planen. Die entwurfsbestimmenden Anforderungen der Aufgabenstellung waren: Kein Arbeitsplatz sollte weiter als 13 m von großflächigen Fenstern entfernt liegen. Die zusammenhängenden Büroflächen sollten eine möglichst große Ausdehnung haben. Die großflächigen Bereiche sollten in überschaubare Raumeinheiten von ca. 1000 m² gegliedert werden.

Die Besonderheit der Lösung ergab sich aus den Überlegungen zur störungsfreien Erschließung: Haupterschließungswege wurden zusammen mit Pausenräumen, Toiletten, Garderoben und Besprechungsräumen in jeweils einem »Service«-Geschoß angeordnet, das ein darüber und darunter liegendes Großraumgeschoß bedient. Das Zwischengeschoß enthält außerdem alle für die Funktionseinheit von drei Geschossen erforderlichen Räume der Haustechnik. Daraus ergaben sich kurze Wege und wirtschaftliche Dimensionen für alle Installationen.

1st Prize in a limited competition for the administrative headquarters of the German health insurance organisation (DKV) in 1966. Over a site area of 18 000 m² and in two stages, some 40 000 m² of office space were to be planned in open-plan form. The design parameters contained in the brief were: no working place should be further than 13 m from large-area fenestration; the continuous office space should have as large an area as possible; the large, continuous areas should be articulated into comprehensible spatial units of approx. 1000 m². The particular characteristics of this solution were derived from the idea of disturbance-free access. The main access routes were grouped together with rest rooms, toilets, cloakrooms and conference rooms to form single »service« storeys, serving one open-plan storey above and one below. The intermediate storey also accommodates all mechanical services rooms required for this three-storey functional unit. The result was short routes and economical dimensions for all installations.

Gegenüberstellung von entflochtenen und nicht entflochtenen Verkehrsbewegungen
oben: nicht entflochten
Beim nicht entflochtenen Grundriß (d.h. Büroflächen, Verkehrszonen und Nebenräume liegen auf einem Geschoß) treten folgende Störungen auf:
- Bei Lage im Gebäudeinnern (oben links) werden die Großraumflächen zerrissen.
- Bei Lage am Fenster werden die Großraumflächen von der Lichtquelle abgeschnitten (oben rechts).
- Im Bereich der Kerne durch Bündelung von mehreren Verkehrsarten entstehen Störbewegungen für die angrenzenden Arbeitsplätze.
- Diese Bündelung der Verkehrsarten verursacht flurartige Verkehrswege auf den Büroflächen und damit Unterbrechungen des Informationsflusses zwischen den Arbeitsplätzen.

unten: entflochten
Beim entflochtenen Grundriß sind sich gegenseitig störende Verkehrsarten in verschiedene Ebenen gelegt, d.h. die Nebenräume liegen in einem Zwischengeschoß, das jeweils das nächsttiefere und -höhere Bürogeschoß versorgt. Eine Treppe in der Mitte des Dreieckmoduls ist die interne Verbindung vom Arbeitsgeschoß zum Servicegeschoß.

Comparison of segregated and non-segregated traffic flow
top: non-segregated
In the case of non-segregated plan, (i.e. office areas, traffic zones and ancillary rooms situated on same floor), the following disturbances occur:
- situation in interior of building (top left): open plan areas fragmented;
- situation next to windows: open plan areas cut off from light source (top right);
- in core areas where various kinds of traffic are grouped together: disturbance to adjacent working areas caused by movement;
- this grouping of various kinds of traffic creates corridor-like routes in office areas and thus causes interruption of flow of information between work places.

bottom: segregated
In the case of plan where functions segregated, mutually disturbing forms of traffic are situated on different levels; i.e. ancillary rooms are positioned on intermediate floors that serve the office floors immediately above and below. A staircase at the centre of the triangular module provides the internal connection from working floor to service floor.

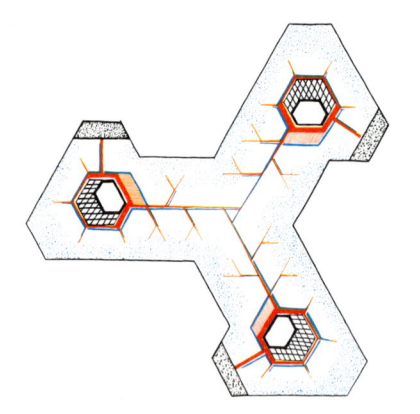

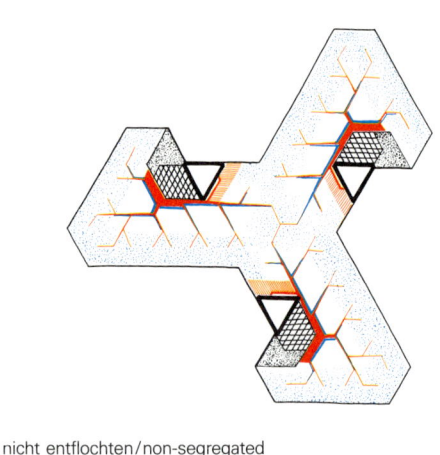

nicht entflochten/non-segregated
△ Verkehrskern/Communications core
Füll- und Leerverkehr/Traffic: arrivals and departures
Kommunikationsverkehr gestreut/Communications, scattered
Kommunikationsverkehr gebündelt/Communications, grouped
Sozialverkehr/Social communications
Garderobe, Waschraum, WC/Cloakroom, toilets, WC
Pausenraum/Rest room

Arbeitsgeschoß/Working floor

Servicegeschoß/Service floor

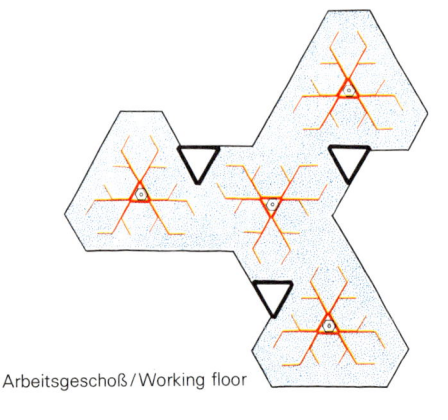

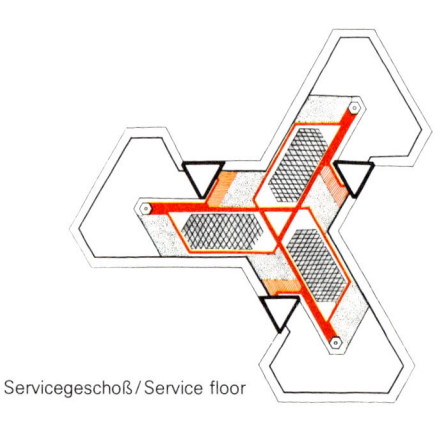

entflochten/segregated
△ Verkehrskern/Communications core
Füll- und Leerverkehr/Trafic: arrivals and departures
Sozialverkehr/Social communications
Garderobe, Waschraum, WC/Cloakrooms, toilets, WC
Pausenraum/Rest room
Kommunikationsverkehr/Communications
Sozialverkehr/Social communications

123

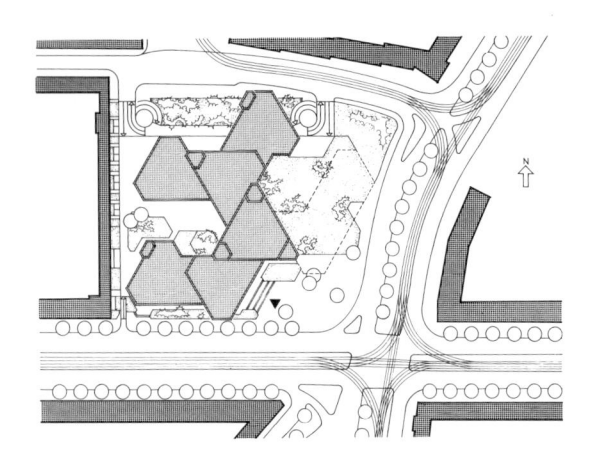

Grundrisse
oben Mitte Untergeschoß
unten Mitte Erdgeschoß
oben rechts Normalgeschoß Großraum
unten rechts Servicegeschoß mit Pausen-, Besprechungsräumen, Toiletten, Garderoben

Plans
top middle Basement
bottom middle Ground floor
top right Typical floor open plan area
bottom right Service storey with rest and discussion rooms, toilets and cloakrooms

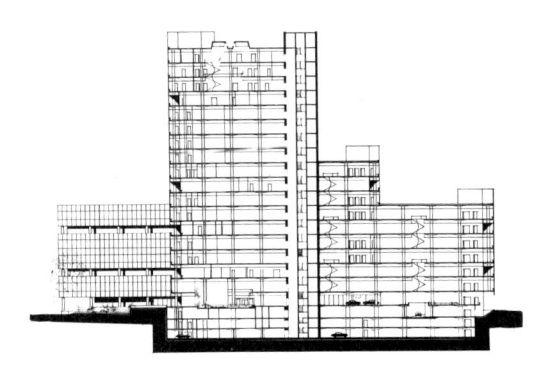

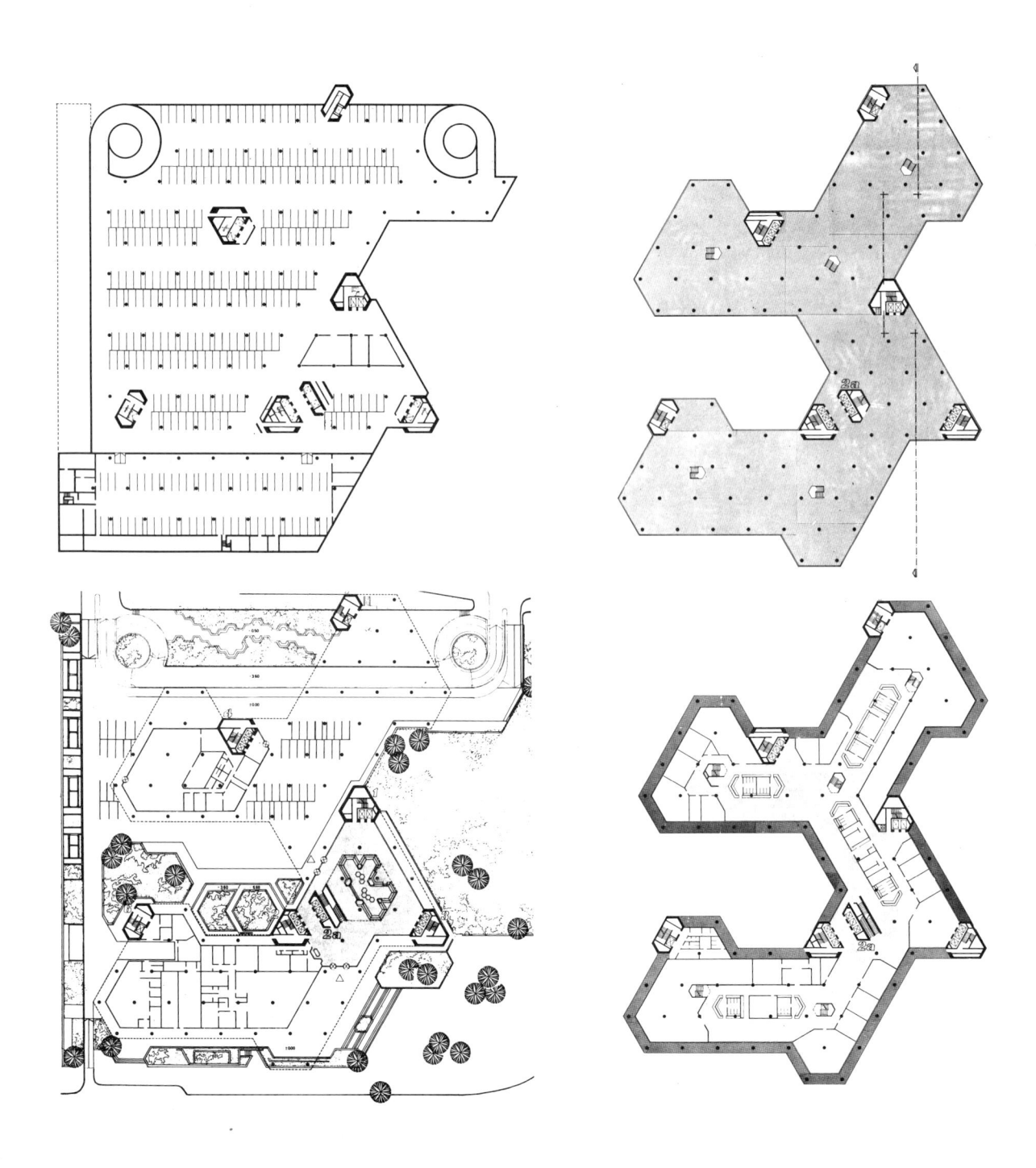

124

Reflexionsglas und Alubrüstung sind so aufeinander abgestimmt, daß sie bei den meisten Beleuchtungszuständen als schimmernde Einheit wirken.

Reflecting glass and aluminium apron cladding are harmonized in such a way that in most lighting conditions they give the impression of a single shimmering whole.

125

Iduna Hamburg

Teil des in Bauherrengemeinschaft mit anderen Unternehmen errichteten Einkaufszentrums Hamburger Straße, bestehend aus einem dreigeschossigen Ladentrakt mit aufgesetzten Bürohochhäusern. Fertigstellung 1970.

Part of a shopping centre in the Hamburger Straße that was erected in conjunction with other firms organized into a tax benefited developers' association (Bauherrengemeinschaft). The centre consists of a three-storey shopping tract with high-rise office blocks on top. Completed 1970.

Rathaus Castrop-Rauxel

Entwurfsbeitrag zum beschränkten Wettbewerb um die Gestaltung eines neuen Zentrums für die Stadt Castrop-Rauxel. Rathaus, Mehrzweckhalle und Sporthalle liegen als lockere Baugruppe an einer Fußgängerachse mit signifikanten Freiräumen.

Entry to a limited competition for the design of a new centre for the town of Castrop-Rauxel. Town hall, multi-purpose hall and sports hall form a loosely-knit group of buildings along a pedestrian axis with important open spaces.

Hauptverwaltung Shell Hamburg

2. Preis im Wettbewerb 1970. Die an die Shell-Muschel erinnernde Grundrißfigur entstand aus der Forderung nach mehreren Bauabschnitten und nach enger Zuordnung von Großraum- und Zellenbüros. Die innere Erschließungsfläche ist knapp und übersichtlich.

2nd Prize in competition, 1970. The layout configuration, which recalls the shape of a sea shell, was derived from the need to divide the structure into a number of building stages and to keep open-plan and individual unit offices in close relationship to each other. The internal access area is relatively small and clearly arranged.

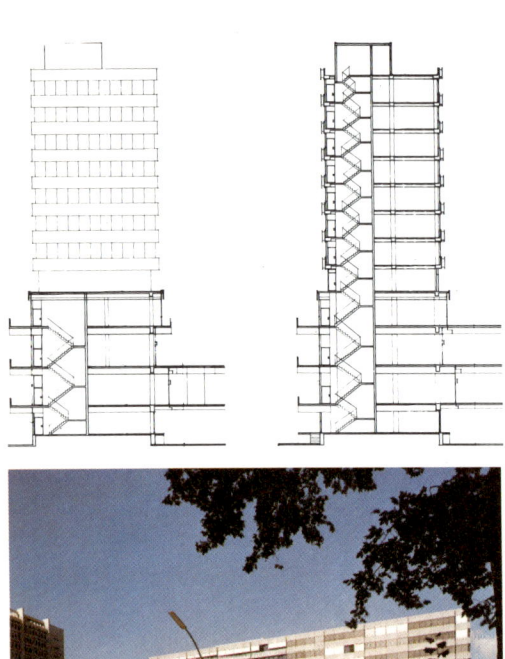

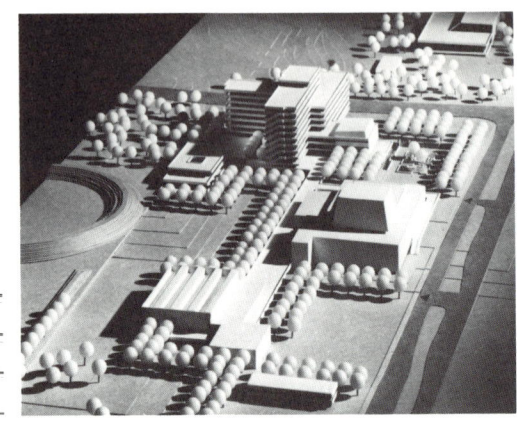

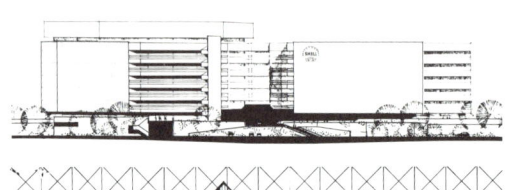

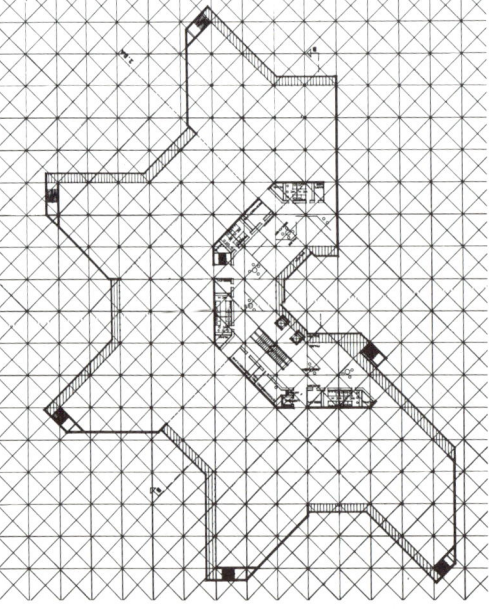

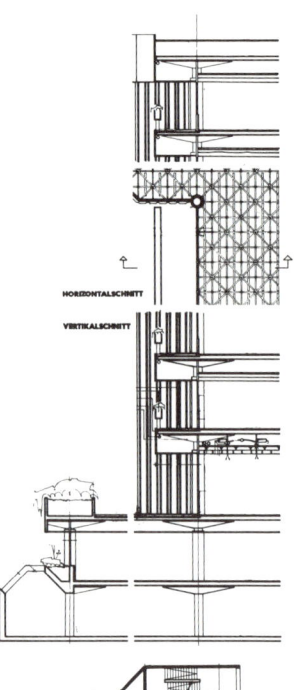

Vorstandsgebäude Bayer Leverkusen

1. Preis im Wettbewerb 1970, nicht ausgeführt. Die Schwierigkeit der Aufgabe bestand darin, dem Vorstandsbau durch Anordnung und Ausformung die ihm zukommende Besonderheit vor dem viel größeren Bau des Vorstandsstabes gewinnen zu lassen.

1st Prize in competition, 1970. Not executed. The difficulty of the project lay in achieving, through siting and design, the special quality appropriate to a building for the executive board against the much larger managerial staff building.

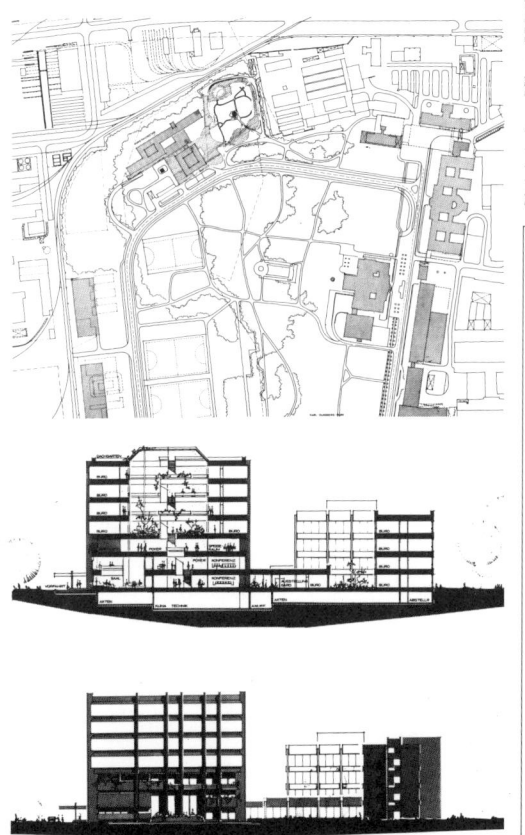

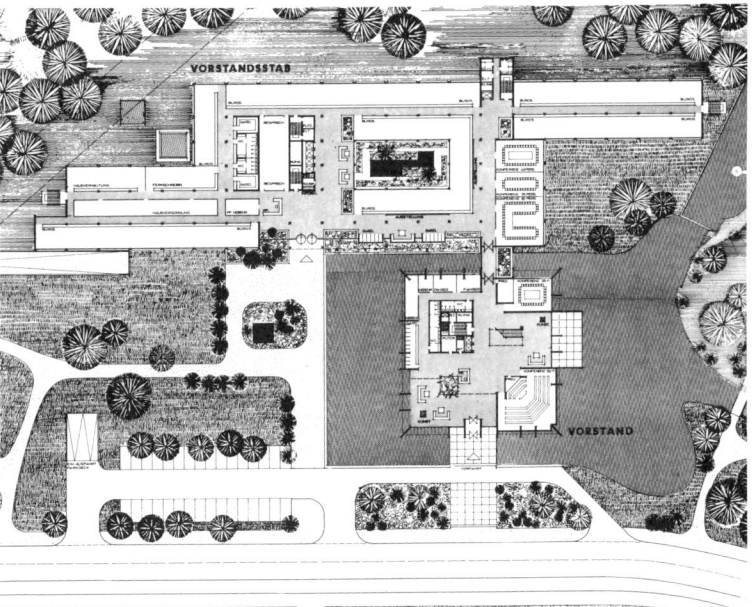

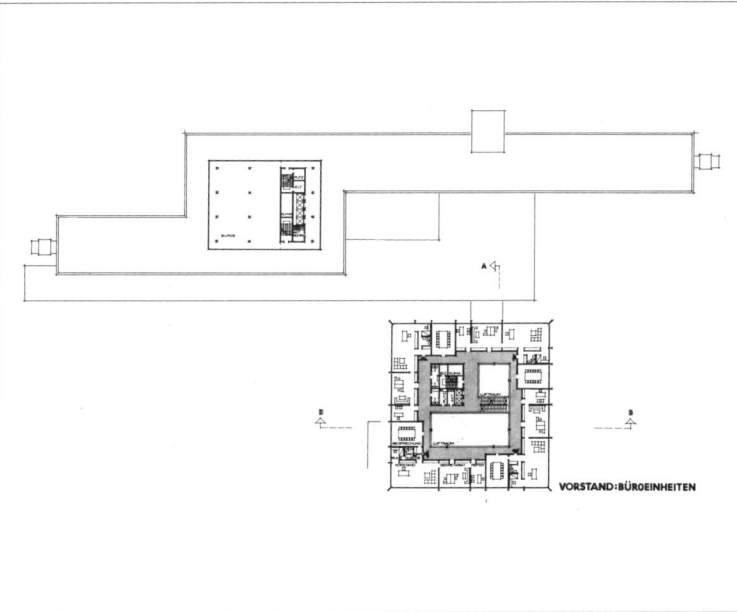

Hauptverwaltung Philips Wien

Vorentwurfsplanung 1974, mit Dr. techn. K. Hlavenitzka, Wien. Die große Bürofläche sollte reversibel und erweiterbar sein. Durch die Anlage einer separaten Verkehrs- und Nebenraumspange, die durch Kerne mit den Büroflächen verknüpft ist, bleiben die Büroflächen voll flexibel und frei vom Horizontalverkehr.

Outline design proposals, 1974, with Dr. techn. K. Hlavenitzka, Vienna. The large office space was to be reversible and extendible. By planning a separate strip for communications and ancillary rooms, linked by core zones to the office areas, the office areas themselves remain completely flexible and free of horizontal traffic.

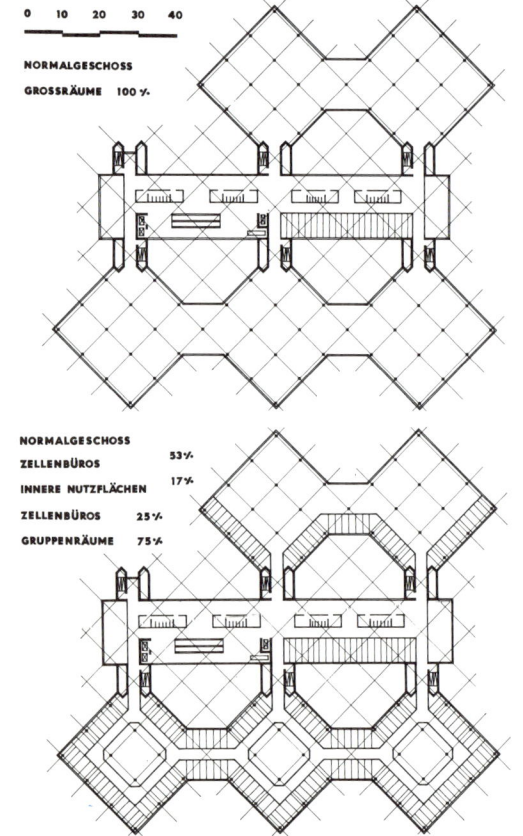

Hauptverwaltung Veba Chemie Gelsenkirchen-Buer

Vom Entwurfsgutachten (1. Rang) wurde nur die Kantine ausgeführt (S. 100), die Hauptverwaltung später an anderer Stelle verwirklicht (S. 166). Reversibles Bürohaus auf Dreiecksgrundriß mit zwei gleichwertigen Erschließungskernen und Sonderflächen im Erd- und Untergeschoß. Grundrißfigur und Zuordnung zur Kantine ergaben sich aus der städtebaulichen Umgebung vorhandener Werkbauten.

Of those elements contained in the design study (1st place) only the canteen was actually executed, (p. 100). The administrative headquarters were subsequently built on a different site, (p. 166). A »reversible« office block on a triangular site, with two access cores of equal weight and with special areas on the ground and lower ground floors. The configuration on plan and the orientation to the canteen were due to the existing industrial buildings in the immediate urban vicinity.

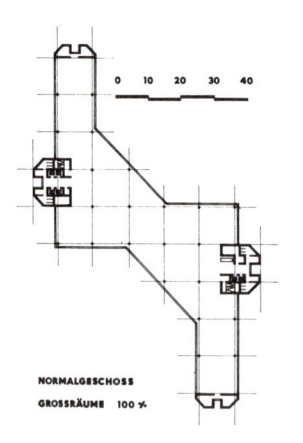

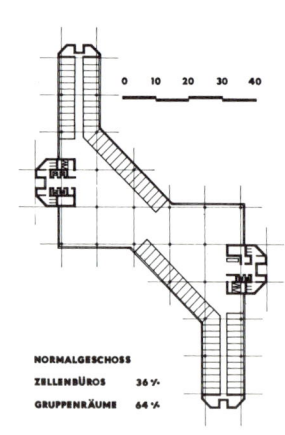

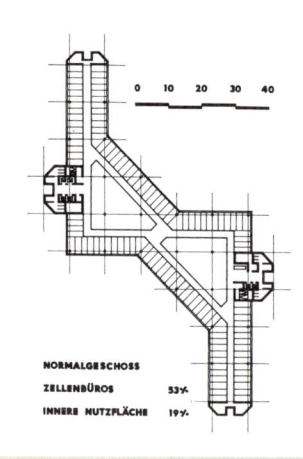

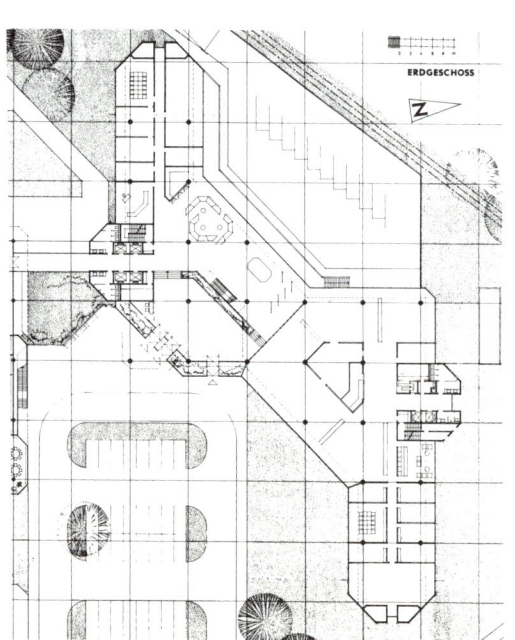

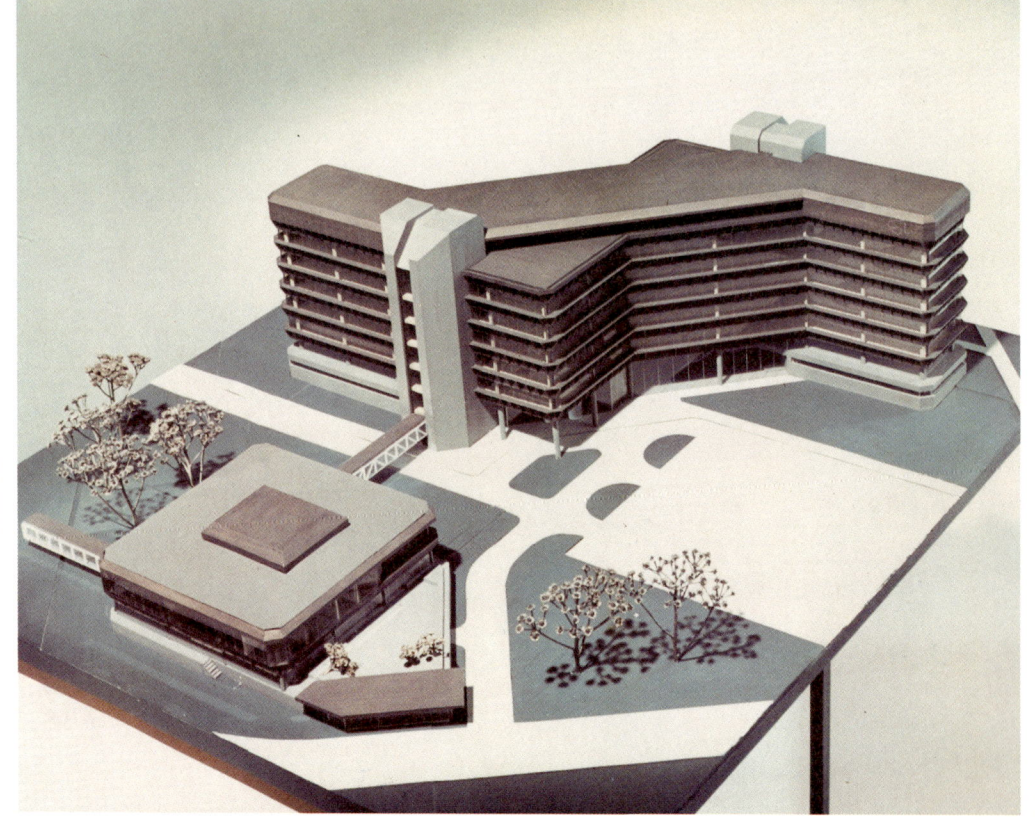

Hauptverwaltung Colonia Versicherung
Köln

1. Preis in beschränktem Wettbewerb 1971. Auf beengtem Grundstück war das Raumprogramm für reversible Büroflächen nur in einem Hochhaus mit Überbauung einer Straße unterzubringen.

1st Prize in a limited competition, 1971. In view of the confined site, the spatial programme of the Colonia Insurance organisation with its demand for reversible office space could only be accommodated in a high-rise development and by building over a street.

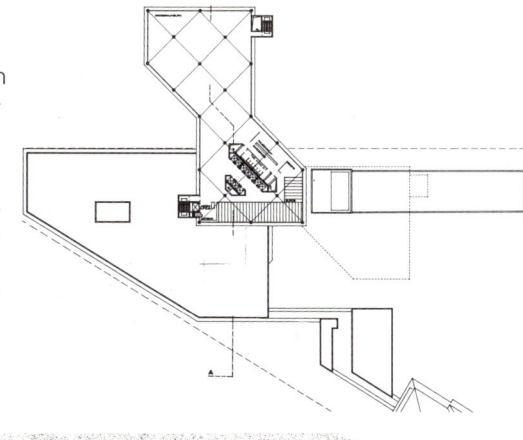

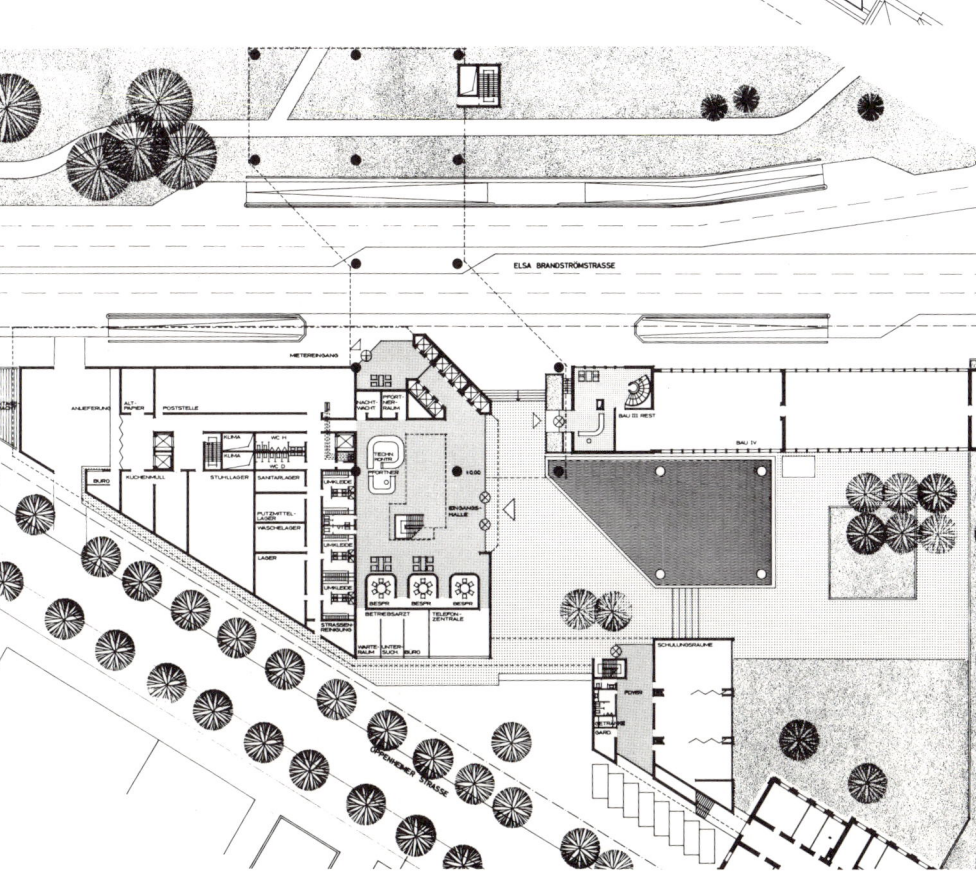

Unternehmensbereich D Siemens
München-Perlach

1. Preis im internationalen Wettbewerb 1970, nicht ausgeführt. Sehr große Bauanlage für ca. 8000 Mitarbeiter mit Büros, Labors, Werkstätten, EDV, Schulungs- und Sozialräumen für Forschung, Entwicklung und Vertrieb. Der Entwurf erfüllt die Forderung nach Reversibilität (auch im Bereich der Labors!) durch Grundrißzuschnitt und Erschließungssystem über Zwischengeschosse, ähnlich dem Entwurf für die Bayer-Verkaufsabteilungen (S. 120) oder das ausgeführte Haus der DKV (S. 122).

1st Prize in an international competition held in 1970; not executed. Very large building complex for approx. 8000 employees, containing offices, laboratories, workshops, data processing areas, training rooms and rooms for social activities for the realms of research, development and marketing. The design complies with the demand for reversibility, (even in the laboratory realm), by means of the plan layout and an access system via intermediate storeys, similar to the design for the Bayer sales department (p. 120), or the complex built for the DKV, (p. 122).

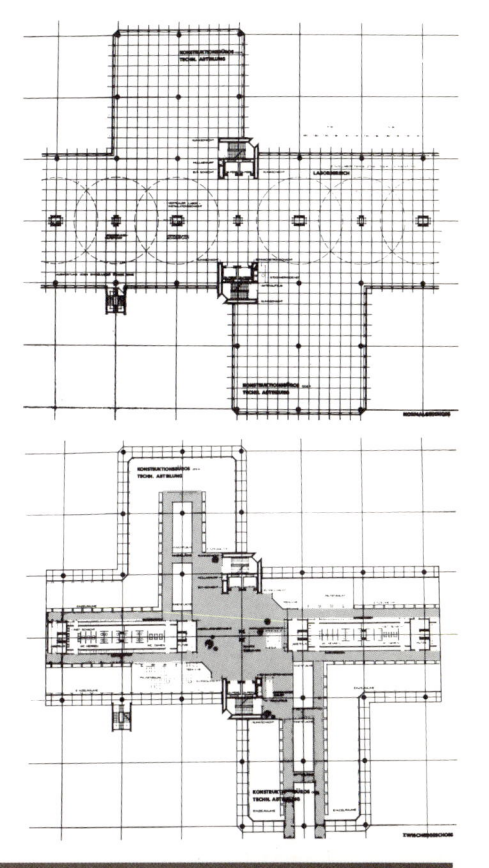

oben Normalgeschoß
unten Zwischengeschoß

top Typical floor
bottom Intermediate floor

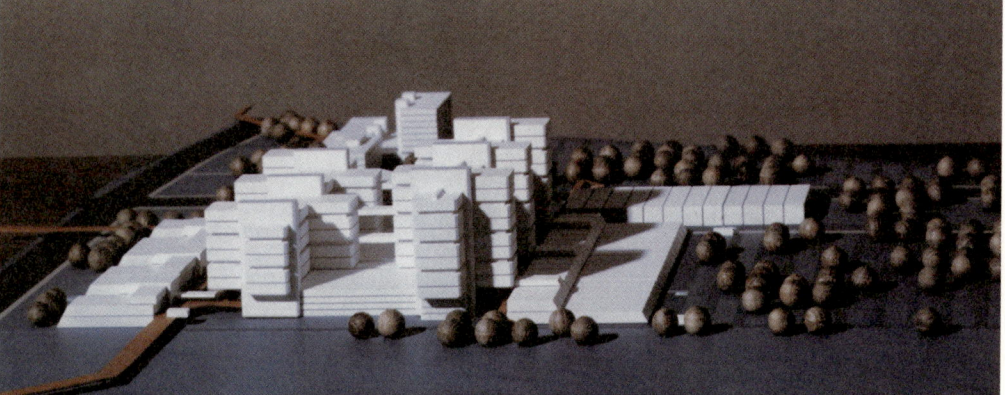

Hauptverwaltung VEW Dortmund

Bauherr: Rheinisch-Westfälische Immobilien-Anlagegesellschaft Düsseldorf. Das reversible Bürohaus der Vereinigten Elektrizitätswerke gestattet die Unterbringung der ca. 1000 Arbeitsplätze sowohl in Zellenbüros als auch in Großraumflächen (derzeitige Nutzung: Zellenbüros). Neben den Normalbüros enthält das Bauwerk sehr umfangreiche Raumgruppen für technische Sonderzwecke, EDV-Anlagen, Kasino, Werkstätten, Lager und Tiefgaragen. Um den Baukörper aus städtebaulichen Gründen nicht zu hoch werden zu lassen, sind die Sonderflächen unter Ausnutzung des fallenden Geländes und durch Absenkung innerer Höfe weitgehend in einem in das Gelände eingelassenen Sockelbauwerk untergebracht. Damit wurde erreicht, daß etwa nur die Hälfte der gesamten Baumasse über Terrain in Erscheinung tritt. Die glatte spiegelnde Außenhaut des Bürohauses aus reflektierendem Sonnenschutzglas soll die umgebende Parklandschaft das Gebäude optisch durchdringen lassen. Fertigstellung 1976.

Building client: Rheinisch-Westfälische Immobilien-Anlagegesellschaft, Düsseldorf. This »reversible« office block provides working space for some 1000 persons, both in office cells and in open-plan office form. (The present use is in the form of individual unit offices.) As well as the normal office space, the building contains extensive groups of rooms for special technical purposes, data processing plant, club rooms, workshops, stores and underground garaging. In order to restrict the height of the building for urban planning reasons, and by using the slope of the site, and lowering the level of internal courtyards, the areas for special purposes are largely accommodated in a plinth structure sunk into the ground. It was thus possible to have approximately only half the entire built volume visible above ground. The smooth, mirror-like outer skin of the office block in reflecting solar glass is intended to allow a visual penetration of the building by the surrounding park landscape. Completion date, 1976.

oben links Technikgeschoß/
top left Services storey
1 Büros/Offices
2 Schaltleitung/Area switch room
3 Telefonzentrale/Telephone switchboard
4 Rechner/Calculating area
5 EDV-Anlage/Computer area
6 Poststelle/Mail room
7 Klimazentrale/Air conditioning plant
8 Kältezentrale/Cooling plant
9 Heizzentrale/Central heating plant
10 Elektrozentrale/Electrical plant
11 Notstromdiesel/Emergency diesel generator

unten links Erdgeschoß/
bottom left Ground floor
1 Vorfahrt/Arrivals
2 Eingangshalle/Entrance hall
3 Betriebsarzt/Company doctor
4 Konferenzzentrum/Conference centre
5 Lichthöfe/Light wells
6 Gästespeiseräume/Visitors' dining rooms
7 Küche/Kitchen
8 Essenausgabe/Meals counter
9 Cafeteria/Cafeteria
10 Betriebsrestaurant/Company restaurant
11 Einfahrt Garage/Garage access
12 Ausfahrt Garage/Garage exit
13 Anlieferstraße/Delivery road
14 Gartenanlage/Gardens

rechts Normalgeschosse/
right Typical floors
oben Großraumnutzung/top Open-plan office layout
unten Zellenbüronutzung/bottom Single unit office layout
1 Bürofläche/Offices
2 Pausenraum/Recreation room
3 Besprechungsraum/Conference room
4 Registratur/Records filing
5 Garderobe/Cloakroom
6 Teeküche/Tea kitchen
7 Putzraum/Cleaners' room

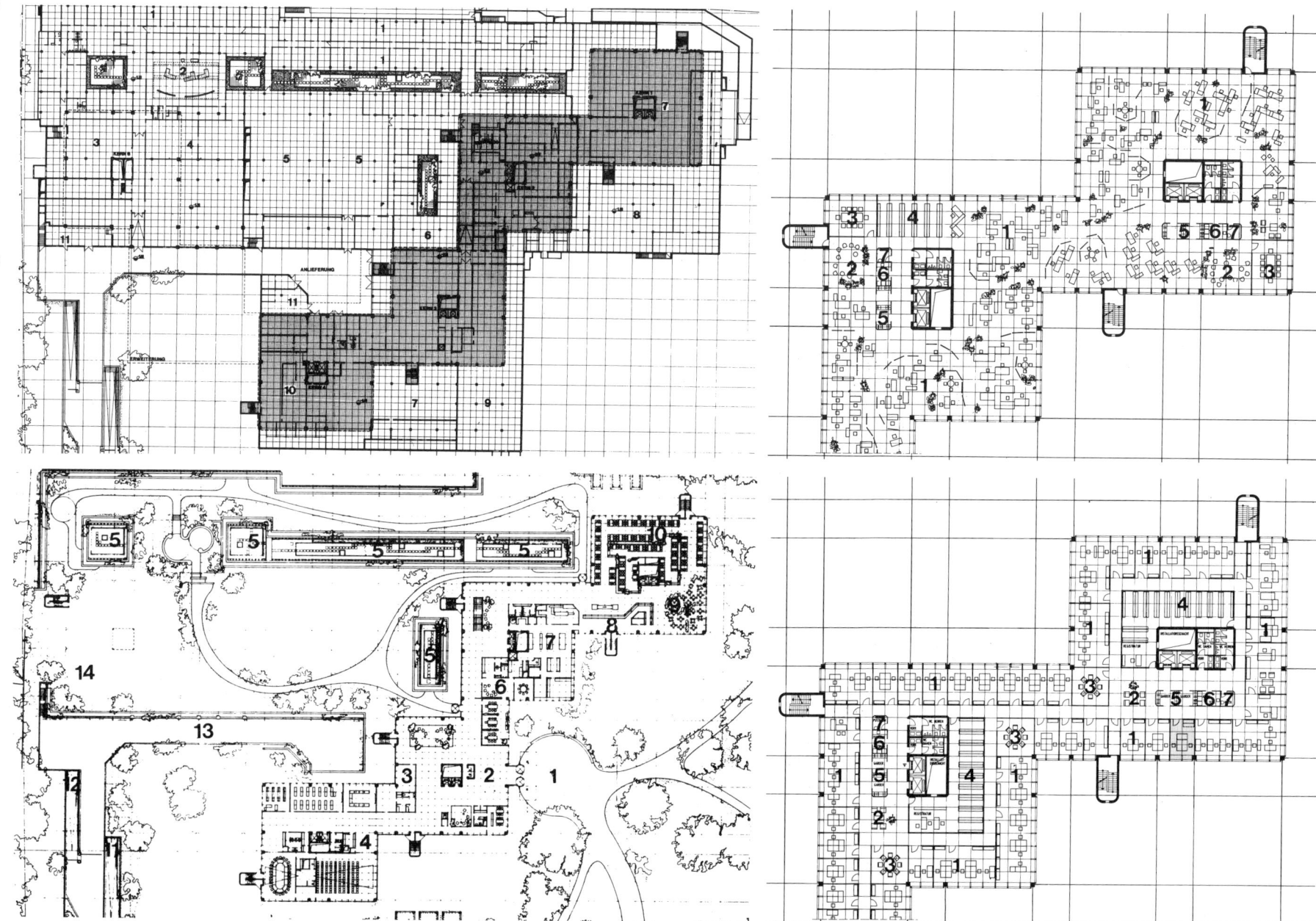

außen links
Blick in einen der Grünhöfe
im Sockelgeschoß

Far left
View into one of the planted
courtyards in plinth structure

132

oben rechts
Um Bauhöhe zu sparen, wurden Stahlverbundträgerdecken mit Regelaussparungen verwendet.

Top right
In order to reduce building height composite steel girder slabs were used with openings at regular intervals.

Das Haus gewinnt einen Teil seiner Geschlossenheit durch das in allen Räumen verwendete einheitliche Deckensystem.

The building acquires part of its sense of unity from the soffit system used in all rooms.

Die Büroflächen können sowohl für Zellen- als auch Großraumnutzung verwendet werden. Die unterschiedlichen Anforderungen beider Büroarten sind im Deckenausbau besonders berücksichtigt. Für das Großraumbüro ermöglicht die Metallkassettendecke die erforderliche Schallabsorption und eine blendfreie Beleuchtung von 800 lx. Für Zellenbüroverwendung ist die Decke als horizontale Schallabschottung (1 mm Stahlblech mit darüberliegender Schluckmatte) ausgebildet, so daß die Bürotrennwände an der Decke enden und im Deckenhohlraum keine zusätzlichen Schallschutzmaßnahmen erforderlich sind. Durchgehende Installationshohlräume in Decke und Doppelboden, mit dem alle Büroflächen ausgerüstet sind, erlauben Anpassung an zukünftige Bürotechnik.

The office areas can serve both individual unit and open-plan office uses. Special allowance is made for the different requirements of these two types in the floor construction. In the case of open-plan offices the metal waffle-type soffit provides the necessary sound absorption and allows non-glare lighting of 800 lux illuminance. Where single cell offices are required the ceiling is constructed as a horizontal sound barrier, (1mm sheet steel with sound absorbent matting on top). The office partition walls stop at the soffit and thus no additional sound absorption measures are necessary for the void between suspended soffit and the structure. The continuous spaces for service runs in the ceiling construction and floating raft floor, which are foreseen in all office areas, provide scope for adaptation to meet future developments in the realm of office technology and services.

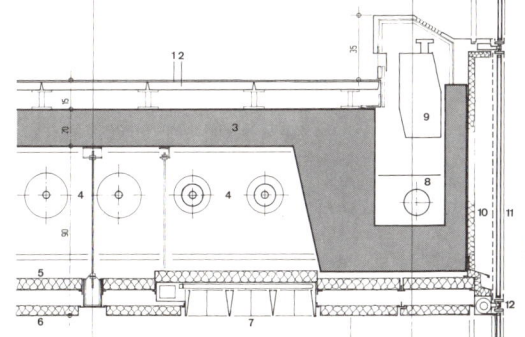

Decken- und Fassadendetail/Details of floor construction and façade
1 Teppich / Carpet
2 Doppelboden / Floating raft floor
3 Stahlverbundträgerdecke / Composite steel girder slab
4 Installationsraum / Services void
5 Schwerauflage / Heavyweight membrane
6 Akustikdecke / Acoustic soffit
7 Einbauleuchte / Lighting fitting
8 Konvektorenschacht / Convector duct
9 Induktionskonvektor / Induction convector
10 Luftraum / Void
11 Glasbrüstungselement / Glass apron panel
12 Alu-Fassadenprofil / Aluminium curtain wall profile

Hauptverwaltung Vorwerk Wuppertal

Aufgelockerter Bürokomplex auf einem Hanggrundstück am Waldrand mit Blick auf das im Tal liegende Wuppertal-Barmen.

A loose complex of offices on a sloping site at the edge of a wood and with a view to Wuppertal-Barmen in the valley below.

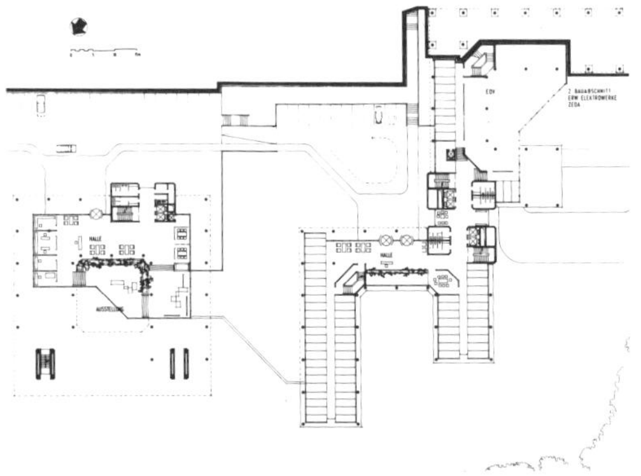

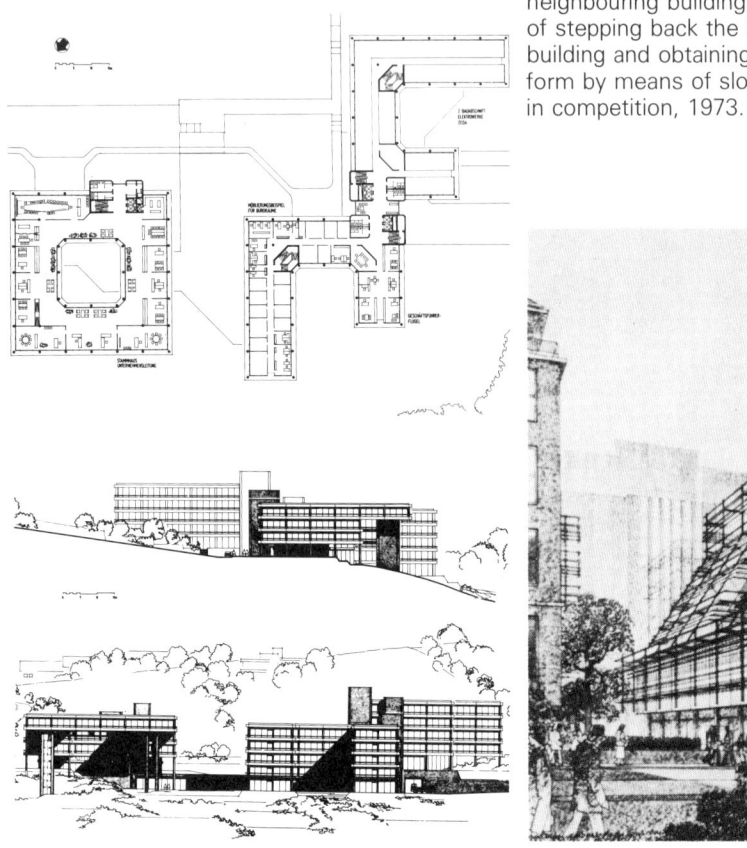

Grundrisse
oben Eingangsgeschoß
Mitte Normalgeschoß

Plans
top Entrance floor
middle Typical floor

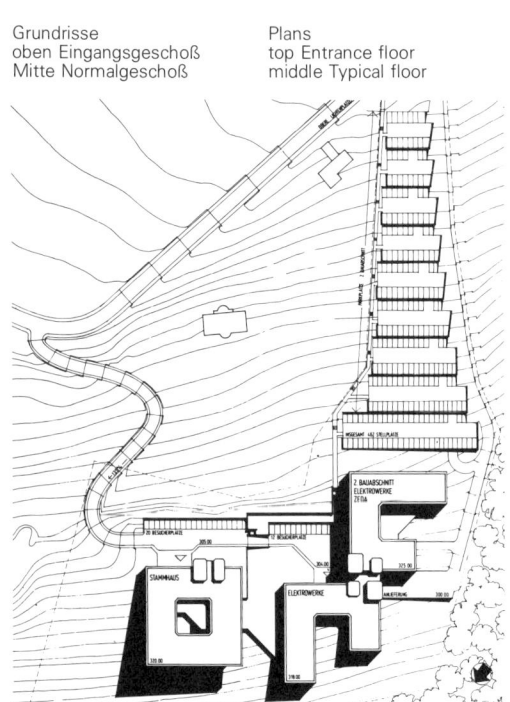

Hauptverwaltung Klöckner Duisburg

Auf einem verwinkelten innerstädtischen Grundstück war ein umfangreiches Raumprogramm für 2000 Büro-Arbeitsplätze unterzubringen. Aus der Schwierigkeit, zu den Nachbarhäusern die erforderlichen Abstandsflächen einzuhalten, entstand der Entwurfsgedanke, die Baukörper zurückzustaffeln und durch Schrägfassaden eine signifikante Gebäudeform zu erzielen. 2. Rang im Wettbewerb 1973.

The extensive spatial requirements of the brief required the accommodation of 2000 office working places on an irregularly shaped site in the town centre. The difficulty involved in maintaining the necessary distance from neighbouring buildings led to the design idea of stepping back the individual parts of the building and obtaining a significant building form by means of sloping façades. 2nd Prize in competition, 1973.

Deutsche Botschaft Helsinki

Wettbewerb 1972, 2. Rang. Versuch, das Gebäude der deutschen Vertretung durch baukörperliche Differenzierung in die reizvolle, hügelige Landschaft und die umgebende Bebauung einzufügen.

Competition, 1972; second place. An attempt to fit this German embassy building into the attractive hilly landscape and the surrounding built environment by means of an articulation and differentiation of the built volumes.

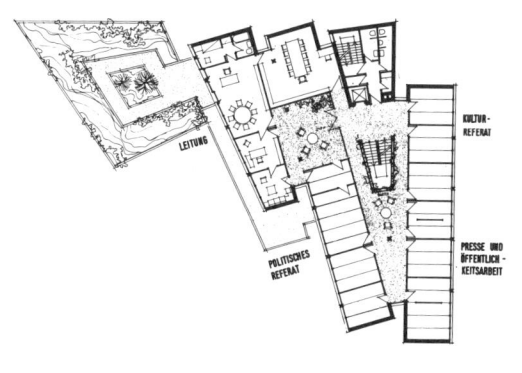

Hauptverwaltung ÖVA-Versicherung Mannheim

2. Stelle im Gutachten 1974. Erstmals wird die neue Büroraumart der Gruppenräume verlangt, die ab 1980 weite Verbreitung erfahren wird. Der Entwurf zeigt bereits alle Merkmale späterer Ausprägungen: viel Außenwandlänge, geringe Innenzonen, Raumtiefen unter 8 m, alle Gruppenräume an der Außenwand. – Die Schwierigkeit dieser Aufgabe lag darin, daß ein zweiter Bauabschnitt gleicher Größe systemlogisch anzufügen war.

2nd Place in design study, 1974. For the first time the new type of office space, the group room, appears on the scene. From 1980 onwards it was to enjoy widespread use. The design already reveals all the features of the later forms it was to take:
considerable lengths of external wall, small inner zones, room depths less than 8 m, and all group rooms situated along external walls. The difficulties of this project lay in the fact that a second stage building of the same size had to be added on in an analogous system.

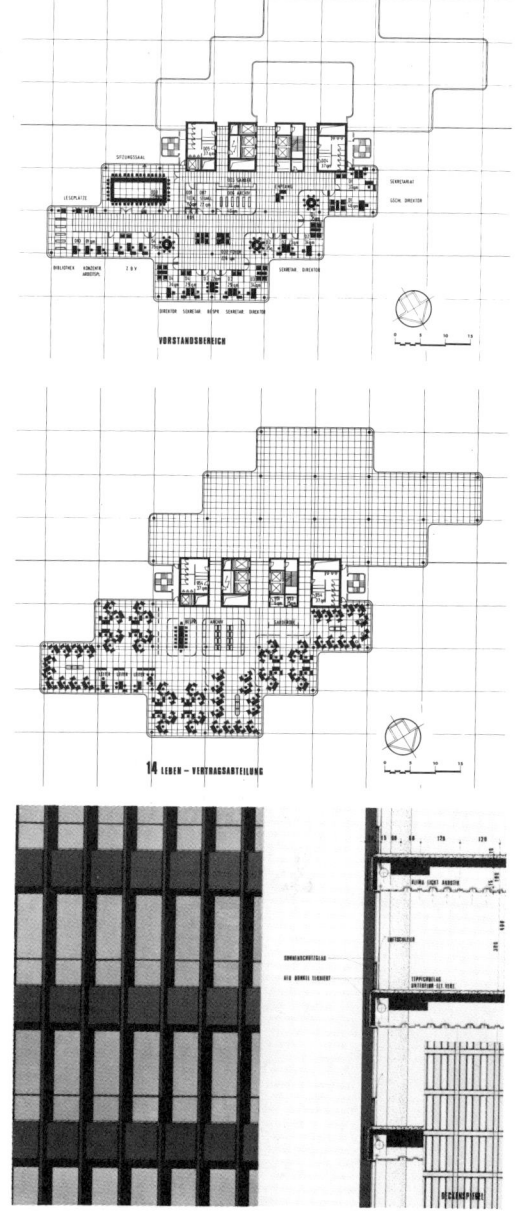

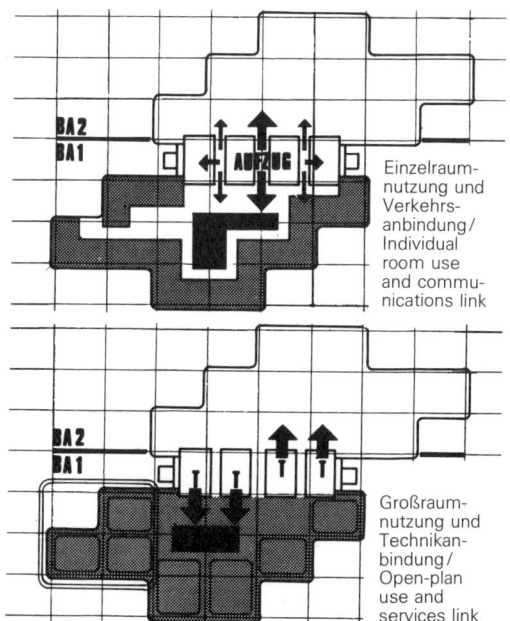

Einzelraumnutzung und Verkehrsanbindung / Individual room use and communications link

Großraumnutzung und Technikanbindung / Open-plan use and services link

Bayern Versicherung München

Hauptverwaltung für ca. 500 Mitarbeiter in schwieriger städtebaulicher Situation inmitten eines Wohngebietes. 1. Preis im Wettbewerb 1973. Ausführungsplanung zusammen mit v. Wertz, Ottow, Bachmann, Marx, München. In jedem Geschoß gruppieren sich drei Großraumbüros, die durch Zellenbüros und Pausenräume voneinander getrennt sind, um eine zentrale Erschließungshalle, die von den Verkehrs- und Nebenraumkernen umgeben ist. Ungewöhnlich großes Nebenraumprogramm mit Sozialeinrichtungen (Turn- und Schwimmhalle, Kegelbahnen) in den Untergeschossen. Die stark plastische Fassade wurde mit Nagelfluh verkleidet.

Administrative headquarters for approx. 500 employees, set in a problematic urban context in the midst of a residential area. 1st Prize in a competition in 1973. Detailed design in collaboration with v. Wertz, Ottow, Bachmann, Marx in Munich. On every floor there are three open-plan offices, separated from each other by office cells and rest rooms, arranged about a central access hall that is in turn surrounded by cores housing communications and ancillary rooms. An unusually large programme of ancillary space, with social facilities, (gymnasium, swimming hall, bowling alleys) on the basement floors. The boldly articulated face of the building was clad in nagelfluh, a conglomerate stone.

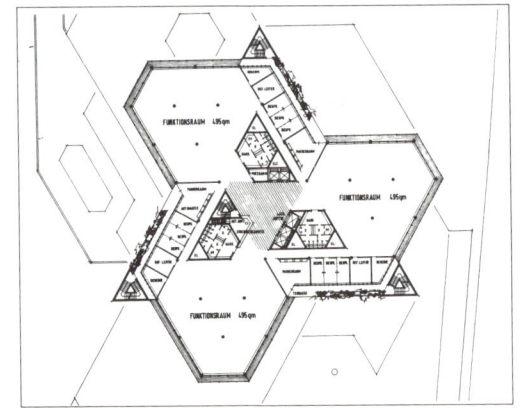

Rathauserweiterung Wolfsburg

Mehrere Planungsstadien von 1972 bis 1977. Nicht ausgeführt. Reversibles Bürohaus für ca. 1000 Mitarbeiter, in dem die in vielen Mietbüros im Stadtgebiet verstreuten Ämter zusammengefaßt werden sollten. Die knappe Grundstücksfläche erforderte die Unter- und Überbauung einer öffentlichen Straße. Die geforderten Bauabschnitte wurden in Fassung 2 (Modell unten) durch Aufstocken, in Fassung 3 (rechts) durch Anbau erreicht.

Several stages of planning between 1972 and 1977. Not built. »Reversible« office block for roughly 1000 persons, in which the various municipal departments in rented office accommodation scattered about the town were to be brought under one roof. The tight space necessitated the building over and under of a public road. The various stages of building required were to be achieved in version 2 (model below) by means of building on additional floors and in version 3 (right) by lateral extension.

Grundrisse / Plans
oben Zellenbüro / top Single unit offices
unten Großraumbüro / bottom Open-plan office
1 Zellenbüro / Single unit office
2 Besprechung / Conference rooms
3 Sonderflächen / Special areas
4 Warten / Waiting area
5 Innenhof / Courtyard
6 Pausenräume + Garderobe / Rest rooms + cloakrooms
7 Großraumbüro / Open-plan office

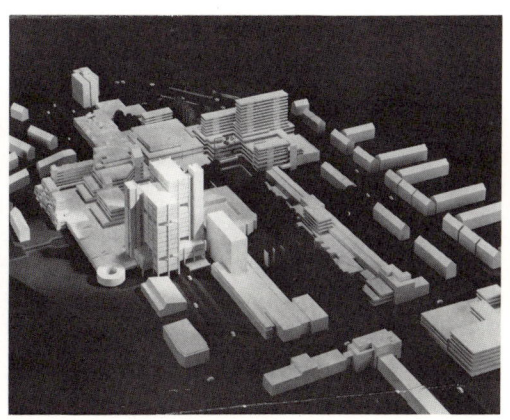

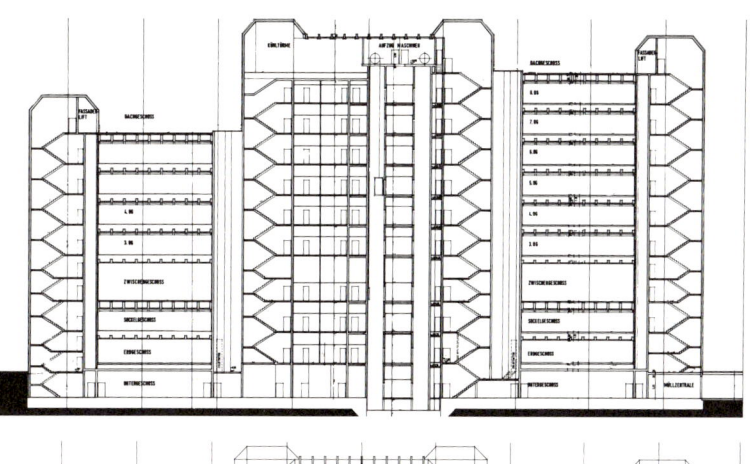

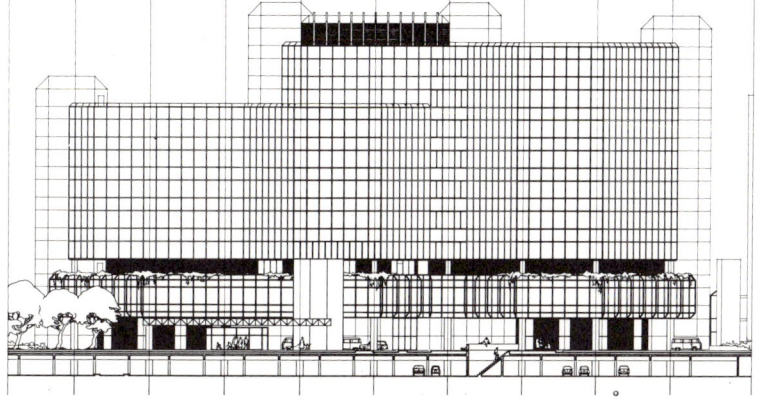

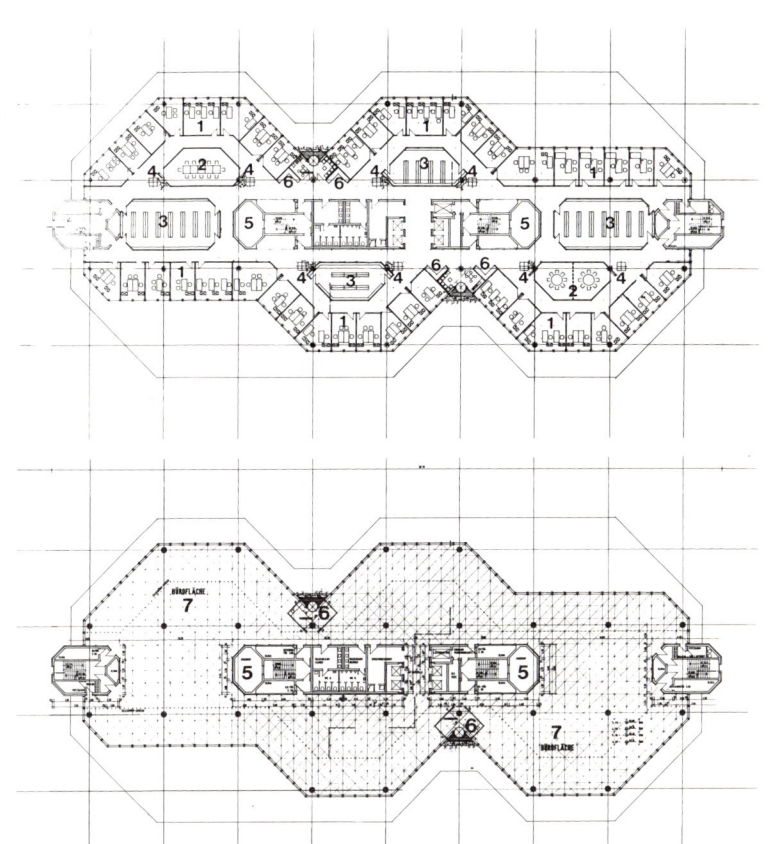

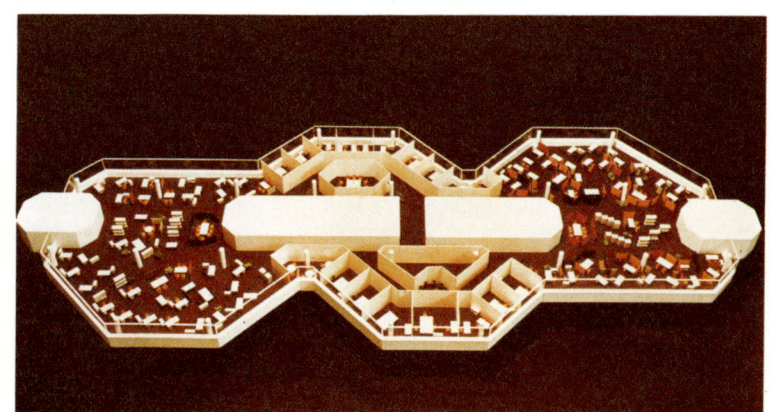

Hauptverwaltung Getreideimportgesellschaft Duisburg

Bürohaus (Mischung von Großräumen und Zellenbüros) und zugehörige Sonderflächen (EDV, Kasino, Hausdienste, etc.) in zwei Bauabschnitten. Vorentwurf 1974, in Arbeitsgemeinschaft mit Laskowski und Schneidewind, Braunschweig.

Office building, (a mixture of open-plan and single cell offices and their ancillary special areas –, data processing, club rooms, internal services, etc.), to be built in two stages. Outline proposals in 1974 in association with Laskowski and Schneidewind, Brunswick.

Hauptverwaltung Tchibo Hamburg

Wettbewerb 1974. Großraumbürohaus mit umfangreichen Sonderflächen in den Sozialbereichen (Sport und Erholung). Fußgängerströme aus drei verschiedenen Richtungen waren mit den per Fahrzeug auf tieferer Ebene Ankommenden zusammenzuführen.

Competition, 1974. Open-plan office building with extensive areas for special uses in the social realm (sport and leisure). Pedestrian routes from three different directions had to be linked up with vehicular arrivals from a lower level.

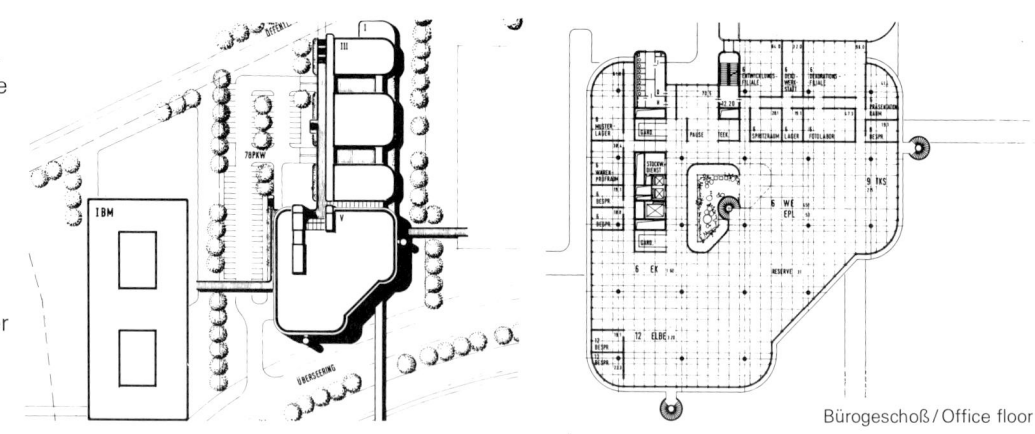

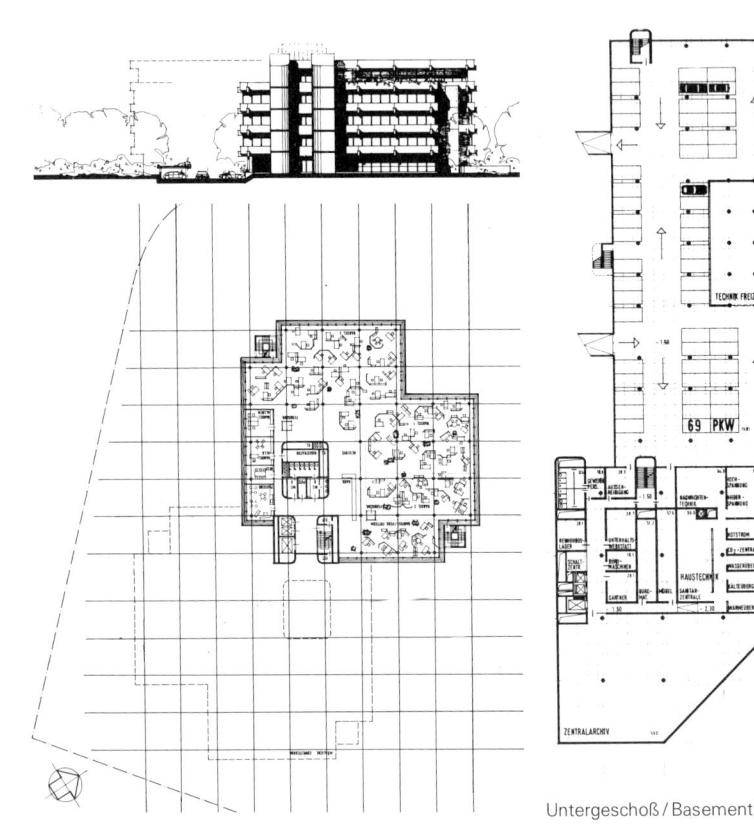

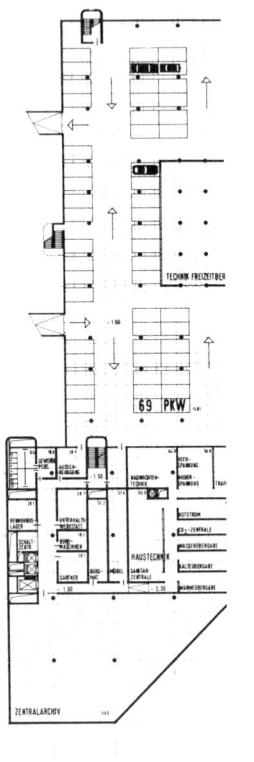

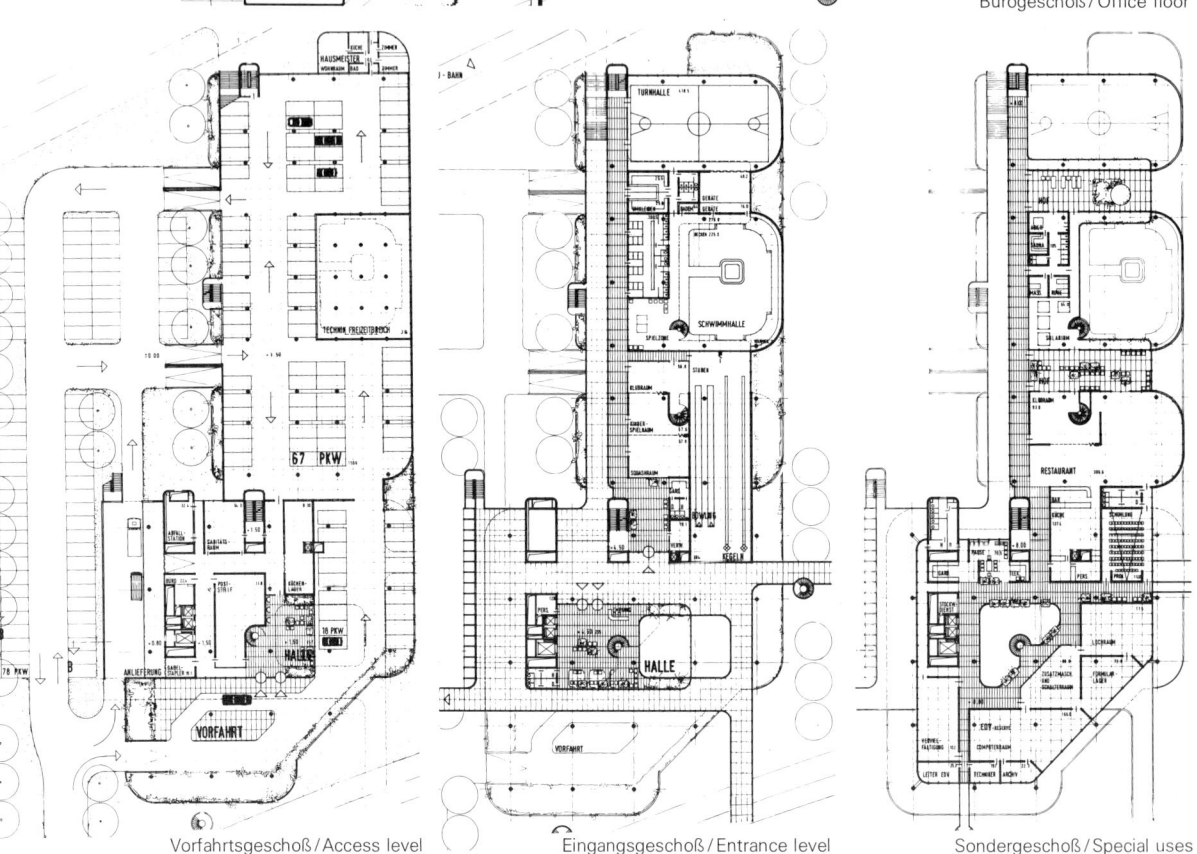

Bürogeschoß / Office floor

Untergeschoß / Basement

Vorfahrtsgeschoß / Access level

Eingangsgeschoß / Entrance level

Sondergeschoß / Special uses

Röhrenwerke Mannesmann Lintorf

Wettbewerb 1974. Verwaltungsgebäude mit 1500 Arbeitsplätzen, je zur Hälfte Zellen- und Großraumbüros. Campusartige Anlage von mehreren Bürogebäuden des Mannesmann-Konzerns auf »der grünen Wiese« in der Nähe von Düsseldorf.

Competition, 1974. Administrative building containing 1500 working places, half as individual cell type, half in the form of open-plan offices. A campus-like complex consisting of several office buildings of the Mannesmann concern set in a »virgin field« near Düsseldorf.

Normalgeschoß mit Zellenbüro- und Großraumbürozone

Typical floor with individual office cells and open plan office zone

Hauptverwaltung Norddeutsche und Hamburg Bremer Versicherung Hamburg

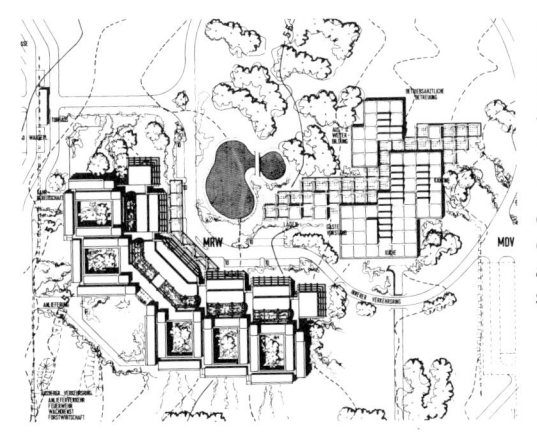

1. Preis im Wettbewerb 1975. Großraumbürohaus auf städtebaulich kompliziertem, hoch ausgenutztem Grundstück mit schwierigen Zugangs- und Abstandsbedingungen. Nicht realisiert.

1st Prize in competition, 1975. Open-plan offices on a site that was, in an urban planning context, complicated and highly developed, and was problematic in terms of access and space between buildings. Not built.

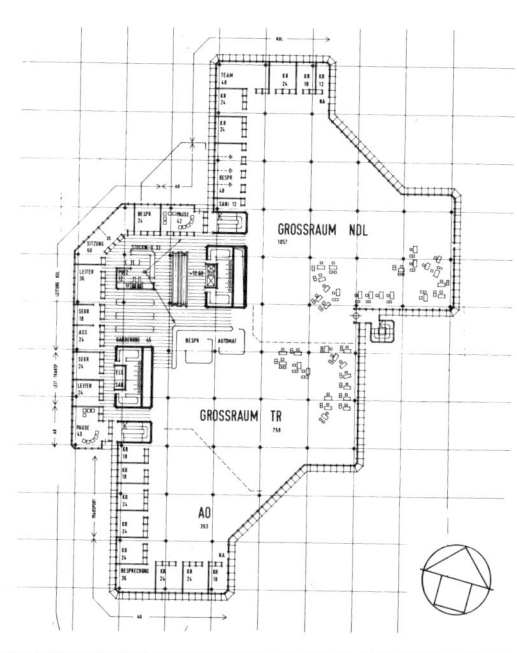

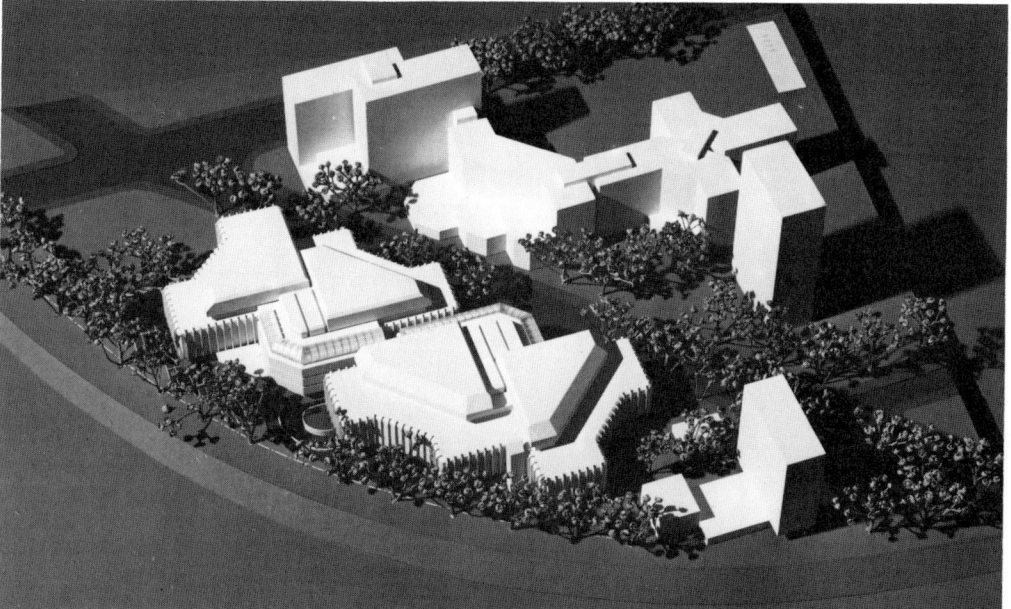

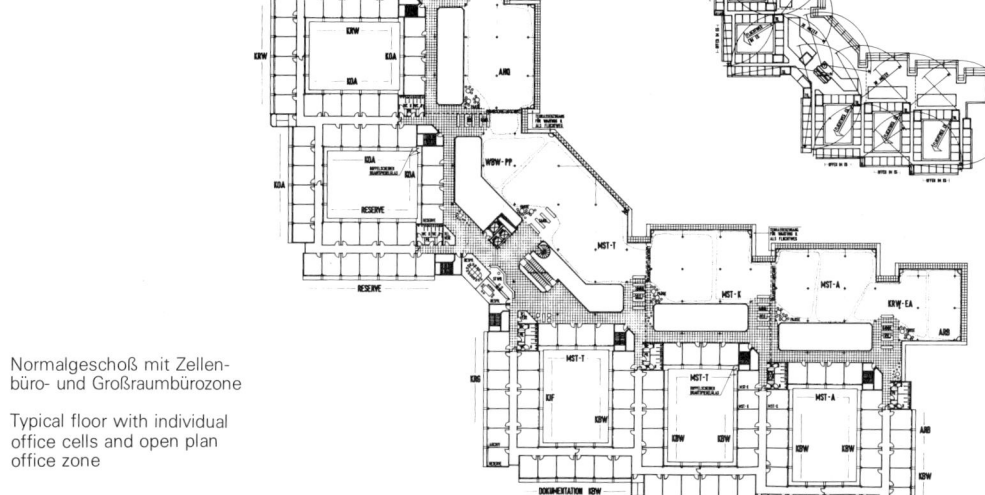

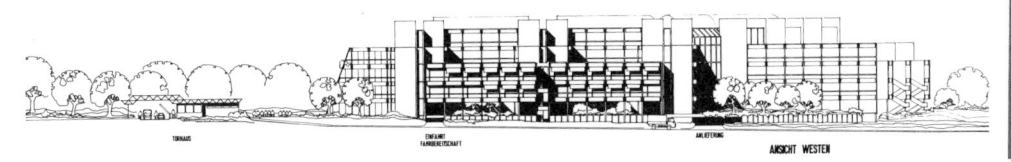

Technisches Rathaus Köln 1. Stufe

Wettbewerb 1975, 4. Preis. Die Besonderheit bestand darin, die sehr große Baumasse in zwei Bauabschnitten auf einem von U-Bahn, Straßen und Parkplätzen unterbauten, sehr knappen Grundstück unterzubringen. 1981 wurden die Preisträger zu einem zweiten Wettbewerb eingeladen (S. 143).

Competition, 1975; 4th prize. The particular feature of the Technical City Hall scheme consisted in fitting the very large building volume in two stages on to an extremely tight site, under which ran the underground, roads and parking spaces. In 1981 the prizewinners were invited to take part in a second competition, (p. 143).

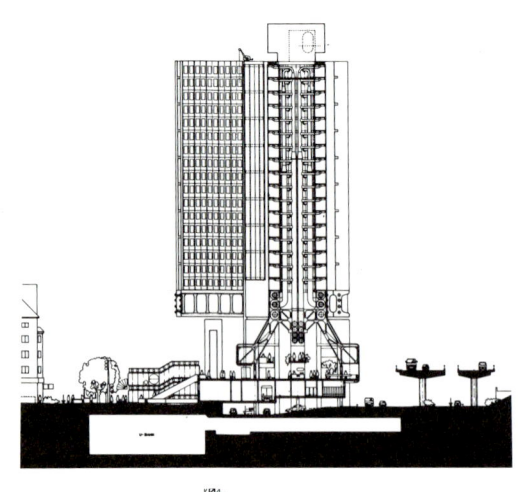

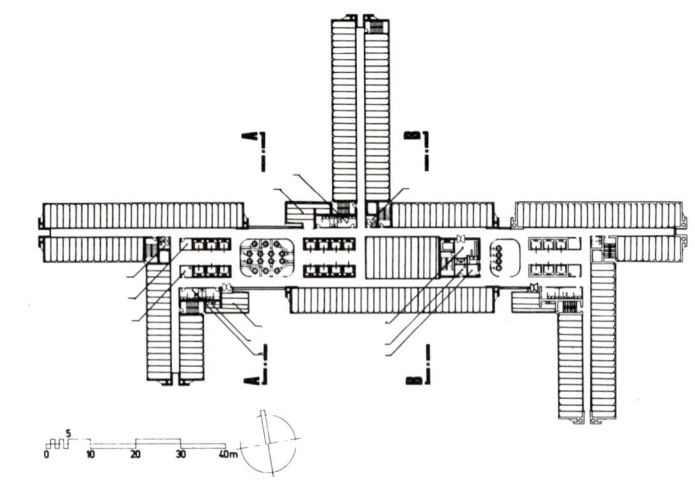

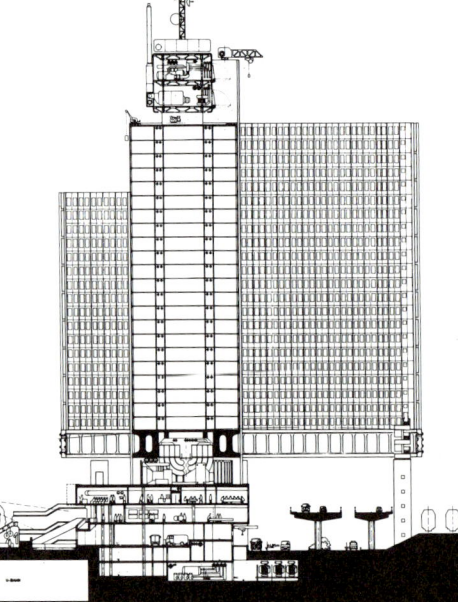

Grundriß Geschoß 1–17
oben Schnitt A–A
unten Schnitt B–B

Plan of floors 1–17
top Section A–A
bottom Section B–B

Technisches Rathaus Köln 2. Stufe

2. Preis im eingeladenen Wettbewerb der Preisträger aus der 1. Stufe 1975 in schwieriger städtebaulicher Situation zwischen Bundesbahn und einer viergeschossigen Gründerzeitbebauung.

2nd Prize in competition by invitation for the Technical City Hall of Cologne, (2nd stage), held amongst the prizewinners from the 1st stage (1975). Difficult urban planning situation between railway and a four-storey building, dating from the end of the last century (Gründerzeit).

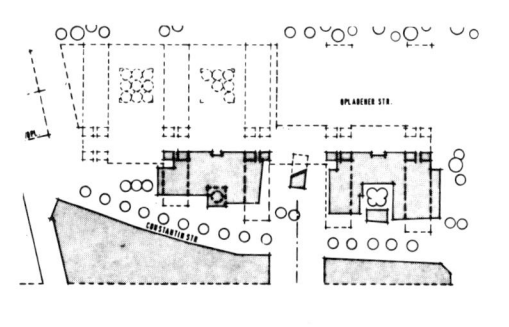

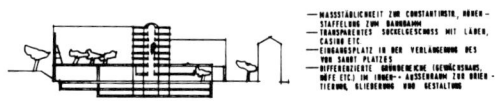

rechts
oben Schnitt A–A mit Ansicht
Mitte Erdgeschoß
unten Normalgeschoß

right
top Section A–A with elevation
middle Ground floor
bottom Typical floor

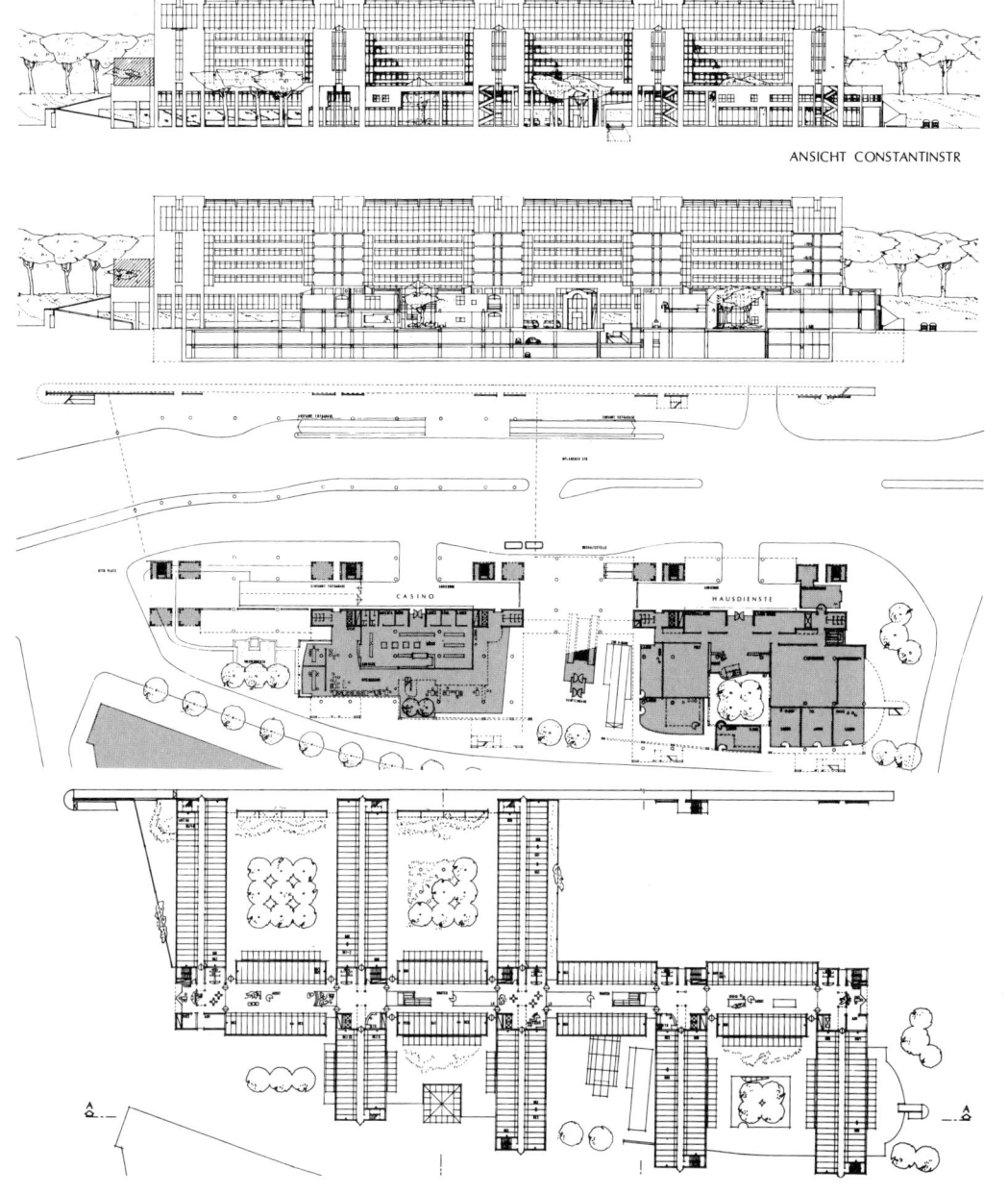

ANSICHT CONSTANTINSTR

Deutsche Botschaft Moskau

Wettbewerb 1975. Die Gesamtanlage umfaßt die Hauptbereiche Kanzlei, Residenz des Botschafters, Sport- und Freizeit (Clubhaus), Schule und die Wohnungen der Botschaftsangehörigen.

Competition, 1975. The entire embassy complex comprises the main areas for official offices, the residence of the ambassador, sport and leisure facilities (a club house), school and dwellings for the embassy staff.

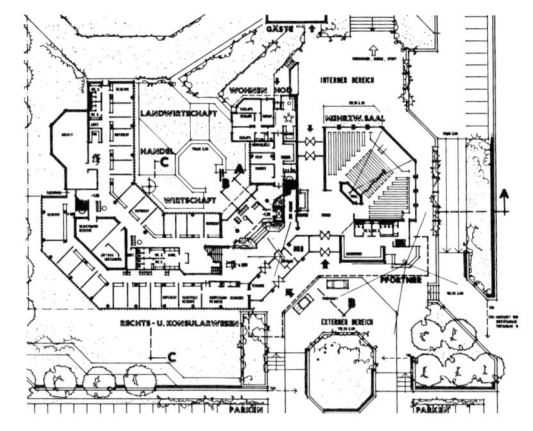

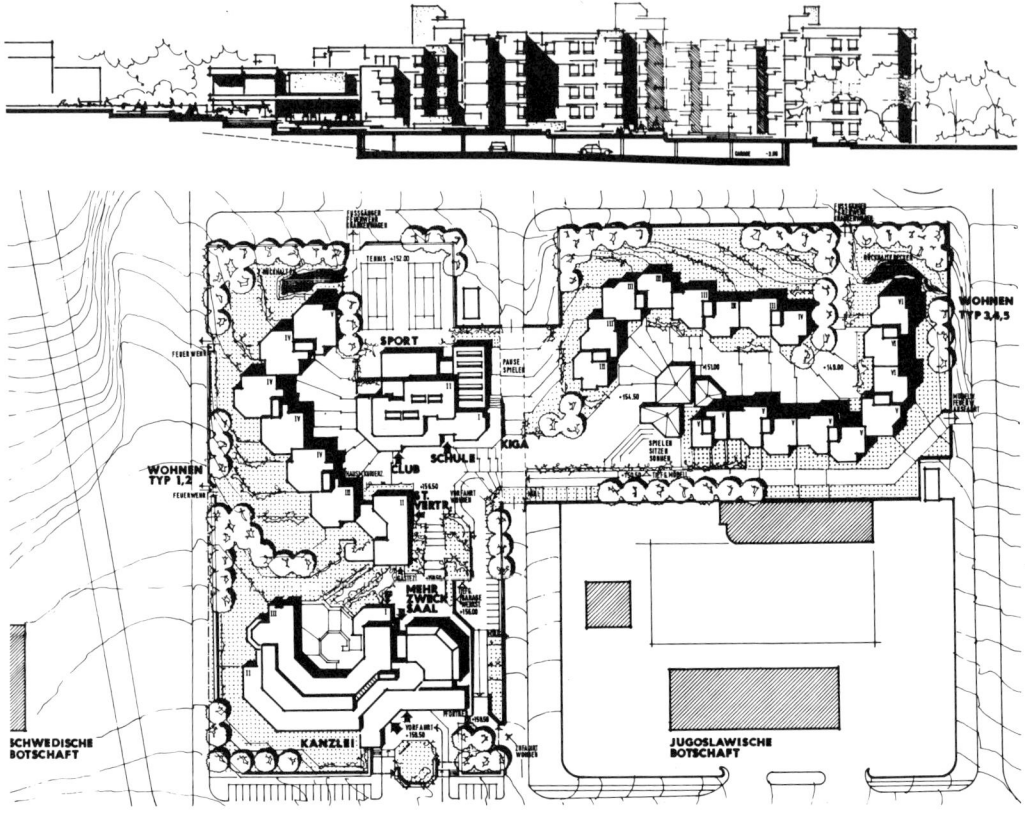

Regionalverwaltung Salzgitter Stahl Düsseldorf

Entwurfsgutachten nach funktionaler Leistungsbeschreibung 1976. Die Lösung für das Bürohaus entstand aus den städtebaulichen Gegebenheiten einer Solitärbebauung in der neuen Düsseldorfer »Geschäftsstadt« beidseits des Kennedy-Damms, den schwierigen Zufahrtsbedingungen und der Forderung, einen zweiten Bauabschnitt fast gleicher Größe später funktionell günstig anfügen zu können.

Design study based on functional description of activities, 1976. The design solution for this office building reflects the urban planning constraints imposed upon an isolated structure in the new Düsseldorf »business city« on both sides of the Kennedy-Damm; it reflects the problematic access conditions and the need to be able to add a second phase building of almost the same size at a later stage and in a functionally convenient way.

A = erster Entwurf
Hochhausscheibe mit dreigeschossigem keilförmigen Unterbau

A = First scheme
High rise slab with three-storey wedge-shaped plinth structure

B = zweiter Entwurf
Zwei quadratische Türme mit gläsernem Gelenk verbunden

B = Second scheme
Two right-angle towers with glass link

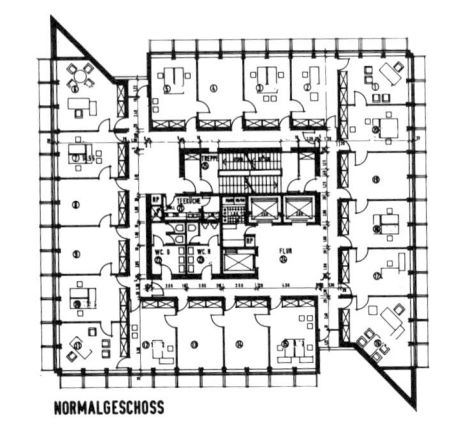

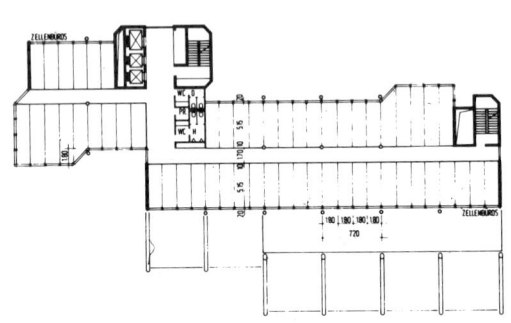

Hauptverwaltung Vereinigte Versicherungsgruppe München-Perlach

Entwurfsgutachten 1976, 2. Rang. Der Entwurf separiert die Normalbürozonen von den umfangreichen Sonderflächen sowohl vertikal wie horizontal. Die Untergeschosse zeigen die Bewältigung der komplizierten Funktionszusammenhänge der Sonderflächen untereinander und zur Ver- und Entsorgung. In den Normalgeschossen ergibt ein hierarchisch geordnetes Wegesystem gute Orientierbarkeit.

Design study, 1976; 2nd place. The design for the administrative headquarters of an insurance group separates the normal office zones from the extensive areas for special uses, both vertically and horizontally. The basement storeys are exemplary in the way they resolve the complicated functional interrelationships of the special use areas amongst themselves and to the service areas. On the standard floors the hierarchically organized system of routes affords good orientation.

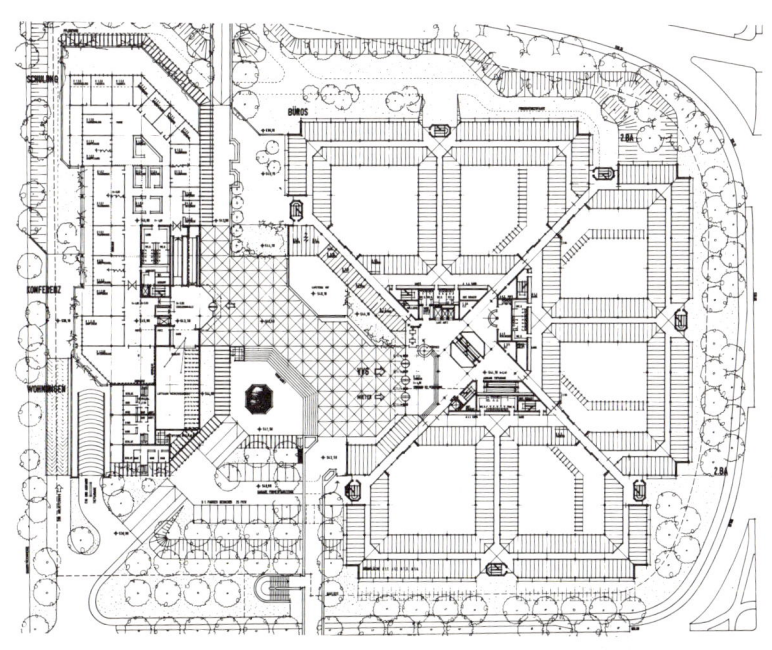

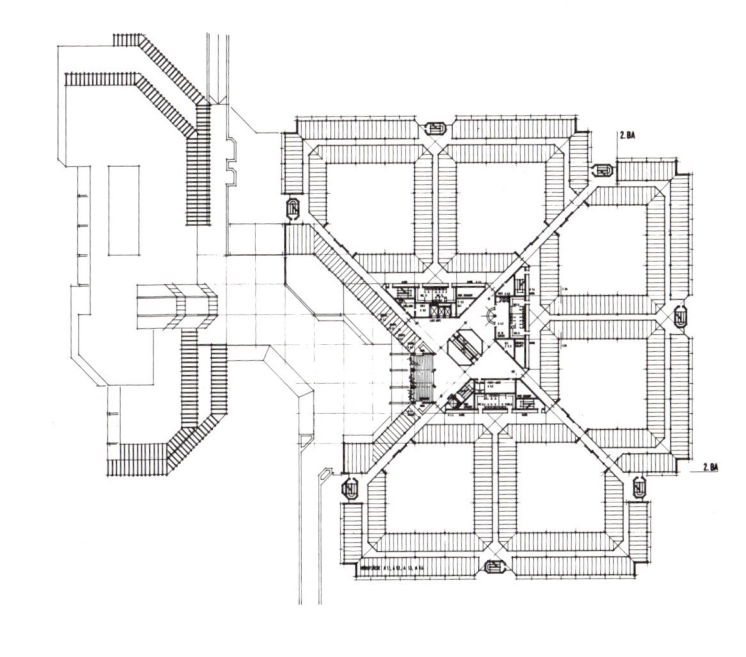

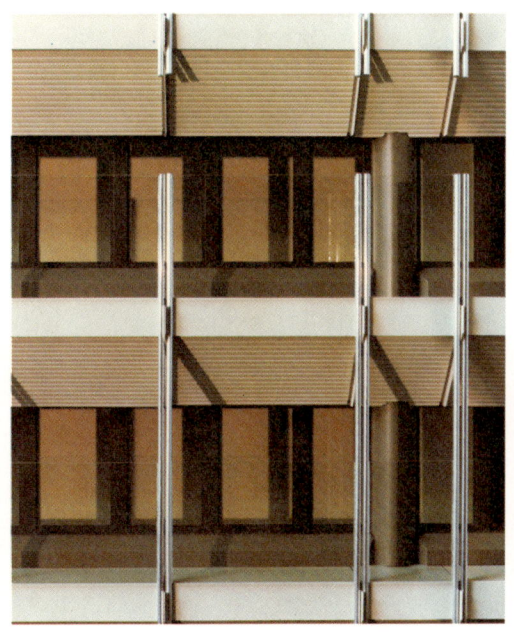

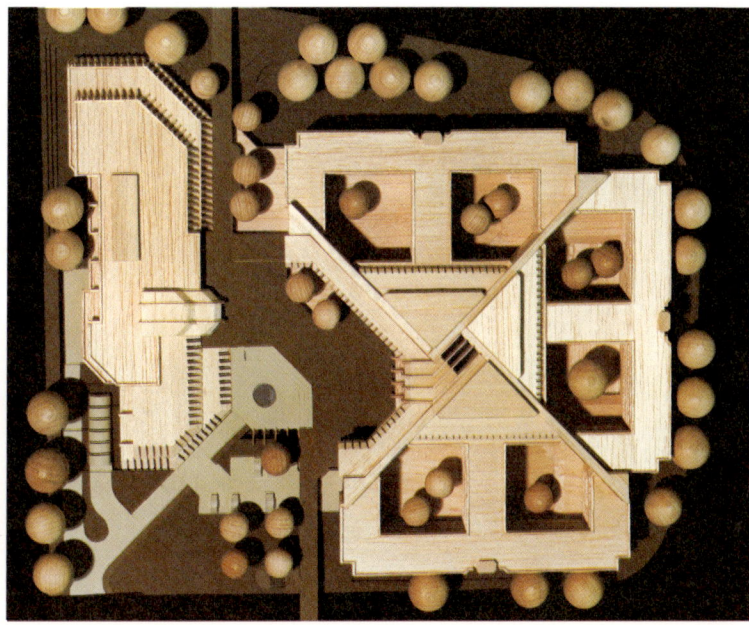

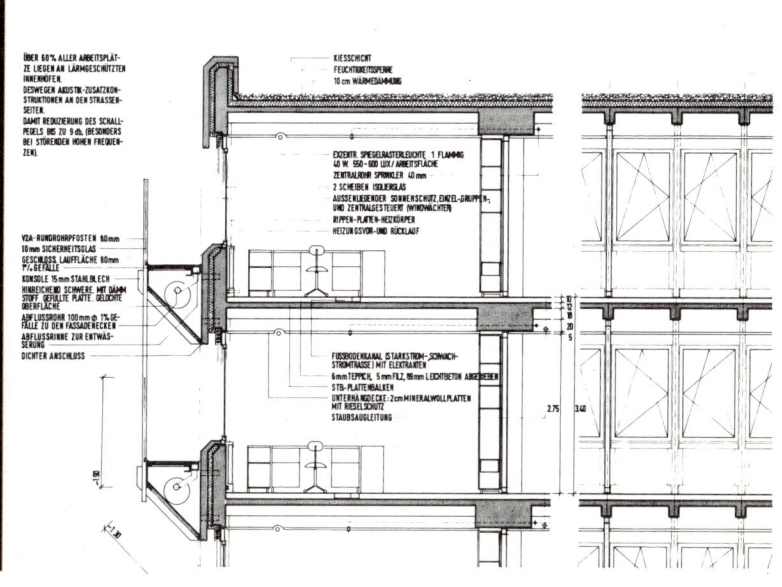

Kreishaus Warendorf

Wettbewerb 1977. Die halbringförmig den Eingangsfreiraum umschließende Baumasse verdeutlicht die Zugangsbedingungen: von einer zentralen Grundstückszufahrt sollten der Haupteingang und viele dezentrale Eingänge erreichbar sein.

Competition, 1977. The half-ring shape of the building bent about the open space of the entrance highlights the access conditions to this district office. From a central approach to the site, access was to be provided to the main entrance and to a number of secondary entrances.

Rathaus Hattingen

Wettbewerb 1977. Der Grundstückszuschnitt und Maßstab der städtebaulichen Umgebung legten das vorgeschlagene System der Addition winkelförmiger Bürotrakte nahe, die auf der Straßenseite von großräumigen, publikumsintensiven Sonderflächenbereichen begleitet werden.

Competition, 1977. The shape of the site and the scale of the surrounding urban fabric suggested the system proposed for the town hall: an additive system using L-shaped office tracts with, on the street face, large-scale areas for special uses, where intense public traffic is to be expected.

Hauptverwaltung DEVK Köln

Wettbewerb 1976, 1. Rang. Großraumbürogebäude der Deutschen-Eisenbahn-Versicherungs-Kasse für ca. 1600 Arbeitsplätze (in zwei Bauabschnitten) auf sehr reizvollem Grundstück unmittelbar am Rheinufer neben der Zoobrücke. Die Büroflächen werden von einer großzügigen Verkehrszone so erschlossen, daß Verkehrsbewegungen im Großraum minimiert werden. Gliederung der Büroflächen durch vertikale Raumverbindungen, um den Saalcharakter herkömmlicher Großraumbüros zu überwinden. (Ausführung S. 178)

Competition, 1976; 1st place. Open-plan office building for the German Railways Insurance Fund, containing working space for some 1600 persons, (in two stages of building), and set on a very attractive site on the banks of the Rhine neer the Zoo Bridge. Access to the office areas is provided via a generously proportioned communications zone in such a way that traffic movement in the open-plan areas is kept to a minimum. The office spaces are articulated by vertical links in an attempt to overcome the hall-like character of conventional open-plan offices. (Actual execution, p. 178)

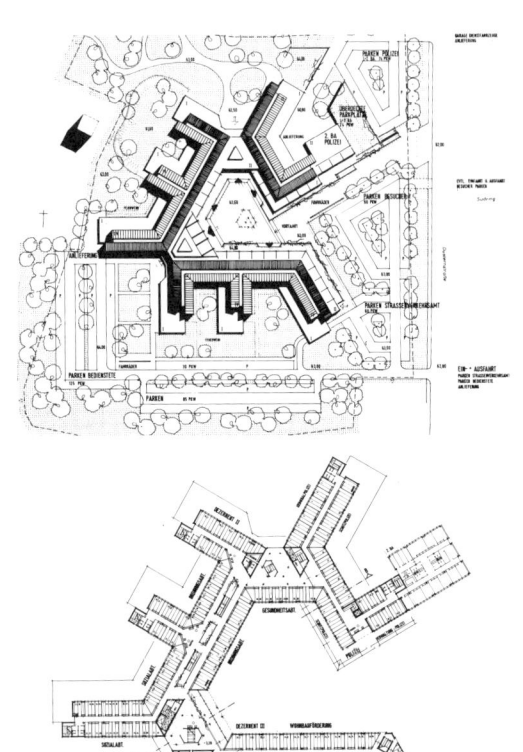

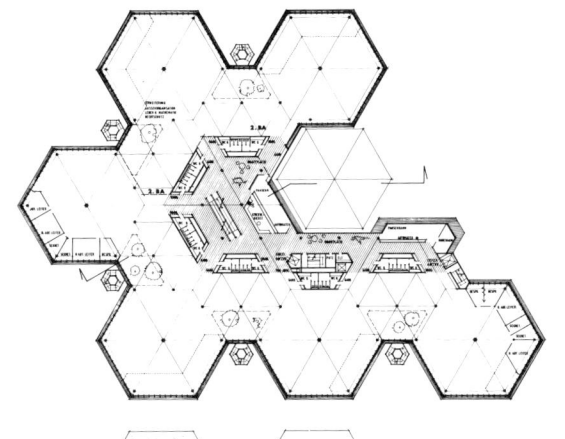

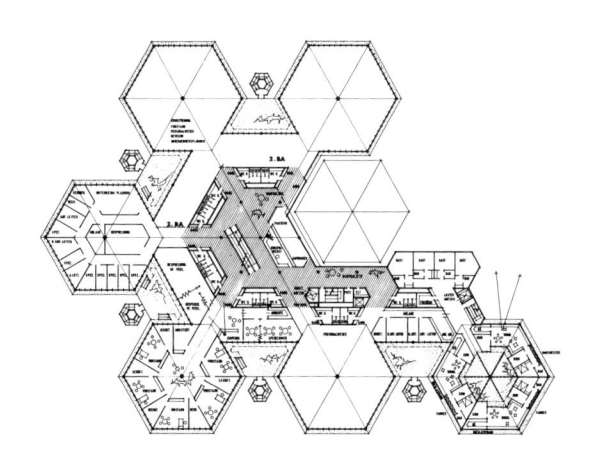

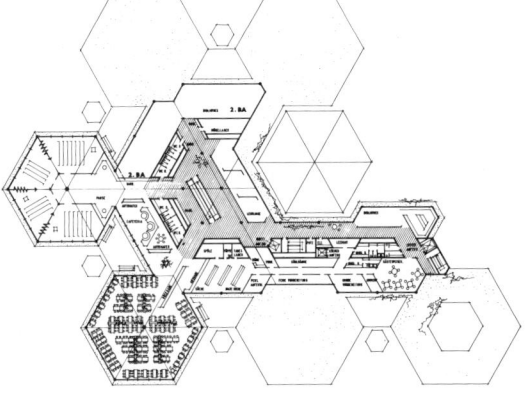

S. 146 Modell Wettbewerbsfassung
Alle Zeichnungen: Überarbeiteter Wettbewerbsentwurf
oben links Normalgeschoß überwiegend Großraumnutzung
oben Mitte Normalgeschoß überwiegend Zellenbüronutzung
links Dachgeschoß mit Schulungsräumen

P. 146 Model of competition entry
All drawings: Revised competition design
top left Typical floor, predominantly open-plan use
top middle Typical floor, predominantly single office use
left Attic storey with rooms for training

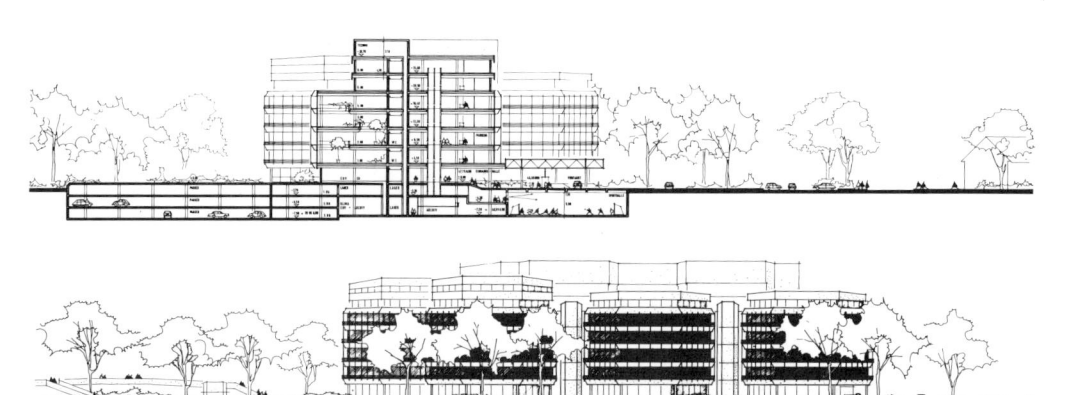

NORMALES GROSSRAUMBÜRO

WETTBEWERBSENTWURF

ÜBERARBEITUNG

147

Hauptverwaltung Thyssengas Duisburg-Hamborn

1. Rang im Entwurfsgutachten 1976. Zellenbürogebäude mit ca. 50 000 m³ umbautem Raum. Der Neubau enthält in den Obergeschossen in einer am Kern versetzten Zweibundanlage die Büroräume. Das Erdgeschoß nimmt in einem Breitfuß Sonderflächen (EDV, Kasino, Schulungs- und Konferenzräume) auf. Das Haus ist wegen der Nähe einer stark befahrenen Straße und der Emissionen der benachbarten Industrie vollklimatisiert. Fertigstellung 1980.

1st Place in design study competition, 1976. Building with individual office units and of approximately 50 000 m³ built volume. The new structure consists of offices on the upper floors in a two-bay layout astride the core. The ground floor contains special areas, (data processing, club rooms, training and conference rooms), in a broad plinth. Because of its proximity to a busy road and the emissions from neighbouring industrial plants, the building is fully air conditioned. Completed 1980.

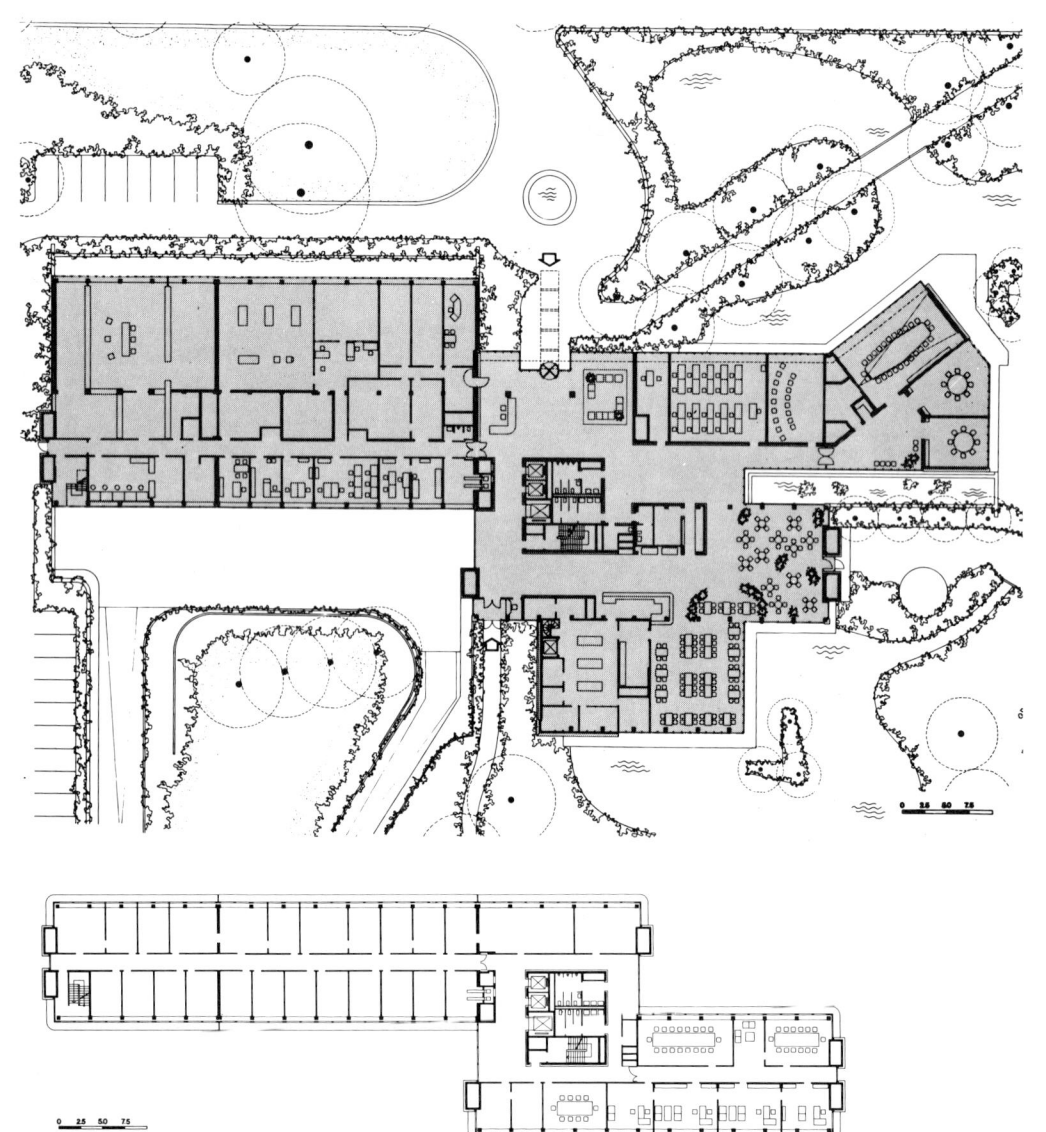

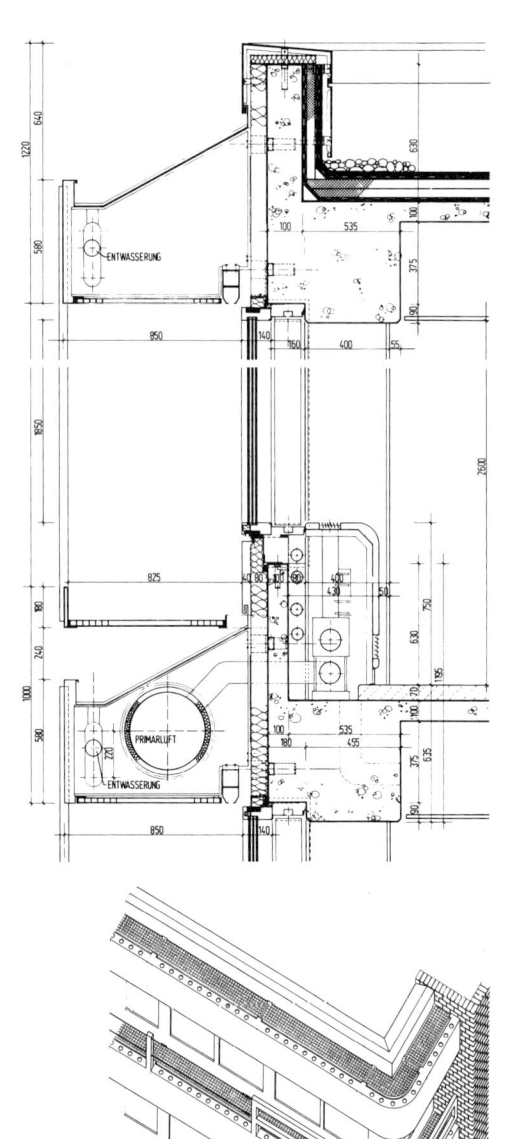

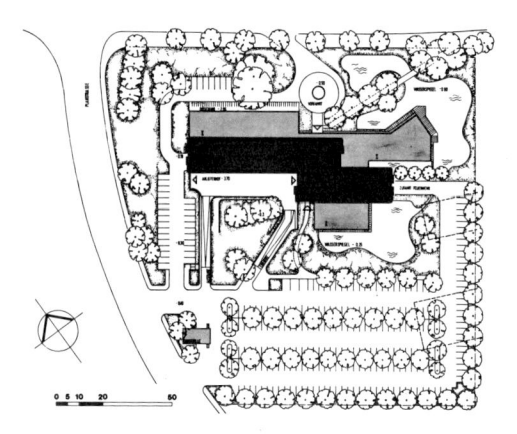

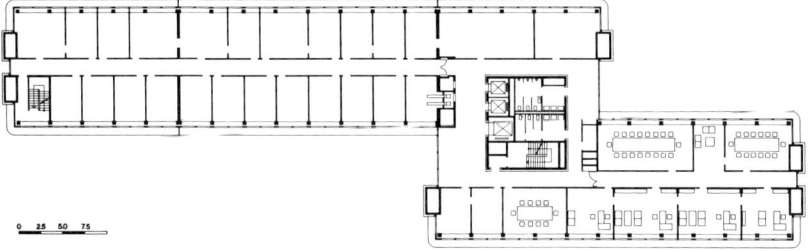

Um Gebäudehöhe zu sparen, wurden die horizontalen Klimakanäle innerhalb des Putzbalkons vor die Fassade gelegt, siehe Axonometrie rechts.

In order to restrict the height of the building, horizontal air conditioning ducts were laid within the service balconies in front of the façade, see axonometric right.

Der schöne alte Baumbestand wurde sorgfältig erhalten und durch Neupflanzungen ergänzt, die durchgehende Verglasung bezieht ihn in die Raumwirkung des Erdgeschosses ein.

The beautiful stock of mature trees on the site was carefully preserved and complemented with new plantings. The continuous strips of glazing allow them to be drawn into and become part of the spatial experience of the ground floor.

Die Gemeinschaftsräume im Erdgeschoß sind von Wasserflächen schützend umgeben.

The rooms for group use on the ground floor are protectively enclosed by areas of water.

Verwaltungszentrum eines Chemiekonzerns

Plangutachten 1975. Für insgesamt ca. 8000 Mitarbeiter wurde eine neutrale Baukörperform vorgeschlagen, die sowohl Zellenbüros wie Großräume und Gruppenräume aufzunehmen imstande ist. Damit wird ein in vielen Bauabschnitten homogener Gesamtkomplex erreicht.

Planning study, 1975. The proposal made was for a neutral building form to house some 8000 employees that would be capable of accommodating individual office cells, open-plan offices and group rooms. In this way a homogeneous building complex would be possible extending over a number of building stages.

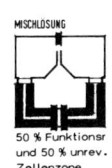

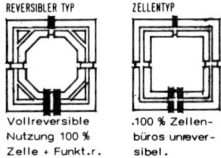

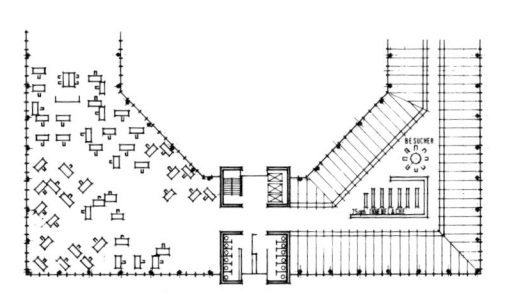

Erweiterung Hauptverwaltung Hamburg
Mannheimer Versicherung Hamburg

Wettbewerb 1978, 1. Preis. Großraumbürohaus, dessen zentrale Erschließung auch nach Erweiterung erhalten bleibt. Nicht ausgeführt, da ein anderes Grundstück für die Erweiterung später geeigneter erschien.

Competition, 1978; 1st prize. Open-plan office building, the central access of which is retained even after extensions. The scheme was not carried out, for at a later date a different site was held to be more suitable for the extension.

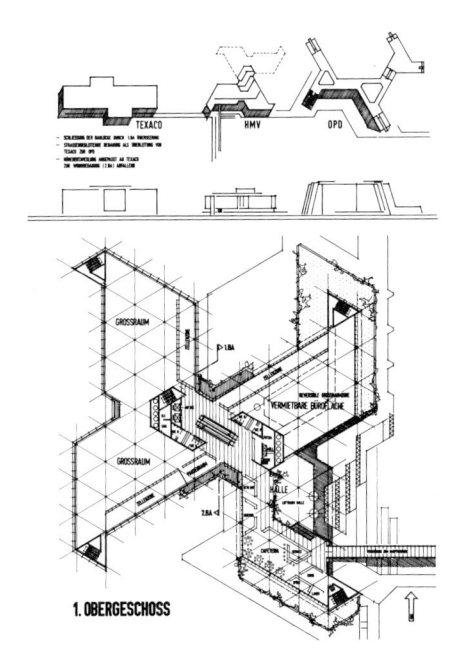

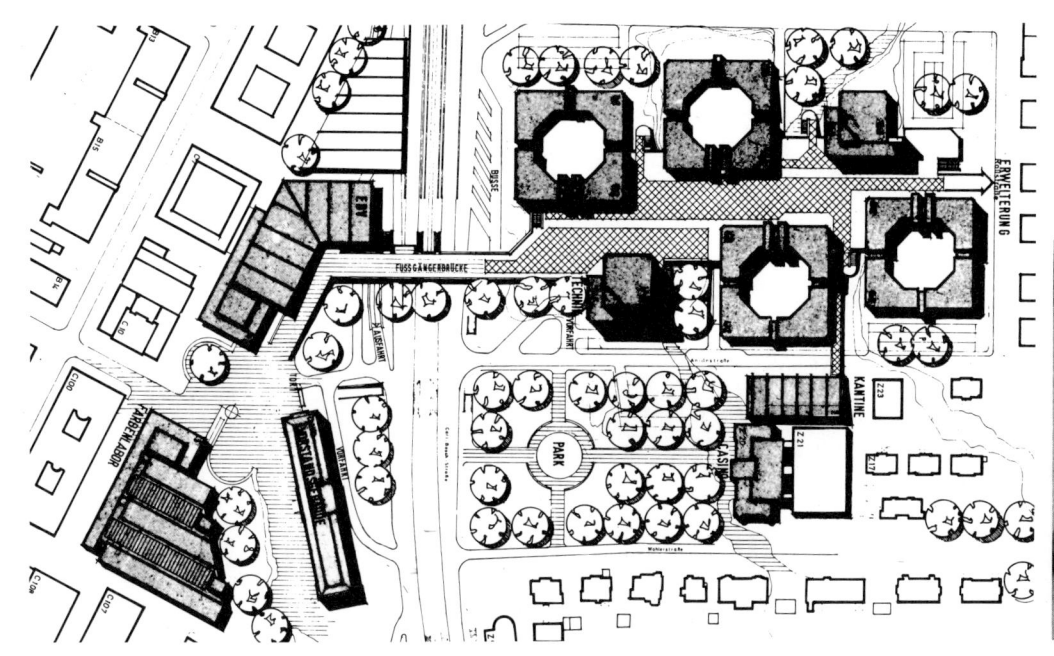

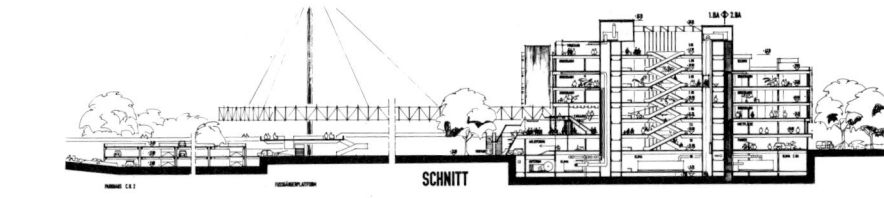

Ministry of Public Works and Housing
Riyadh Saudi-Arabien

1. Rang im Entwurfsgutachten 1977, nach drei verschiedenen Entwurfsphasen Ausführungsplanung bis 1980, Baubeginn Dezember 1982. Das Ministerium enthält ca. 3500 Arbeitsplätze in Zellen- und Gruppenbüros sowie Versammlungs-, Empfangs-, Speise- und Ausstellungsräume, einen Labortrakt und eine Cafeteria. Tiefgaragen und haustechnische Räume sind in zwei Sockelgeschossen untergebracht. Der Bürotrakt des Ministers liegt im Zentrum der fünf miteinander verbundenen Bürotürme (die auf sieben erweitert werden können), eine Konferenzhalle mit 500 Sitzplätzen flankiert den Eingang. Angleichung an örtliche Architekturtradition wurde nicht mit dekorativen Details, sondern durch tektonische Elementarformen versucht, die in dieser Region anzutreffen sind: Quadratgrundrisse, turmähnliche Baukörperform, stark geschlossene Außenwände, helles Material. Die oberen Gebäudeabschlüsse sollen entfernt an die Zinnenkränze der alten Paläste in Riyadh erinnern.

1st Place in a design study competition, 1977. Detail planning after three different phases of design, lasting until 1980, commencement of construction, December 1982. The ministry building contains working space for approx. 3500 persons in both individual cell form and group offices, in addition to assembly, reception and dining rooms, exhibition space, a laboratory tract and a cafeteria. Basement garages and rooms for internal services are contained in two plinth storeys. The minister's office tract is situated at the centre of the five interconnected office towers, (which can be extended to seven at number). A conference hall with seating for 500 persons flanks the entrance. Adoption of the local architectural tradition was not attempted in the form of decorative details, but by the use of the elemental tectonic forms that one finds in this region —, square shaped plans, tower-like structural forms, external walls with few openings, light-coloured materials. The upper edges of the building remind one vaguely of the crenellations of the old palaces of Riyadh.

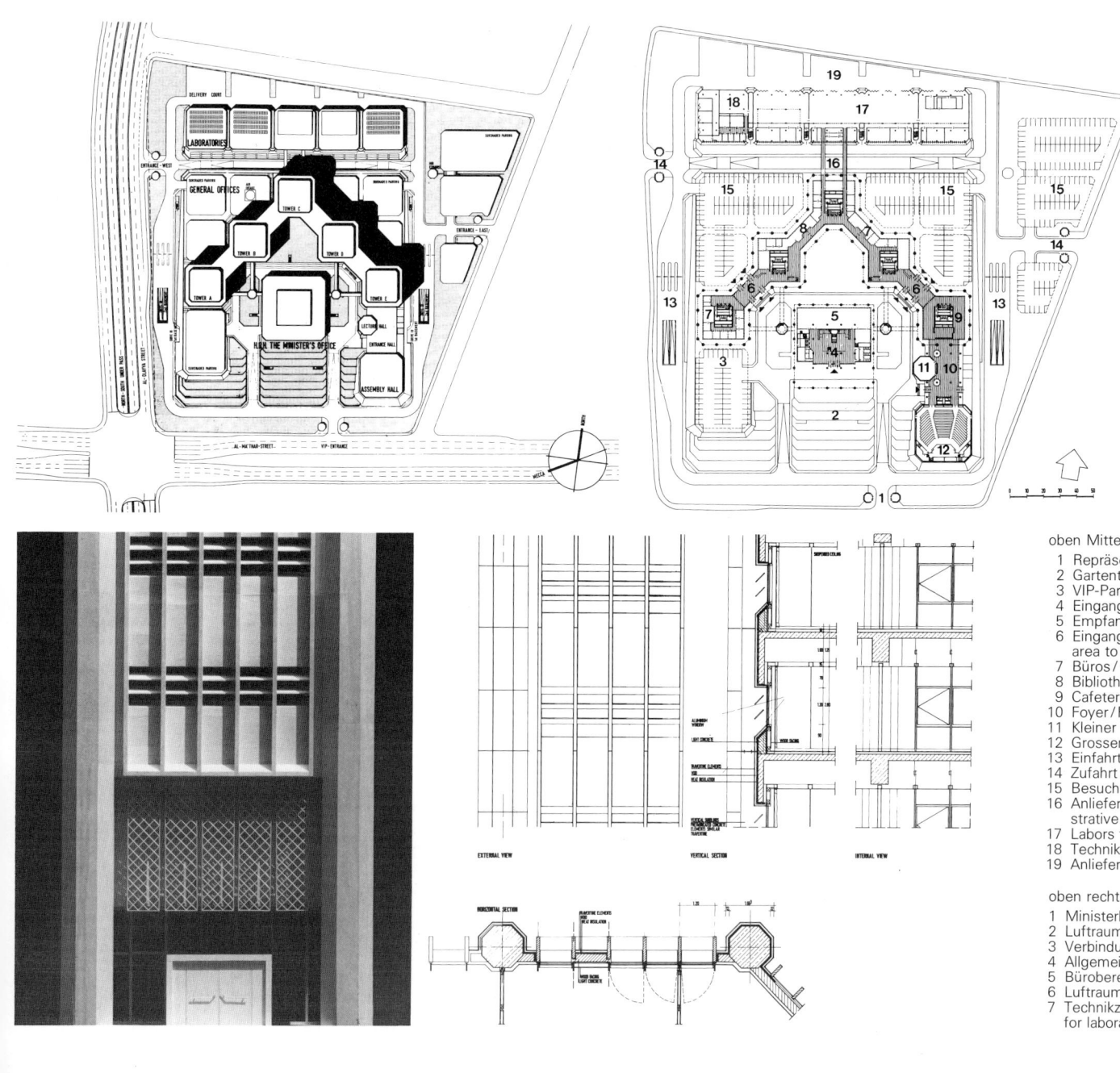

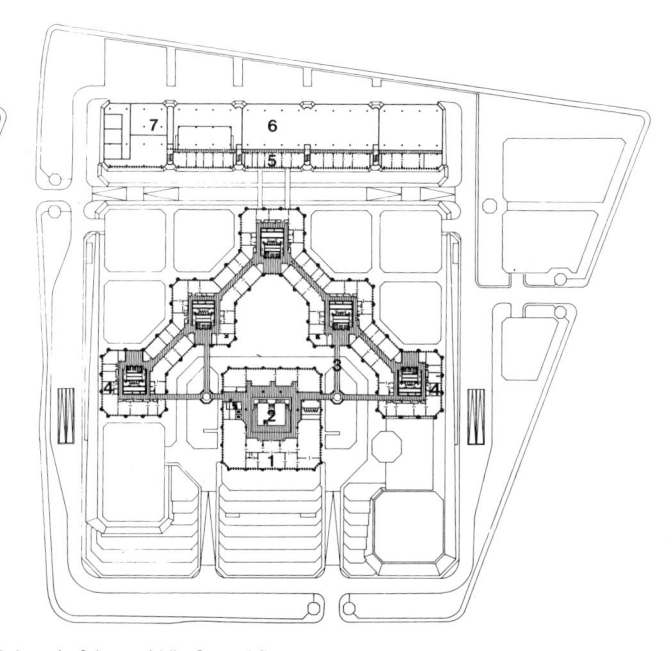

oben Mitte Erdgeschoß / top middle Ground floor
1 Repräsentative Zufahrt / Official drive
2 Gartenterrassen / Terraced gardens
3 VIP-Parkplätze / VIP parking
4 Eingangshalle Ministerbüro / Entrance hall to minister's office
5 Empfangs- + Speisesaal / Reception + dining hall
6 Eingangshalle und Ausstellungsbereich der Bürohochhäuser / Entrance hall and exhibition area to office towers
7 Büros / Offices
8 Bibliothek / Library
9 Cafeteria / Cafeteria
10 Foyer / Foyer
11 Kleiner Vortragssaal / Small lecture hall
12 Grosser Vortragssaal / Large lecture hall
13 Einfahrt Tiefgarage Verwaltung / Basement garage access for administration
14 Zufahrt für Mitarbeiter + Besucher / Access for staff + visitors
15 Besucherparkplätze / Visitors' parking
16 Anlieferung Verwaltungsgebäude + Einfahrt Tiefgarage Labors / Deliveries for administrative building + basement garage access for laboratories
17 Labors für Baustoffprüfung / Laboratories for testing building material
18 Technikzentrale Laborbereich / Mechanical services centre for laboratory area
19 Anlieferung Laborbereich / Deliveries for laboratory area

oben rechts 1. Obergeschoß / top right 1st Floor
1 Ministerbüro / Minister's office
2 Luftraum Eingangshalle / Void over entrance hall
3 Verbindungsgänge / Connecting corridors
4 Allgemeiner Bürobereich / General office area
5 Bürobereich Labors / Office area for laboratories
6 Luftraum Laborhallen / Void over laboratories
7 Technikzentrale Laborbereich / Mechanical services centre for laboratory area

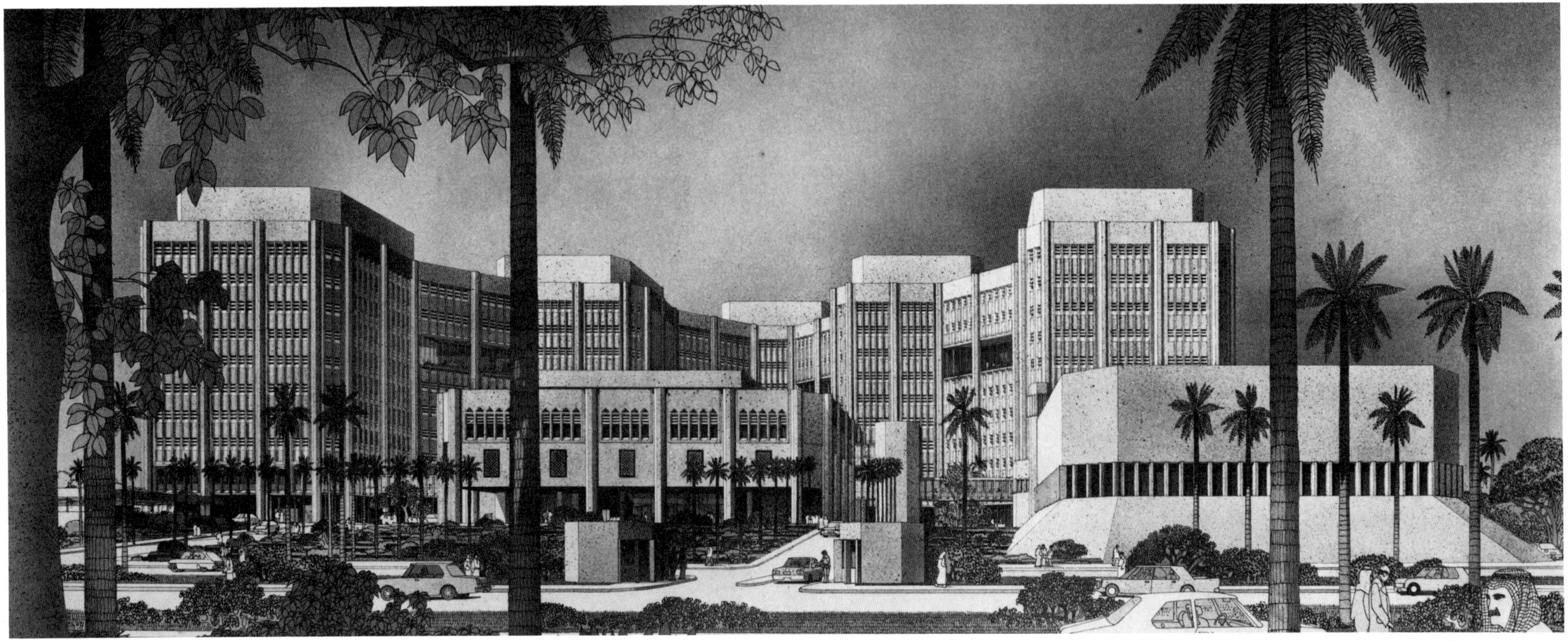

155

Verwaltungsgebäude GEW Köln

Wettbewerb 1976, 1. Preis
Fertigstellung 1980

Das Projekt ist ein Beispiel dafür, wie ein unter klaren Zielvorgaben des Auslobers entstandenes Wettbewerbsprojekt ohne wesentliche Veränderung gebaut werden konnte.

Das Verwaltungsgebäude der Gas- und Elektrizitätswerke der Stadt Köln ist Teil eines außerhalb der Innenstadt errichteten Betriebszentrums, das Werkstätten, Lager, Rechenzentrum und Verwaltung an einer Stelle zusammenfaßt. Wir erhielten den Auftrag nach beschränktem Wettbewerb.

Das Planungskonzept für das Verwaltungsgebäude wurde von zwei Zielvorstellungen des Bauherrn wesentlich bestimmt:
- gegliederte, kleinteilige Bürolandschaften mit humanen Arbeitsplätzen zu schaffen,
- für ein kommunales Versorgungsunternehmen ein Gebäude mit vorbildlicher Energieverwendung zu errichten.

Der Wunsch des Bauherrn nach gegliederten, kleinteiligen Bürolandschaften bestimmte die Grundidee der architektonischen Gestaltung, das Gebäude von einer Wabenstruktur von Achteck-Elementen mit je 200 m² zusammenzusetzen. Die in dem Flächenmuster entstehenden Quadrate wurden in den Bürogeschossen zu glasüberdachten Innenhallen ausgebaut, die auch den innengelegenen Gebäudebereichen Tageslicht verschaffen. Einblicke in andere Geschosse, individuelle Bepflanzungen, Wendeltreppen als Verbindung der Geschosse untereinander schaffen vielfältige Raumgliederungen. Mit dem Kölner Architektur-Preis 1980 und dem Mies-van-der-Rohe-Preis 1981 ausgezeichnet.

Competition entry 1976, 1st Prize
Completion 1980

This project is an example of how a competition entry, designed to a clear brief on the part of the clients, can be built without undergoing major changes.

This administrative building for the City of Cologne's gas and electricity works is part of a works centre built outside the inner city and integrating workshops, stores, data processing centre and administration in a single location. We received the commision following a limited competition.

The planning concept for this administrative building was largely determined by two requirements on the part of the client:
- the creation of small unit, articulated office landscapes with humane working conditions;
- the erection of a building with a model use of energy for a public utility organisation.

The client's wish for small size, articulated office landscapes determined the basic idea behind the architectural design, i.e. forming a building out of a honeycomb structure of octagonal elements, each 200 m² in area. The residual squares thus created in the pattern of the layout plan were developed into glass-roofed interior halls on the office storeys, bringing daylight into even the interior realms of the building. Views to other floors, individual planting arrangements and spiral staircases as connecting links between floors all serve to create a variety of spatial experiences. Awarded the Architectural-Prize of the City of Cologne in 1980 and the Mies van der Rohe Prize in 1981.

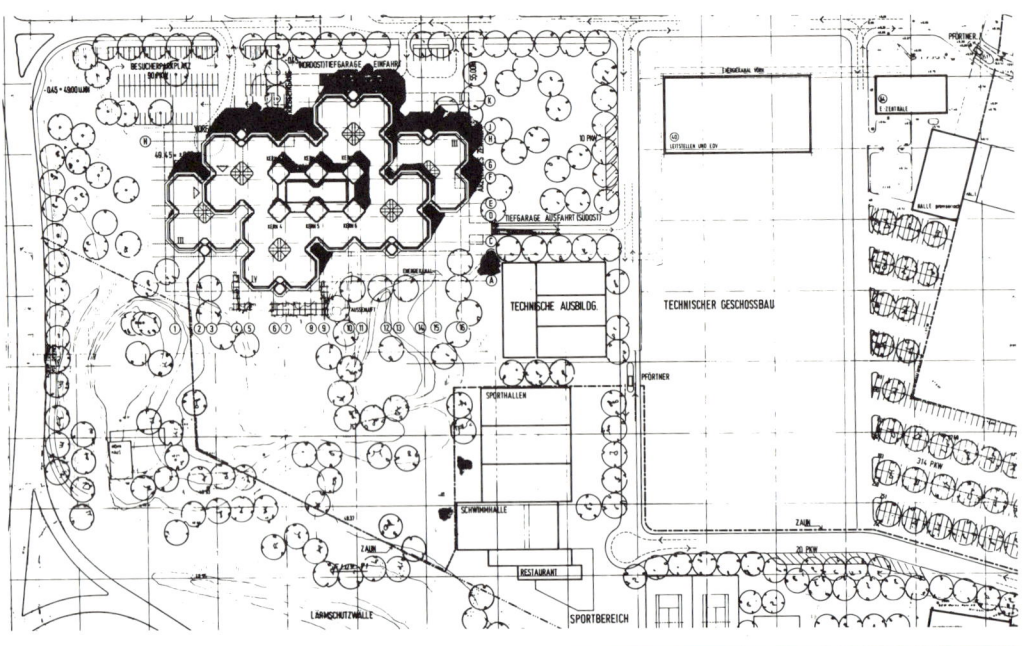

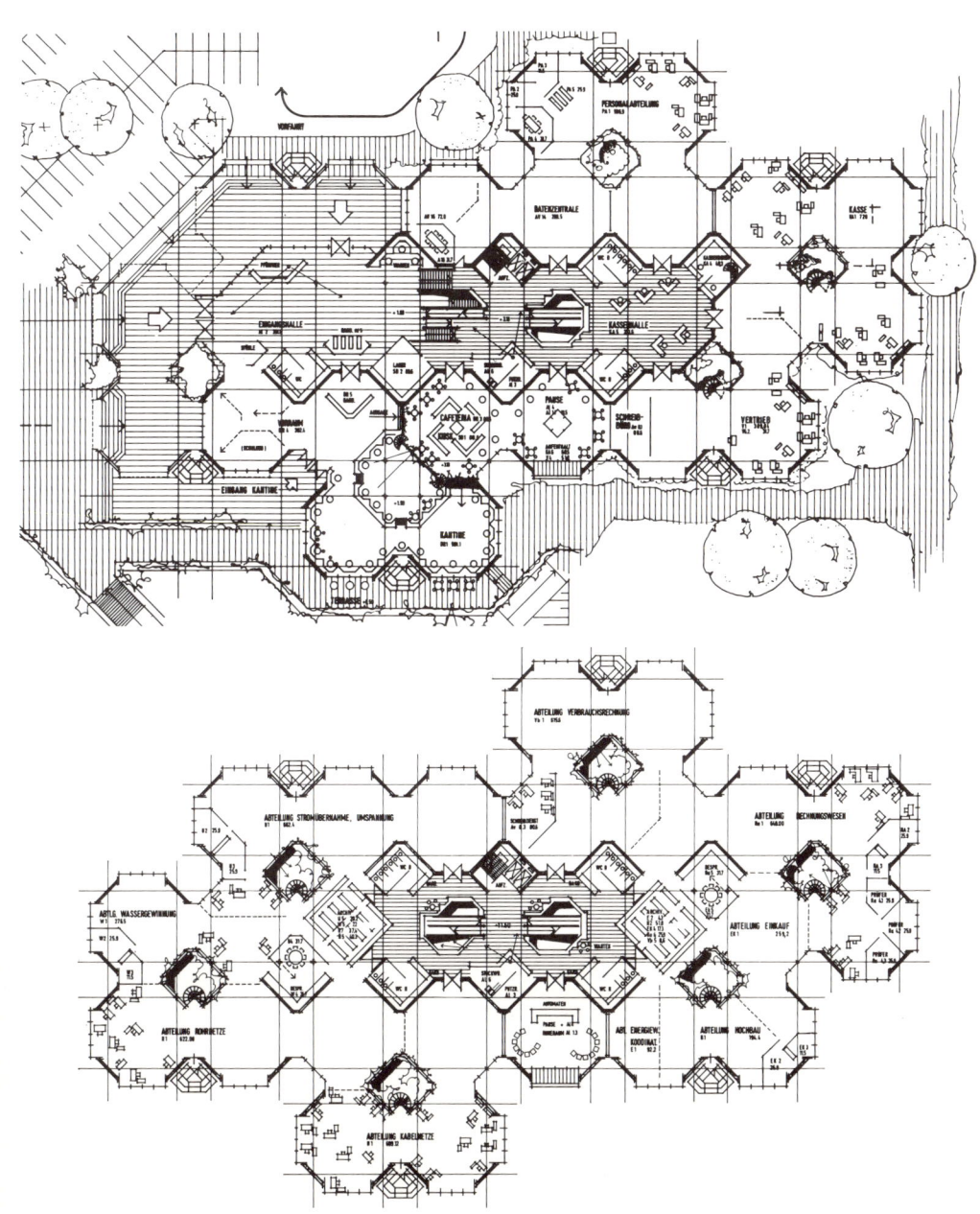

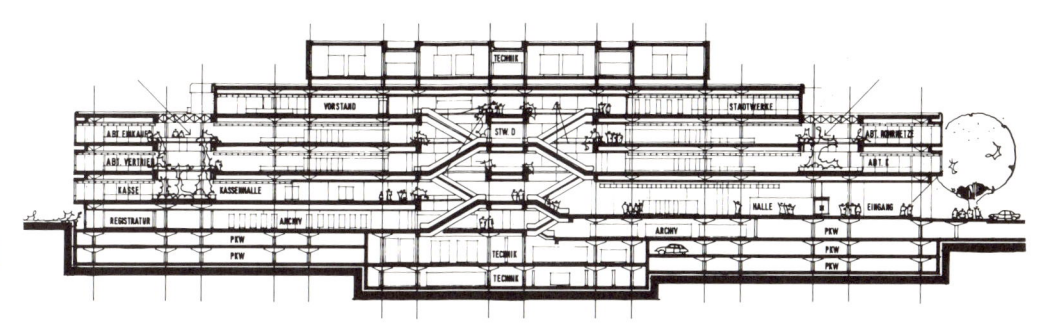

Wettbewerbsprojekt
Competition project

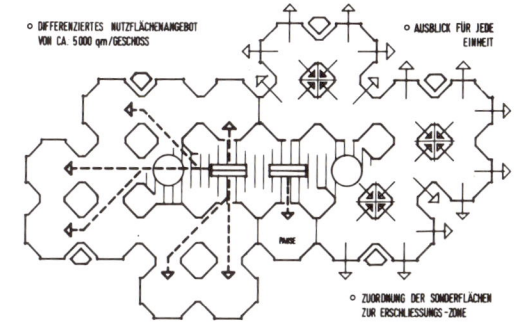

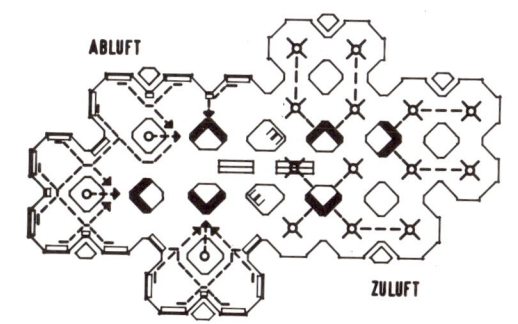

Nutzung / Function

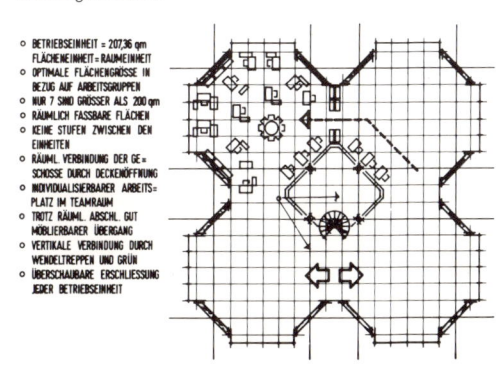

Technik / Services

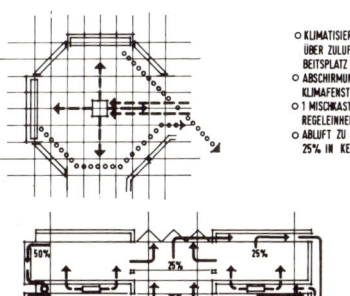

Betriebseinheit / Working unit

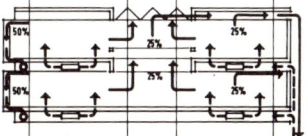

Betriebseinheit = Technische Versorgungseinheit /
Working unit = Services unit

157

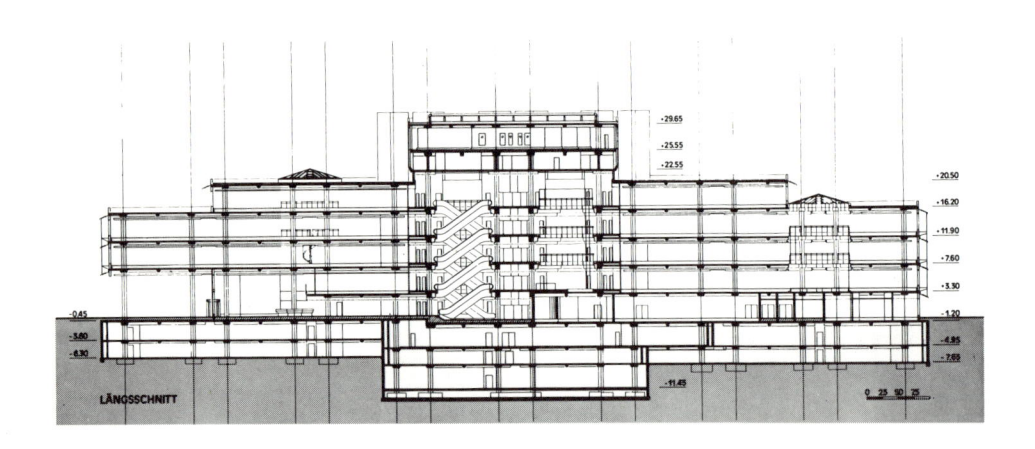

Ausgeführtes Projekt
Project as executed

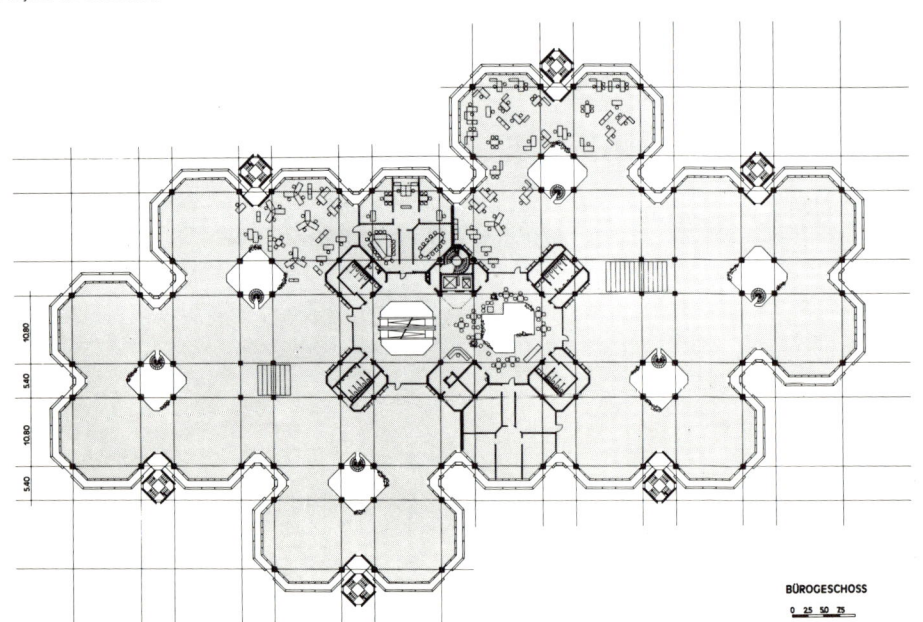

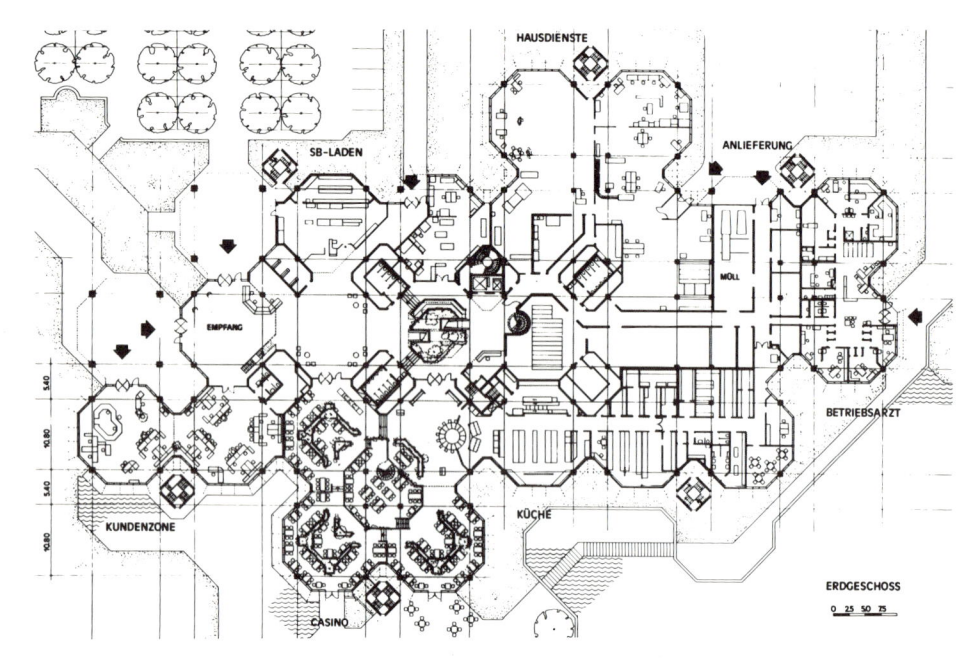

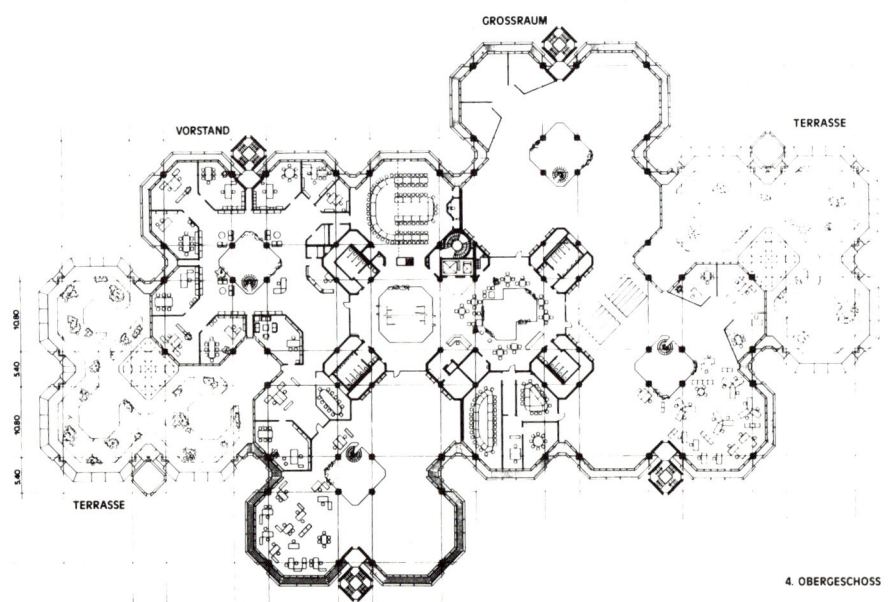

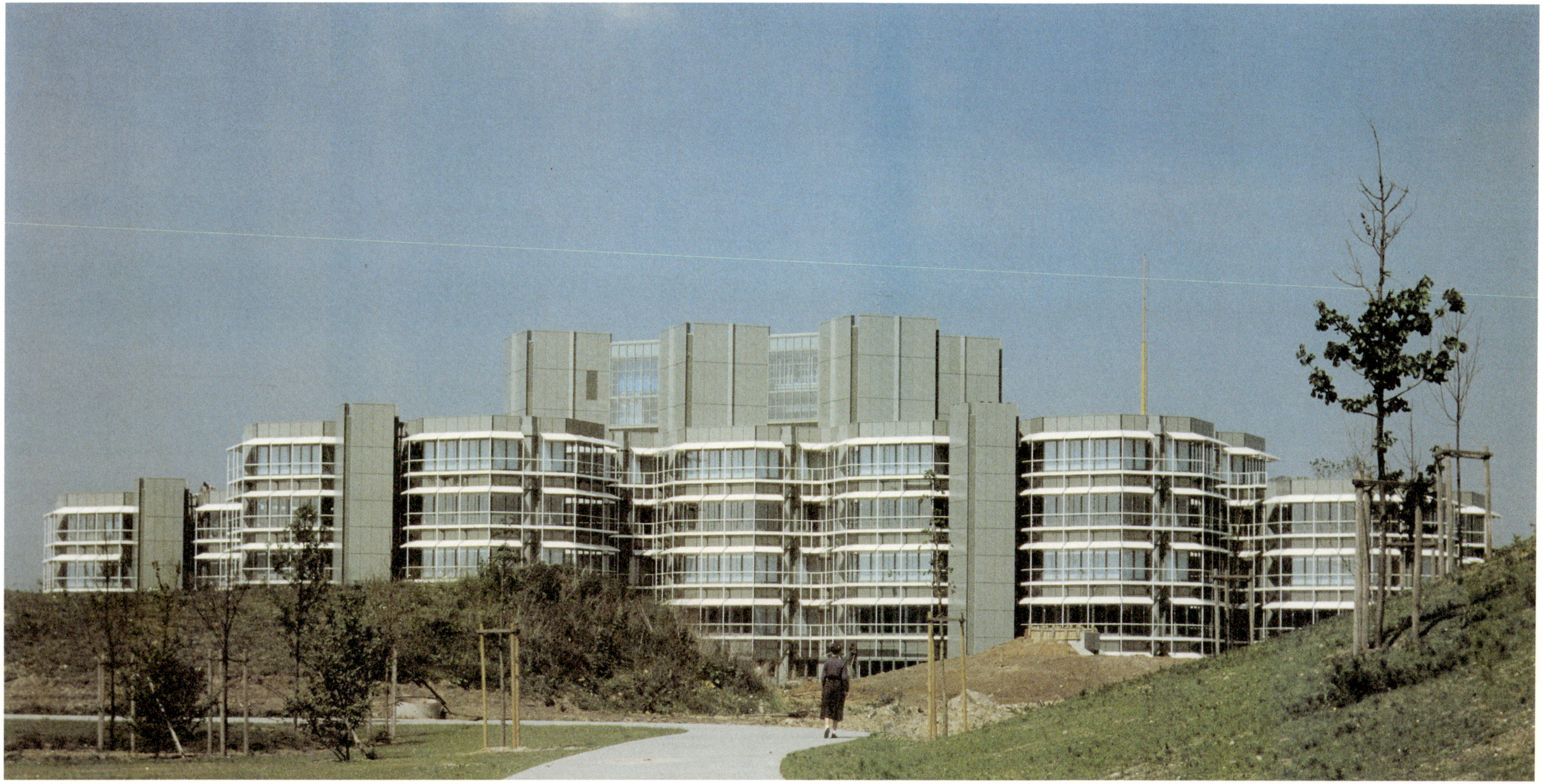

Fassade

Die Fassade ist als Abluftfassade ausgebildet, bei der im Luftraum zwischen äußerer Dreifachscheibe und innerer Scheibe Abluft von oben nach unten geführt wird. Der Wärmedämmwert der Fassade entspricht dadurch einer 36,5 cm starken Mauerwerkswand. Es war daher möglich, nahezu raumhoch zu verglasen, damit ein Maximum an Tageslicht in die Büroräume gelangen kann.

The façade

This is constructed to serve as an extract ventilation façade. Extracted air is conducted from top to bottom in the space between the external triple-layer skin and the inner skin. The thermal insulating value of the façade thus corresponds to a 36.5 cm thick brick wall. As a result of this, it was possible to have glazing virtually the full height of rooms and thus ensure a maximum level of daylighting in the office areas.

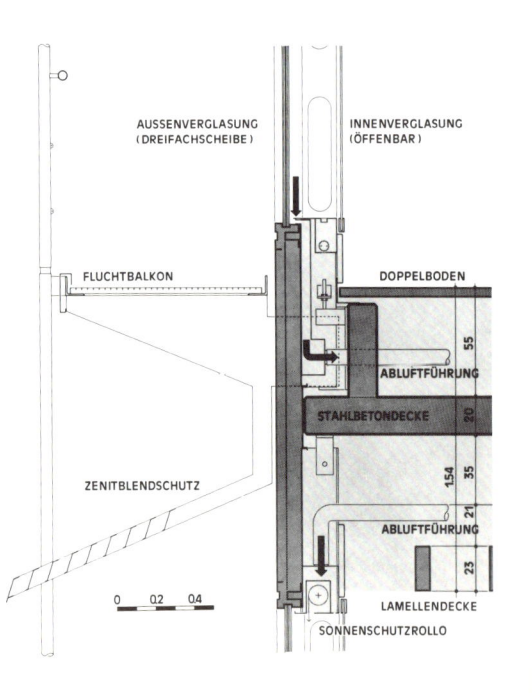

Energiesparende Maßnahmen im Konzept der Haustechnik

Um für die Klimatisierung und Beleuchtung ein energiesparendes und zugleich den individuellen Bedürfnissen der Mitarbeiter gerecht werdendes System zu finden, wurde eigens ein Technikwettbewerb durchgeführt.
Für die Klimatisierung wurde das System »unten-oben« gewählt, bei dem im Fußboden und am Schreibtisch die Luft eingebracht und an der Decke abgesaugt wird. Die Frischluft tritt dadurch im Aufenthaltsbereich ein; die Luftführung entspricht dem natürlichen Auftrieb bei Erwärmung der Luft.
Die Beleuchtung kommt mit einer installierten Leistung von nur 17 W/m² bei 1000 Lux am Arbeitsplatz aus, erzielt durch eine zweite Komponentenbeleuchtung aus Spiegelrasterdecken in der abgehängten Decke und abgependelten, individuell einschaltbaren Leuchten über dem Schreibtisch.
Damit wurden zwei wichtige Ergebnisse erzielt:
- Die Reduzierung der eingebauten Wärmelast und damit Verringerung der aufzuwendenden Kühlleistung,
- Verringerung des Stromverbrauches.

Darüber hinaus werden – tageslichtabhängig gesteuert – die zwei äußeren Beleuchtungsreihen bei genügender Helligkeit ausgeschaltet.

Measures to conserve energy in mechanical services

In order to find systems of air conditioning and lighting that would be both energy saving and also meet the needs of the individual employee, a special technical competition was held. For the air conditioning a »bottom to top« system was selected, whereby air is introduced at floor level next to desks and extracted via the ceiling. The fresh air supply is thus fed in at a level where people are working, and the direction of flow corresponds to the natural movement of air on being heated.
The lighting suffices with an installation capacity of only 17 W/m² providing 1000 lux at the working place. This is achieved by means of a second component light source from a mirror grid soffit in the suspended ceiling, plus hanging, individually controlled lamps over desks.
In this way two important things were achieved:
- the reduction of the level of in-built heat and thus the reduction of the cooling capacity required;
- reduction of electricity used.

In addition, the lighting is coupled to daylight conditions; the two outer rows of lighting are switched off when there is sufficient natural light.

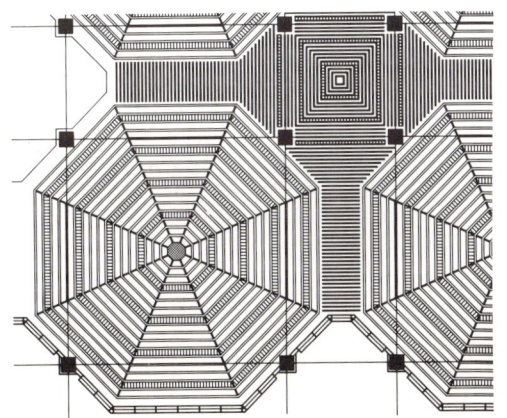

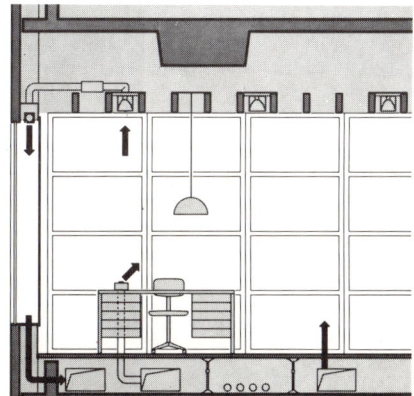

162

Über dem Bereich der Verkehrshallen und Kerne liegt die Lüftungszentrale für die Büroflächen (Abbildung S. 159). Den damit verhinderten Blick in den Himmel ersetzt ein Deckenbild von Sigi Zahn.

The ventilation plant serving the office areas is situated over the access halls and cores, (ill. p. 159). The view beyond to the sky, which is thus obscured, is replaced by a ceiling fresco by Sigi Zahn.

Arbeitsamt Hannover

Wegen seiner günstigen Lage am Rande des Stadtkerns am Leine-Bogen entschloß man sich, das 1950 gebaute und nicht mehr ausreichende Arbeitsamt zunächst durch Flügelbauten zu erweitern, dann auch den bestehenden Hauptbau neu zu gestalten.

Because of its advantageous position at the edge of the city centre on the bend of the River Leine, it was decided initially to extend the now inadequate employment exchange by adding two wings to the original building, erected in 1950. Subsequently it was decided to reorganize the existing main building as well.

links Ergeschoß / left Ground floor
1 Eingangshalle / Hall
2 Wartebereich / Waiting area
3 Antragsannahme / Applications
4 Aktenhaltung / Document storage
5 Vordrucklager / Printed forms store
6 Gruppenräume / Group rooms
7 Mediothek / Media centre
8 Einführungsbereich / Introductory area
9 Vortragssaal / Lecture hall
10 Innenhof / Courtyard

2–5 Leistungsabteilung / Payments + support department
6–9 Berufsinformationszentrum (BIZ) / Careers informations centre

rechts Obergeschoß / right Upper floor
1 Erhaltener Altbau / Existing building retained

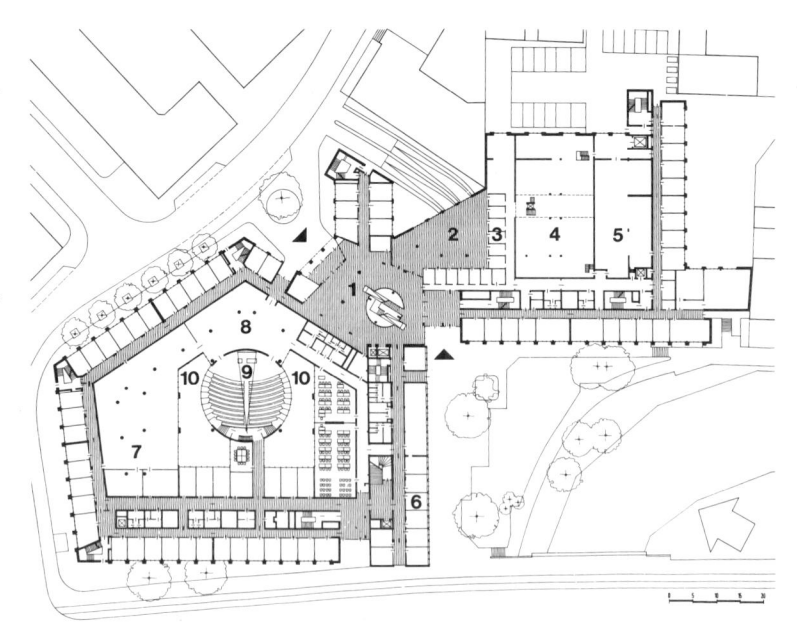

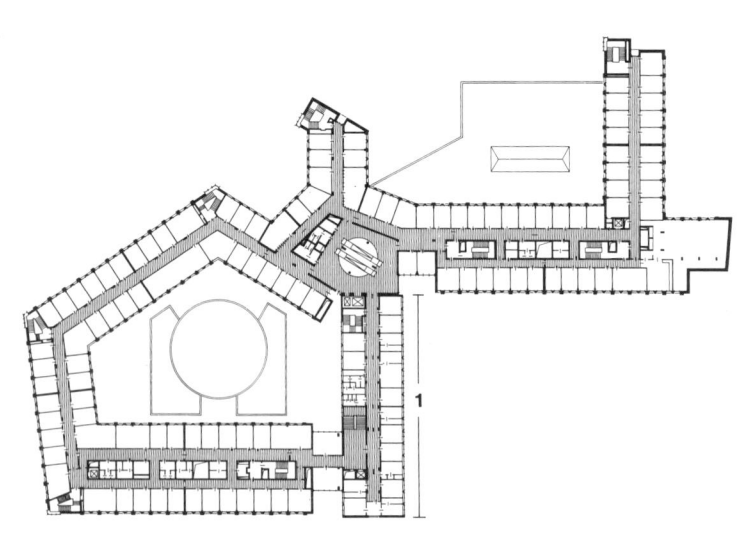

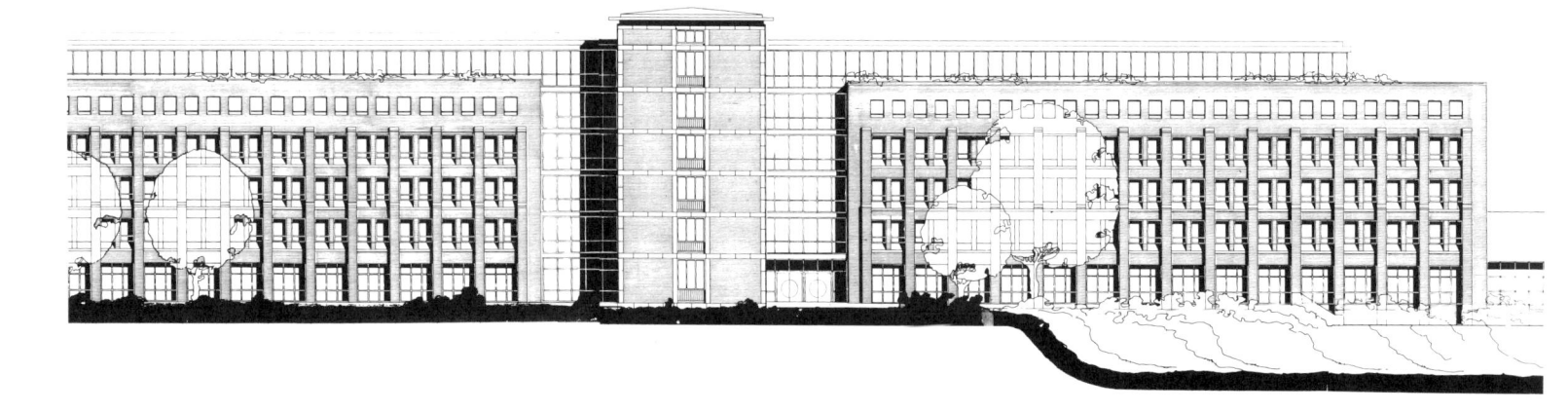

Hillmannkomplex Bremen

Gutachten 1979, 3. Rang. Mietbürohaus mit Läden und Restaurants im Unter-, Erd- und 1. Obergeschoß. Eine diagonale Passage folgt dem zu erwartenden Fußgängerstrom; sie führt durch eine mehrgeschossige Innenhalle. Die Fassadenausbildung nimmt tektonische Charakteristika der Erscheinung des an gleicher Stelle im Kriege zerstörten, Hotels »Hillmann« auf.

Study, 1979; 3rd place. Block of rented offices with shops and restaurants on basement, ground and first floors. A diagonal arcade follows the line of the expected flow of pedestrian traffic. It leads through an internal hall that rises over several storeys. The façade construction adopts certain of the architectural features that once characterized the Hillmann Hotel, which stood on the same spot and was destroyed in the war.

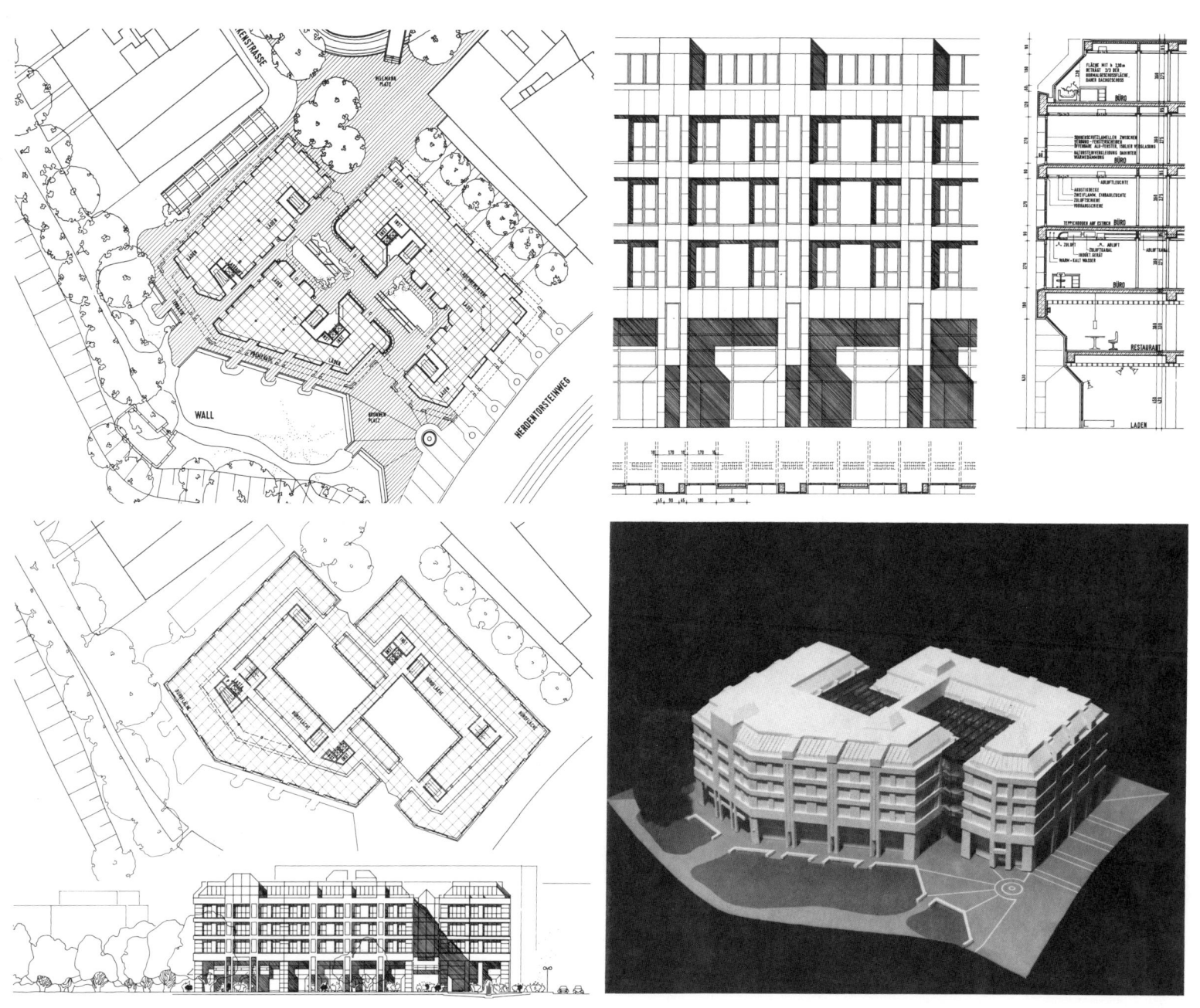

Hauptverwaltung Veba Oel AG Gelsenkirchen

Baubeginn 1981. Zusammen mit Dipl.-Ing. Stjepan Çadéz. Hauptverwaltung für ca. 1100 Mitarbeiter, erweiterungsfähig um weitere 200 Arbeitsplätze, in Zellenbüroweise mit umfangreichen Sonderflächen für Vorstand, EDV, Schulung, Konferenz, Kasino, Gästespeiseräume, Hausdienste. Die flache, weitläufige Anlage nimmt die Entwicklungsmöglichkeiten des sehr großen Grundstücks wahr. Die damit mögliche Fensterlüftung bedingte Lärmschutzwälle zu den umgebenden stark befahrenen Straßen, die eine willkommene Möglichkeit zur Verzahnung des Bauwerks mit seiner plastischen Landschaftsumgebung bot. Die äußere Erschließung wird durch die Baumpflanzungen sinnfällig unterstrichen. Im Inneren sind die drei viergeschossigen Bürowaben durch eine großzügige Verkehrsspange mit den Sonderräumen im klimatisierten Kopfbau auf kurzen, räumlich reizvollen Wegen mit Einblicken in die unterschiedlich gestalteten Gartenhöfe verbunden. In Zusammenarbeit mit Gartenarchitekten, bildenden Künstlern und dem Lichtplaner wurde die Integration von Bauwerk, Gartenplanung, Belichtung, Beleuchtung, Kunst und Leitsystem versucht.

Commencement of construction, 1981. In collaboration with Dipl.-Ing. Stjepan Çadéz. Administrative headquarters with space for approx. 1100 employees. Can be extended to accommodate an additional 200 work places. Individual office cells with extensive areas for special uses for the executive board, data processing, training, conferences, club rooms, guest dining rooms, and internal services. This low-rise, extensive complex takes advantage of the development potential of a very large site area. The window ventilation that thus became possible necessitated the building of embankments to screen off the noise from the busy surrounding roads; these acoustic screens in turn provided a welcome opportunity of interlocking the building with the bold relief of the surrounding landscape. The external access is clearly underlined by the tree planting. Internally, a spacious communications strip links the three 4-storey office honeycombs to the areas for special uses in the air conditioned head building along short, spatially attractive routes that afford views into garden courtyards of different design. In collaboration with landscape architects, artists and lighting experts, an attempt was made to integrate building structure, garden planning, daylighting and artificial lighting, art and communications systems.

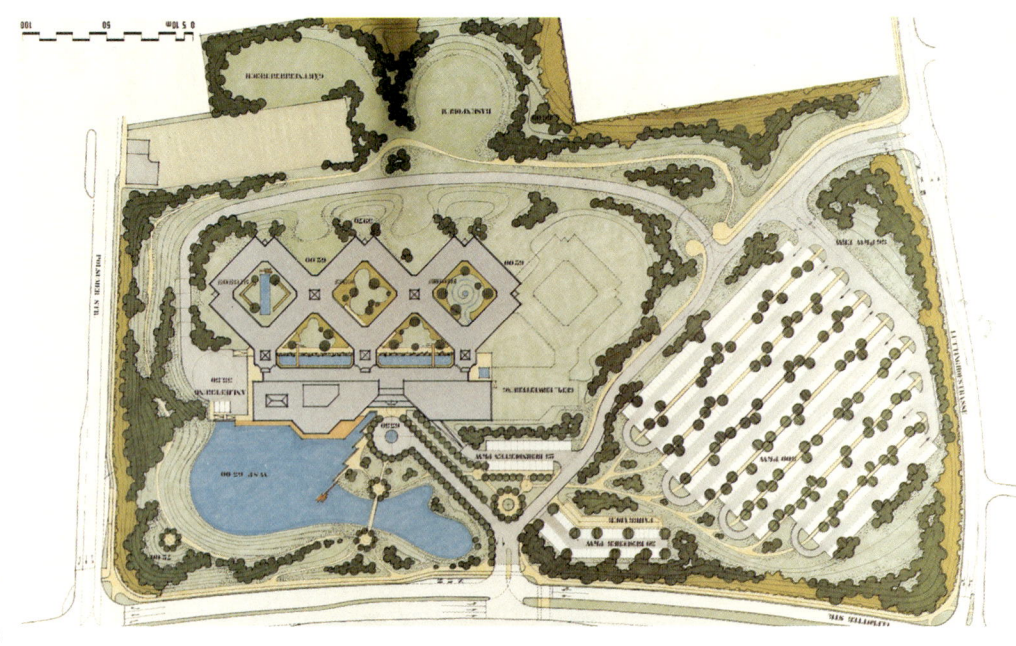

Erdgeschoß / Ground floor

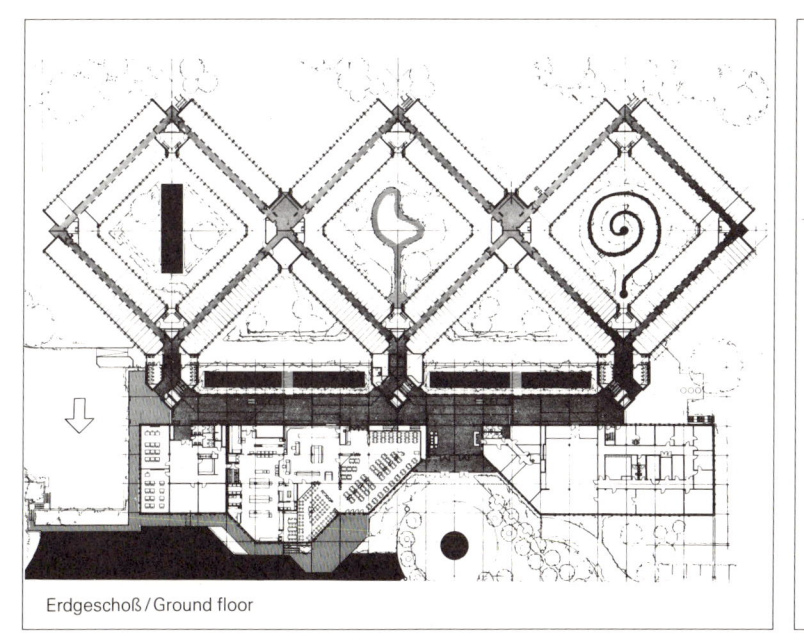

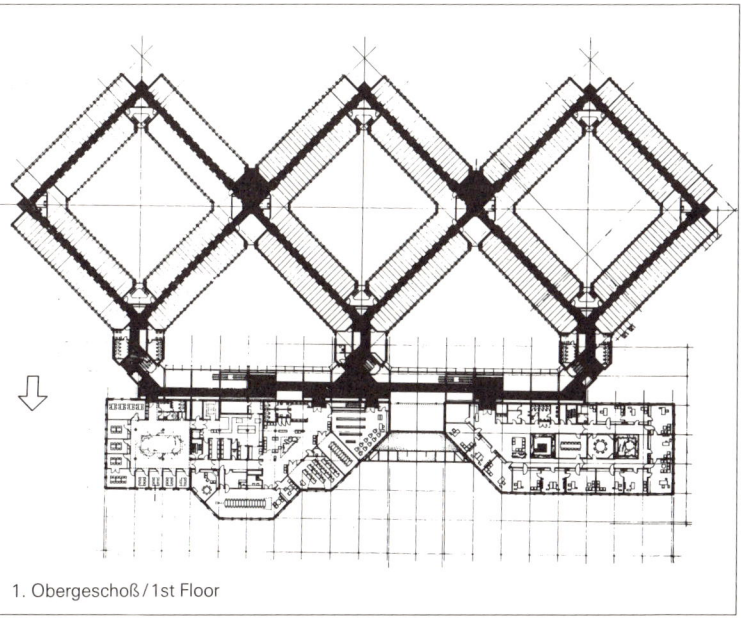

1. Obergeschoß / 1st Floor

Die Materialwahl für die Fassade beschränkt sich auf ortsübliche Klinker aus Gründen der Einheitlichkeit und Durabilität, kombiniert mit einer Stahlkonstruktion für die Verkehrsspange und einbrennlackierten Leichtmetallfenstern.

The selection of materials for the façade is limited to local bricks, chosen for reasons of unity and durability, combined with a steel construction for the communication strip and stove-enamelled aluminium windows.

168

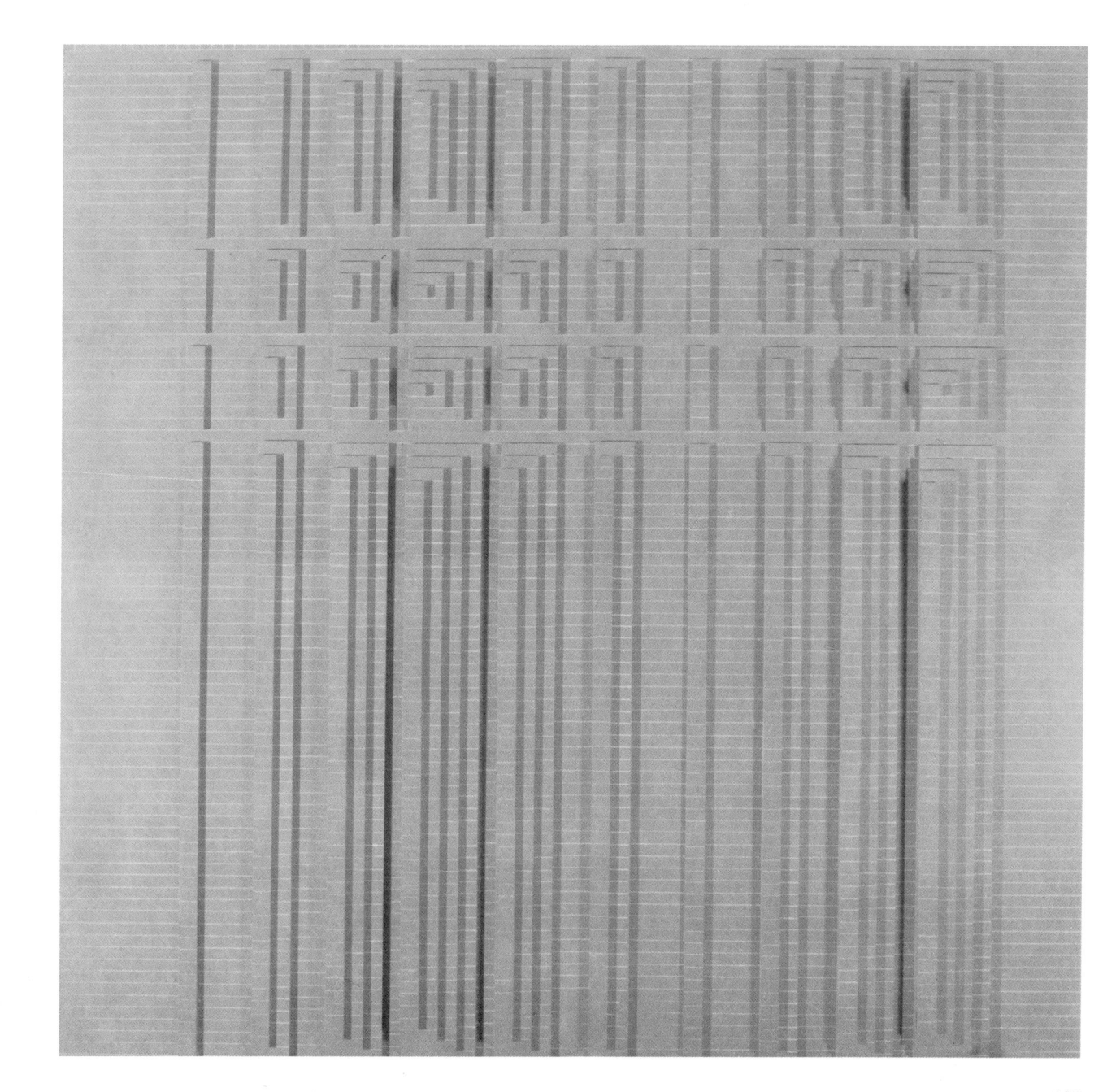

In der Verkehrsspange zwischen den Normalbüros und den Sonderräumen sorgt ein graphisches Informations- und Leitsystem von Kriwet für einfache Orientierung. Die Backsteinwände werden von Prof. Boehm künstlerisch gestaltet.

In the communications link between the standard offices and the areas for special uses a graphic information and directional system by Kriwet provides simple orientation. The artistic treatment of the brick walls is by Prof. Boehm.

VW Wolfsburg

Wettbewerb 1980, 4. Preis. Verwaltungskomplex außerhalb des Werksgeländes für ca. 2600 Mitarbeiter in vier Bauabschnitten. Die Anordnung der reversiblen Zellen- und Gruppenbüros in, durch eine Verkehrsspange verbundenen, Baukörpereinheiten verdeutlicht die Baustufen.

Competition, 1980; 4th prize. Administrative complex outside the actual works for approx. 2600 employees in four building stages. The distribution of the reversible cell-type and group offices over the individual built volumes, linked together by a communications strip, illustrates the actual phases of building.

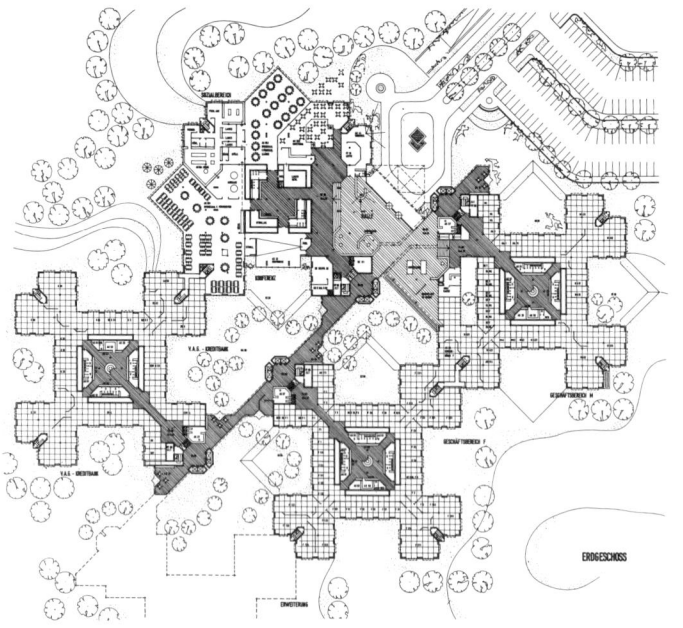

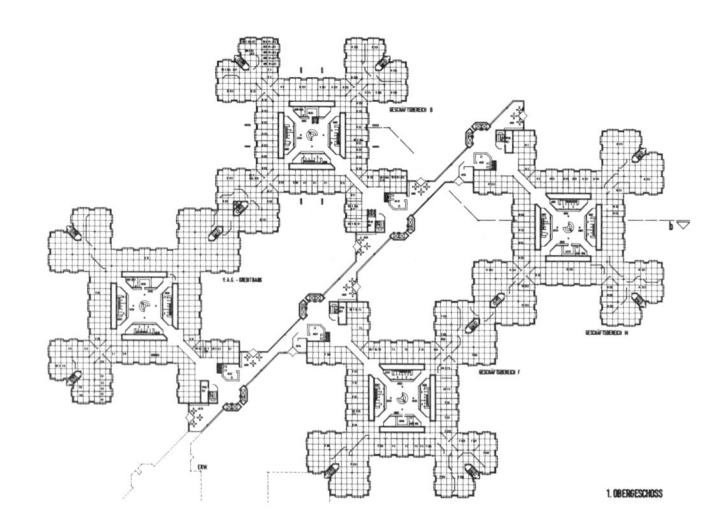

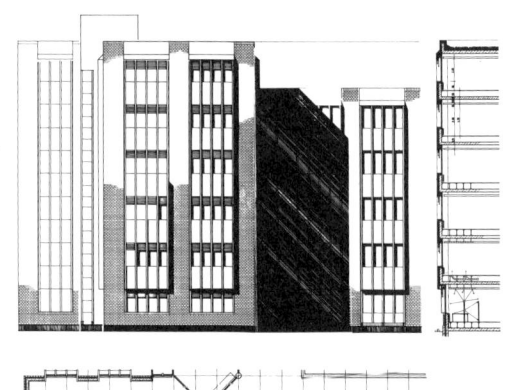

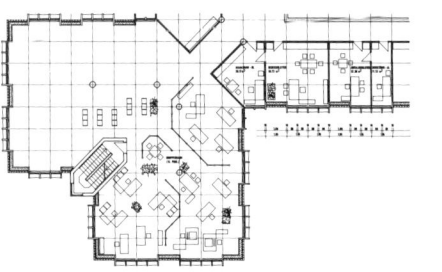

Municipality Abu Dhabi

4. Preis im internationalen Wettbewerb 1979, bearbeitet mit Dr. Walter Overseas, einem Zusammenschluß mit zwei Ingenieurbüros. Die Zellenbüros und Sonderräume der Stadtverwaltung von Abu Dhabi umgeben einen allseits zugänglichen Platz, der von einem riesigen Schattendach überspannt ist.

4th Prize in an international competition, 1979, developed through the firm Dr. Walter Overseas, an amalgamation with two engineering offices. The individual office cells and rooms for special uses in this building surround an open space that is accessible from all sides and that is spanned by an enormous roof shade.

Kreishaus Hofheim

Wettbewerb 1980, Ankauf. Die Baukörpergruppierung folgt aus der Erschließungssituation und der Ausrichtung der Hauptmenge der Arbeitsplätze zum schönen Ausblick nach Süden.

Competition entry, 1980, which won a purchase award. The grouping of the elements of the building for the district offices, Hofheim, resulted from the access situation and the orientation of the majority of working places towards the attractive aspect to the south.

Bundespostministerium Bonn

Wettbewerb 1981. Die Baukörperanordnung folgt aus der Funktion (verschiedene Sicherheitsstufen) und den städtebaulichen Gegebenheiten. Sie modifiziert das Anordnungssystem des benachbarten Ministeriums.

Competition, 1981. The layout of this building for the Federal Ministry of Post and Telecommunications is an expression of functions, (different levels of security), and the urban context. It represents a modification of the layout system of the neighbouring ministry.

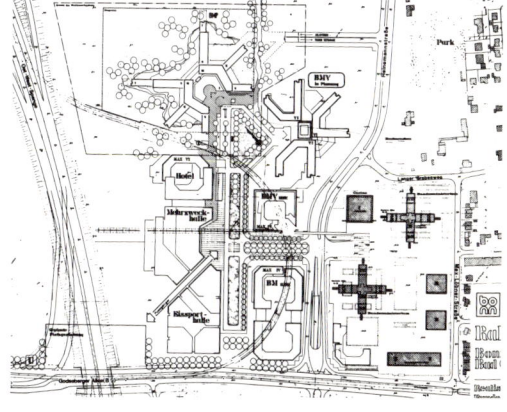

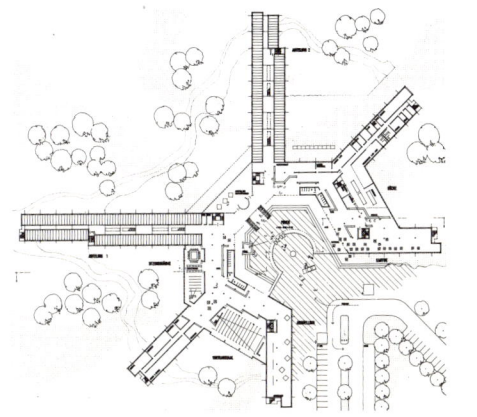

Arbeitsamt Bochum

1. Preis im Wettbewerb 1980 mit bauform, Köln. Vier um einen Innenhof angeordnete Baukörper beinhalten jeweils Bereiche unterschiedlicher Funktionen. Die Erschließung erfolgt über eine zentrale Verteilerhalle im Erdgeschoß zu dem Vertikalkern jedes Traktes. Sondernutzungszonen sind nahe dem Haupteingang angeordnet und durch besondere baukörperliche Ausformung betont. Das Gebäude erhält eine Ziegelsichtmauerwerk-Verkleidung. Fertigstellung 1984.

1st Prize in a competition for the Employment Exchange, Bochum, 1980, in conjunction with bauform, Cologne. Each of the four building structures grouped about an internal courtyard contains different functional realms. Access is via a central distributing hall on the ground floor, linked to the vertical core of each tract. Zones for special uses are situated near to the main entrance and are emphasized by the special design of the built form. The outer skin of the building is of facing bricks. Completion date, 1984.

Erdgeschoß / Ground floor
1 Eingangsbereich / Entrance area
2 Innenhof / Courtyard
3 Wartebereich / Waiting area
4 Antragsannahme / Applications
5 Aktenhaltung / Document storage
6 Bibliothek + Mediothek / Library + media centre
7 Eingangsbereich BIZ / Entrance area
8 Gruppenräume / Group rooms

3 –5 Leistungsabteilung / Payments + support department
6 –8 Berufsinformationszentrum (BIZ) / Careers information centre

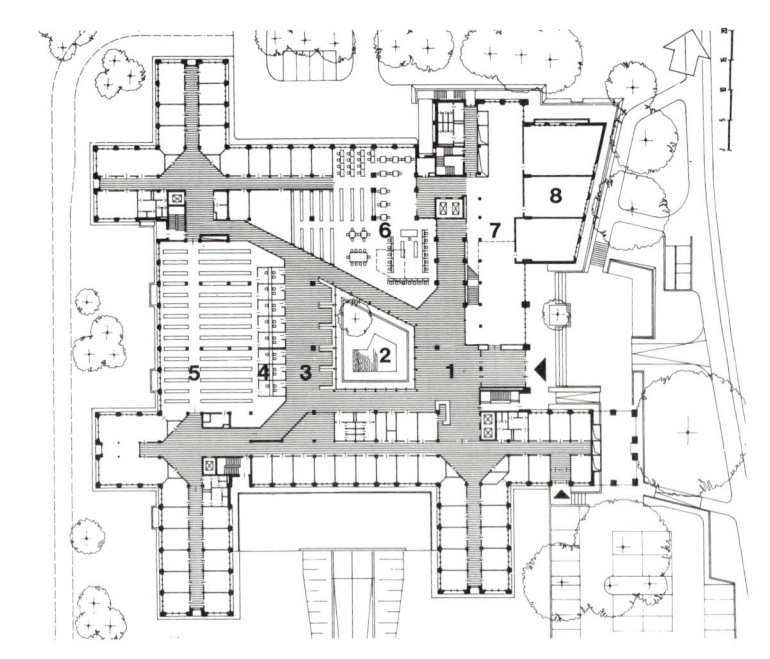

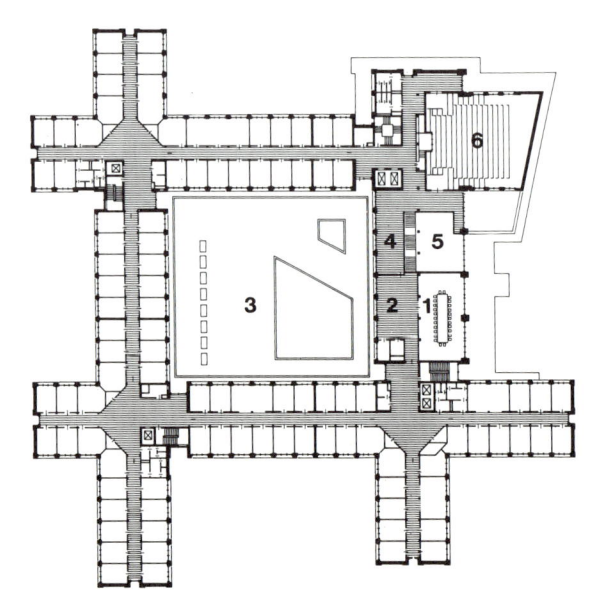

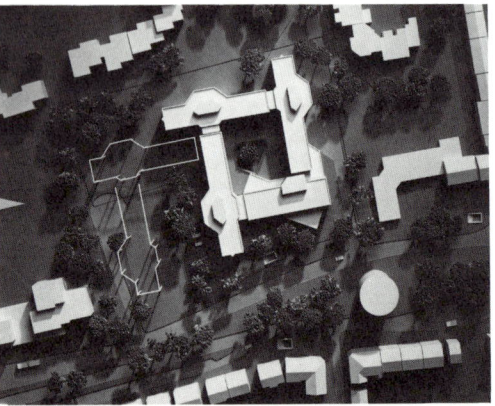

1. Obergeschoß / 1st Floor
1 Sitzungssaal / Conference room
2 Foyer / Foyer
3 Begrünte Dachflächen / Planted roof areas
4 Garderobe / Cloakroom
5 Luftraum Eingangsbereich BIZ / Void over entrance
6 Großer Hörsaal / Large lecture hall

4 –6 Bildungsinformationszentrum (BIZ) / Careers information centre

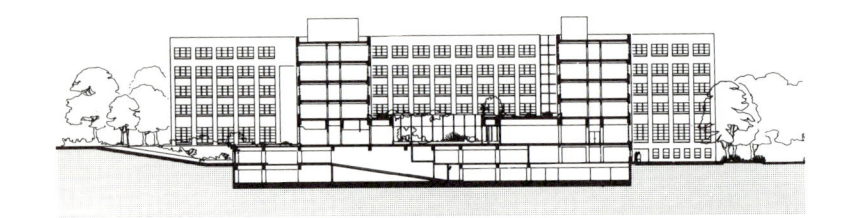

173

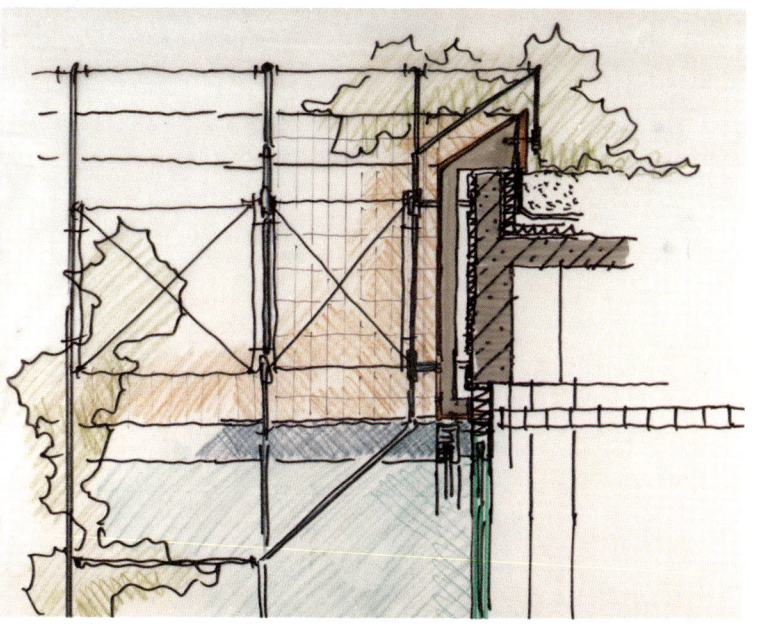

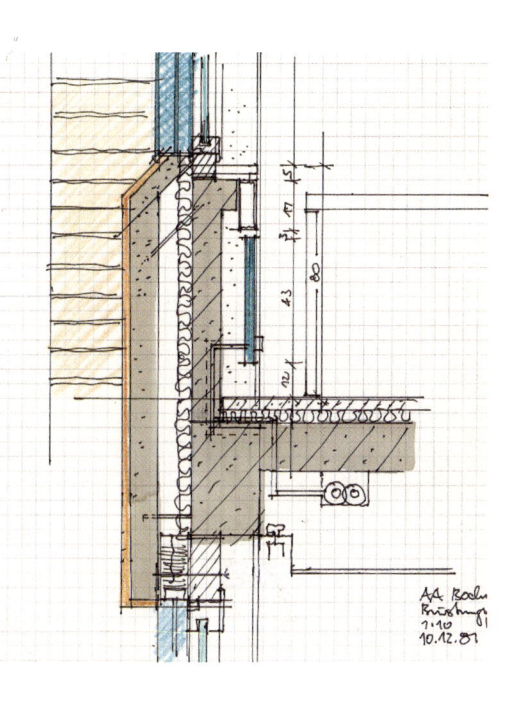

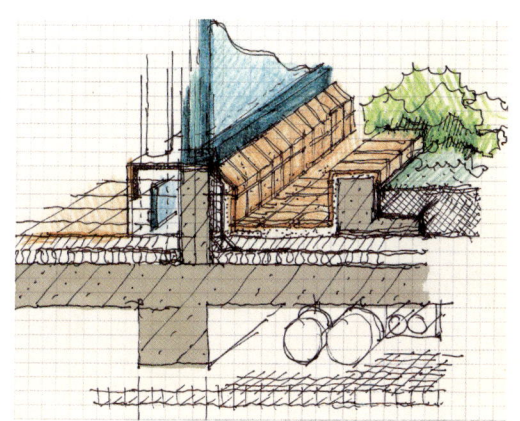

Rathaus Oldenburg

Wettbewerb 1981. Versuch, mit der Anordnung und Gliederung der großen Baumasse die städtebaulichen Bezüge sinnfällig deutlich zu machen.

Competition 1981. An attempt to make urban relationships transparent through the disposition and articulation of the large building volume of the Oldenburg town hall.

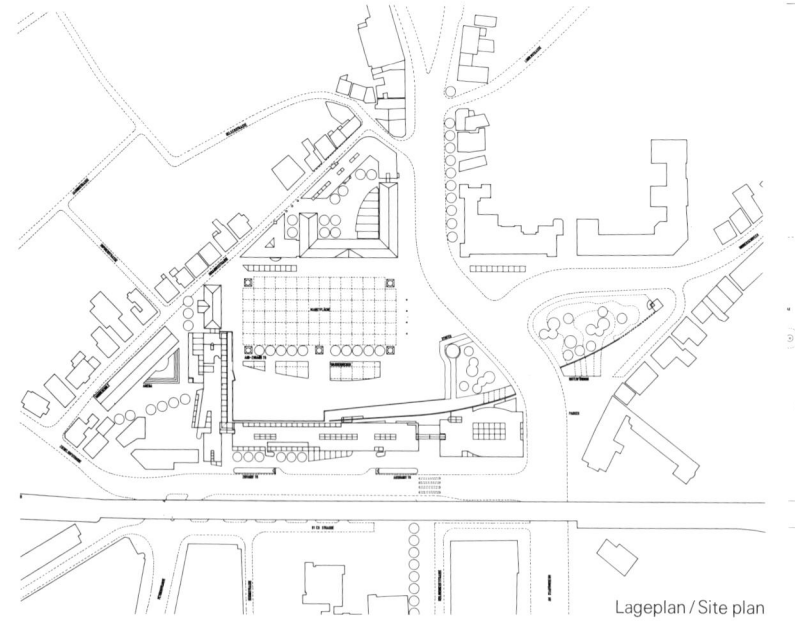

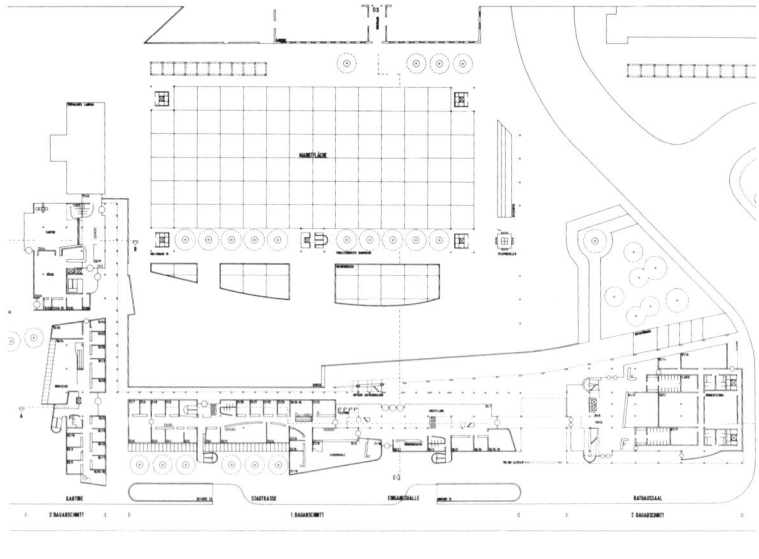

Lageplan / Site plan

oben Erdgeschoß / top Ground floor
unten 2. Obergeschoß / bottom 2nd Floor

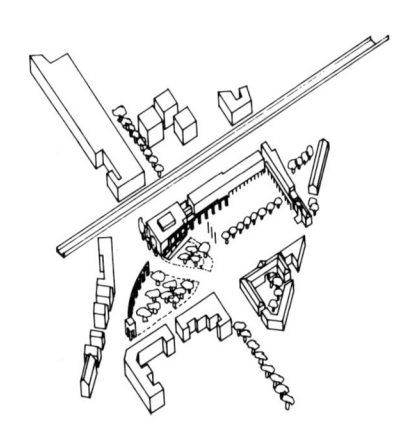

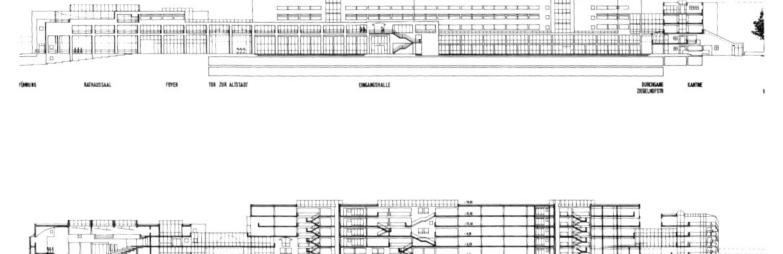

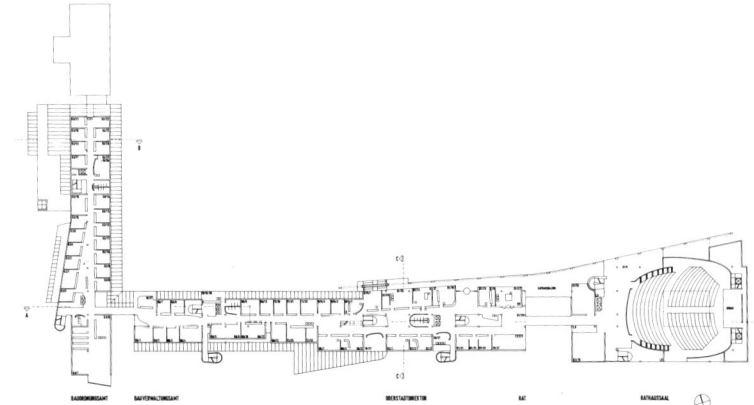

Arbeitsamt Hagen

Auf dem Grundstück eines für die Iduna Hagen 1963–70 geplanten Mietbürohaus-Komplexes wurde nach dessen Verkauf das Arbeitsamt Hagen errichtet. Fertigstellung 1981. Das 21-geschossige Hochhaus mit zweigeschossigen Sockelbauten liegt im Ortskern Hagens, umgeben von zwei- bis fünfgeschossiger Bebauung. Es komplettiert die Situierung von Hochhäusern entlang des Innenstadtringes (Stadtverwaltung, Sparkasse) in Bahnhofsnähe.

After the sale of the site on which a complex of rented office accommodation for the Iduna company in Hamburg had originally been planned, (1963–70), the Employment Exchange Hagen was erected there. Completion date, 1981. The 21-storey tower block with its two-storey plinth structures is situated at the centre of Hagen, surrounded by 2- to 5-storey buildings. It marks the conclusion of a series of tower blocks along the inner ring of the city, (municipal administration, savings bank), in the vicinity of the station.

unten links Modell Iduna Hagen (Planung 1963–70)
Mitte und rechts Modell und Ausführung des Arbeitsamtes

bottom left Model of Iduna Hagen (Planning 1963–70)
middle and right Model and actual execution of the employment exchange

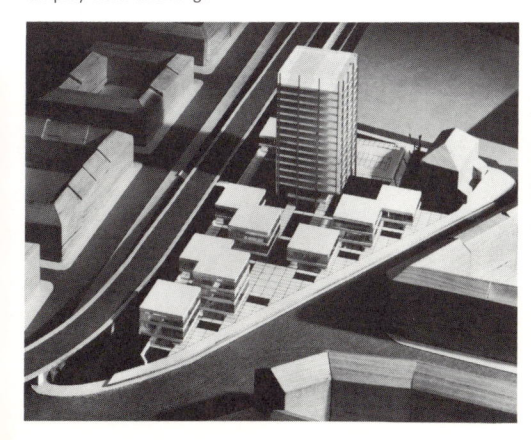

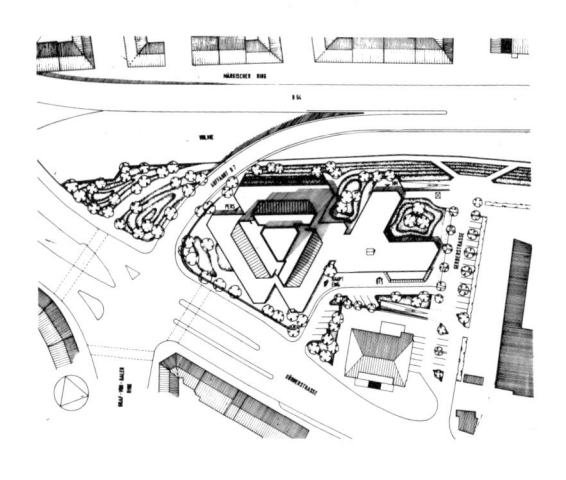

oben Mitte Längsschnitt / top middle Longitudinal section
unten Mitte Erdgeschoß / bottom middle Ground floor
unten links Normalgeschoß mit 20 Zellenbüros je Geschoß /
bottom left Typical floor with 20 single offices per floor

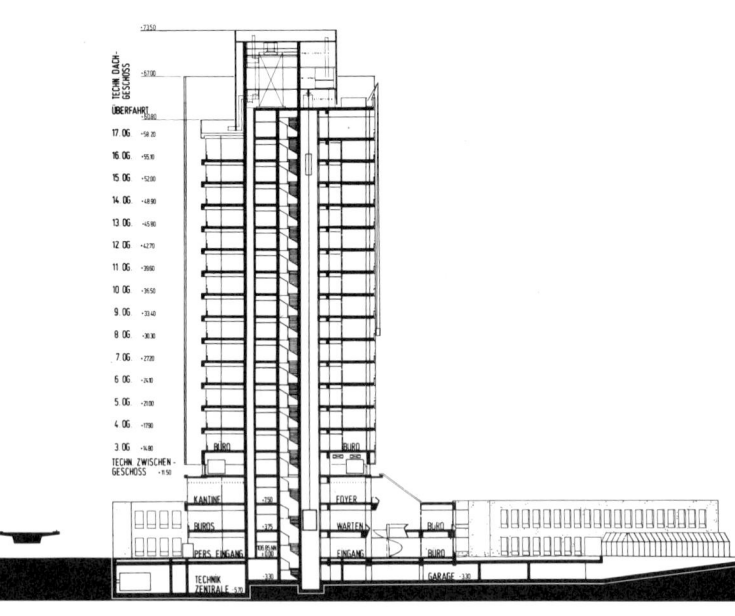

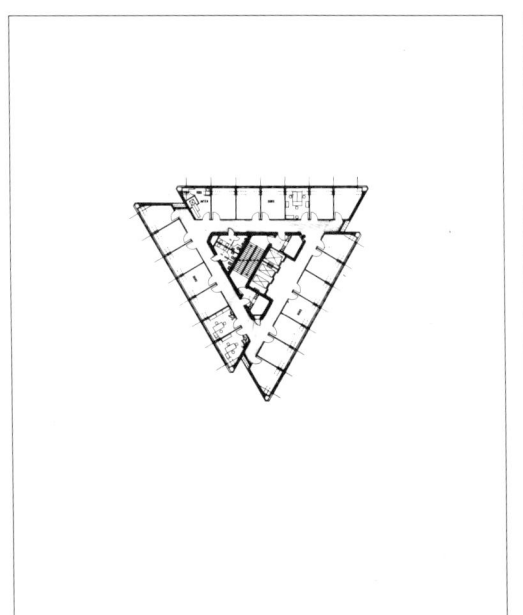

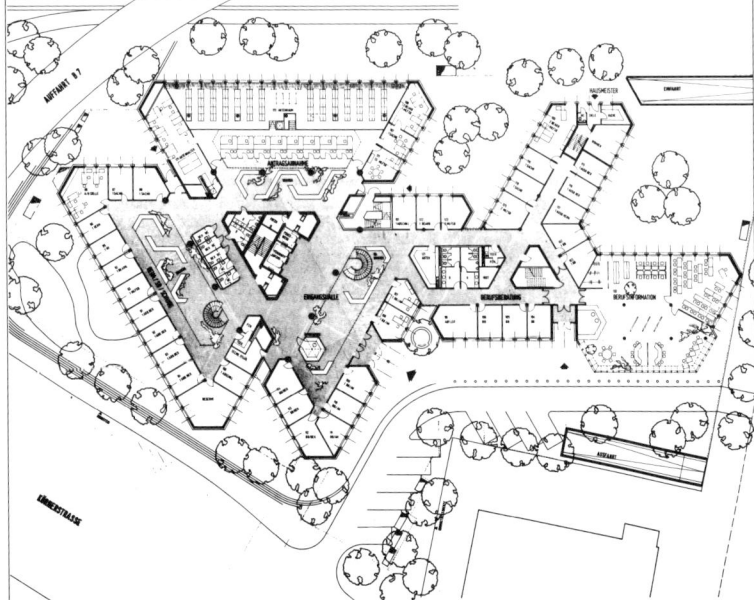

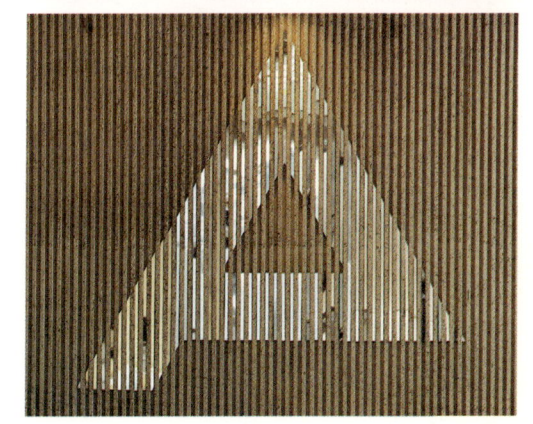

links Eingangshalle mit Prismen von Prof. Luther
Mitte und unten rechts Leitsystem von Szabo

left Entrance hall with prisms by Prof. Luther
middle and bottom right Directional system by Szabo

Hauptverwaltung DEVK Köln Ausführung

Aufgrund der Wettbewerbsentscheidung für die Deutsche-Eisenbahn-Versicherungs-Kasse aus dem Jahre 1976, (S. 146) bei dem zwei 1. Preisträger hervorgingen, entstand eine Arbeitsgemeinschaft mit Novotny-Mähner und Assoziierte, Offenbach. Der gemeinsame Entwurf versucht die Vorteile der beiden Wettbewerbsarbeiten zu kombinieren: klare Disposition der Büroflächen als gegliederte Großräume um eine Innenhalle und eine Kernzone, dann Gliederung der großen Baumasse, an hervorragender Stelle in Köln, unmittelbar an Rhein und Zoobrücke, um die Erscheinung eines monumentalen Solitärs zu vermeiden. Baubeginn 1982.

As a result of the competition for the German Railways Insurance Fund building in 1976 (p. 146) in which two first prizes were awarded, a project partnership was formed with Novotny-Mähner and Associates, Offenbach. The joint design attempted to combine the advantages of both competition entries: the clear layout of the office areas, in the form of articulated open-plan spaces located round an internal hall and core zone; the articulation of the large building volume, in a prominent position in Cologne, (directly adjacent to the Rhine and the Zoo Bridge), in order to avoid any appearance of a monumental, isolated, single building. Commencement of construction, 1982.

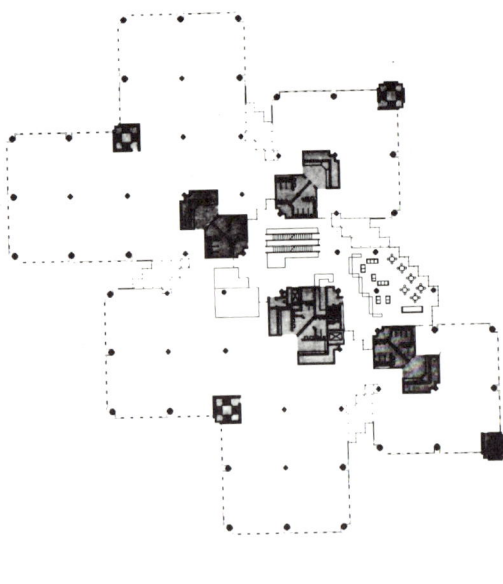

oben rechts
Normalgeschoß (Geschoß 1–4) mit Großraumbürozonen, Rolltreppenanlage und Pausenzonen am Hauptkern
oben links Innenraummodell mit Beleuchtung von Bartenbach

top right Typical floor (floors 1–4) with open plan office zones, escalators and rest zones in main core area
top left Model of interior space, lighting by Bartenbach

Boehringer Mannheim

Gutachten 1980. Erweiterungsplanung bestehender Verwaltung in mehreren Bauabschnitten für insgesamt ca. 2000 Arbeitsplätze. Die reversiblen Büros sind sowohl als Zellenbüros wie auch als Gruppenräume nutzbar.

Study, 1980. Planning for the extension of an existing administration over a number of building stages and to provide working space for approximately 2000 persons in all. The reversible office space can be used for individual cells or for group rooms.

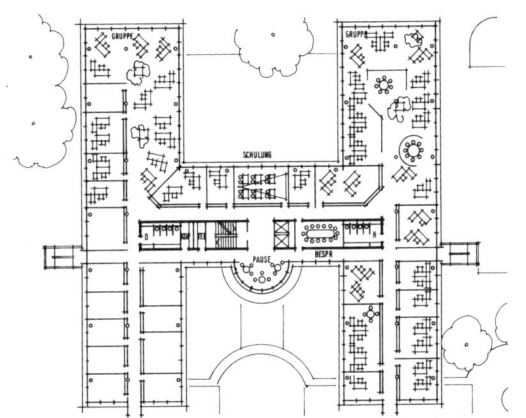

Landratsamt Goslar

Wettbewerb 1980. Aufnahme des Maßstabs der Umgebung und Auseinandersetzung mit den schwierigen Grundstücksverhältnissen ergaben die vorgeschlagene Lösung.

Competition, 1980. The adoption of the scale of the surrounding area and a battle with difficult site conditions resulted in this proposal for local government district offices in Goslar.

Arbeitsamt Bielefeld

Wettbewerb 1981, zusammen mit bauform, Köln. Versuch, das komplizierte Funktionsprogramm (Trennung der Benutzerkategorien, Bauabschnitte) mit den städtebaulichen Gegebenheiten (Abriegelung nach Norden, Öffnung zum Park) in Einklang zu bringen.

Competition, 1981, in conjunction with bauform, Cologne. An attempt to reconcile the complicated functional programme of an employment exchange, (separation of different categories of visitor, and building stages), and the existing urban situation: (cut off to the north; the opening to the park).

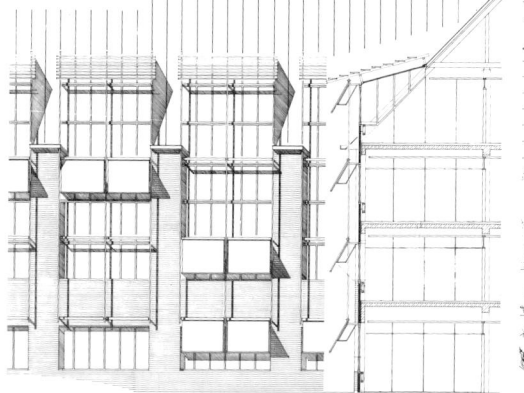

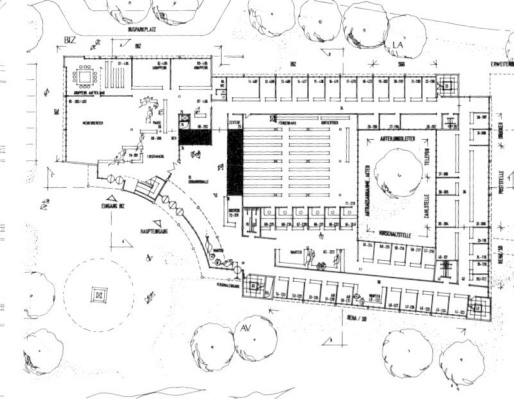

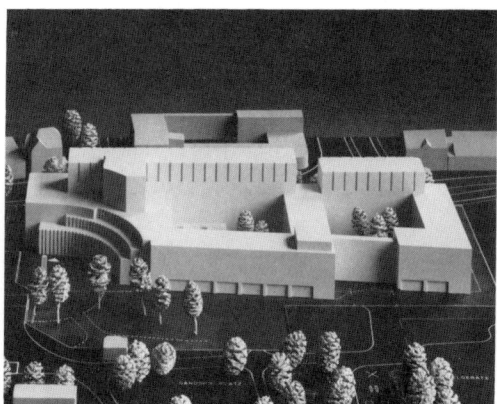

BASF Espagnola Barcelona

Entwurfsgutachten 1980. Neubau der Hauptverwaltung des deutschen Chemiekonzerns in Spanien. Reversibles Gruppenbürohaus auf baurechtlich schwierigem innerstädtischen Grundstück mit sehr hoher Ausnutzung.

Design study, 1980. New construction for the administrative headquarters of the German chemical concern in Spain. A block containing reversible group offices on a city centre site with high site use factor and subject to difficulties in respect of building regulations.

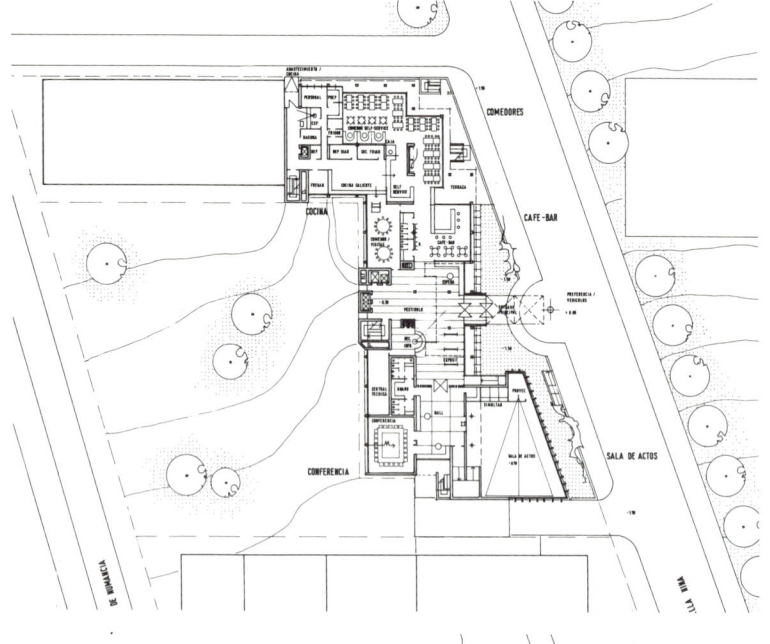

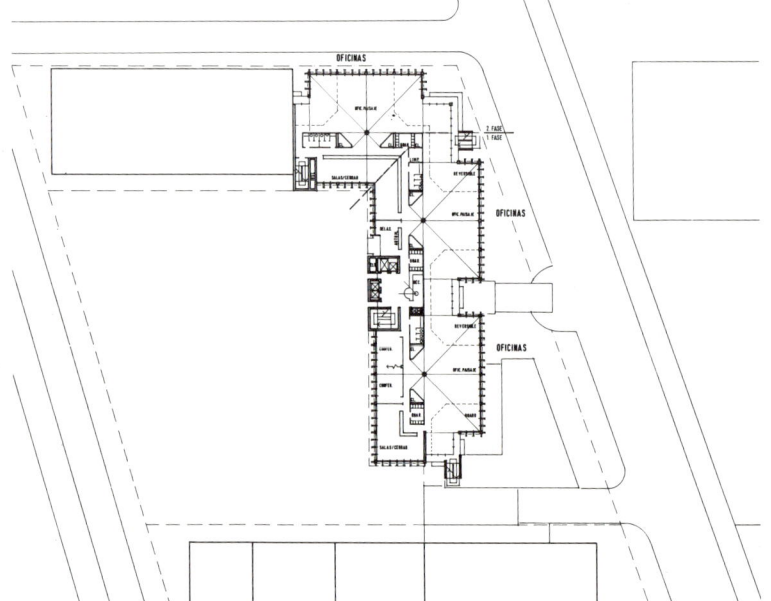

Rathauserweiterung Wilhelmshaven

Bundesoffener Stufenwettbewerb 1980. Die Besonderheit der Aufgabenstellung lag darin, die Baumasse der Rathauserweiterung in stadträumlich-baukörperlichem Bezug zum Högerschen Backsteinbau von 1929 zu setzen.

A competition of more than one stage open to all architects in the Federal Republic of Germany in 1980. The special requirement of the brief lay in finding a spatial relationship in terms of urban solids and voids between the built volume of the town hall extension and the Höger brick structure dating from 1929.

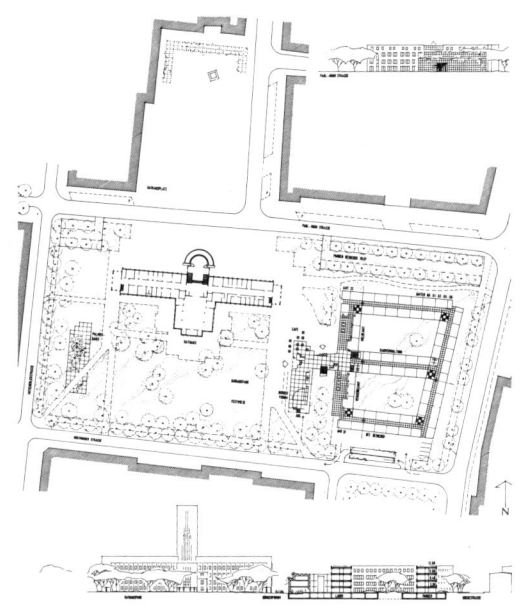

Landratsamt Starnberg

Wettbewerb 1981. Die Arbeit befand sich im Vorderfeld zahlreicher ähnlicher Lösungen des regional ausgeschriebenen Wettbewerbs, zu dem wir zusätzlich eingeladen waren.

Competition, 1981. This scheme for the local government district offices in Starnberg was amongst the leading entries in a regionally restricted competition, to which we were invited in addition and to which a number of similar solutions were submitted.

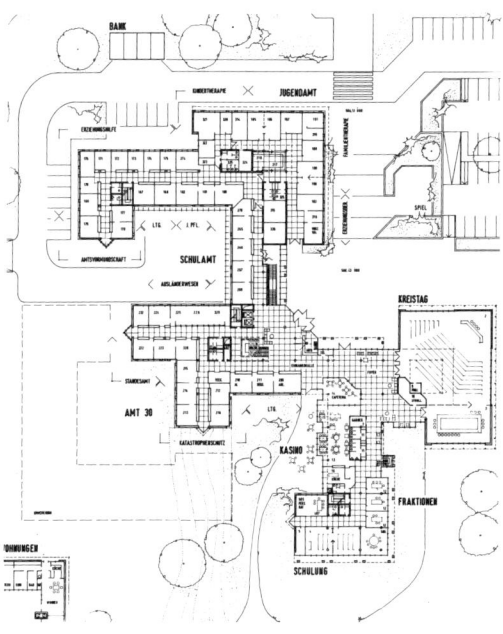

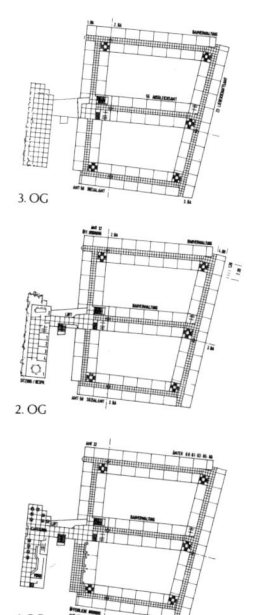

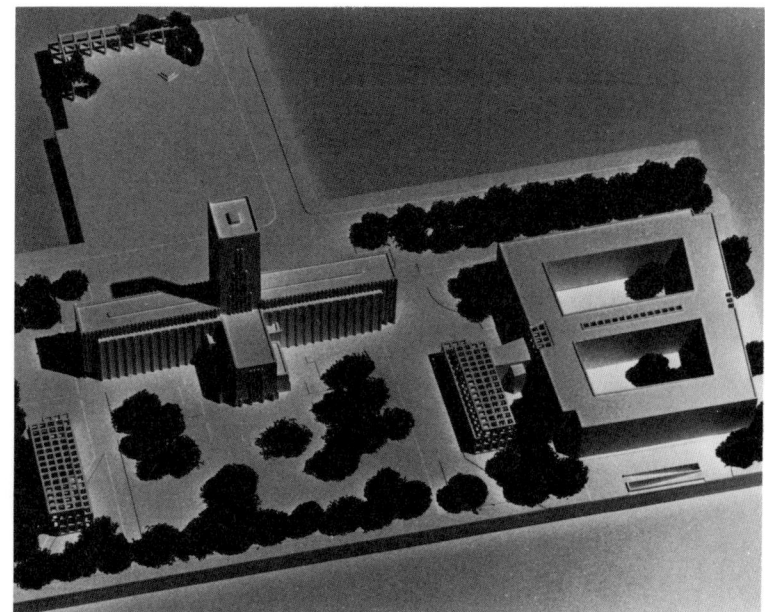

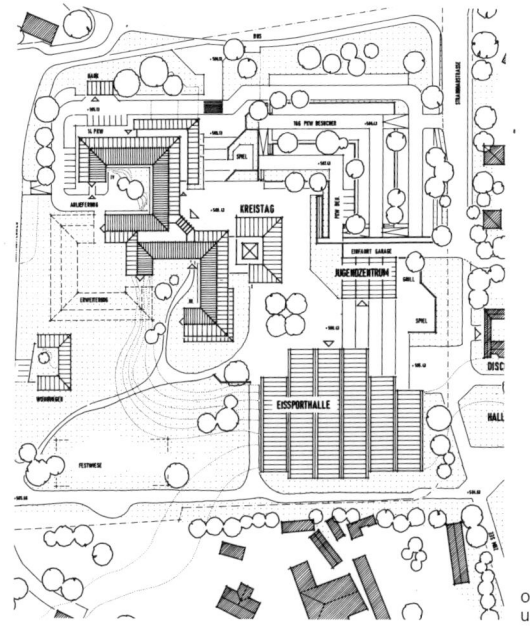

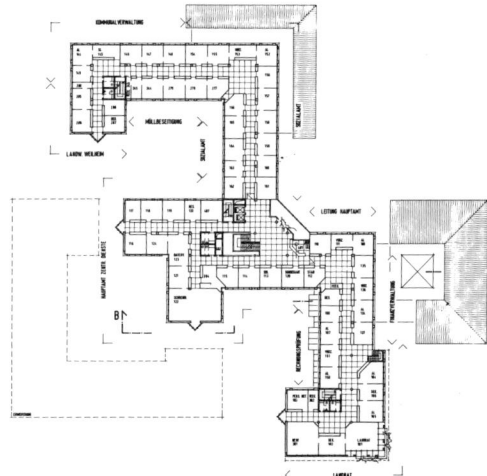

oben Erdgeschoß
unten Normalgeschoß

top Ground floor
bottom Typical floor

Verwaltungsgebäude 3 Krupp AG Essen

Entwurfsgutachten 1981 für die Unterbringung von Gruppenraumbüros mit ca. 1000 Arbeitsplätzen für ein Tochterunternehmen und 400 Arbeitsplätzen in Zellenbüros für ein Dienstleistungsunternehmen der Krupp AG, ein zentrales Rechenzentrum, eine Zentralkantine sowie die erforderlichen Einstellplätze. Mit diesem Vorschlag wurde versucht, den neuen Bürohauskomplex zusammen mit den vorhandenen Bürogebäuden zu einem neuen Verwaltungszentrum zu konzentrieren.

Design study, 1981, for group offices for a subsidiary company with approx. 1000 working places, plus a further 400 places in individual unit offices for a service undertaking of the Krupp AG; in addition, a computing centre, a central canteen and necessary parking. This proposal sought to integrate the new office complex and the existing office buildings into a new administrative centre.

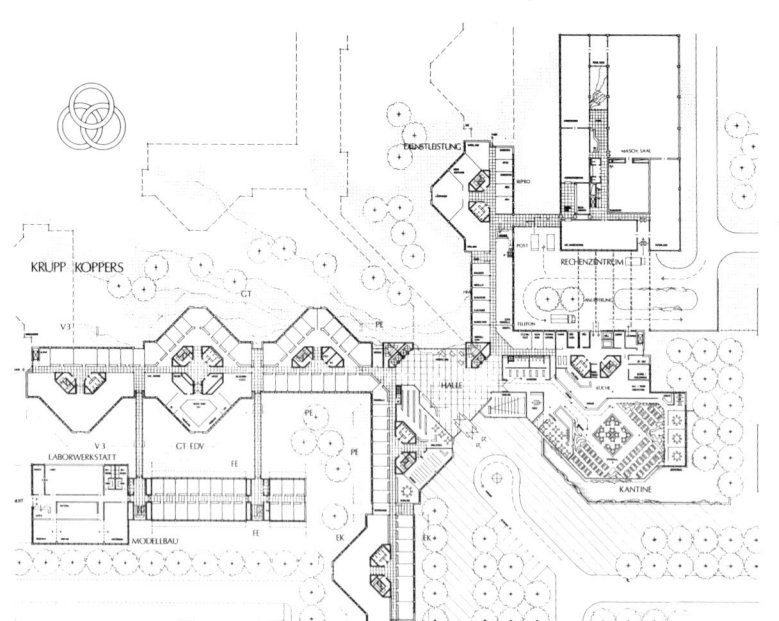

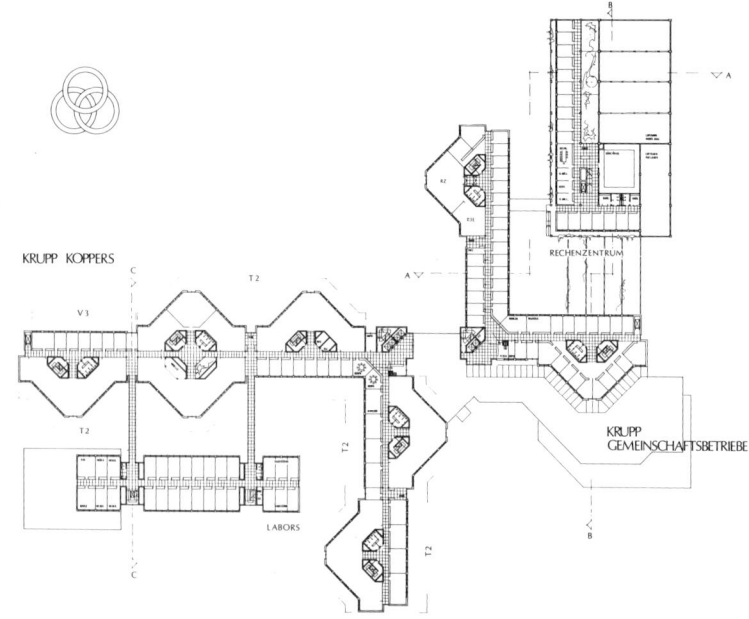

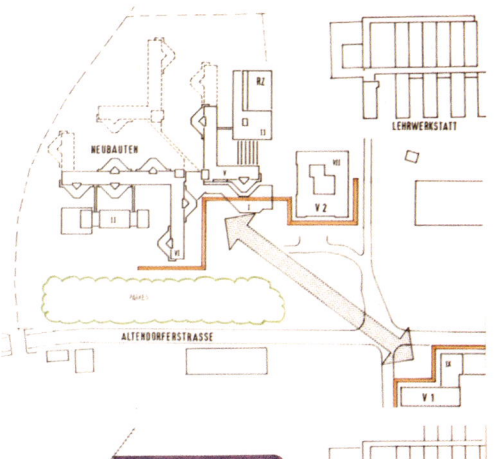

Städtebauliche Einfügung und Höhenentwicklung
- Fortführung des vorhandenen Prinzips der Solitärbauten
- Zugleich Zusammenfügung der Solitäre zum Ensemble: Verwaltungszentrum Krupp
- Verringerung der Gebäudehöhen von V1 und V2 zu den Neubauten als Überleitung zu niedriger Nachbarschaftsbebauung im Westen

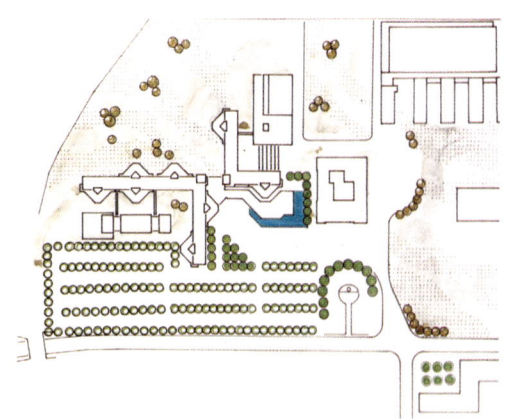

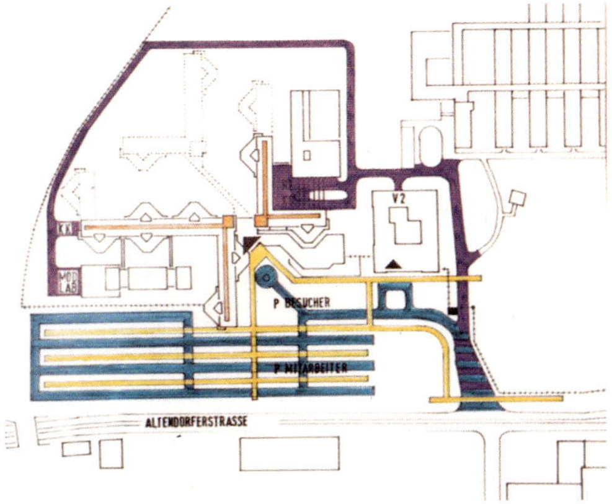

Erschließung
Fahrverkehr blau:
Alle Fahrzeuge benutzen Einfahrt von der Altendorferstr. und teilen sich auf in Besuchervorfahrt, Vorfahrt V2, Parkplatz Besucher, Parkplatz Mitarbeiter längs der Altendorferstr. als Lärmpuffer
Anlieferverkehr violett:
Anlieferstraße – zugleich Feuerwehrumfahrt – von vorhandener Pförtnerschranke zu den verschiedenen Anlieferhöfen der einzelnen Bereiche
Fußgängerverkehr gelb:
Vom Fahrverkehr getrennte Führung zu Eingangshalle, Kernen und internen Hauptverkehrswegen (orange)

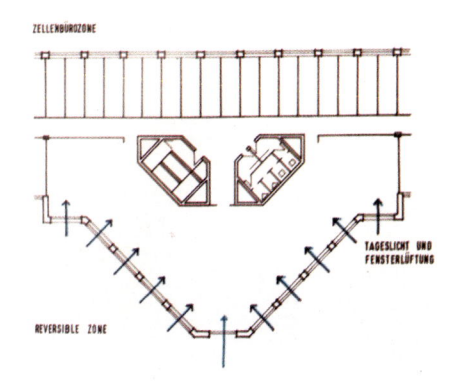

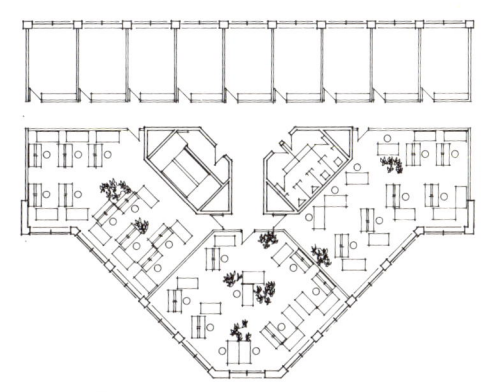

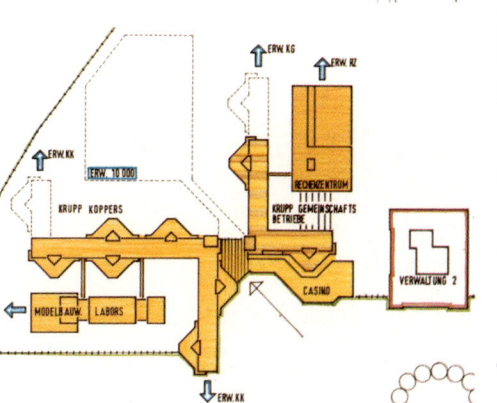

Flächennutzung, Erweiterungen, Sicherheit
- nur eine Eingangshalle
- verschiedene Gebäude für Krupp-Koppers und Krupp Gemeinschaftsbetriebe (gelb)
- verschiedene Ebenen, im EG Serviceeinrichtungen, in den Obergeschossen Büros
- alle Gebäude sind erweiterbar (blau), die 10 000 m² Erweiterungsfläche sind ebenfalls von der zentralen Eingangshalle erschlossen
- alle Gebäude liegen geschützt hinter Zaun (grün), Rechenzentrum besonders geschützt

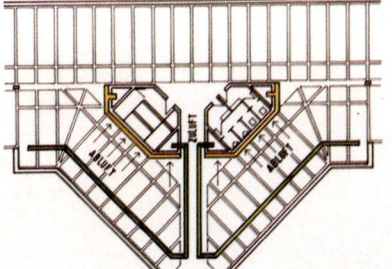

Landschaftsgestaltung
Fortführung des vorhandenen Prinzips der landschaftsgärtnerisch gestalteten Grünräume mit
- hohen Kugelbaumgruppen (voll grüne Kreise)
- niedrigen Parkplatzbewuchses (grün umrandete Kreise)
- Rasenflächen mit Gesträuch und Bodendeckern (punktierte Flächen mit braunen Kreisen)
- Wasserbecken als Abschirmung des Kasinos (blau)

Arbeitsplatzqualität
Die Gruppenräume zeichnen sich durch hohe Arbeitsplatzqualität aus:
- Tageslichtfreundlichkeit
- Fensterlüftung
- gute Akustik
- Gleichwertigkeit der Arbeitsplätze durch Fensternähe und minimierte Störbewegungen

Zusatzlüftung
Sollte die ausschließliche Fensterlüftung nicht ausreichen z. B. an besonders kalten oder warmen Tagen, kann durch einfache Nachrüstung die Lüftung durch die dargestellten Klimakanäle ergänzt werden:
- Zuluft (grün) durch Zuluftrohr mit Drallauslässen
- Abluftabsaugung (gelb) über Kanal als Blende innerhalb der schalldämmenden Kernwandverkleidung
- Platz für Schächte und Zentralen wird vorgehalten, Zellenbürozone ist mit reiner Fensterlüftung vorgesehen

EINZELRÄUME

GRUPPENRÄUME

GRUPPENRÄUME

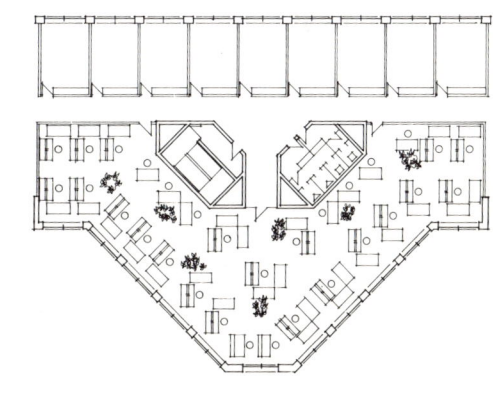

Arbeitsamt Essen

Planung 1981/82. Die städtebauliche Situation legte eine Baumasse von fünf Geschossen nahe, die die stadträumlichen Abschlüsse der weitflächigen Umräume bildet. Sie wird aus zwei Höfen gebildet, an deren Schnittpunkt die Eingangshalle sich den Zugängen von zwei entgegengesetzten Seiten öffnet. Ein dritter Hof kann als zweiter Bauabschnitt angefügt werden. In der Eingangshalle werden die drei verschiedenen Besucherkategorien (Berufsberatung, Arbeitsvermittlung, Unterstützungsempfänger) in die verschiedenen Trakte und Verkehrskerne getrennt.

Planning, 1981–82. The urban context of the Employment Exchange, Essen, suggested a building 5 storeys in height, which would form a conclusion to the broad area of surrounding urban space. It is composed of two courtyards, at the intersection of which the entrance hall opens out to provide access to two opposite sides. A third courtyard can be added on as a second stage of building. In the entrance hall the three different categories of visitor, (those seeking careers advice, those seeking jobs, and recipients of support), are channelled into the relevant tracts and communications cores.

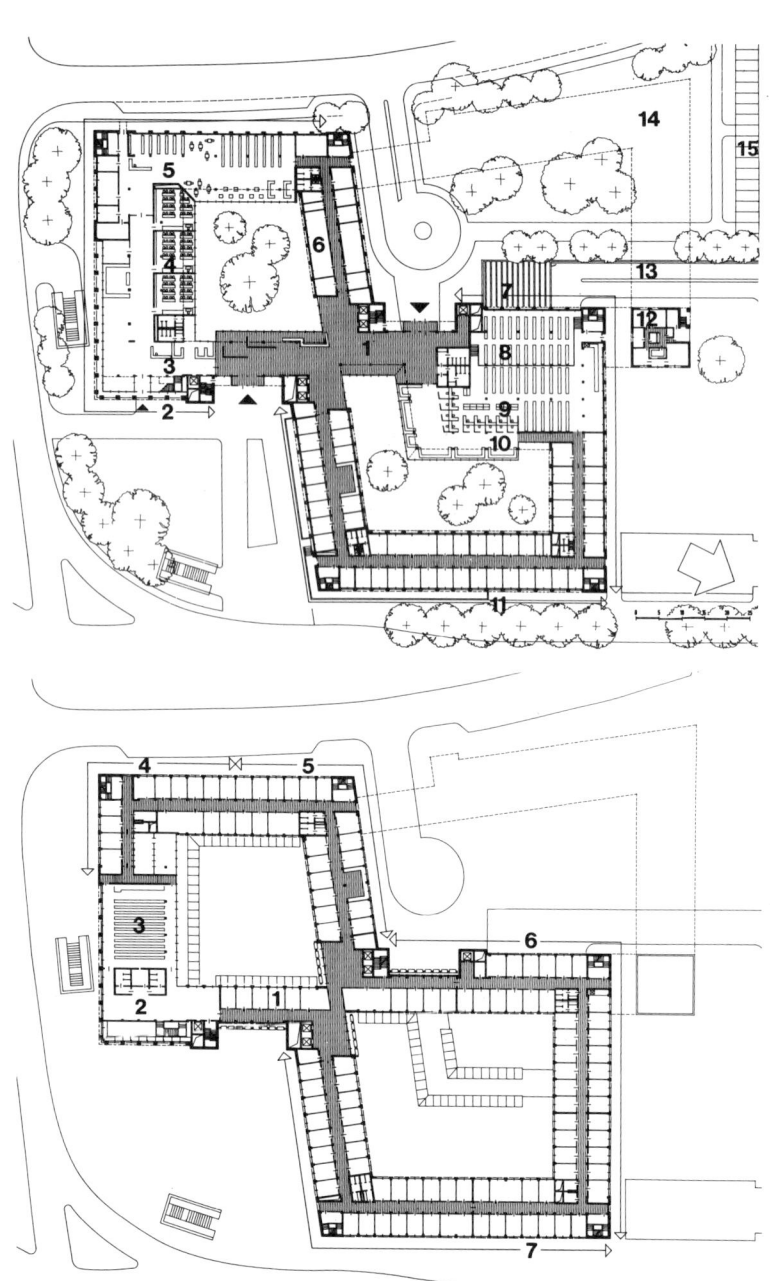

Erdgeschoß / Ground floor
1 Eingangshalle / Entrance hall
2 Berufsinformationszentrum / Careers information centre
3 Einstimmungsbereich / Introductory area
4 Gruppenräume / Group rooms
5 Bibliothek + Mediothek / Library + media centre
6 Telefon + Poststelle / Switchboard + mail
7 Leistungsabteilung / Payments + support department
8 Aktenhaltung / Document storage
9 Antragsannahme / Applications
10 Wartebereich / Waiting area
11 Arbeitsvermittlung / Job placement
12 Hausmeister / Caretaker
13 Anlieferung + Einfahrt Tiefgarage / Deliveries + basement garage access
14 Erweiterung / Space for extensions
15 Besucherparkplätze / Visitors' parking

1. Obergeschoß / 1st Floor
1 Zahlstelle / Payments desk
2 Foyer / Foyer
3 Vortragssaal / Lecture hall
4 Fachtechnischer Dienst / Specialist services
5 Berufsberatung / Careers advice
6 Leistungsabteilung / Payments + support department
7 Arbeitsvermittlung / Job placement

Erweiterungsbau VIAG Bonn

Planung 1981/82. Ergänzung eines vorhandenen Verwaltungskomplexes auf beengtem Grundstück für den Raumanspruch eines neuen Kasinos, von Gästespeiseräumen, Normalbüros und Büros der Geschäftsleitung.

Planning, 1981–82. Additions to an existing administrative complex on a tight site to provide space for new club rooms, visitors' dining rooms, standard offices and offices for the management.

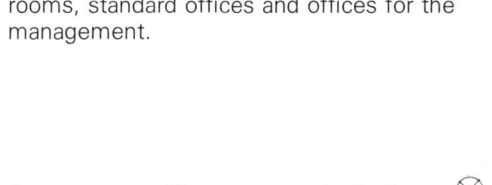

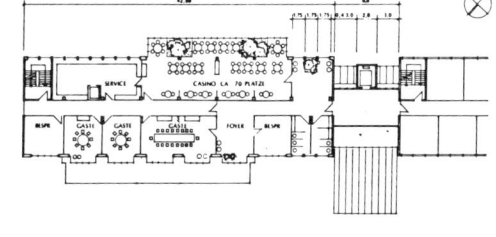

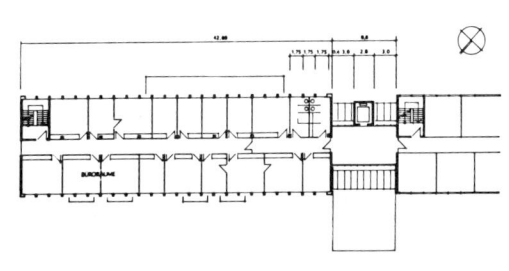

Bürogebäude St. Augustin

Gutachten 1981 für die Unterbringung der Hauptverwaltung eines Verbandes der gewerblichen Berufsgenossenschaften auf einem Grundstück, das bereits Prüflabors des gleichen Unternehmens beherbergt, auf die bei der baukörperlichen Lösung Rücksicht zu nehmen war.

Design study, 1981, for the administrative headquarters of an alliance of trade co-operative associations on a site that already housed test laboratories of the same organisation, which had to be taken into account in the new building proposals.

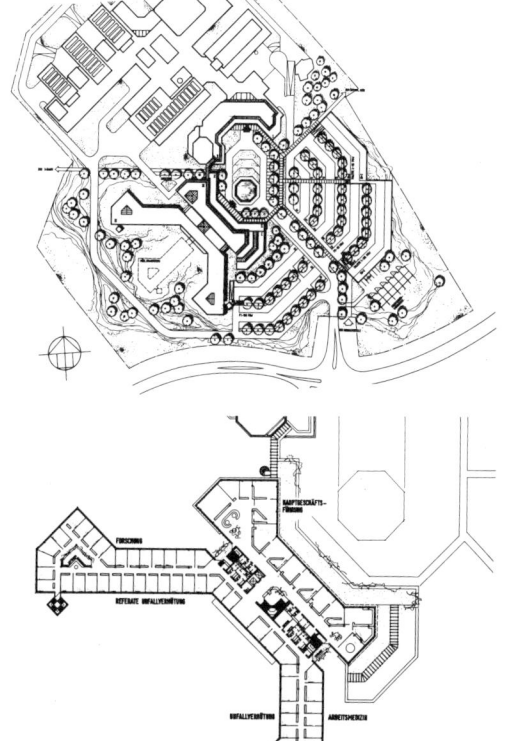

Residential Commercial Complexes of Abu Dhabi

3. Preis in internationalem Wettbewerb 1982, innerstädtische Büro-, Geschäftshaus- und Wohnbebauung.

3rd Prize in international competition, 1982; urban centre office, commercial and housing development.

**Hauptverwaltung Schloemann-Siemag
Düsseldorf**

2. Preis im Wettbewerb, 1981. Für den Hauptsitz einer Ingenieurgesellschaft mit ca. 1000 Arbeitsplätzen. Eines der vielen Beispiele für Gruppenbürohäuser ohne Klimaanlagen, wie sie in dieser Zeit geplant werden.

2nd Prize in a competition in 1981 for the headquarters of an engineering company to contain approximately 1000 working places. One of many examples currently being planned of an office building with group rooms and without air conditioning.

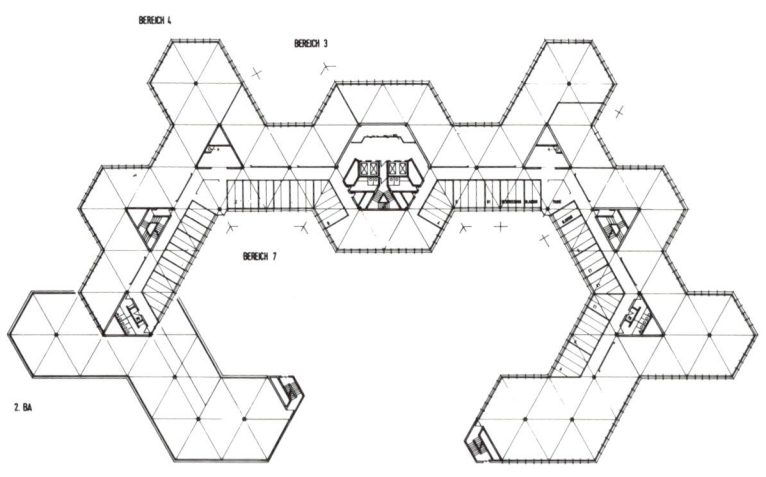

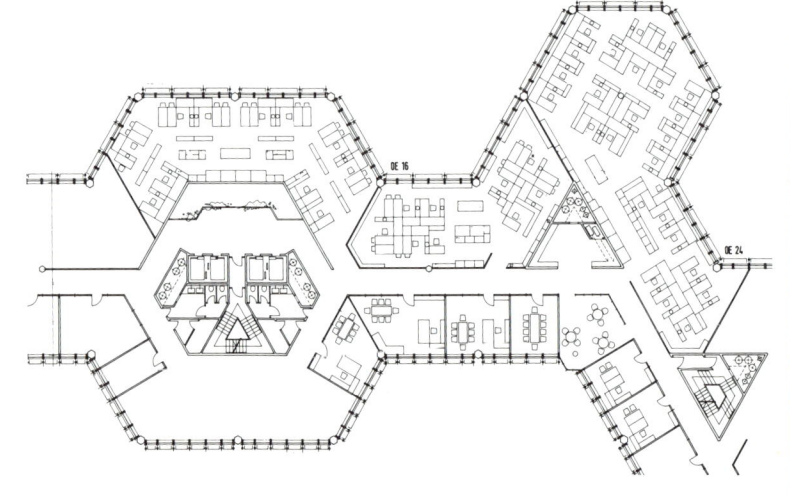

Grundrisse
oben Normalgeschoß
unten Möblierung von Gruppenräumen und Zellenbüros, bzw. Besprechungsräumen
Modelle
oben 1. Bauabschnitt
unten 1. + 2. Bauabschnitt

Plans
top Typical floor
bottom Furnishing of group rooms and individual office cells or conference rooms
Models
top 1st Phase of building
bottom 1st + 2nd Phase of building

Hauptverwaltung Lurgi Frankfurt

Gutachten 1982 für die Hauptverwaltung einer Ingenieurgesellschaft mit 4500 Arbeitsplätzen in reversiblen Zellen- und Gruppenbüros. Hierarchisches System der Verkehrserschließung über Eingangshalle und Verbindungsgänge zu den drei Hauptkernen, von dort über Haupt- und Nebenflure zu den Büros. Die Sonderflächen sind den Bürotrakten winkelförmig vorgelagert.

Design study, 1982, for the administrative headquarters of an engineering company with space for 4500 employees in reversible individual office cells and group offices. Hierarchic system of traffic access via entrance hall and linking corridors to three main cores; from here access via main and subsidiary corridors to offices. The special areas are set at an angle in front of the office tracts.

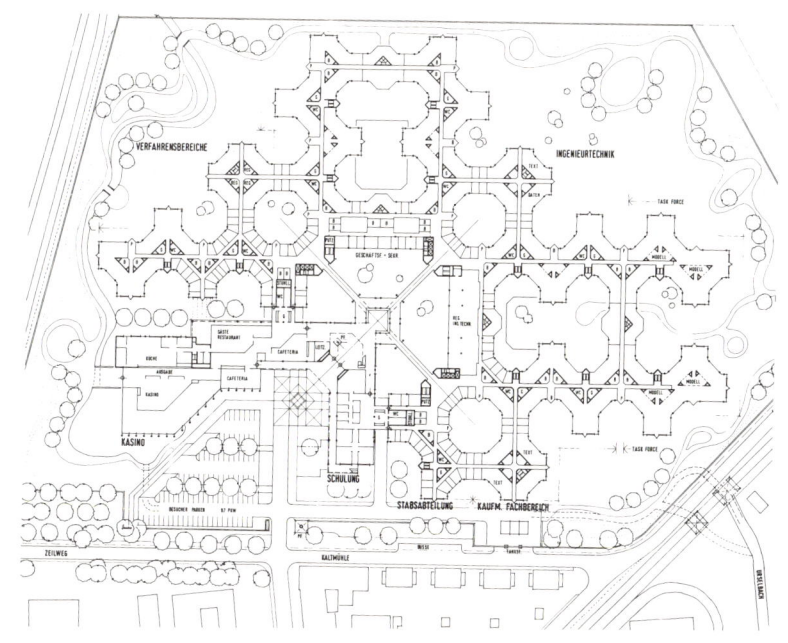

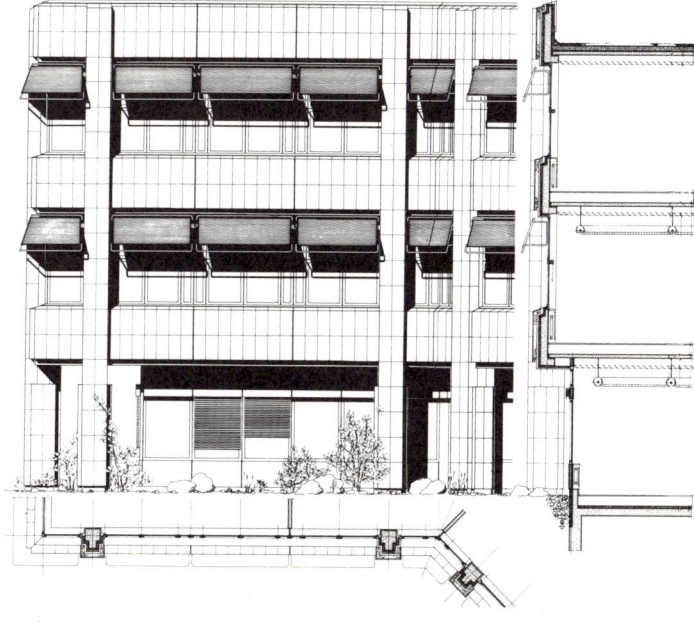

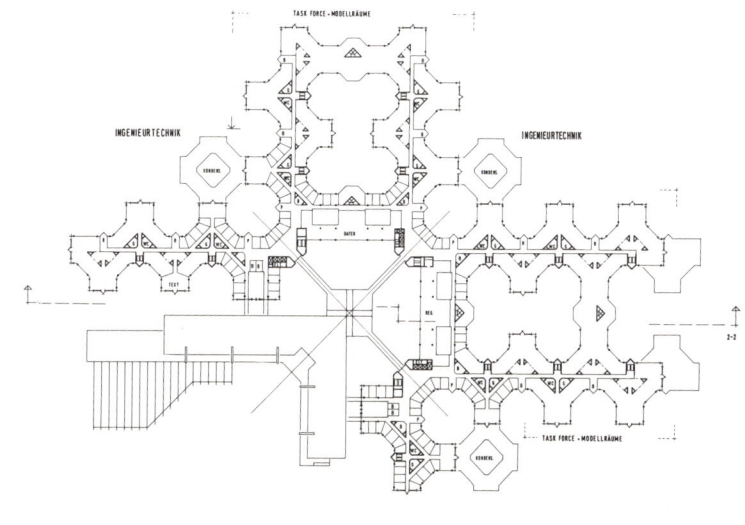

Grundrisse
oben Erdgeschoß
unten 2. Obergeschoß

Plans
top Ground floor
bottom 2nd Floor

Banken/Banks

Braunschweigische Staatsbank Lebenstedt

Zweigstelle einer Regionalbank, bestehend aus dem zweigeschossigen Bankbau, dessen Kassenhalle mit Oberlicht durch beide Geschosse reicht, und einem Zusatztrakt, in dem Büros, Praxen und Wohnungen untergebracht sind.

Branch of a regional bank, consisting of a two-storey bank building, (the main banking hall extending over both floors with a top light), and an additional tract comprising offices, consulting rooms and flats.

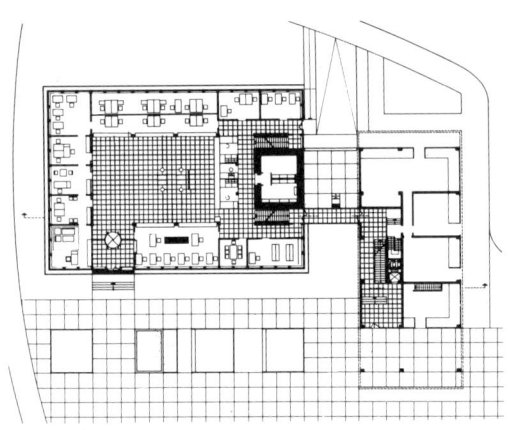

Stadtsparkasse Düsseldorf

Wettbewerbserfolg 1958. Ausführung gemeinsam mit Rosskotten, Tritthardt und Partnern, Düsseldorf. Die zwei Programmteile Hauptstelle und Hauptverwaltung zeichnen sich baukörperlich ab: die Hauptstelle nimmt den Flachbau ein, die Hauptverwaltung das Hochhaus. Wegen der geschäftsgünstigen Lage an einer innerstädtischen Einkaufsstraße wurde die Kassenhalle in das 1. Obergeschoß gelegt, (bequem mit Fahrtreppen zu erreichen), und damit das Erdgeschoß für Läden frei. Eine Lösung, die später bei der Simonbank (S. 193) wiederholt wurde, da sie sich bewährte.

Successful competition entry, 1958. Executed in collaboration with Rosskotten, Tritthardt and Partners, Düsseldorf. The building forms of the two parts of the brief, the main banking area and the administrative headquarters of the City Savings Bank, are contrasted with each other. The main banking area occupies the low-rise building; the administrative headquarters are situated in the tower block. In view of the good business location on a shopping street in the centre of the city, the banking hall was placed on the 1st floor, (easily reached by escalators), and the ground floor was thus left free for shops. It was a solution that proved successful and was later repeated in the Simon Bank, (p. 193).

Erdgeschoß, 1. OG + 16. OG / Ground floor, 1st + 16th floor

1 Kassenhalle / Main banking hall
2 Rolltreppen / Escalators
3 Schließfächer / Safe deposit
4 Laden / Shop
5 Passage / Arcade
6 Post / Mail
7 Autoschalter / Car check
8 Wertpapiere / Securities
9 Daueraufträge / Standing orders
10 Beratung / Advice
11 Vorstand / Executive offices
12 Verwaltung / Administration
13 Sitzungssaal / Conference hall
14 Speiseraum / Dining room
15 Giroabteilung / Credit transfer department
16 Holerithmaschinen / Punch-card machines

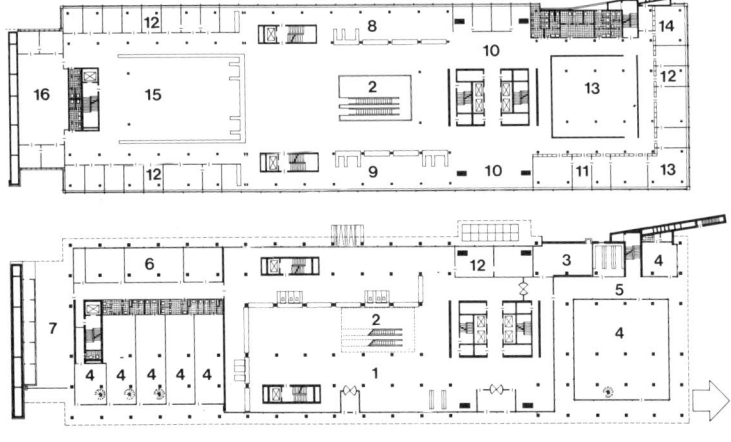

Landeszentralbank Nordrhein-Westfalen
Düsseldorf

1. Preis im Wettbewerb 1957, fertiggestellt 1964. Die Baukörpererscheinung widerspiegelt die Anordnung der Organisationseinheiten im Gebäude: in den unteren zwei Geschossen die Hauptstelle, die den Kundenverkehr, Geldtransporte, Geldbearbeitung und -aufbewahrung erledigt, in den oberen Geschossen die Verwaltung der LZB mit den Räumen des Vorstandes und einem großen Sitzungsraum im Dachgeschoß. Dazwischen liegt die von beiden Organisationseinheiten gemeinsam genutzte Kantine in einem baukörperlich eingezogenen Zwischengeschoß. Ein Seitenflügel beherbergt Wohnungen. Mit dem BDA-Preis Nordrhein-Westfalen 1965 ausgezeichnet. Die kleine Perspektive zeigt die Wettbewerbsfassung mit dem Kassenhallenflachbau vor dem gebogenen Bürohaus.

1st Prize in competition, 1957. Completed 1964. The appearance of the building reflects the arrangement of the organisational units of the Land Central Bank contained within it. Situated on the lower two floors are the main areas for customers' service, money transports, money handling and safe-deposit. The administration of the bank is on the upper floors, with the rooms of the board of management and a large conference room on the top floor. The canteen, used jointly by both these organisational units, is situated on a recessed intermediate floor. There is also a wing of flats. Awarded the BDA Prize of North Rhine Westphalia in 1965. The small perspective view shows the competition version with the low-rise banking hall in front of the curved office block.

links Erdgeschoß / left Ground floor
1 Kassenhalle / Main banking hall
2 Rampen zur Tiefgarage / Ramps to basement garage
3 Innenhof / Courtyard
4 Wirtschaftshof / Service yard
5 Eingangshalle / Entrance hall
6 Büroräume / Offices

oben Mitte 7. Obergeschoß / top middle 7th Floor
1 Normalbüro / Standard offices
2 Arbeitsräume des Vorstandes / Management offices
3 Foyer / Foyer
4 Sitzungszimmer / Conference room

unten Mitte 8. Obergeschoß / bottom middle 8th Floor
1 Lüftungsmaschinen / Air-conditioning plant
2 Anrichte / Pantry
3 Stuhlmagazin / Chair store
4 Großer Sitzungssaal / Large conference room
5 Foyer / Foyer
6 Garderobe / Cloakroom
7 Dachgarten / Roof garden

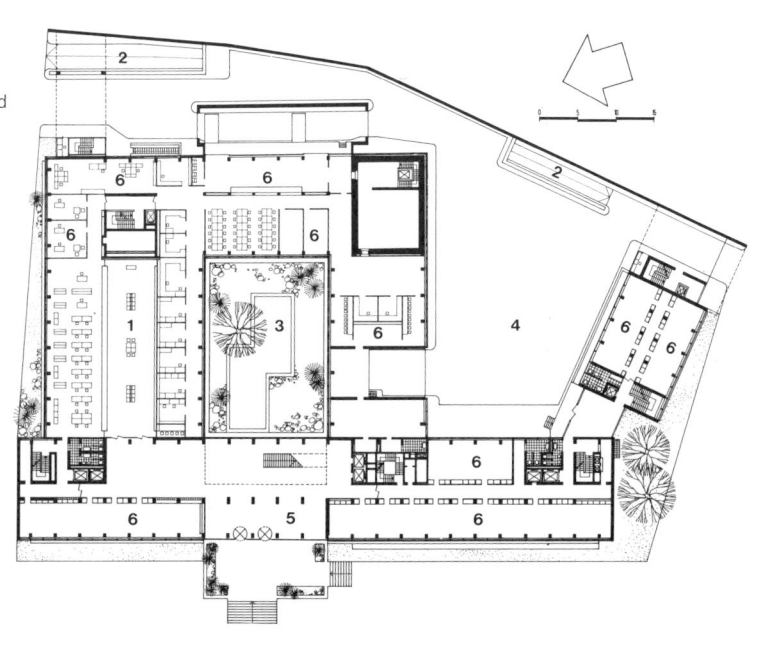

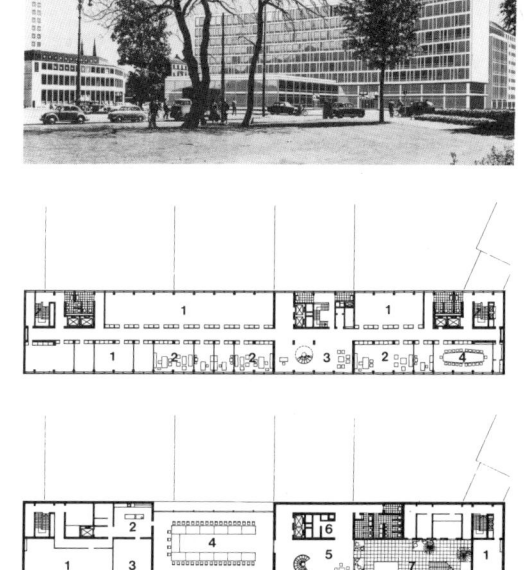

Stadtsparkasse Einbeck

1. Preis im Wettbewerb 1964. Durch Abriß einer baufälligen Kirche war in der Stadtmitte Einbecks ein Platz entstanden. Er war zusammen mit dem Neubau einer Filiale der Stadtsparkasse zu gestalten. Die Lösung, fertiggestellt 1966, bestand in der Anwendung eines formal einheitlichen Gestaltungskonzepts für Platz und Sparkasse durch die Komposition U-förmiger Sichtbetonwandelemente für Wände, Beeteinfassungen und Wasserbecken.

1st Prize in competition, 1964. The demolition of a dilapidated church had created an open space at the centre of the town of Einbeck. This open space was to be laid out in conjunction with the erection of a new branch of the savings bank. The solution, which was completed in 1966, consisted of applying a single formally unifying design concept to the open space and the savings bank, with the use of U-shaped exposed concrete wall elements to form walls, flower beds and water pools.

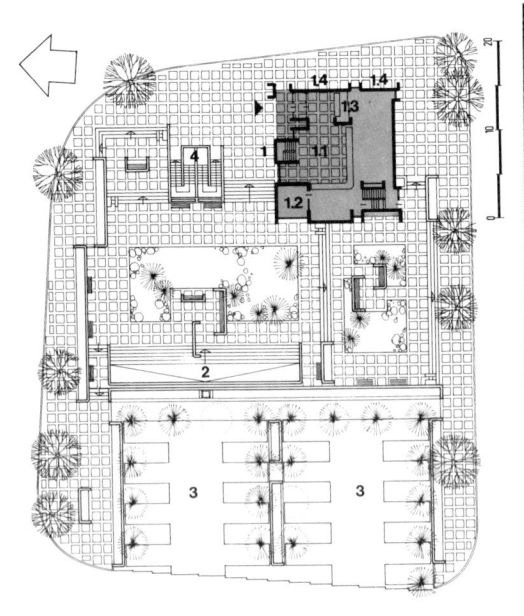

1 Sparkassen- + Verkehrsamtgebäude / Savings bank + tourist information office
1.1 Kassenhalle / Banking hall
1.2 Leiter / Manager
1.3 Information / Information desk
1.4 Vitrinen + Nachttresor / Showcases + night safe
2 Wasserbecken / Water pool
3 Parkplatz / Parking
4 WC-Anlage, Trafo + Schaltraum / WCs, transformer station + switch room

Simonbank Düsseldorf

1. Preis im Wettbewerb 1966. Das weiterentwickelte Projekt liegt in der City von Düsseldorf an anspruchsvoller Stelle. Das Grundstück ist durch die fast vollständige Überbauung sehr hoch ausgenutzt. Das Gebäude enthält neben den Räumen der Bank Mietbüros, ein Café, Läden und Tiefgaragen. Durch die Ladengeschosse führen Passagen, die an die Fußgängerzonen des benachbarten Kö-Centers anschließen. Die Fassade besteht aus bronzefarben anodisiertem Aluminium und braun getöntem Sonnenschutzglas. Fertigstellung 1970.

1st Prize in competition, 1966. This development of an earlier project for the Simon Bank is situated in the city centre of Düsseldorf in a demanding location. The almost complete coverage of the site by the building meant a very intensive use. The building contains, apart from the bank rooms, rented offices, a café, shops and basement parking. Arcades lead through the shopping storeys, linking up with the pedestrian zones of the neighbouring Kö Centre. The façade consists of bronze-coloured anodized aluminium and brown-tinted solar protective glass. Completed 1970.

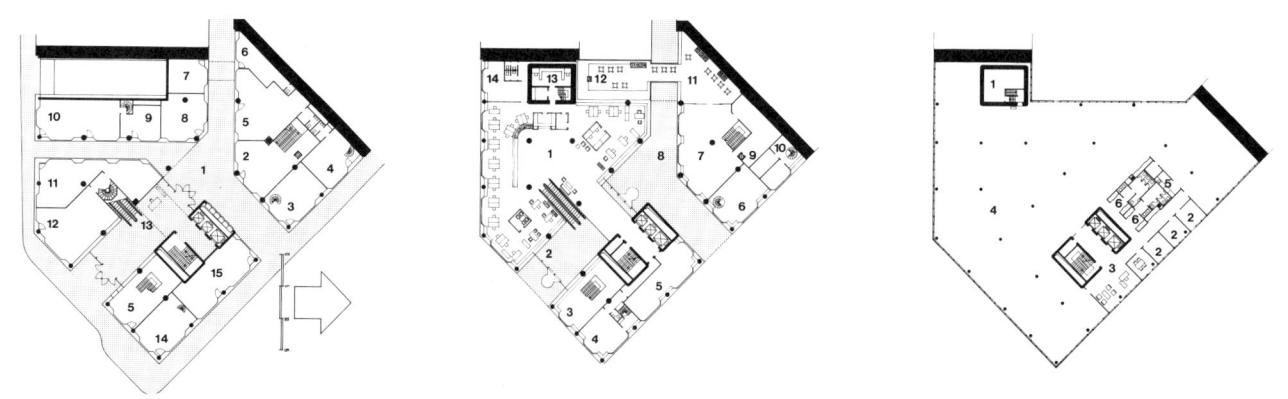

links Erdgeschoß /
left Ground floor
1 Passage / Arcades
2 Konditorei / Pastry shop
3 Optik / Optician
4 Juwelier / Jeweller
5 Moden / Fashion
6 Bijoutique / Bijouterie
7 Teppich-Galerie / Carpet gallery
8 Tabak / Tobacconist
9 Boutique / Boutique
10 Teppiche / Carpets
11 Kindermoden / Childrenswear
12 Antiquitäten / Antiques
13 Eingangshalle / Entrance hall
14 Pelze / Furs
15 Lebensmittel / Food store

Mitte 1. Obergeschoß /
middle 1st Floor
1 Kassenhalle / Main banking hall
2 Luftraum Eingangshalle / Void over entrance
3 Moden / Fashion
4 Pelze / Furs
5 Bank / Bank
6 Optik / Optician
7 Café / Café
8 Luftraum Passage / Void over arcade
9 Küche / Kitchen
10 Juwelier / Juweller
11 Überdeckte Terrasse / Covered roof garden
12 Offene Terrasse / Open roof garden
13 Kundentresor / Customers' safe deposit
14 Poststelle / Mail room

rechts 2.+3. Obergeschoß /
right 2nd + 3rd Floors
1 Tresor / Strong room
2 Besprechungsräume / Conference rooms
3 Empfang / Reception
4 Großraumbüro / Open-plan office
5 Teeküche / Tea kitchen
6 Garderoben / Cloakrooms

Eingangshalle und Ladenpassage
Entrance hall and arcade with shops

Materialien, Detailausbildung und Lichtatmosphäre entsprechen dem repräsentativen Anspruch des Hauses.

Materials, details and lighting atmosphere reflect the representational demands of the building.

Deutsche Bank Düsseldorf

Aus dem Erfolg in einem Planungsgutachten 1976, bei dem nur die Fassade eines Erweiterungsflügels zu gestalten war, entstand die umfangreiche Aufgabe der Neu- und Umgestaltung des ganzen Straßenblocks zwischen Königsallee, Bastionstraße, Breite Straße und Benrather Straße. Die Neubauten enthalten Büroflächen für die 2500 Mitarbeiter, eine 2000 m² große zweigeschossige Kundenhalle, (sie wurde von Professor Ellen Birkelbach innenarchitektonisch gestaltet), eine für den ganzen Baublock einzige Ein- und Ausfahrt, von der im 1. Untergeschoß eine Anlieferstraße (Straßenschleife von 185 m Länge) erreicht wird, die alle Ver- und Entsorgungspunkte erschließt; weiter werden von hier 3 Park-Tiefgeschosse für Kunden und Mitarbeiter mit 300 Parkplätzen erreicht, die so konstruiert sind, daß sie als Zivilschutzräume für rd. 3000 Personen genutzt werden können. In einem fünften Untergeschoß befinden sich Klimazentrale, Archive und Lagerräume. Organisatorische Erfordernisse verlangten den Abbruch des Nachkriegsgebäudes Königsallee 47; der zwischen historischen Fassaden (Königsallee 49 und 51, Um-, Ausbau und Restaurierung S. 18) einzufügende Neubau wurde als neuer Haupteingang mit Zugang zur Kundenhalle ausgebildet. Die festliche Einweihung erfolgte am 12. 5. 1982

The comprehensive brief to design and convert the entire street block between the Königsallee, Bastionstraße, Breite Straße and Benrather Straße resulted from the success of the original planning study of 1976, in which the scheme was limited to designing the façade to an extension wing. The new buildings contain office space for the 2500 employees of the Deutsche Bank, a 2000 m² two-storey high banking hall, (interior design Prof. Ellen Birkelbach), a single vehicular access point serving as entrance and exit to the entire block and linking up with a delivery-service road on the 1st basement level, (a 185 m long loop), which in turn provides access to all servicing points; from here, 3 basement parking levels with 300 parking spaces for customers and staff are reached. They are so constructed that they can also be used as civil defence shelters for roughly 3000 persons. On a fifth basement level the air conditioning plant, archives and store rooms are situated. Organisational constraints necessitated the demolition of the post-war building, Königsallee 47; the new building, which had to be inserted between historic façades, (Königsallee No. s 49 and 51, a combination of conversion, redevelopment and restoration work p. 18), was designated the new main entrance, providing access to the banking hall.

Bastionstraße, Wettbewerbszeichnung und Ausführung
Bastionstraße, competition drawing and actual execution

oben links Längsschnitt Nord-Süd / top left Longitudinal section north-south
oben rechts Erdgeschoß / top right Ground floor
unten links 1. Untergeschoß / bottom left 1st Basement level
unten rechts 2. Obergeschoß / bottom right 2nd Floor

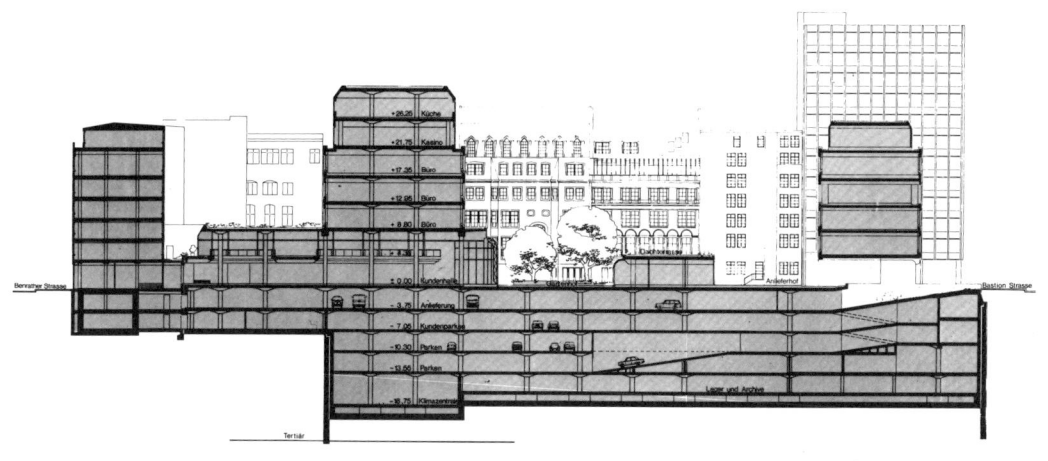

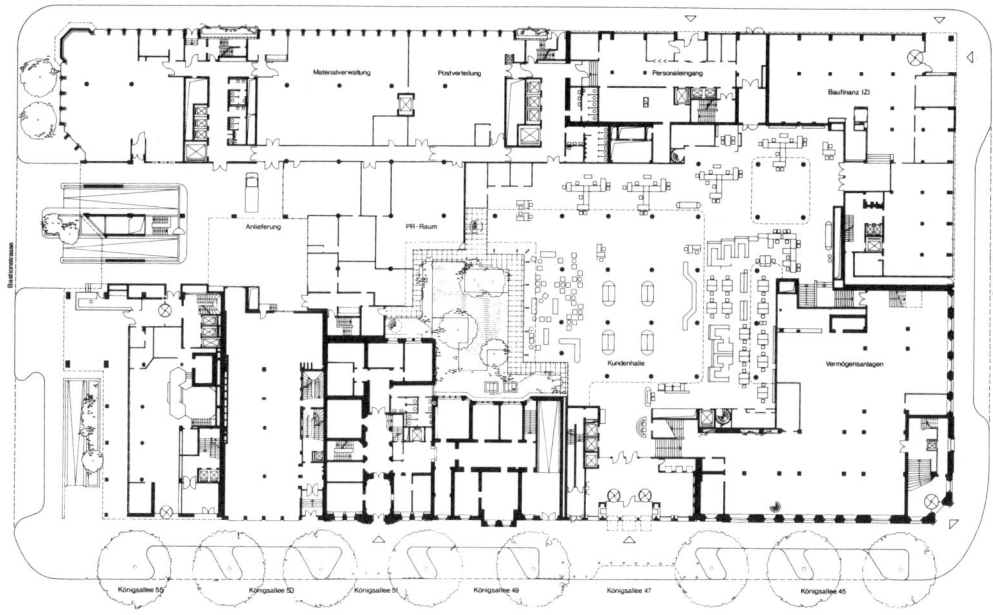

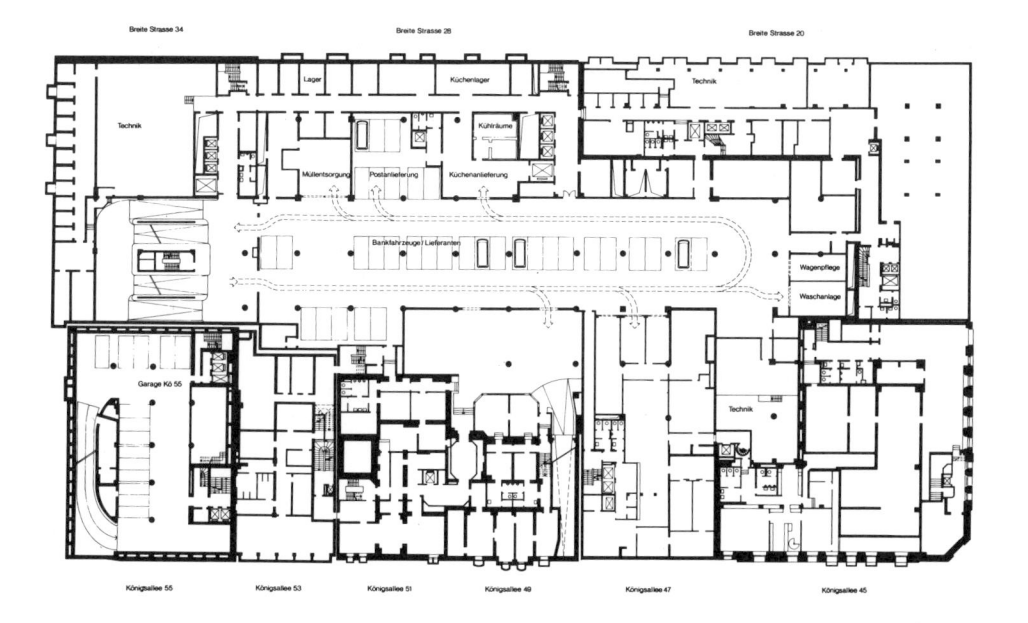

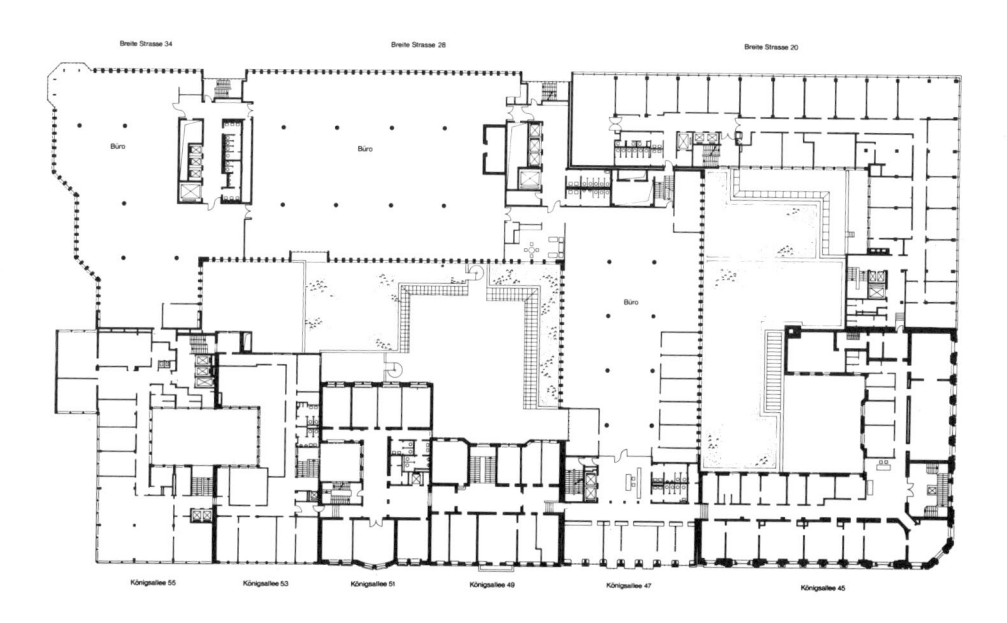

Zustand der Fassaden in der Königsallee vor dem Umbau   Königsallee façades prior to conversion

Die Mansarddächer auf den Altbauten (Kö 49 + 51) – durch Kriegseinwirkung zerstört – wurden wieder aufgebaut und dadurch zwei Vollgeschosse gewonnen. Auf dem Neubau (Kö 47) wurde dasselbe Motiv aufgenommen und ein Foyer- und Saalgeschoß geschaffen.

The mansard roofs to the existing buildings (Kö 49 + 51), – destroyed in the war, – were reconstructed, thus enabling two full storeys to be gained. The same motif was adopted for the new building (Kö 47), to create a double-height storey with foyer and hall.

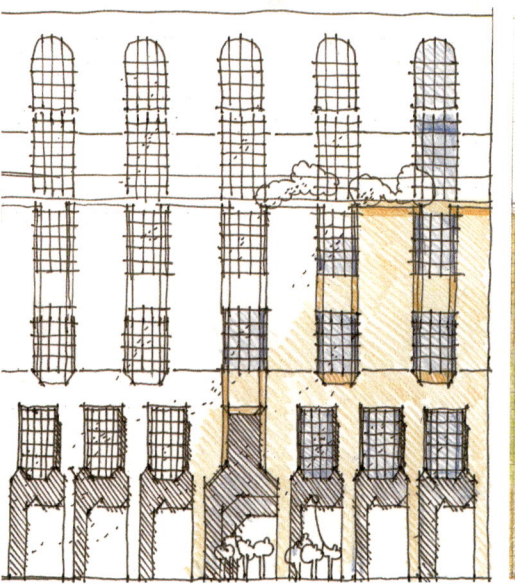

links Vorstudien für die neue
Eingangsfront der Kö 47
rechts
1982 fertiggestellte Fassade

left
Preliminary studies for the
new entrance front of Kö 47
right
Façade completed in 1982

Die großräumige, von Arbeitsemporen (im Foto nicht sichtbar) umschlossene Kassenhalle öffnet sich über eine Erfrischungszone (Investors' corner) zum Gartenhof (Gartenarchitekt Roland Weber) mit Wasserbecken, worin die Bronzeplastik Capricorn von Max Ernst aufgestellt ist.

The spacious banking hall surrounded by raised (balcony) level working areas (not visible in the photo) opens out above a refreshment area (Investors' Corner) and into a garden courtyard, (landscape architect, Roland Weber), containing a water pool in which Max Ernst's bronze sculpture Capricorn stands.

Die neugeschaffenen 18 000 m² Bürofläche sind aus den Zwängen der Grundstücksausnutzung und der damit entstandenen großen Gebäudetiefen überwiegend Gruppenräume. Doppelboden ermöglicht langfristig eine der Entwicklung angepaßte veränderbare technische Ausstattung.
Für die klimatisierten Räume wurde ein Deckensystem entwickelt, in das Luftauslässe und blendfreie Spiegelrasterleuchten integriert sind.

The newly created 18000 m² of office space are the product of the need to obtain maximum site usage; the great depth of building resulting from this is predominantly taken up by service areas.
A double floor construction allows for long-term adaptation to changing developments in technical installations. For the rooms with air conditioning a ceiling system was developed, in which air outlets and non-glare mirror grid soffit lighting are integrated.

links
Foyer 4. OG Kö 47 mit Aufgang zum Saal

rechts
Die Hoffront des Flügels Breite Straße vom Querriegel Kö 47 aus

left
4th Floor foyer, Kö 47, with stairs to hall

right
Courtyard face of Breite Straße wing seen from rear cross-link of Kö 47

Dresdner Bank Düsseldorf

Veranlaßt wurde die Baumaßnahme durch den Neubau einer U-Bahn-Linie, die den Baublock der Dresdner Bank von der Breite Straße zur Königsallee unterquert. Da der U-Bahnbau in offener Bauweise wirtschaftlicher war als im Tunnelverfahren und dazu den Abbruch eines Teiles der Altbausubstanz erforderte, entschloß sich die Bank zu einem General-Um- und Neubau mit dem Ziel der Zusammenfassung der bis dahin auf mehrere Gebäude verteilten Verwaltung. Das Charakteristikum des Entwurfs liegt darin, daß der Innenhof zwischen den Alt- und Neubauten über dem 6. Obergeschoß mit einem Glasdach geschlossen wird, worunter die neue Kassenhalle entsteht. Die an ihr gelegenen neu gewonnenen Büroflächen sind als offene Galerien ausgebildet. Die Umwandlung des Innenhofes zur Innenhalle bringt durch Reduzierung der Gebäudeaußenfläche Einsparungen an Investitions- und Betriebskosten für die Klimaanlage. Ausführungsplanung: Schiel, Possekel und Partner, Düsseldorf.
Bauzeit 1982–85.

The construction work was brought about by the building of an underground railway line, which passes beneath the Dresdner Bank block from the Breite Straße to the Königsallee. As open excavation proved to be a more economical method of construction for the underground line than tunnelling, and as this meant that part of the existing building fabric had to be demolished, the bank decided on a general programme of conversion and new construction for their house, with the aim of bringing together in one location an administration that had hitherto been scattered over a number of buildings. The design is characterized by an internal courtyard between the old and the new structures that is covered with a glass roof above 6th floor level. Beneath this the new main banking hall was situated. The newly gained office space adjacent to this is laid out in the form of open galleries. The transformation of the courtyard into an internal hall and the resulting reduction in the external surface area of the building enabled savings to be made in the capital and running costs for the air conditioning. Construction date 1982–85.

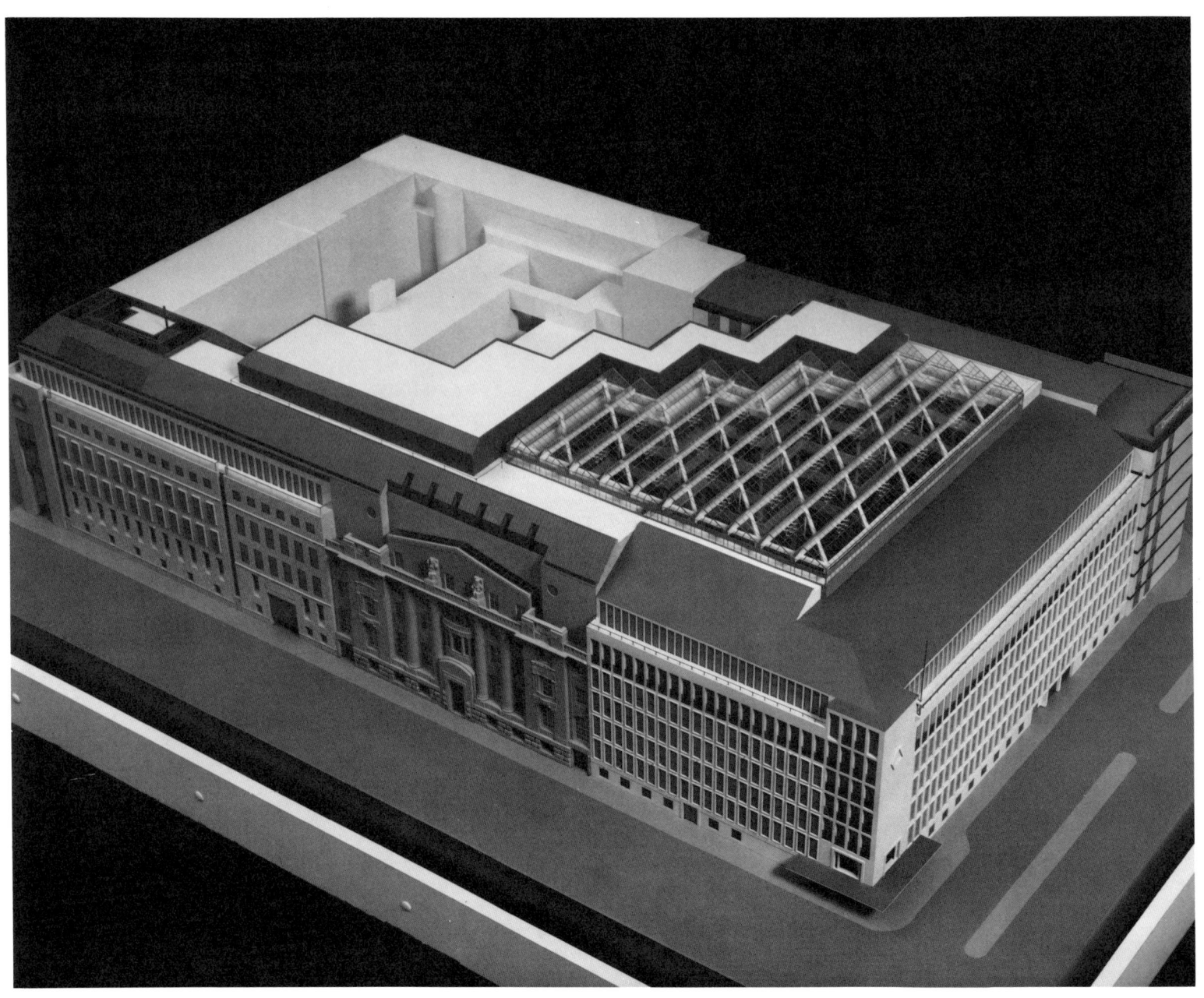

Kassenhallengeschoß / Main banking hall level

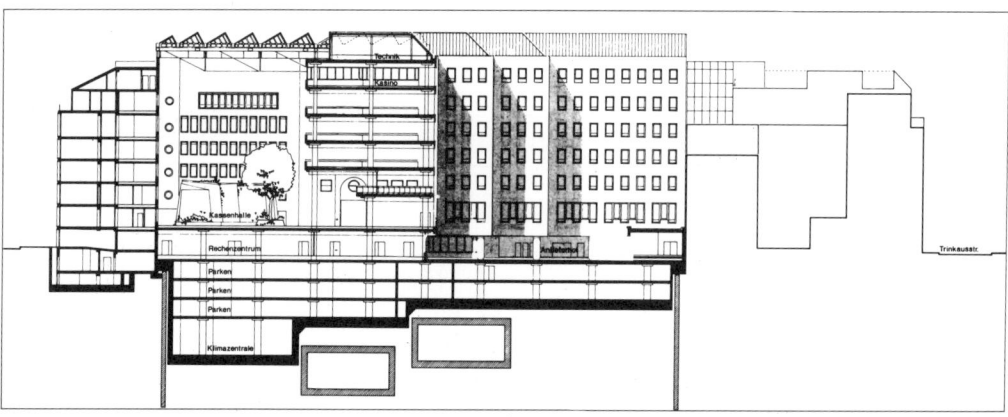

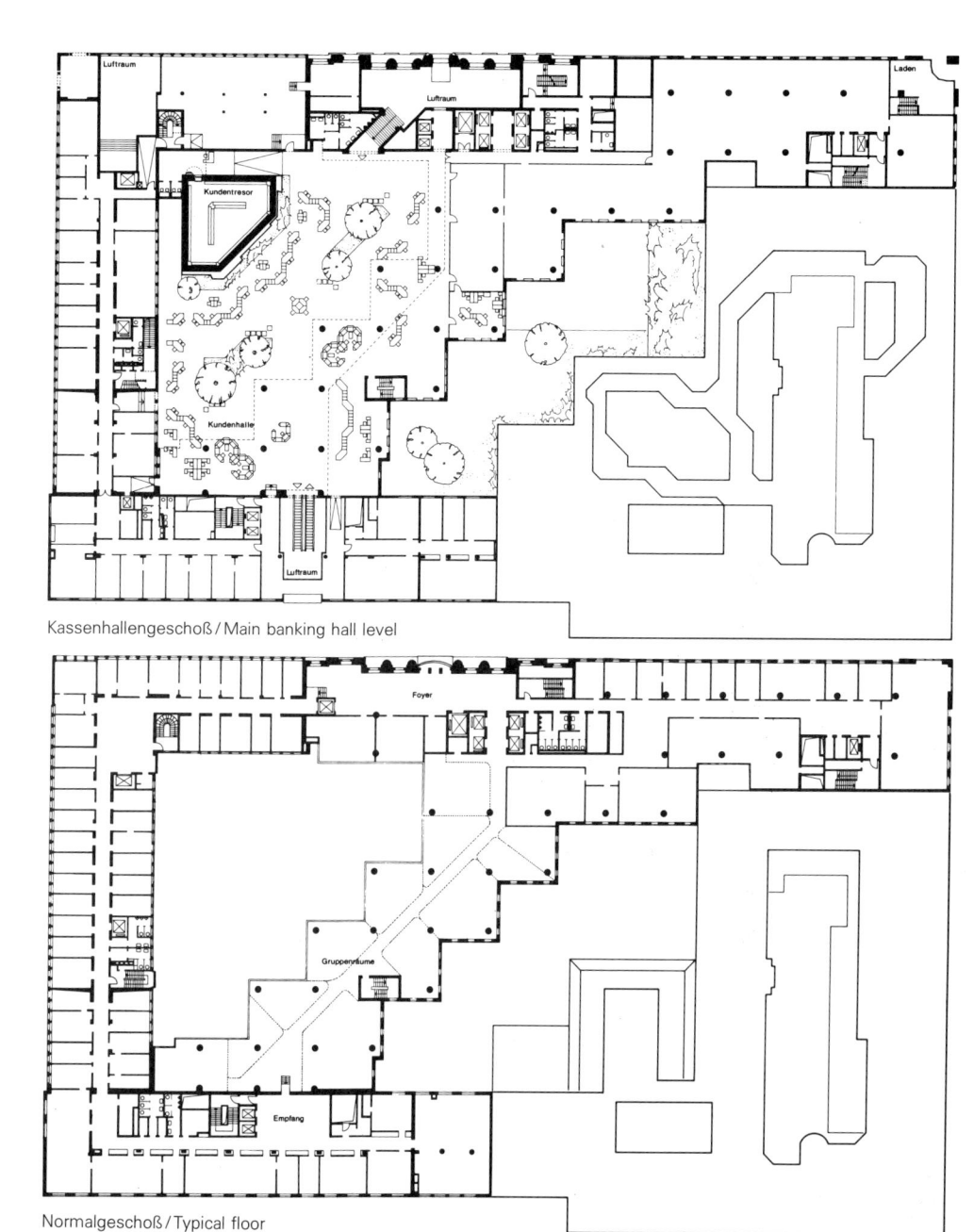

Normalgeschoß / Typical floor

Die Ausformung der Neubaufassade an der Breite Straße orientiert sich an der historischen Parzellenstruktur und versucht mit heutigen Mitteln den Charakter der historischen Fassade aufzunehmen.

The design of the façade to the new building in the Breite Straße reflects the fragmented nature of the historic land structure and attempts to adopt the character of the historic façade using modern means.

Bremer Bank Bremen

Wettbewerb 1974. An städtebaulich prominenter Stelle am Bremer Domshof war die notwendige Erweiterung der Bank für Büroflächen und Kassenhalle behutsam und maßstäblich zwischen den Altbau aus der Gründerzeit und benachbarte historische Bausubstanz einzufügen.

Competition, 1974. Occupying a prominent urban situation in the cathedral close in Bremen, the necessary extensions to the bank to provide additional office space and a main banking hall had to be inserted with great care and a sense of scale between an existing building, dating from the end of the 19th century, and other neighbouring historic building fabric.

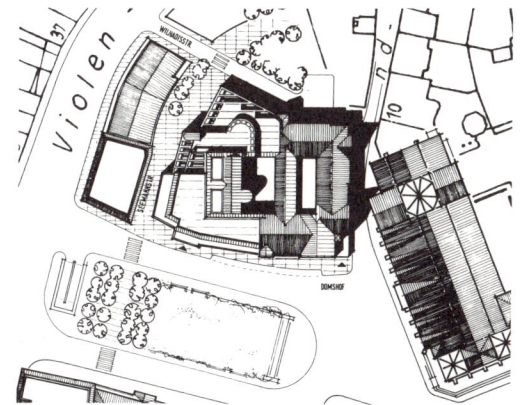

Landeszentralbank Wiesbaden

Wettbewerb 1979, 2. Rang. Die große Baumasse einer Nebenstelle der Landeszentralbank war in einem Wohngebiet mit offener Bauweise unterzubringen. Deshalb liegen große Teile des Bauprogramms, die funktionell dazu geeignet sind, unter der Erde. Die Gestaltung der Fassaden und Baukörper fügt sich in die Villen-Nachbarschaft ein.

Competition, 1979; 2nd place. It was necessary to place the large built volume of a branch of the Land Central Bank in a residential area with predominantly detached buildings. For this reason, where it is functionally justifiable, large parts of the building programme are housed below ground. The design of the façades and the actual structure is attuned to the surrounding villas.

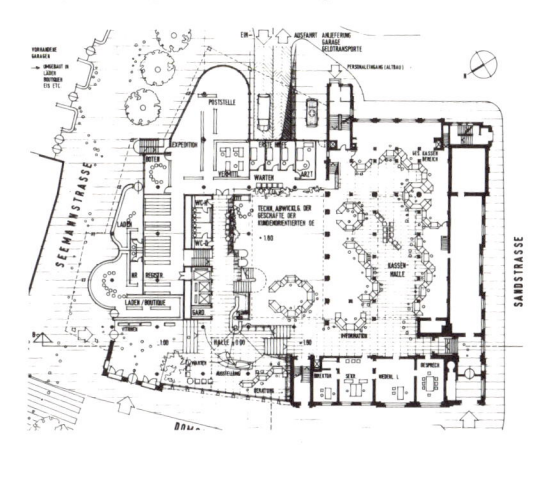

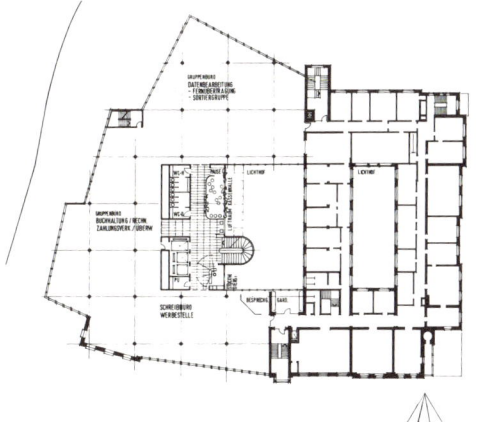

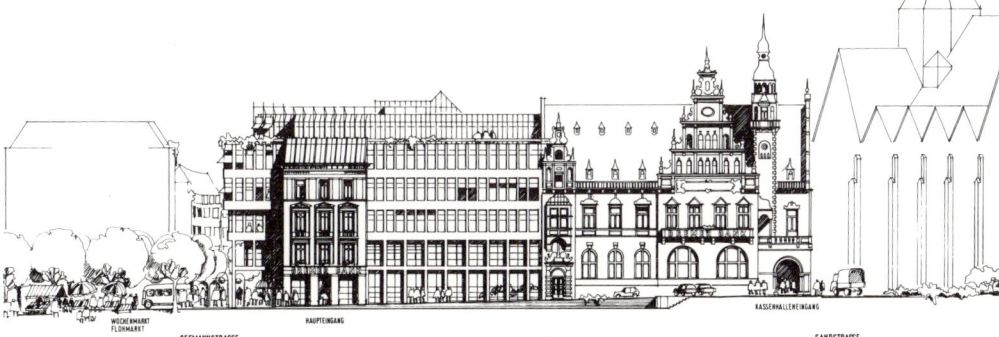

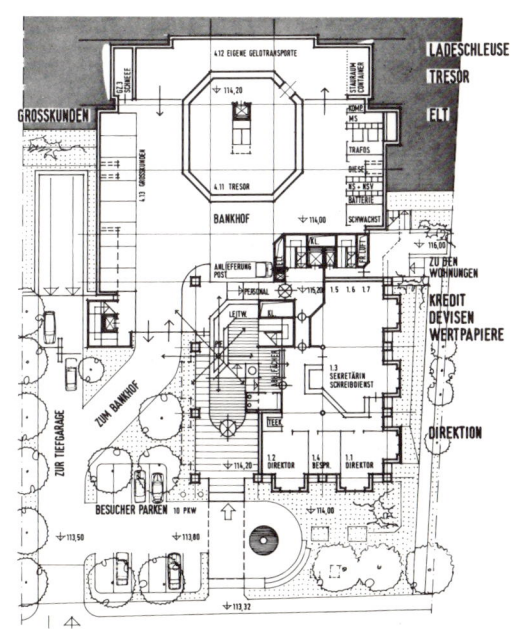

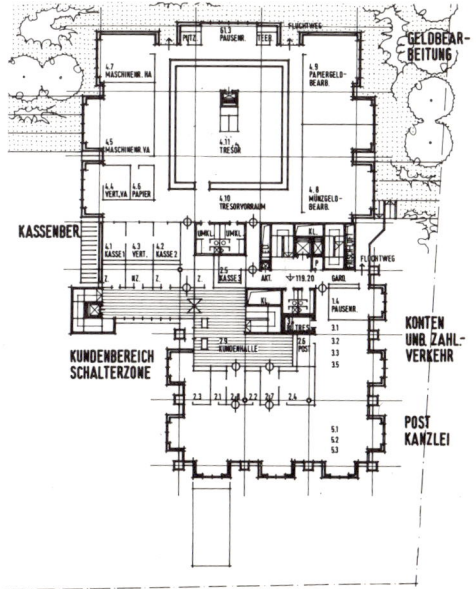

**Kulturbauten/
Buildings for the arts and cultural activities**

**Norddeutscher Rundfunk Funkhaus
Hannover**

Das aus einem noch vor der Währungsreform ausgeschriebenen Wettbewerb hervorgegangene Projekt (zusammen mit Oesterlen und Lichtenhahn) am Maschsee enthält einen Sendesaal und Hörfunkstudios, die sich um einen begrünten Innenhof gruppieren. Mit der Laves-Medaille der Stadt Hannover 1957 ausgezeichnet.

The project (in conjunction with Oesterlen and Lichtenhahn) dates back to a competition, held before the currency reform, for a broadcasting house for North German Radio on Maschsee, Hanover. It comprises a medium sized transmitting hall and a number of sound broadcasting studios, set about a planted internal courtyard. Awarded the Laves Medal of the City of Hanover in 1957.

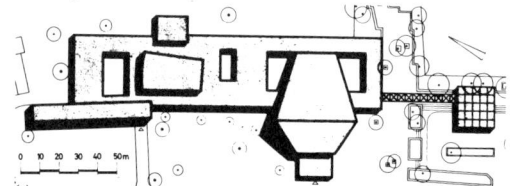

Norddeutscher Rundfunk
Großer Sendesaal Hannover

Ein großer Sendesaal für 1000 Personen wurde als zweiter Bauabschnitt dem Funkhaus am Maschsee angefügt. Wegen seiner aus akustischen Rücksichten gewählten Form wird es von der Bevölkerung »die Baßgeige« genannt.

A large broadcasting hall with room for 1000 persons was added on to Broadcasting House on Maschsee at a second stage of building. Amongst the population it is known as the »bass fiddle«, on account of its form, which was chosen for acoustic reasons.

Studiobühne Universität Kiel

Zusammen mit dem Komplex der Mensa und des Studentenhauses (S. 50) wurde eine Studiobühne mit allen erforderlichen technischen Einrichtungen und Nebenräumen in einem gesonderten Baukörper geplant.

Together with the dining hall and student building complex, (p. 50), a studio stage was planned in a separate building with all necessary technical facilities and ancillary rooms.

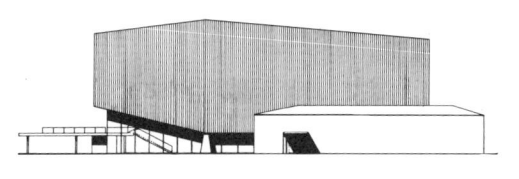

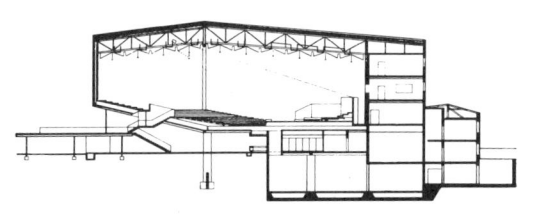

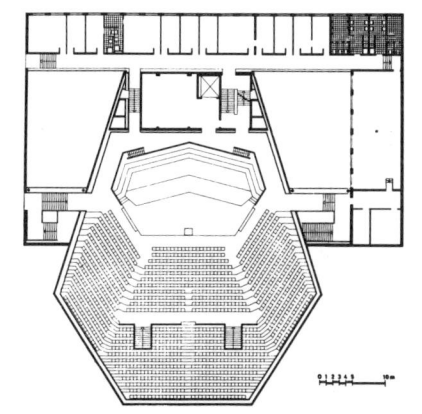

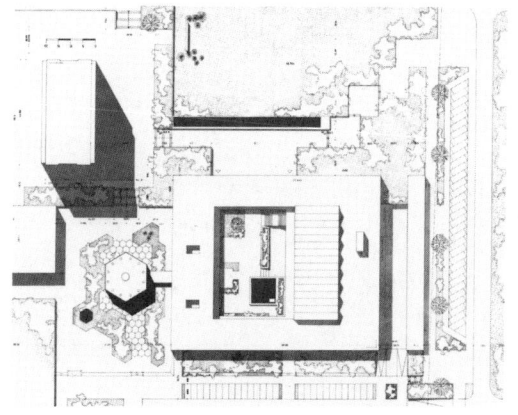

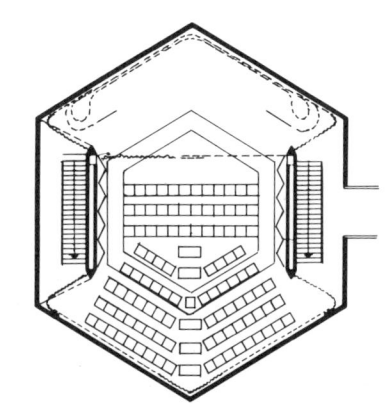

Neue Pinakothek München

Wettbewerb 1966. Versuch, trotz aller räumlichen Differenzierung und Vielfalt einen sich einfach anbietenden »Zwangs«-Rundgang zu schaffen.

Competition, 1966. An attempt, in spite of all the spatial differentiation and variety, to create a circulation route that has a quality of inevitability about it.

Sprengel Museum Hannover

Wettbewerb 1972.

A competition for the Sprengel Museum in Hanover, 1972.

Wilhelm Hack Museum Ludwigshafen

Wettbewerb 1972 in Zusammenhang mit der städtebaulichen Aufgabe, neben dem Museum ein städtisches Service-Gebäude und eine Platzanlage mit Ladenzentrum über einer Tiefgarage zu schaffen.

Competition, 1972, to a planning brief for a municipal service building and a public open space with shopping centre over basement parking next to the museum.

Wallraf Richartz Museum und Museum Sammlung Ludwig Köln

Wettbewerb 1975. Zwischen Kölner Dom und Rheinufer waren neben den Museen ein Konzertsaal für 2000 Personen und Tiefgaragen unterzubringen. Der Lösungsvorschlag nimmt Rücksicht auf die beherrschende Größe des Domchors und ordnet sich dem Maßstab der Kölner Rheinfront ein.

Competition, 1975. Set between Cologne Cathedral and the banks of the Rhine, a museum, a concert hall for 2000 persons and an underground garage were required. The proposed solution takes into account the dominant size of the cathedral choir and also manages to maintain the scale of the Cologne Rhine waterfront.

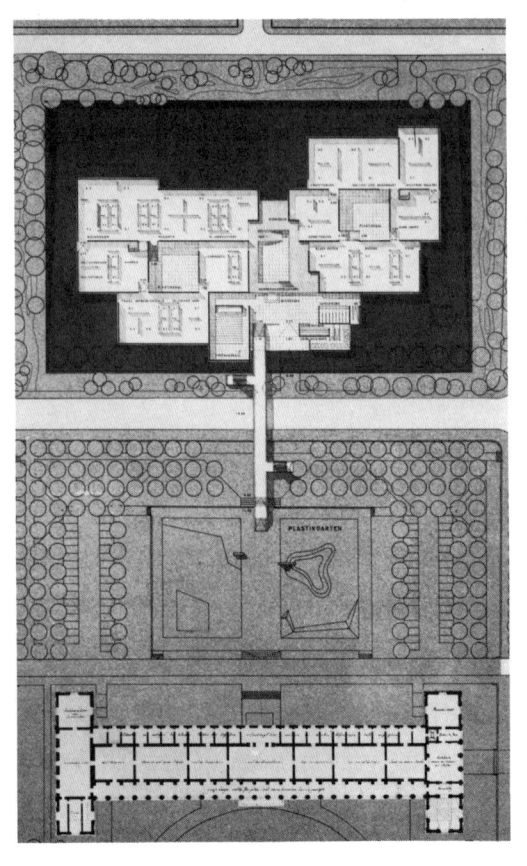

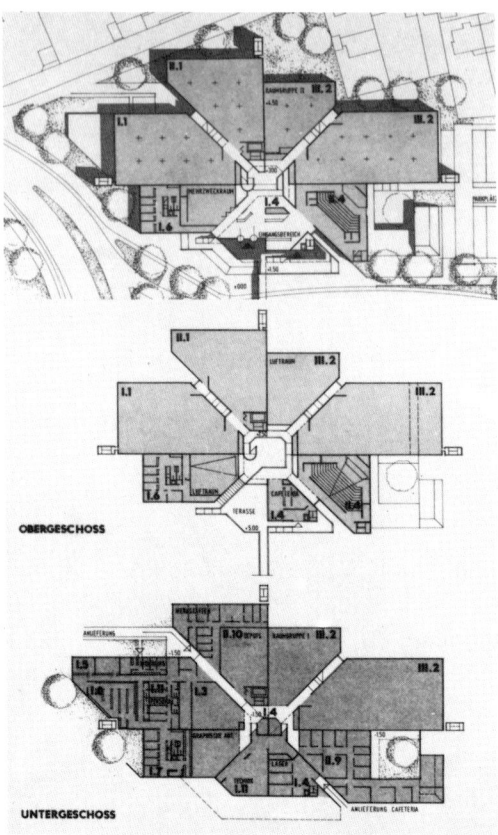

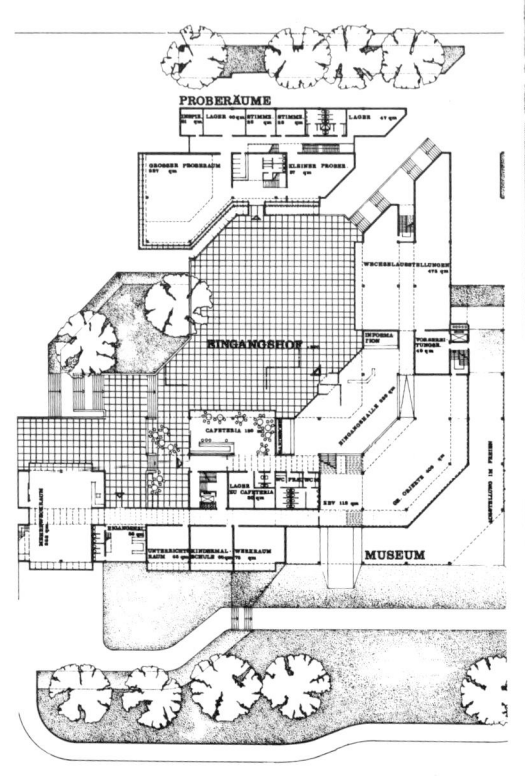

Jahrhunderthalle Hoechst

Aus dem 1. Preis in einem internationalen Wettbewerb ging das 1963 in Betrieb genommene Mehrzweckgebäude hervor. Es bietet Raum für die vielfältigsten Aktivitäten: Theater, Konzert, Schauspiel, Ballett, Versammlungen, Feste, Sport (Tennis, Boxen, Eislauf, Turnen), Ausstellungen, Kongresse, Film etc. Die Bestuhlung kann zwischen 1850 und 4000 Plätzen variiert werden. Das Bauwerk enthält neben der Festhalle Foyers, Garderoben, Speisesäle, Casino, Gästeräume, Kegelbahnen, Hotel und Verwaltung. Die 80 m freigespannte Kuppel – auf sechs Auflagern abgestützt – ist im Scheitel nicht mehr als 13 cm dick. Mit dem Kunstpreis des Landes Hessen 1965 ausgezeichnet.

This multi-purpose building, which was taken into service in 1963, was the result of a first prize-winning entry to an international competition. It provides space for the most varied of activities, – theatre, concerts, plays, ballet, assemblies, festivities, sports, (tennis, boxing, ice skating, gymnastics), exhibitions, congresses, films, etc. The number of seats can be varied from 1850 to 4000.
In addition to the auditorium, the building also contains foyers, cloakrooms, dining halls, club rooms, guest rooms, bowling alleys, a hotel and administration. The dome, of 80 m clear span, resting on six supports, is not more than 13 cm thick at the top. Awarded the Arts Prize of Hessen in 1965.

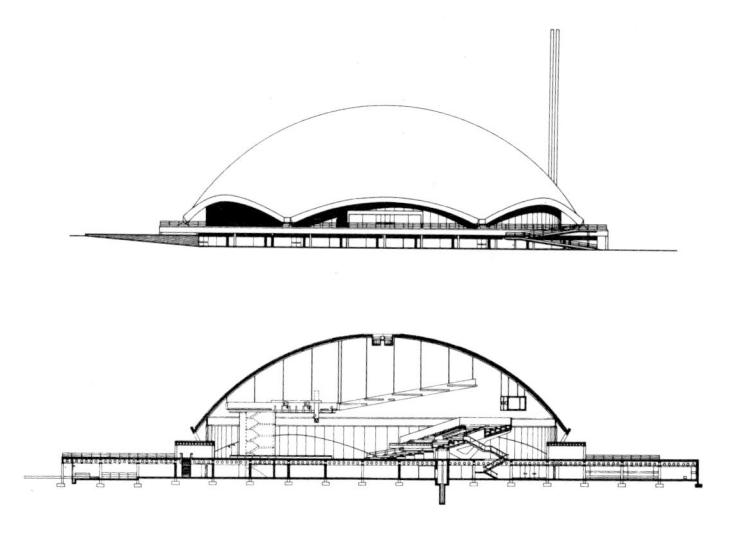

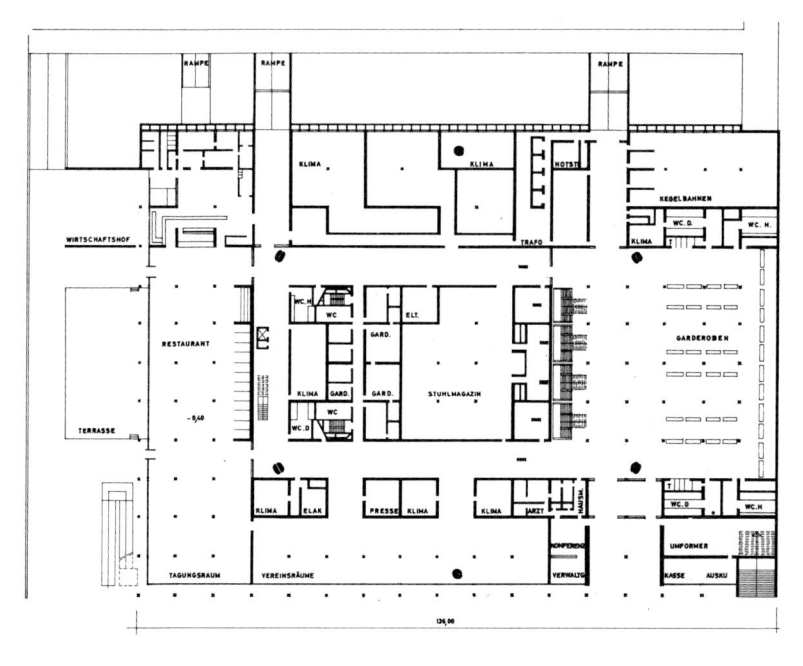

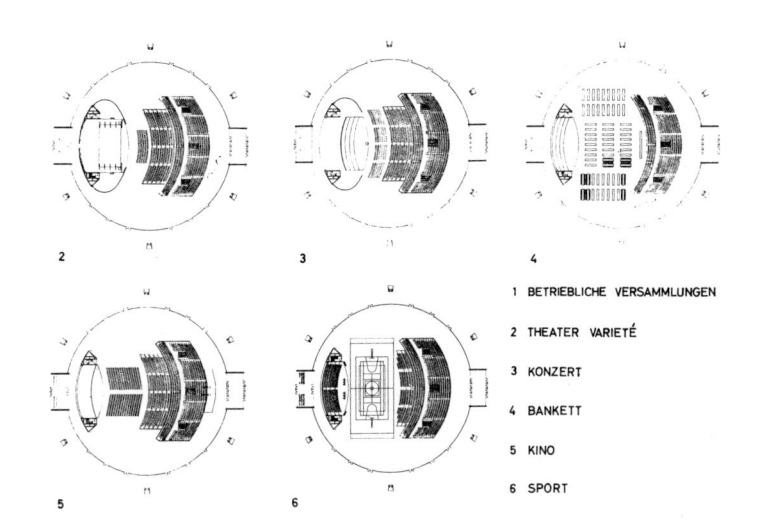

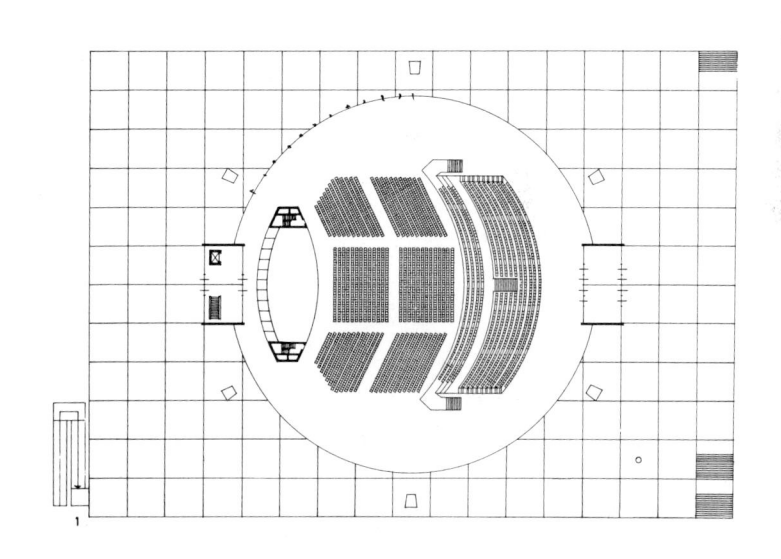

Grundrisse
oben Sockelgeschoß
unten Saalgeschoß

Plans
top Plinth storey
bottom Hall level

1 BETRIEBLICHE VERSAMMLUNGEN
2 THEATER VARIETÉ
3 KONZERT
4 BANKETT
5 KINO
6 SPORT

212

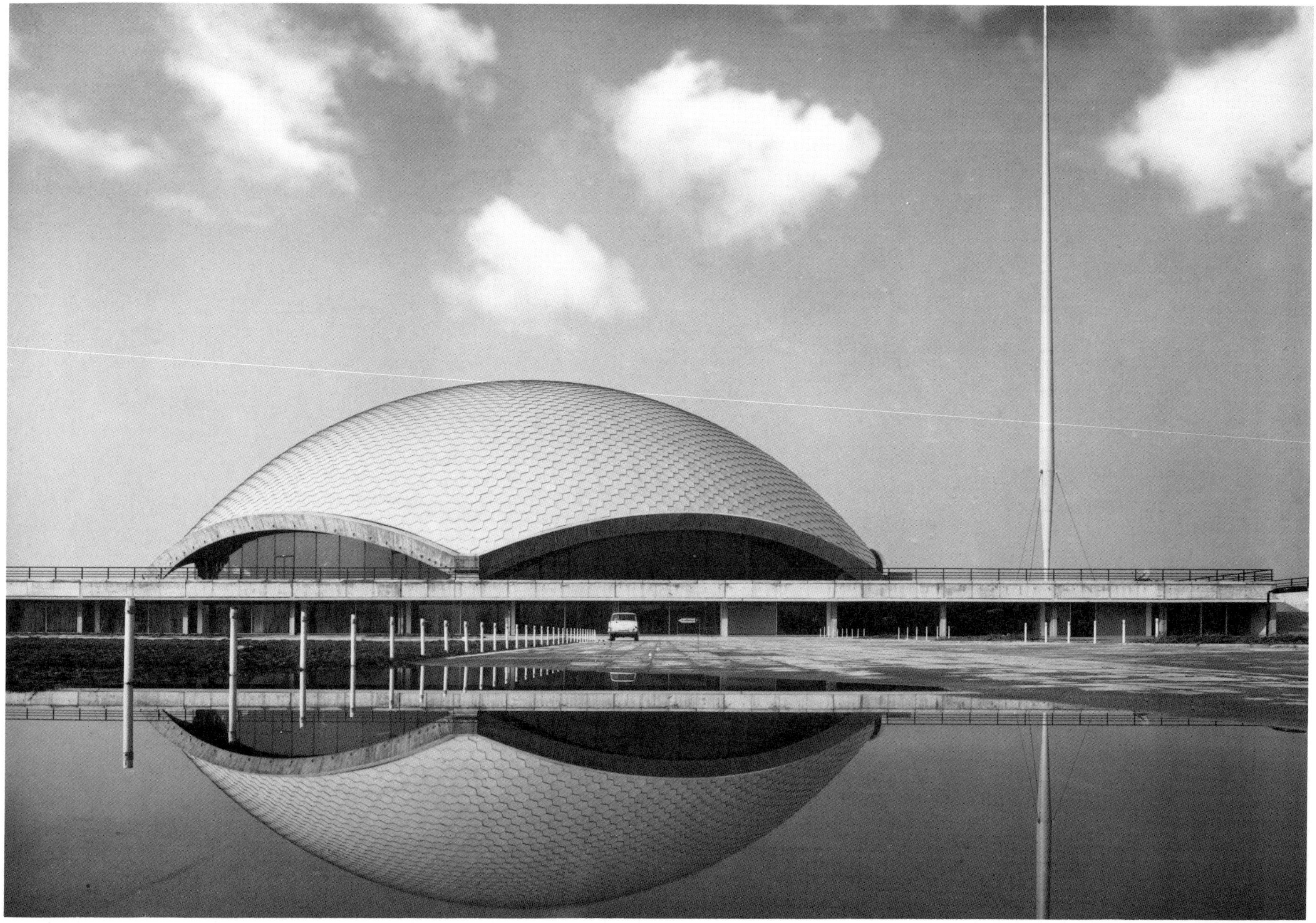

Anhang

KSP	Kraemer Sieverts & Partner
Büros	in Braunschweig und Köln mit den Adressen: Wolfenbütteler Straße 45 3300 Braunschweig Telefon 0531/6 55 21-24 Am Römerturm 3 5000 Köln 1 Telefon 0221/23 62 46
Partner	Professor Dr.-Ing. Friedrich Wilhelm Kraemer Dr.-Ing. Ernst Sieverts Dipl.-Ing. Karl Friedrich Gerstenberg Professor Dr.-Ing. Heinz Henning Huth Dipl.-Ing. Lutz Käferhaus Dipl.-Ing. Kurt Wolf
Projektpartner	Frau Dipl.-Ing. Aleksandra Nitschke-Stefanović Dipl.-Ing. Hans Dieter Reichel Dipl.-Ing. Dieter Schapitz

Werksverzeichnis

Die im Werkverzeichnis verwendeten Abkürzungen bedeuten:

FWK : Architekt Prof. Dr.-Ing. Friedrich Wilhelm Kraemer (1936 – 1960)
KPS : Architekten Prof. Kraemer – Pfennig – Sieverts (1960 – 1974)
KSP : Architekten Prof. Kraemer Sieverts & Partner (seit 1975)

Als Mitarbeiter sind die wesentlich Beteiligten, in der Regel die verantwortlichen Projektleiter und Oberbauleiter aufgeführt. Die jeweils zuständigen Partner sind nicht genannt, es sei denn, sie waren vor ihrer Partnerschaft als Projektleiter tätig. Den inzwischen ausgeschiedenen Partnern schulden wir die Nennung ihrer Zuständigkeit bei folgenden, in diesem Buch dargestellten, Bauten, Projekten und Wettbewerben (WBW):

Dipl.-Ing. Stjepan Çadéz BDA

Hauptverwaltung Thyssengas, Duisburg-Hamborn
Deutsche Bank Düsseldorf, 1. BA
WBW Bremer Bank, Bremen
Bildungszentrum Südwest, Karlsruhe
WBW Sprengel Museum, Hannover
WBW Wilhelm Hack Museum, Ludwigshafen

Arch. Eike Wiehe BDA

WBW Heidelberger Druckmaschinenfabrik, Heidelberg
Rathauserweiterung Wolfsburg
WBW Regionalverwaltung Salzgitter-Stahl, Düsseldorf
WBW Rathaus Hattingen
WBW Verwaltungszentrum eines Chemiekonzerns
WBW Erweiterung Hamburg-Mannheimer-Versicherung, Hamburg
WBW Hauptverwaltung GEW, Köln
Arbeitsamt Hagen
WBW Arbeitsamt Bochum
WBW Paul Ehrlich Institut, Langen
WBW Pharmazeutische Institute TU Braunschweig
Research and Study Centres, Saudi-Arabien
Wohn- und Geschäftszentrum Kastanienhof, Köln

Übersetzer Peter Green München

Wir danken an dieser Stelle ganz besonders Frau Dr.-Ing. Hildegund Brandenburg, Karlsruhe, die die Zusammenstellung und das Lay-out des Buches übernahm und in harmonischer Zusammenarbeit mit dem Karl Krämer Verlag die Schlußarbeit besorgte.

Seite	Bauten + Projekte	Architekten/ Kooperationen	Verantwortliche Mitarbeiter
	Bauten der Denkmalpflege		
10	Gewandhaus Braunschweig	FWK	Haas, Heier, Herrenberger, Jebens
12	Herzog August Bibliothek Wolfenbüttel	KPS im Auftrage des Landes Niedersachsen, vertreten durch das Staatshochbauamt Wolfenbüttel (vor 1969) und Staatshochbauamt I Braunschweig (nach 1969), Oberleitung/ Bauleitung.	Asendorf, Meier, Rippke
16	Büro- und Wohnhaus Am Römerturm 3 Köln	KSP	Heuveldop, v. Solodkoff
14	Zeughaus Wolfenbüttel	KPS/KSP Auftraggeber siehe Herzog August Bibliothek	Nieschalk, Pini-Weingand
13	Lessinghaus Wolfenbüttel	KPS-Planunion/KSP Auftraggeber siehe Herzog August Bibliothek	Käferhaus, Barz, Pini-Weingand
20	Hörfunkzentrale WDR Köln	KSP	Gabriel, Hoven, Schmiedecke
18	Deutsche Bank Düsseldorf (Königsallee 49/51)	KSP unter Mitwirkung von Klaus Ehrensberger Hamburg	Ahnesorg, Viehrig
	Wohnungsbauten, Heime, Hotels		
24	Haus Wolff-Limper Braunschweig	FWK	Bingel
24	»Unter den Eichen« Bad Harzburg	FWK	Westermann
24	Haus Hoeck Braunschweig	FWK	Werker
25	Haus Luther Braunschweig	FWK	Haas, Luckhardt, Asendorf
24	Haus Hess Braunschweig	FWK	Luckhardt, Asendorf
25	Haus Flebbe Braunschweig	FWK	Schäfer, Asendorf
28	Haus Kraemer 1 Braunschweig (1937)	FWK	Werker
26	Haus Sandforth Braunschweig	FWK	Hoge, Vitua
27	Haus Roedenbeck Stöckheim	KPS	Puell, Meißgeier
25	Kaserne Nienburg-Langendamm	FWK/KPS	Beier
27	Haus Munte Braunschweig	KPS	Schulze, Meißgeier
28	Haus Kraemer 2 Braunschweig (1955)	FWK	Hoge, Asendorf
29	Studentenwohnheime Berlin	KPS	Kersten, Wolf, John
30	Atriumhotel Braunschweig	KPS	Schulze, Meißgeier
33	Wohnbebauung am Alsterufer Hamburg (WBW)	KPS	Stahrenberg
34	Studentenwohnheim Berlin-Schlachtensee	KPS-Planunion	Reichel
33	Hotel Holiday-Inn Wolfsburg	KPS unter Mitwirkung von Holiday Inns Inc./Frankfurt (Innengestaltung/ Bauleitung)	Hovestadt, Käferhaus, Schroeder
39	Musikerhaus in Monte Leon bei Maspalomas Gran Canaria	KPS	Majewski
36	Studentenwohnheim Würzburg-Keesburg	KPS unter Mitwirkung von Spindler sen. München (Bauleitung)	Reichenbach
36	Studentisches Wohnen (WBW)	KPS unter Mitwirkung von Jana-Bau AG Tauber- bischoffsheim (Generalunternehmung)	M. Käferhaus
34	Eifelhöhenklinik Marmagen	KSP in Arbeitsgemeinschaft mit Prof. Huth Köln	
36	Studentenwohnheim Würzburg Zweierweg	KSP unter Mitwirkung von Spindler jun. München (Bauleitung)	v. Gramatzki

Seite	Bauten + Projekte	Architekten/ Kooperationen	Verantwortliche Mitarbeiter
35	Studentenwohnheim Bamberg	KPS/KSP unter Mitwirkung von Neundorfer + Seemüller Bamberg (Bauleitung)	Reichenbach, v. Gramatzki
38	Wohn- und Geschäftshaus Am Römerturm 2 Köln	KSP unter Mitwirkung von Cento-Wohnbau Köln (Oberleitung/Bauleitung)	Gabriel, K. Kraemer, Regenhard, Goebel
39	Altenheim St. Vinzenz Köln (WBW)	KSP	K. Kraemer, Schwickert
	Schulen, Universitäten, Bibliotheken		
42	Oberschule Wolfsburg	FWK	Jebens, Sieverts, Monse
43	Mittelschule Peine	FWK	Broos, Lehmann
43	Handelsschule Heidelberg	FWK	Menzel, Monse, Geister
42	Aufbau- und Abendgymnasium Dortmund	FWK	Menzel, Wolf
44	Auditorium Maximum TH Braunschweig	KPS	Stammeier, Schulze, Wolf
45	Rektorat und Fakultät 1 TH Braunschweig	KPS	Schulze, Esau
46	Bibliothek TH Braunschweig	KPS in Zusammenarbeit mit Neue Heimat Hamburg (Oberleitung/Bauleitung)	John
48	Elektrotechnische Institute TH Braunschweig	KPS	Breidenbend, Esau
48	Volksschule Dortmund-Rahm	KPS	Jürgens, Vitua
50	Mensa und Studentenhaus Universität Kiel	KPS	Dziadzka, Vitua
49	Fakultät III TH Braunschweig (WBW)	FWK	Huth
49	Hörsaalgebäude Universität Münster	KPS	Stammeier, Harms
62	WDR College Gebäude Köln-Bocklemünd	KPS	Hovestadt
51	Sportforum Universität Kiel (WBW)	KPS	Birner
52	Ingenieurschule Gelsenkirchen	KPS	Jürgens, Juraschek
49	Universität Bremen (WBW)	KPS	Martinoff
49	Universität Bielefeld (WBW)	KPS	Nitschke-Stefanović
54	Bildungsstätte Nümbrecht	KPS-Planunion	Käferhaus, Heyden, Rippke
62	Schulzentrum Hankensbüttel (WBW)	KSP	Pramann
56	Schulzentrum Gifhorn	KSP in Zusammenarbeit mit A + I Wolfsburg (Oberleitung/Bauleitung)	Pramann, v. Gramatzki
58	Bildungszentrum Südwest Karlsruhe	KSP in Zusammenarbeit mit Schulz Karlsruhe (Bauleitung)	Pramann, Schmidt-Joswig, Viehrig
60	Internal Security Forces College Riyadh Saudi-Arabien (Gutachten)	KSP im Rahmen von AGC Associated German Consultants Essen	Nitschke-Stefanović
62	Bundesakademien Brühl (WBW)	KSP	Nitschke-Stefanović
62	Paul Ehrlich Institut Langen (WBW)	KSP	
63	Civil Defence Institute Riyadh Saudi-Arabien	KSP im Rahmen von AGC Associated German Consultants Essen unter Mitwirkung von Osnova Belgrad und Jones-McCoach London (Ausschreibung)	Zahn, Grund
74	Imam Mohammad Bin Saud Islamic University Riyadh Saudi Arabien (WBW)	KSP	Nitschke-Stefanović, Reichel
68	Pharmazeutische Institute der TU Braunschweig	KSP in Zusammenarbeit mit Strabag-Bau AG Hannover (Generalunternehmung) unter Mitwirkung von Staatshochbauamt I Braunschweig (Oberleitung)	M. Käferhaus
70	Forschungsgebäude Leibnizhaus Wolfenbüttel	KSP Auftraggeber siehe Herzog August Bibliothek	Neumann, K. Kraemer, M. Käferhaus, v. Gramatzki, Pini-Weingand, Duerre
72	Hochschule für Bildende Künste Braunschweig	KSP unter Mitwirkung von Staatshochbauamt I Braunschweig (Oberleitung)	Zahn, Kloster, Schapitz, Ludwig, Duerre

Seite	Bauten + Projekte	Architekten/ Kooperationen	Verantwortliche Mitarbeiter
74	Technische Universität Hamburg-Harburg (WBW)	KSP	Zachmann, Kuck
75	Girls' College Riyadh Saudi-Arabien (WBW)	KSP	Nitschke-Stefanović
	Städtebau, Innerstädtische Zentren, Sanierungen		
78	Iduna-Zentrum Braunschweig	KPS	Hovestadt, Heyden
79	Fußgängerbrücke Berliner Platz Braunschweig	KPS	Käferhaus, Heyden
80	Altstadtsanierung Karlsruhe (WBW)	KPS	Garbrecht, Diekmann
81	Innerstädtisches Zentrum Neustadt/Weinstraße	KPS-Planunion Bauherr: Deutsche Bau- und Grundstücks AG – Baugrund – Bonn	Çadéz, Viehrig
80	Wohnbebauung Fontenay Hamburg (WBW)	KSP	Nitschke-Stefanović, Briesemeister
82	Research and Study Centres Saudi Arabien	KSP unter Mitwirkung von Mews u. Teichmann, Berlin und Harden, Braunschweig (Ausschreibung)	Reichel, Ludwig
88	Wadi Saqra Circle Project Amman Jordanien (WBW)	KSP	Ahola
90	Berliner Platz Mülheim/Ruhr (WBW)	KSP	Zachmann, Kuck
91	Kleiner Schloßplatz Stuttgart (WBW)	KSP in Arbeitsgemeinschaft mit Meyer-Hakala, Braunschweig	
92	Gürzenich I Köln (WBW)	KSP in Arbeitsgemeinschaft mit Prof. Huth, Köln	
92	Gürzenich II Köln (WBW)	KSP in Arbeitsgemeinschaft mit Prof. Huth, Köln	
86	Wohn- und Geschäftszentrum Kreishaus Galerie St.-Apern-Straße Köln	KSP	Tyrell, Hahn
	Industriebauten, Sozialbauten		
96	Fabrikanlage Unger und Sohn Braunschweig	FWK	Luckhardt, Asendorf
96	Rolleiflex Werkstattgebäude VII Braunschweig	FWK	Sieverts, Pfennig
96	Sozialgebäude Büssing Braunschweig	FWK	Askanazy, Asendorf
97	Volkswagen-Großhandlung Max Voets Braunschweig	FWK	Sieverts, Asendorf
96	NSM Spielautomatenfabrik Bingen	FWK	Lehmann
98	Rolleiflex Werkstattgebäude VIII Braunschweig	FWK	Pfennig
98	Rolleiflex Werkstattgebäude IX Braunschweig	FWK	Pfennig
99	Maschinenfabrik Wohlenberg Hannover	KPS	Sieverts, Meißgeier
99	Gemeinschaftshaus Aluminium-Walzwerke Singen	KPS	in der Mühlen, Lange
99	Prüflabor Rheinisch-Westfälische Kalkwerke Dornap	KPS	Kafka
100	Kantine Veba Chemie Gelsenkirchen	KPS unter Mitwirkung von Harms + Partner Hannover (Bauleitung)	Çadéz, Muschalla, Bernstorf
101	Heidelberger Druckmaschinenfabrik Heidelberg (WBW)	KSP	M. Käferhaus
102	Braunschweiger Zeitung Braunschweig	KSP unter Mitwirkung von Rüping GmbH Düsseldorf (Projektsteuerung/Bauleitung)	Reichel, Schapitz
101	Fernmeldeturm Düsseldorf (WBW)	KSP in Arbeitsgemeinschaft mit Deutsche Baugrund Bonn	Gabriel
	Büro- und Verwaltungsgebäude, Geschäftshäuser		
108	Flebbe Braunschweig	FWK	Luckhardt, Pfennig
109	Pfeiffer & Schmidt Braunschweig	FWK	Askanazy, Asendorf

Seite	Bauten + Projekte	Architekten/ Kooperationen	Verantwortliche Mitarbeiter
109	Wasser- und Schifffahrtsdirektion und Kataster- und Vermessungsamt Bremen	FWK	Welp, Menzel
108	Vereinigte Leben Bremen	FWK	Sieverts, Stammeier, Bohl
108	Hamburg Mannheimer Versicherung Hannover Friedrichswall	FWK	Sieverts, Diedrichsen
112	Wullbrandt & Seele Braunschweig	KPS	Hovestadt, Speck, Asendorf
113	Iduna Versicherung Braunschweig	FWK	Sieverts, Schulze, Dönges
114	Perschmann Braunschweig	KPS	Pfennig, Meißgeier, Asendorf
110	Hauptverwaltung Unterharzer Berg- und Hüttenwerke Goslar	FWK	Welp, Broos, Sieverts, Pysall, Geister
113	Iduna Versicherung Osnabrück	KPS	Stammeier, Bohl
113	Iduna Versicherung Münster	KPS	Stammeier, Bohl
113	Iduna Versicherung Essen	KPS	Dönges
108	Staatskanzlei Hannover (WBW)	KPS	Huth
115	Rechenzentrum eines Chemiekonzerns	KPS	Askanazy, Wolf
114	Erweiterungsbau Preussag Hannover	KPS	Huth
114	Iduna Versicherung Schweinfurt	KPS in Zusammenarbeit mit Joachim Haberland (Oberleitung/Bauleitung)	Wittenberg, Struhk
118	Hauptverwaltung BP Hamburg	KPS	Schulze, Vitua, Wolf II
116	Rathaus Essen (WBW)	KPS	Kafka
121	Preussag Berlin	KPS	Huth
126	Rathaus Castrop-Rauxel (WBW)	KPS	Huth
120	Bayer Verkaufsabteilungen Leverkusen (Gutachten)	KPS	Nitschke-Stefanović, Stahrenberg
121	Iduna Versicherung Gelsenkirchen	KPS	Stammeier
122	Hauptverwaltung DKV Köln	KPS	Huth, Harms, Viehrig
126	Iduna Versicherung Hamburg	KPS	Stammeier, Muschalla
121	Stadthaus Bonn (WBW)	KPS	Stahrenberg
127	Vorstandsgebäude Bayer Leverkusen (WBW)	KPS	M. Käferhaus, Nitschke-Stefanović
126	Hauptverwaltung Shell Hamburg (WBW)	KPS	M. Käferhaus, Nitschke-Stefanović
128	Hauptverwaltung Veba Chemie Gelsenkirchen-Buer (Gutachten)	KPS	Muschalla, Çadéz, Boskamp
136	Hauptverwaltung Vorwerk Wuppertal	KPS	Gerstenberg
136	Hauptverwaltung Klöckner Duisburg (WBW)	KPS	Gerstenberg
128	Hauptverwaltung Philips Wien (WBW)	KPS in Arbeitsgemeinschaft mit Dr. Hlavenitzka, Wien	Cadez
129	Unternehmensbereich D Siemens München-Perlach (WBW)	KPS	Nitschke-Stafanović, Stahrenberg
137	Deutsche Botschaft Helsinki (WBW)	KPS	M. Käferhaus, Nitschke-Stefanović
138	Hauptverwaltung Bayern Versicherung München	KPS in Arbeitsgemeinschaft mit von Wertz, Prof. Ottow, Bachmann, Marx, München unter Mitwirkung von Konold, München (Bauleitung)	Nitschke-Stefanović, Reichel
130	Hauptverwaltung VEW Dortmund	KPS-Planunion unter Mitwirkung von Harms + Partner Hannover (Bauleitung)	Gerstenberg, Bernstorf
139	Rathauserweiterung Wolfsburg	KPS-Planunion	Schapitz
137	Hauptverwaltung ÖVA-Versicherung Mannheim (Gutachten)	KPS	Çadéz
140	Hauptverwaltung Getreideimportgesellschaft Duisburg	KPS in Arbeitsgemeinschaft mit Laskowski und Schneidewind Braunschweig	Reichel, Nitschke-Stefanović

Seite	Bauten + Projekte	Architekten/ Kooperationen	Verantwortliche Mitarbeiter	Seite	Bauten + Projekte	Architekten/ Kooperationen	Verantwortliche Mitarbeiter
141	Hauptverwaltung Röhrenwerke Mannesmann-Lintorf (WBW)	KPS	Gabriel	156	Hauptverwaltung GEW Köln	KSP	Barz, Bernstorf, Schmiedecke
140	Hauptverwaltung Tchibo Hamburg (WBW)	KSP	Hirche	175	Arbeitsamt Hagen	KSP in Zusammenarbeit mit bauform GmbH Köln (Projektsteuerung) und Dr. Kammel, Hagen	U. Tyrell
142	Technisches Rathaus, Köln 1. Stufe (WBW)	KSP	Baum				
141	Hauptverwaltung Norddeutsche und Hamburg Bremer Versicherung Hamburg (WBW)	KSP in Zusammenarbeit mit E. Wiehe, Hamburg	Schaub	164	Arbeitsamt Hannover	KSP in Zusammenarbeit mit bauform GmbH Köln (Projektsteuerung/ Bauleitung) und E. Wiehe Hamburg (Planung) unter Mitwirkung von Staatshochbauamt II Hannover	
144	Deutsche Botschaft Moskau (WBW)	KPS	Nitschke-Stefanović				
145	Hauptverwaltung Vereinigte Versicherungsgruppe München-Perlach (Gutachten)	KSP	Nitschke-Stefanović				
				171	Municipality Abu Dhabi (WBW)	KSP	Nitschke-Stefanović
144	Regionalverwaltung Salzgitter Stahl Düsseldorf (Gutachten)	KSP	Gabriel, Streibel	165	Hillmannkomplex Bremen (Gutachten)	KSP	Nitschke-Stefanović
129	Hauptverwaltung Colonia-Versicherung Köln (WBW)	KPS	Gerstenberg, Nitschke-Stefanović, Heinemann	166	Hauptverwaltung Veba Oel AG Gelsenkirchen	KSP in Arbeitsgemeinschaft mit Stj. Çadéz Köln Gartenarchitekten: Boedecker, Beyer, Wagenfeld Beleuchtung: Bartenbach	Bernstorf, Goray
146	Kreishaus Warendorf (WBW)	KSP	Nitschke-Stefanović				
146	Hauptverwaltung DEVK Köln (WBW)	KSP	Nitschke-Stefanović				
146	Rathaus Hattingen (WBW)	KSP	Schmidt	170	Hauptverwaltung VW Wolfsburg (WBW)	KSP	Nitschke-Stefanović
151	Verwaltungszentrum eines Chemiekonzerns (Gutachten)	KSP	Barz	172	Arbeitsamt Bochum (WBW)	KSP in Arbeitsgemeinschaft mit bauform GmbH Köln (Projektsteuerung/Bauleitung) unter Mitwirkung von Finanzbauamt Dortmund	K. Kraemer
148	Hauptverwaltung Thyssengas Duisburg-Hamborn	KSP unter Mitwirkung von DAL Mainz (Projektsteuerung)	Baum, Schmidt-Joswig				
152	Ministry of Public Works and Housing Riyadh Saudi Arabien (Gutachten)	KSP unter Mitwirkung von Mews u. Teichmann Berlin und Symonds u. Tramor Cardiff (Ausschreibung)	Reichel	184	Arbeitsamt Essen	KSP in Zusammenarbeit mit bauform GmbH Köln	Reichel, Ahola
				171	Bundespostministerium Bonn (WBW)	KSP	Zachmann, Kuck
151	Erweiterung Hauptverwaltung Hamburg Mannheimer Versicherung Hamburg (WBW)	KSP	M. Käferhaus	174	Rathaus Oldenburg (WBW)	KSP	Meyer, Leonhardt
				171	Kreishaus Hofheim (WBW)	KSP	Schmidt

Seite	Bauten + Projekte	Architekten/ Kooperationen	Verantwortliche Mitarbeiter
178	Hauptverwaltung DEVK Köln Ausführung	KSP in Arbeitsgemeinschaft mit Novotny Mähner + Ass., Offenbach	Viehrig, Eikermann
179	Arbeitsamt Bielefeld (WBW)	KSP in Arbeitsgemeinschaft mit bauform GmbH Köln	Reichel, Ahola
179	Landratsamt Goslar (WBW)	KSP	Zahn
179	Boehringer Mannheim (Gutachten)	KSP	Zahn, Nitschke-Stefanović
180	BASF Espagnola Barcelona (WBW)	KSP	Nitschke-Stefanović
143	Technisches Rathaus Köln 2. Stufe (WBW)	KSP	Meyer, Leonhardt
186	Hauptverwaltung Schloemann-Siemag Düsseldorf (WBW)	KSP	Zachmann, Kuck
181	Landratsamt Starnberg (WBW)	KSP	Hennies
181	Rathauserweiterung Wilhelmshaven (WBW)	KSP	Zachmann, Kuck
185	Bürogebäude St. Augustin (Gutachten)	KSP	M. Käferhaus, Nitschke-Stefanović
182	Verwaltungsgebäude 3 Krupp AG Essen (Gutachten)	KSP	M. Käferhaus, Nitschke-Stefanović
185	Erweiterungsbau VIAG Bonn	KSP	Schapitz, Seifert, Beckmann
185	Residential Commercial Complexes of Abu Dhabi (WBW)	KPS im Rahmen von AGC	Reichel
187	Hauptverwaltung Lurgi Frankfurt (Gutachten)	KSP	Nitschke-Stefanović

Banken

Seite	Bauten + Projekte	Architekten/ Kooperationen	Verantwortliche Mitarbeiter
190	Braunschweigische Staatsbank Lebenstedt	FWK	Woldt
191	Landeszentralbank Nordrheinwestfalen Düsseldorf	FWK/KPS	Menzel, Pysall, Geister
190	Stadtsparkasse Düsseldorf	KPS in Arbeitsgemeinschaft mit Rosskotten und Tritthardt Düsseldorf	Wenger
192	Stadtsparkasse Einbeck	KPS	Strohe
193	Simonbank Düsseldorf	KPS mit Schütze, Düsseldorf (Bauleitung)	Gerstenberg
196	Deutsche Bank Düsseldorf	KSP unter Mitwirkung von Frau Prof. Birkelbach Wuppertal (Innengestaltung)	Weber, Beckmann, K. Kraemer, Eikermann
202	Dresdner Bank Düsseldorf	KSP in Zusammenarbeit mit Schiel/Possekel, Düsseldorf (Ausführungsplanung/Bauleitung)	Brendel, Schmidt-Joswig
205	Bremer Bank Bremen (WBW)	KSP	Gabriel, Neumann
205	Landeszentralbank Wiesbaden (WBW)	KSP	Nitschke-Stefanović

Kulturbauten

Seite	Bauten + Projekte	Architekten/ Kooperationen	Verantwortliche Mitarbeiter
208	Norddeutscher Rundfunk Funkhaus Hannover	FWK in Arbeitsgemeinschaft mit Oesterlen und Lichtenhahn Hannover	Garten, Marlow, Heier
211	Jahrhunderthalle Hoechst	KPS	Beier, Juraschek
209	Norddeutscher Rundfunk Großer Sendesaal Hannover	FWK in Arbeitsgemeinschaft mit Oesterlen und Lichtenhahn Hannover	Beier
209	Studiobühne Universität Kiel	KPS	Dziadzka, Vitua
210	Neue Pinakothek München (WBW)	KPS	Birner
210	Sprengel Museum Hannover (WBW)	KSP	
210	Wallraf Richartz Museum und Museum Sammlung Ludwig Köln (WBW)	KSP	Baum
210	Wilhelm Hack Museum Ludwigshafen (WBW)	KSP	

Publikationen (Zeitschriften und Bücher)

Kraemer	Walter Gropius	Westermanns Monatshefte 8/57 S. 75
Kraemer	Richard Neutra	Westermanns Monatshefte 11/59 S. 53
Kraemer	Das Braunschweiger Schloß als Architektur-Prospekt	Bauwelt 13/60 S. 350
Kraemer	Universität Bremen	Weser-Kurier Nr. 48 2/61 S. 17
Kraemer	Brief zum 10jährigen Bestehen der Zeitschrift	glasforum 2/61 S. II
Kraemer	Der Arbeitsplatz	Deutsche Zeitung 5/61 S. II
Kraemer	Die Abhängigkeit des Raumklimas von Sonnenschutz und Fensterlüftung	Baumeister 11/61 S. 1129
Kraemer	Der Auftrag der Baukunst	DAI 12/61 S. 489
Kraemer	Entscheidend ist am Bau die innere und äußere Übereinstimmung	Detail 1/62 S. 9
Kraemer	Von drei Bereichen, die den Weg der Baukunst bestimmen	Handbuch des Bauwesens 62
Kraemer	Industriebau und Baukunst – Bedeutung der Grenzen	Bauen und Wohnen 5/62 S. 189
Kraemer	Die baukonstruktiven Grundgedanken der Stilepochen	Westermanns Monatshefte 12/62 S. 54
Kraemer	Uns alle trägt die gleiche Schöpfung	Materia Medica Nordmark 3. Sonderheft 1963
Kraemer	Mietbürohäuser	Deutsche Bauzeitung Sonderdruck 2/63 S. 87
Kraemer	Gute Hörsamkeit ist heute nicht nur Geheimnis	Detail 5/63 S. 548
Kraemer	Gewißheit und Ahnung in der Baukunst	Sonderdruck zur Einweihung Bürohaus Grün & Bilfinger 8/63
Kraemer	Moderne Industrie und Geschäftsbauten	DAI Sonderdruck 10/63
Kraemer	Gespräch zwischen den Fakultäten	Stadtbauwelt 3 38–39/64 S. 214
Kraemer	Gedanken zur Planung des Mietbürohauses	glasforum 4/64 S. 2
Kraemer	Staatstheater Braunschweig Neubau Kleines Haus	omnibus 10/64 S. 11
Kraemer	Zu 9 Diplomarbeiten	Bauwelt 1–2/65 S. 11 + 18
Kraemer	Ein Rathaus in unserer Zeit- Wettbewerbsentwurf für das Essener Rathaus	glasforum 3/1965
Kraemer	Die Wandlung der Baukunst durch den Industriebau	BP-Kurier IV/65 S. 8 Architektur und Wohnform 3/66 S. 62
Kraemer	Erfahrungen bei der Planung und Ausführung verglaster Hörsaalwände	Detail 5/65 S. 1002
Kraemer	Industriebau, der große Anreger für die Baukunst	Der Mensch und die Technik 14. 3. 66 A101
Kraemer	Das Großraumbüro, eine neue Bauaufgabe unserer Zeit	Deutsche Bauzeitung 4/66 S. 283
Kraemer	Die Stadt von heute für den Menschen von morgen	Auszug: Hochschultage 1967 (Lübeck) S. 62
Kraemer	Ordnung und Gestalt im Industriebau	Zentralblatt für Industriebau 10/67 S. 398
Kraemer	Die Gestalt von Bürohäusern	Bauwelt 1/68
Kraemer im Forumgespräch	Neue Tendenzen der Büroplanung	Büroplanung und Organisation 1968 (Pohlschröder)
Kraemer, Sieverts, Huth	Großraumbüro – dargestellt am Beispiel der DKV Köln	Krämer Verlag 1968
KPS	Gedanken über die Planung von Industriebauten	Bürodruck 1968/69
Sieverts	Büroarbeit von morgen	md 5/69 S. 70
Sieverts, Stahrenberg	Reversibilität Großraumbüro – Einzelraumbüro	Bauwelt 33/70 S. 1274

Autor	Titel	Quelle
Sieverts	Großraumbüros / Der Einfluß von Geschoßform und Geschoßgröße auf die Nutzungsvariabilität	Bauwelt 43/70 S. 1642
Sieverts	Über die Zergliederung komplexer Problemstrukturen	Bauen und Wohnen 12/70 S. XII 1 3/71 S. III 1
Sieverts, Wolf	Die Gefahren der Zahlenspiele	Bauwelt 14/71 S. 558
Sieverts	Erfahrungen mit der ZERKOS-Methode	Bauen und Wohnen 7/71 S. 314
Kraemer	Gegenwärtiger Stand der Planung von Verwaltungsbauten	Der Architekt 11/71 S. 271
Kraemer	Kriterien der Raumplaung für Büroarbeit	Fachtagung CeBit 71 S. 87
Sieverts	Variabilität, Flexibilität, Reversibilität	congena Texte 3/72
Kraemer	Vom Großraumbüro zur reversiblen Grundrißstruktur	Architektur und Wohnwelt 3/72, S. 149–151 + 188
Kraemer	Ist der Bürogroßraum der Weisheit letzter Schluß?	Deutsche Bauzeitschrift 4/72 S. 529
Sieverts	Reversible Bürobauten	bürotechnik, Automation und Organisation 11/72 S. 1393
Sieverts	Lagebedingungen der Konstantflächen bei reversiblen Bürobauten	Bauwelt 3/73 S. 124
Sieverts	Erfahrungen mit Großraumbüros. Sind 12 Quadratmeter zuwenig?	Rationelles Büro + EDV 11/73 S. 30
Kraemer	Erfahrungen mit Großraumbüros	Tagungsberichte Pro + Contra Großraumbüro
Sieverts	Die Zukunft der Großraumbüros – Mögliche Alternativen	Veranstalter: Verlag Moderne Industrie Febr. 1974
Sieverts Kraemer	Wirtschaftliche Aspekte der Gebäudeplanung Humane Aspekte der Gebäudeplanung	Tagungsberichtsband Cebit 1974 S. 135
Kraemer, Meyer	Bürohausgrundrisse	Alexander-Koch-Verlag 1974
Kraemer Sieverts	Serie: Künftige Tendenzen Humane Aspekte der Bürohausplanung Wirtschaftliche Verwaltungsgebäude	Bauen + Wohnen 1/75 S. 12 + S. 17 Bauen + Wohnen
Sieverts	Die unberechtigte Kritik am Großraumbüro	Büro + EDV 4/75 S. 18
Sieverts, Wolf	Die unbekannte Hypthek / Auswirkungen der Bauplanung auf die Kosten der Büroarbeit	Büro + EDV 10/75 S. 36
Sieverts, Wolf	Richtwerte für Kosten von Bürohäusern	Bauwelt 37/75 S. 1032
Kraemer	Reversibilität von Bürobauten	Bauen + Wohnen 12/75 S. 477
KSP	Großraumbüro (Neue Erkenntnisse, Erfahrungen, Verbesserungen)	Verlag Moderne Industrie 1975
Sieverts	Entwicklungen im Bürohausbau	Bauwelt 14/76 S. 440
Sieverts	Rathaus Wolfsburg – Das Rathausprojekt und seine Geschichte	Büro + EDV 1977
KSP	Das erste vollreversible Bürohaus	Büro + EDV 4/77 S. 22
Sieverts (Mitverfasser)	Personalenzyklopädie	Verlag Moderne Industrie Band 1 1977 Band 2 1978
Sieverts	Probleme der Reversibilität	Der Architekt 10/78 S. 461
KSP	Open plan offices, new ideas, experience and improvement	Mac Graw-Hill 1978
Sieverts	In kleinen Schritten weg vom Großraumbüro	Büro + EDV 4/79 S. 30

Autor	Titel	Quelle
Sieverts	Bürohaus von Morgen	Bürotechnik Jubiläumsheft Sep. 79 BTA + BTO (Bürotechnik) 12/1979 S. 1452
Sieverts	Bürohausbau morgen – Neue Erkenntnisse, neue Ziele, neue Schwierigkeiten – aus der Sicht des Architekten	
Sieverts	Großraumbüros: Erfahrungen, Erkenntnisse, Entwicklungen	Aktuelles Bauen 1979
Wolf	Kollege Computer im Architekturbüro – ein Erfahrungsbericht	Deutsche Bauzeitung 3/80 S. 69
Sieverts	Bürohausbauten der 80er Jahre	Baumeister 9/1980 S. 863
Sieverts	Gruppenräume: Individualisierung der Arbeitsplatzumwelt	Deutsches Architektenblatt 9/80 S. 1157
Sieverts	Bürohaus- und Verwaltungsbauten	Kohlhammer-Verlag 1980
Sieverts	Alternative- im Büro – so sehen Büros der Zukunft aus	AIT 5/81
Sieverts	Büroarchitektur im Wandel – Gruppenbüros erschließen Rationalisierungsreserven	Europa Industrie Revue 3/81 S. 19
Sieverts	Sonnenschutzsysteme Planungs- und Ausführungsprobleme	Der Architekt 7–8/1981 S. 367
Sieverts	GEW-Gruppenräume realisiert	Büro + EDV 9/81 S. 12
Sieverts, Langohr (Mitverfasser)	Büroraum- und Arbeitsplatzgestaltung Organisatorisch bedingte Arbeitsplatzumsetzungen – Ergebnis einer Repräsentativerhebung	Arbeitskreis im Verband der Privaten Krankenversicherungen Erfahrungsbericht 6 gemäß Protokoll der Sitzung am 24./25. 10. 1981
Sieverts	Sanierung von Bürogebäuden	Deutsches Architektenblatt 4/82 S. 473 Office Management 6/1982 S. 660
Sieverts	Alternativen im Büro – so sehen Büros der Zukunft aus	AIT 5/82 S. 387 HK-international Holz + Kunststoff 9/82 S. 780–786
Sieverts (Mitverfasser)	Bürogestaltung und Gesundheit	FBO Verlag 1982
Sieverts	Konzepte für Büros mit Zukunft Tagungsband mit konkreten Anregungen für Büroraumplanung und Büroorganisation Richtungsweisende Lösungen der Architektur für das gewählte Büroraumkonzept	Verlag Akzente Studiengemeinschaft 1982

Mitarbeiter / Assistents

Reihenfolge annähernd chronologisch entsprechend dem Eintritt in die jeweiligen Büros FWK, KPS, KSP

André, Martha
Asendorf, Friedrich
Askanazy, Gert
Ackermann, Peter
Axhausen, Joachim
Achenbach, Albrecht
Ameling, Walter
Argen, Erol
Auerlich, Ursula
Asuquo, Offioug
Albert, Hans-Jürgen
Abhau, Hans-Peter
Altemark, Barbara
Angerstein, Ulrike
Arnecke, Angelika
Ahnesorg, Margit
Ahnesorg, R.-Dieter
Albert, Clemens
Ahrens, Heike
Andreas, Ulrike
Andresen, Eva
Ahola, Antti
Afchar, Masoud

Bingel, Wolfgang
Bahlhorn, Horst
Birker, Karl
Broos, Hans
Beckhoff, Friedr. Wilhelm
Burckhard, Götz
Bellenworth, Marianne
Böhm, Johannes
Brügge, Rolf
Becker, Ines von
Bertges, Ludwig
Blenkle, Rolf
Bartels, Dietrich
Bührmann, Norbert
Becker, Udo
Brenner, Brigitte
Barlen, Dieter
Beier, Horst
Brakebusch, Tile
Brandi, Jochen
Breidenbend, Bert
Bahr, Peter
Bente, Ulrich
Blume, Andrea
Bohl, Rolf Rudi
Bacher, Ursula
Beckmann, Ilse
Blaich, Ulrike
Brinkmann, Reinhold
Brunnert, Hans Georg
Bechtloff, Gerhard
Bönig, Elfriede
Breimeier, Dörte
Becker, Gudrun
Bittel, Günther
Blank, Wilfried
Bofinger, Helge Grote

Balassa, Resso
Berke, Arnold
Bernotat, K. H.
Boldt, Walter
Busch, Ingrid
Beuthan, Barbara
Bischoff, Sabine
Braxator, Brigitte
Bellin, Günther
Brüntrup, Josef
Brügmann, Karin
Birner, Christoph
Brüggeboss, Heidemarie
Behrens, Monika
Bernstorf, Dietrich
Bischoff, Gerhard
Buchholz, Susanne
Büttner, Hans-Joachim
Beddies, Renate
Bischoff, Edith
Bliemeister, Alfred
Burghardt, Hannelore
Bartel, Anette
Brandes, Ursula
Becker, Regine
Barth, Lothar
Barth, Margarete
Brannies, Günvor
Blychert, Ingvar
Beekmann, Ben
Brandenburg, Hildegund
Beckmann, Jörg
Bock, Hans Egger
Barz, Almut
Baum, Mirko
Breuer, Peter
Brandes, Karin
Blank, Hannelore
Breucha, Christa
Bauss, Angelika
Blüming, Egon
Brendel, Gustav
Briesemeister, Rainer
Beu, Johanna
Berling, Claudia
Behrens, Karin
Bahl, Klaus-Dieter
Burger, Eduard
Bremer, Kallika

Czech, Richard
Chot, Irene
Castell-Rüdenhausen, Ferdinand-Otto Graf zu
Cokorillo, Miro
Cunningham, Bernard
Coellen, Hans-Dieter
Cimiotti, Johann-Peter
Çadéz, Stjepan

Dempwolff v., Hermann
Diedrichsen, Hans-Peter
Dasselaar, Friedrich
Dönges, Hans-Rolf
Duis, Jan
Dziadzka, Alfred
Dalokay, Yalcin

Daamen, Hans Gisbert
Drüsedau, Heide
Dönges, Christa
Doose, Volker
Drohn, Wolf-Dieter
Döring, Dieter
Dienelt, Gisela
Diekmann, Jürgen
Dirks, Ruth
Dökel, Elfie
Dietrich, Verena
Delonge, Sieglinde
Decker, Ulrich
Dobcvisek, Alenka
Dransfeld, Ursula
Dümchen, Karin
Drux, Ferdinand
Dublanka, Ursula
Dorrioy, Lois
Duerre, Rolf

Ehrlich, Gerald
Eichstädt, Peter
Esau, Peter
Estorff v., Wilhelm
Eichstaedt, Wolfgang
Ernst, Hans-Joachim
Eschner, Werner
Ernst, Klaus
Erling, Manfred
Etscheid, Gisela
Eichstädt, Elfie
Ebeling, Ingo
Gravert, Uwe
Ewert, Gerda
Eikermann, Hartmut
Eysel, Ekkehard

Fritz, Walter
Fröde, Kurt
Funke, Hermann
Fischer, Heinz
Fleck, Walter
Faßhauer, Ullrich
Freudemann, Gerhard
Förster, Renate
Fuchs, Alfred
Faßmann, Joachim
Fournier, Gilbert
Franzke, Kl.-Dieter
Fischer, Dietrich
Fiedler, Peter
Fricke, Heinz
Feußner, Uta
Francke, Klaus
Feldhusen, Bernd
Friebe, Benno
Friese, Mechelt
Feuser, Karin
Frey, Dirk
Fiebig, Michael
Faber, Christian
Frank, Michael
Fleher, Gudrun
Friebe, Benno
Flamm, Ulrich

Forsbach, Jürgen
Freudenthal, Peter
Fussbroich, Josefine
Felten, Michael
Franke, Elke
Frings, Hubert
Folwatschni, Christine
Felbrich, Elisabeth
Fischer, Günter

Garten, Gerolf
Goritz, Günter
Gut, Johann
Geister, Gottfried
Gayer, Jean
Geister, Brigitte
Gerlach, Klaus,
Gleich, Edda
Gehrich, Margrit
Guther, Christian
Gallwitz, Peter
Griesenberg, Rolf
Gehle, Evelyn
Götsch, Herwil H. W.
Gross, Ute
Grünke, Alfred
Girndt, Gisela
Goldammer, Gotthard
Garbrecht, Dietrich
Geutsch, Erhard
Glockentöger, Otto
Gerstenberg, K. F.
Grommeck, Christiane
Gibbins, Olaf
Grosz, Helga
Gabriel, Klaus
Grote v., Brigitte
Günter, Ruth
Goeckens, Wolfgang
Grimm, Burghard
Graf, Ulrich
Gramatzki v., Klaus
Gieson, Monika
Gutmann, Horst-D.
Goldammer, Rita
Grigat, Kurt-Ernst
Gratze, Herbert
Gumminny, Bärbel
Grund, Sylvester
Grandjean, Johan
Gschwilm, Heinrich
Gasson, Marion
Goerentz, Rainer
Glöckler, Gerlinde
Gueloez, Levent
Goray, Helmut
Gabler, Uwe
Göbel, Sabine
Ganswind, Margarethe

Haas, Otto
Habermann, Willi
Hermann v., Paul
Harbert, Traute
Herrenberger, Justus
Herda, Fritz

Heier, Heinz
Herda, Maria
Hübötter, Peter
Hallmann, Sabine
Heinemann, Alois
Heufer, Klaus
Hoge, Rüdiger
Hahn, Hans-Peter
Hoffmann, Rudolf
Huth, Heinz-Henning
Heuser, Karl-Christian
Hundertmark, Dieter
Hausmann, Ulrich
Hacke, Joachim
Haß, Günter
Hilse, Gertrude
Hohmann, Katrin
Hansen, Jürgen
Heddenhausen, Ekkehard
Huth, Dietrich
Huuck, Hermann
Harms, Robert
Henning, Hedwig
Höstermann, Dieter
Hovestadt, Günther
Hogrebe, Eckardt
Heintz, Claus-Anselm
Hunsdörfer, Roderich
Hahn, Hannelore
Hampel, Manfred
Heyden, Horst
Heinzer, Joachim
Hatipoglu, Afsin
Hoffmann, Artur
Hennig, Adolf
Hoffmeister, Barbara
Hausmann, Gabriele
Hild, Michael
Heinemann, Armin
Heuveldop, Rudolf
Hilf, Friedegund
Hilgert, Gertrud
Hoven, Rainer
Hasenfuß, Christa-Bärbel
Heiser, Gerd
Heinecke, Joachim
Hornung, Kornelia
Hirche, Bernhard
Herz, Udo
Hennies, Ehrenfried
Hagen, Wolfgang
Härtel, Meike
Hartwig, Rolf
Hermann, Ulrich
Hornei, Thorsten
Hoffmann, Dieter
Heißenbüttel, Karin
Heckenberg, Ute
Heinen, Siegfried
Hafer, Hannelore
Heuer, Robert

Igert, Jens
Iselt, Marion
Jauns, Gisela
Jebens, Claus-Peter

Jürgens, Bernd
Juraschek, Peter
Joneikis, Johann
John, Hans-Ludger
Jensen, Uwe
Jozat, Hans
Jünke, Roswitha
John, Peter

Kottwitz, Herbert
Kreyß, Karl-Friedrich
Kudoke, Christa
Kaufmann, Caterina
Klevenhusen, Helmut
Kreyß, Ilse
Koller, Peter
Kruth, Bernhard
Kaminiarz, Heinz
Koeppen, Jost
Korb, Hans-Georg
Kappe, Hans Hermann
Karpel, Robert
Koch, Dieter
Klatt, Günter
Kätge, Heike
Karnagel, Helga
Kokkelink, Günter
König, Rodolph
Kramer, Otto
Krusnik, Ivan
Kafka, Ulrich
Kersten, Volker
Kiehl, H. J. H.
Kirchhoff, Peter
Kleineberg, Jürgen
Klocke, Horst
Kloth, Ernst Adolf
Krause, Ingrid
Kronberg, Wolfgang
Kamper, Hannes
Kasprzyk, Gerhard
Kley, Manfred
Kubicki, Sven
Kock, Renate
Koch, Wiltrud
Kuhne, Helga
Kurzweg, Rolf
Karrenfuehr, Günter
Krüger, Monika
Kubota, Tadayoshi
Käferhaus, Lutz
Käferhaus, Maren
Kiel, Detleff
Kiel, Berthold
Kliemt, Gudrun
Klug, Johannes
Kümper, Klaus-Mich.
Kuben, Petra
Kraemer, Kaspar
Koppe, Christa
Krubasik, Michael
Krüger, Elke
Kullik, Karin
Kerle, Franz-Jürgen
Koch, Beate
Kaiser, Ingrid
Krüger-Heyden, Karsten

Kemmerling, Karl-Heinz
Kraska, Karin
Krabiell, Manfred
Krämer, Regina
Küster, Heide-Marie
Kiesel, Angela
Karell, Hans-Rolf
Kabus, Klaus
Kühne, Reinhild
Kleine-Ruschkamp, Angela
Krause, Regina
Kausche, Ilona
Kramer, Christina
Krammelbein, Bernd
Krücken, Heinz
Kunert, Udo
Kumm, Horst
Kopp, Anja
Köhler, Helmut
Kloster, Konrad
Krumbe, Michael
Kuck, Gotthard

Luckhardt, Klaus
Ledeboer, Lambertus
Lehmann, Werner
Lauritzen, Uwe
Lehmann, Christine
Lange, Claus
Lange, Crista
Lindekugel, Inge
Lange, Dieter
Lerch, Albert
Lange, Hans-Joachim
Laude, Renate
Liehn, Klaus-Ekkeh.
Landscheiten, Hans T.
Lehotzky, Hans-Joachim
Lorenz, Claudia
Lenz, Jürgen
Lepper, Joachim
Lieb, Mathias
Lochner, Edelgard
Lackner, Roswitha
Luig, Wilhelm
Lieb-Braunagel, Edeltraud
Lücken, Hildegard
Levy, Angela
Leistenschneider, Christoph
Licht, Barbara
Leistenschneider, Claus
Lohmann, Martin
Ludwig, Claus-Günter
Lüth, Sabine
Lackum v., Wolfgang
Lutz, Martin
Lewen, Barbara
Lorenz, Jürgen
Lübbert, Klaus

Mewes, Liselotte
Markabrunn, Ursula
Marlow, Jürgen
Müller, Alfred
Menzel, Karl-Heinz

Moschner, Johannes
Monse, Wolfgang
Müller, Kirsten
Muschalla, Michael
Müller-Susemihl, Lisa
Maurer, Christel
Maurer, Käthe
Medefindt, Karl-Ludwig
Mann, Gotje-Marie
Müller, Günter
Mämpel, Peter
Meyer, Helene
Meyer-Bruck, Heinz
Mühlen in der, J.W.
Meißgeier, Ernst
Müller, Wolfgang
Meyer, Barbara
Meysen, Fried
Mühlen in der, Stana
Mack, Gerd
Mander, Antonio
Marek, Gert-Dieter
Meisels v., Istvan
Mier, Erich
Mels, Elfriede
Meyer, Antje
Meier, Friedr.
Martinoff, Erich
Moseler, Heinz-Peter
Müller-Röwekamp, Heiko
Martins, Egbert
Mathey, Heinrich
Majewski, Immo
Müller, Ursula
Matsche, Christian
Mc. Cue, James
Michaelis, Hildegund
Mathiesen, Johannes
Malessa, Rolf
Möbius, Egon
Müller, Jörg
Müller, Reinhard
Müller, Barbara
Meinecke, Almuth
Marwede, Thies
Maike, Cornelia
Müller, Brigitte
Müller, Alois

Neuhaus, Alfons
Niegisch, Herta
Nossing, Hermann
Nagel, Elke
Neumann, Joachim
Neumann, Peter
Noris, Jürgen
Nölke, Dirk
Niehoff, Anneliese
Nieschalk, Ulrich
Nieschalk, Brigitte
Neumann, Mathias
Neunzig, Gisela
Nolte, Elmar
Nentwig, Claudio

Ovendi, Eberhard

Fotografen / Photographs by

Oelschig, Christine
Obstoy, Karl-Peter
Oberst, Arnold
Otthoff, Charlotte
Otte, Renate
Osterloh, Christian
Oppermann, Reinhard

Pahlke, Ursula
Passie, Waldemar
Pfennig, Günter
Pysall, Hans-Joachim
Pfennig, Helene
Pieper, Heinrich
Plump, Therese
Peters, Raymond
Puell, Richard
Pfeil, Axel
Post, Ulrich
Peemöller, Heinke
Preussner, Horst
Porsiel, Uta
Pasel, Ursula
Pesonen, Martti
Piepenschneider, Hanna
Pocklitz, Heinz
Porzelt, Werner
Pustolla, Werner
Patzke, Dieter
Pinnekamp, Erwin
Paulitsch, Norbert
Pawliska, Rainer
Pfadt, Konrad
Ponet, Ingo
Pfennig, Raimund
Pieper, Hans-Joachim
Pini-Weingand, Jutta
Pramann, Friedrich
Powroschnik, Christina
Pinnau, Ursula
Prinz, Wolfgang
Preusteck, Johannes
Pfeffer, Klaus-Jürgen
Peckmann, Albert
Pülz, Annette
Pohl, Manfred
Prönnecke, Marion
Preiss, Regina
Pape, Margret
Priller, Andrea
Preußler, Vera
Pieper, Matthias

Querner, Dorle
Quarg, Gotthard

Rühle, Karl
Romero, Rolf
Retzki, Horst
Raths, Götz
Rehkate, Werner
Riedemann, Agnes
Rollenhagen, Eike
Rühland, Claus
Renke, Christine
Ruff, Eckard

Redell, Brigitta
Roos, Werner,
Rose, Wolfgang
Runge, Hildegund
Rahne, Fritz
Rollenhagen, Ingeborg
Riegelbeck, Hedwig
Rautenstrauch, Bernd
Rutz, Frank-Michael
Reichel, Dieter
Reinebeck, Otto
Richter, Heinrich
Rippke, Jürgen
Reif, Ingeborg
Reinicke, Ilse-Johanna
Richter, Heiko
Rüde, Erika
Reichenbach, Dieter
Rittig, Dieter
Reichard, Heidrun
Ritter, Dagmar
Rötel v., Max
Roesch, Marion
Roß, Melitta
Rink, Christian
Ruić, Ante
Röttelbach, Heike
Rogmann, Erwin
Rudloff v., Susanne
Reulein, Gertrud
Rössing, Hans W.
Raddatz, Theodor
Russek, Lothar
Rudloff v., Florian
Regenhardt, Stephan

Schmidt, Frank-Rud.
Seidel, Karl-Heinz
Schäfer, Fritz
Schlote, Wolfram
Sieverts, Ernst
Sifrin, Werner
Sommerfeld, Frank
Stammeier, Günter
Schneider, Hans
Scherill, Theodor
Steinhoff, Heinz
Schuld, Fritz
Schindelhauer, Joachim
Schneider, Gisela
Schulze, Reinhard
Storch, Heinrich
Schulze, Wolfgang
Speck, Klaus
Sommer, Helmut
Stroncek, Renate
Schnell, Johann-Georg
Strüber, Gert
Scholz, Herbert
Schade, Karl
Schlüter, Theo
Schröder, Peter
Stache, Wilfried
Stahn, Friedrich
Schartner, Erika

Salm, Hannelore
Schröder, Hans
Schulze, Barbara
Schulze, Renate
Schwarze, Karin
Sebastian, Dieter
Spatzier, Ursula
Splettstoßer, H.J.
Schlüter, Agathe
Schlüter, Evelyn
Schneyer, Manfred
Schmidt, Renate
Spruck, Dieter
Strohe, Gerhard
Struhk, Hans
Stenger, Jost
Schlemmer, Lothar
Schön, Waltraud
Schultz, Wolfgang
Schulz, Manfred
Sebastian, Irmgard
Sardjono, Meicy
Serwe, Ursula
Selle, Astrid
Sandforth, Edgar
Siuda, Ladislaus
Seidel, Karin
Schmidt, Horst-Bernd
Schumacher, Walborg
Stoletzki, Margrit
Schapitz, Dieter
Stahrenberg, Peter-Otto
Stelljes, Dierk
Samtleben, Anneliese
Strobel, Ingeborg
Schanz, Gertrud
Schäffel, Gunter
Schroetter, Helga
Stefanović, Aleksandra
Szymkowiak, Günter
Schmersahl, Friedrich
Schlüssler, Irmgard
Solodkoff v., Leonid
Schulz, Monika-Marietta
Stertenbrink, Petra
Streibel, Christian
Schmidt, Gabriele
Simandi, Edith
Schulze, Barbara
Schwarz, Klaus
Schaub, Walter
Schwede, Hennes
Schlicht, Edeltraud
Sattar, Christina
Schmidt, Egon
Schmidt, Inge
Schmidt-Joswig, Willi
Schwickert, Hans
Schulte, Ulrike
Schön, Ekkehardt
Saal, Gerhard
Scheer, Margarete
Schenderlein, Betina
Schnabel, Andi
Schulte, Guido
Schuster-Schekatz, Beate

Schweinoch, Horst-Bodo
Schmidt, Lothar
Schmidt, Marita
Schmiedecke, Rolf
Scheiffarth, Ursula
Schütz, Christine
Sausen, John
Stoecker, Heinz
Schalon, Ernst
Schmidt, Bernhard
Seiffert, Ursula

Thamm, Florian
Tarradi, Georg
Thoms, Manfred
Tusch, Gudrun
Thieleker, Erwin
Thrun, Wolfgang
Tech, Ulrich
Tangermann, Hannelore
Thiele, Bärbel
Timm, Carsten
Tooren, Geerd
Thiele, Wolfgang
Tavernier, Karl
Tuchscherer, Klara
Tyrell, Ulrike
Tyrell, Werner
Tjärks, Gerhard
Thust, Heike
Teherani, Sayed Hadi
Teuber, Harry
Toubanakis, Ingrid

Uhl, Eberhard
Ullrich, Heinz-Joachim
Uellendahl, Frank

Vogel, Elvira
Vitua, Manfred
Viehrig, Günther
Vollmer, Wilhelm
Vohrmann, Herbert
Volf, Miroslav
Vollmann, Helmut
Vopel, Evelin
Valda-Estra, Federico
Vassiliov, Eleftheria

Werkar, Wilhelm
Warzelhan, Horst
Welp, Karl-August
Wellershaus, Bernd
Westphal, Wolfgang
Wellershaus, Hartmut
Weseler, Günther
Wolf, Kurt
Winnenburg, Günter
Woldt, Gustav
Wege, Otto
Wolff, Friedemann
Wenger, Fritz-Hans
Wilke, Ernst
Wolffram, Günther
Wischke, Helge
Wittig, Gerhard

Weigand, Erich
Werner, Jörg
Wiencke, Hans-Peter
Wilke, Waltraud
Wittenberg, Hartmut
Wittke, A.O.F.
Weigel, Klaus
Wichmann, Monika
Wilke, Gisela
Wolf, Hans-Ulrich
Wiencke, Waltraud
Winter, Hans-Heinz
Wittenberg, Axel
Witt, Hans-Joachim
Wolf, Eckard
Winter, Hartmut
Werner, Rudolf
Wünschmann, Michael
Wagler, Harald
Windolf, Jürgen
Westphal, Berta
Willmünder, Peter
Windheuser, Wolfgang
Wenzel, Klaus-Dieter
Wilkening, Friedrich
Wolff, Sigrun
Weber, Volkhard
Weigel, Klaus
Wonneberg, Michael
Weber, Martina
Wolzenburg, Hans-Jürgen
Wessolek, Ingrid
Werheit, Christa
Wiechert, Michael
Wolf, Bettina
Westenberg, Hans P.
Weggen, Ulrich
Welp, Uwe
Wendt, Franz

Zaufke, Siegrun
Zillich, Carsten
Zimmermann, Angela
Zankl, Gerda
Zahn, Ulrich
Zaddach, Susanne
Zistler, Helene
Zimmermann, Michael
Zachmann, Hans-Christian

Bartenbach 178
Beckert 49, 51, 99, 192, 209
Bleyl 32, 62, 114, 120, 126, 128, 129
Büse 132, 133
Carstensen 141
Dodenhoff 109
Führ Raumdesign 38
Goertz-Bauer 136, 190
Gösel (Deutsche Bank) 18
Gramann 139, 152
v. Gramatzki 13, 15, 33, 35, 36, 37, 55, 57, 62, 64, 65, 66, 67, 68, 69, 71, 73, 74, 75, 80, 83, 84, 85, 88, 89, 101, 103, 104, 105, 145, 146, 153, 165, 179, 184, 186, 187, 205,
Grohs 143, 149, 159, 162, 178, 210
Hagen 194, 195
Hanisch 87, 160, 161, 162, 163, 202, 203, 204
Hartzenbusch 123
Harz 196, 198, 199, 200, 201
Hauschild 209
Heidersberger 10, 11, 13, 24, 25, 26, 28, 31, 42, 43, 44, 45, 46, 47, 48, 53, 79, 96, 97, 98, 99, 108, 109, 110, 111, 113, 114, 121, 123, 125, 130, 132, 133, 134, 135, 190, 191, 193, 208, 209, 212, 213
Heise 208
Jahr 38, 156
Huth 49, 93
Kabus 99
Kessler 121
Kloth 32, 121
Kortegast 27
KPS 62, 80, 127
Kralisch 167, 169
Krause 134
Kreuter 27
Kuck 90, 180, 181
KSP 16, 55, 134
Leiska 74
Mechau 58, 59, 81
Medau 204
Monse 25, 42, 43
Ohlsen 25, 48, 108, 112, 113, 114
Orgel-Köhne 29
Pape 171
Pegels 39
Rheinländer 118
Schmölz 24, 25, 28
Schmölz-Huth 16, 18, 19, 21, 200, 201
Schöne 12, 15
Schreiber 156
Sitte 48, 175
Söhn 126
Stahl 87, 172, 175, 177
Stephan 125
Strenger 113
Täubner 86, 87, 166, 168, 169

Thomas 17, 100
Wrubel 113, 114
Bilddienst Stadt Braunschweig 45
Bilddienst Landeshauptstadt Stuttgart 91
DKV Archiv 125
Finanzbauamt Bielefeld 179
Hamburger Aero Lloyd GmbH 196
Hamburger Luftbild KG 118
WDR Archiv 20
Werksfoto eines Chemiekonzerns 115
Werksfoto Gartner 149, 150
Architketen v. Wertz, Ottow, Bachmann, Marx 138

Perspektivenzeichner / Perspectives by

Ahola 88, 89
Huth 49, 167
Jacoby 21, 75, 136, 147, 154, 176, 178, 180, 185, 196
Kraemer, K. 172, 173
Kubicki 117, 120
Meyer-Hakala 91
Raddatz 60, 65, 155, 182
Struhk 114
Zachmann 90